UNIVERSAL ORLANDO

2015

The Ultimate Guide to the Ultimate Theme Park Adventure

Kelly Monaghan

THE INTREPID TRAVELER

Universal Orlando
The Ultimate Guide To The
Ultimate Theme Park Adventure

Published by
The Intrepid Traveler
P.O. Box 531
Branford, CT 06405
http://intrepidtraveler.com

Copyright © 2015 by Kelly Monaghan
Fourteenth Edition
Printed in the United States
Book design by Jana Rade; photo inserts by Susan Chwae
Cover photo © 2015 Kelly Monaghan
Theme park maps designed by Eureka Cartography
Orlando area map on page 16 by MapGorilla.com
ISSN: 1543-6233
ISBN: 978-1-937011-39-0
Library of Congress Control Number: 2014937994

Publisher's Cataloguing in Publication Data.
    Monaghan, Kelly
    Universal Orlando: the ultimate guide to the ultimate theme park adventure.
Branford, CT: Intrepid Traveler, copyright © 2015.
    Revised and updated edition of Universal Studios Escape (2000).
    Includes five maps.
    PARTIAL CONTENTS: Universal Studios Florida. -Islands of Adventure. Seuss Landing. Lost Continent. Jurassic Park. Wizarding World of Harry Potter. -CityWalk. -Luxury Resorts.
    1. Universal Orlando--Description and travel--Guidebooks. 2. Theme parks--Orlando region, Florida--Guidebooks. 3. Hotels--Orlando region, Florida--Guidebooks. I. Title. II. Intrepid Traveler.
    917.5924

Trademarks, Etc.

Photo Credits

About the Author

Kelly Monaghan has been covering the "other Orlando" for twenty years. In addition to this book, he is the author of *Seaworld, Discovery Cove, & Aquatica: Orlando's Salute to the Seas.* Over the years he has written other travel-oriented books about how to travel on the cheap and how to be a home-based travel agent. He offers a home study course for those who wish to expand their travel horizons with — and profit from — their own travel marketing business at **HomeTravelAgency. com**

Table of Contents

List of Maps

CHAPTER ONE:

PLANNING YOUR ESCAPE

Have you heard about the magical kingdom in the middle of Florida? There, the halls of an enchanted castle echo not with the squeals of little girls playing princess, but the screams of teens and adults having the ride of their lives. And you can find dozens of other adventures within walking distance of this one, inside an intimate resort that epitomizes new urbanism. For Orlando visitors willing to wander beyond the usual World, an extraordinary new Universe is waiting.

You're forgiven if Mickey immediately came to mind as you read the preceding paragraph. After all, the Mouse has been the Big Cheese of Florida tourism ever since 1971, when Walt Disney World opened on 43 sprawling square miles of scrubland southwest of Orlando in Lake Buena Vista. Two decades later, Disney's domination of Orlando's attraction industry was still essentially unchallenged. By then, this new and improved version of California's Disneyland had been expanded to include hotels, water parks, nightclubs, and multiple theme parks. But when Universal Studios, in distant California, announced plans for an East Coast edition of their famous Hollywood tour, Mickey was spooked enough to rush the Disney/MGM Studios (today known as Disney's Hollywood Studios) into construction.

Universal's entry in the Florida theme park sweepstakes was dubbed Universal Studios Florida. When it opened in 1990 it quickly became Orlando's number-two attraction, but it was just one theme park to Disney's many and seemed doomed to perpetual also-ran status.

That all changed in 1999 when Universal Studios Florida reinvented itself as Universal Orlando Resort, adding a second theme park, a nighttime entertainment complex, and several hotels. For the first time, Walt Disney World had competition worthy of the name and Orlando had its second multi-park, multi-hotel, multi-activity, all-in-one, never-need-to-leave-the-property vacation destination. Then, in June 2010, almost exactly 20 years after opening its original park, Universal Orlando introduced "The Wizarding World of Harry Potter," a highly anticipated expansion that reset the bar for theming and thrills. Four years later, in 2014, came a second Potter-themed area and another round of frenzied excitement. The resort isn't resting on its newfound laurels either; new owner Comcast has purchased substantial acreage in the surrounding area for potential expansion and announced accelerated capital investments worth over $1.1 billion in their resorts this year. There are even rumors it might buy SeaWorld!

Universal Orlando, then, represents a new departure in theme park and resort destinations that is very shrewdly positioned in the marketplace to build its own following and capitalize on any decline of the Disney brand. It is sure to capture the imagination of both theme park veterans and a new generation of vacationers hungry for entertainment experiences designed with the twenty-first century in mind.

Just What Is 'Universal Orlando'?

Universal Orlando and Walt Disney World are both multi-park, multi-resort vacation destinations. But whereas Disney sprawls over a vast area, Universal Orlando is comfortably compact, allowing its guests to spend less time getting around and more time enjoying themselves. And while Disney World harkens back to an earlier time, Universal is very much of the moment, with an eye to the future.

There are two theme parks here. The original movie-studio-themed **Universal Studios Florida** (USF) is still going strong. It continues to add new thrills using the very latest in technology. Almost literally next door is **Islands of Adventure** (IOA), an attraction that takes the whole notion of "theme park" to the next level, with awesome rides and hyper-detailed environments.

CityWalk is an entertainment and restaurant complex that lies between the theme parks. This is very much an adult experience, with a cross-cultural sampling of dining and entertainment (although several restaurants will also appeal to the younger set). And CityWalk rocks, thanks to the world's largest Hard Rock Cafe and Hard Rock Live, a performance space that hosts some of pop music's biggest names.

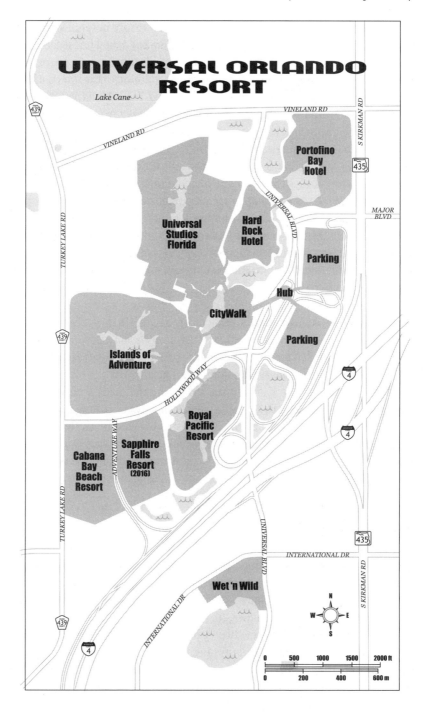

Universal's quartet of themed, on-property resort hotels likewise go toe-to-toe with Mickey's best lodgings. Portofino Bay Hotel has established itself among Orlando's premiere resort hotels. This ultra-luxury property is a photographic reproduction of that favorite destination of the international jet set, Portofino, Italy. More casual is the Hard Rock Hotel, which radiates a hip California sensibility and is just steps away from the front gate to Universal Studios Florida. The Royal Pacific Resort evokes the romance of far-off Bali, just minutes away from the theme parks by foot or boat. The value-priced Cabana Bay Beach Resort is an affordable alternative to off-site motels with family-friendly features and a retro-modern flair.

Across the Interstate on an adjacent parcel sits **Wet 'n Wild**, a water park that Universal owns. It has not been fully rolled into the "Universal Orlando" brand, but it is included in some ticket options and free shuttle service from the on-site hotels makes it easy to visit. In 2013 Universal purchased the land under and around Wet 'n Wild, fueling speculation that the resort may soon expand into that area.

Universal Orlando is a family destination. But, unlike some parks, Universal seems to recognize that "families" come in all sorts of different packages. Parents with little ones will find this an almost ideal place for their kids. And yet families with teenagers will not have to worry about complaints that the rides are "lame." Best of all, adults who have yet to have kids, or who have grown kids, or who have left the kids at home, or who never plan to have kids at all can come to Universal Orlando without feeling that they're in a kiddie park. And those snobbish sophisticates who think theme parks are beneath them may find themselves won over by the dazzling architecture, the luxurious accommodations, the gourmet food, and the wide array of nighttime entertainment.

When to Come

There are three major questions you must ask yourself when planning a visit to Universal Orlando: How crowded will it be? What will the weather be like? When will my schedule allow me to go? For most people, the third question will determine when they go, regardless of the answers to the other two. That's too bad because, for those who can be flexible, carefully picking the time of your visit will offer a number of benefits. During slow periods, the crowds at Orlando's major theme parks are noticeably thinner than they are at the height of the summer or during the madness of Christmas week. On top of that, hotel rates are substantially lower and airfare deals abound.

Likewise, Orlando in winter can seem positively balmy to those from the North, although it's unlikely you will find the temperature conducive to swimming (except in heated pools). Spring and fall temperatures are close to ideal. Avoiding the "rainy season" (roughly June through September) is also a good idea. You are not only avoiding the worst of the heat and humidity, but locals swear those afternoon thunderstorms are more frequent, more intense, and last longer than they used to.

Let's take a look at these two variables: the tourist traffic and the weather. Then you can decide which dates will offer your ideal Orlando vacation.

Orlando's Tourist Traffic

Most major tourist destinations seem to have two seasons — high and low. For most of Florida, the high season stretches from late fall to early spring, the cooler months up North. Low season is the blisteringly hot summer, when Floridians who can afford it head North. Orlando, thanks to its multitude of family-oriented attractions, has five or six distinct "seasons," alternating between high and low, reflecting the vacation patterns of its prime customers — kids and their parents.

The heaviest tourist "season" is Christmas vacation, roughly from Christmas Eve through January 1. Next comes Easter week and Thanksgiving weekend. The entire summer, from Memorial Day in late May to Labor Day in early September, is on a par with Easter and Thanksgiving. There are two other "spikes" in attendance: Presidents' Week in February and College Spring Break. Various colleges have different dates for their Spring Break, which may or may not coincide with Easter; the result is that the period from mid-March through mid-April shows a larger than usual volume of tourist traffic. The slowest period is the lull between Thanksgiving and Christmas. Next slowest (excluding the holidays mentioned earlier) are the months of September, October, November, January, and February. Tourism starts to build again in March, spiking sharply upward for Easter/Spring Break, then dropping off somewhat until Memorial Day.

It would be nice to know how theme park attendance rises and falls from month to month. That information is a closely guarded trade secret, but fairly reliable annual estimates are available. Here are annual attendance figures for Orlando area parks for 2013 as estimated by the trade groups TEA and AECOM Economics:

Rank*	Park	Attendance
1	The Magic Kingdom	18,588,000
3	EPCOT	11,229,000
4	Disney's Animal Kingdom	10,198,000
5	Disney's Hollywood Studios	10,110,000
7	Islands of Adventure	8,141,000
8	Universal Studios Florida	7,062,000
10	SeaWorld Orlando	5,090,000

*Numbers represent the parks' **national** rankings. Disneyland in California was number two, Disney California Adventure was number six, Universal Studios Hollywood was ninth.

In other words, on any given day, the largest crowds will tend to be at the Disney parks. If you've been a Disney regular, Universal Orlando will seem quite manageable by comparison.

The best advice is to avoid the absolutely busiest times of the year if possible. The slow months of fall and spring are ideal. Even January can be enjoyable if you're not the sunbathing type. If you come during the summer, as many families must, plan to deal with crowds when you arrive and console yourself with the thought that Disney is likely even busier.

■ The Best Day of the Week to Visit

A fair bit of advice has been written about the best days of the week to visit the various Orlando area theme parks, but such guidance has shown itself to be of limited use. The problem with predictions is that you could arrive on the "slowest" day of the week to find there's been an atypical blip in attendance.

That being said, Sunday is typically the least-crowded day to visit Universal Orlando, theoretically because most visitors to Orlando start their vacations on the weekend and go to Disney first. Crowds increase Tuesday through Friday, with Thursday often the busiest; Saturdays can be surprisingly slow. The surest predictor of crowds on any particular day is the online price of Universal Express Plus passes (see later in this chapter for details).

Finally, there is no reason to cram a visit into a day or two (although many people insist on doing just that). The per-day cost of multi-day tickets (see *The Price of Admission*, below) is quite reasonable and they remove the insane pressure that comes with a park-a-day touring schedule.

■ The Best Time of Day to Visit

Though it's hard to guess which day of the week is best, it is easy to advise on what time of day to come to the parks, regardless of the day of the week or the time of year: as early as humanly possible.

The parking garage opens at least 90 minutes before the parks' official opening time, and the park gates may open 60 minutes early (for "early entry" guests) and 15 to 30 minutes early for the general public. During peak periods, optimum touring requires being among the first through the turnstiles, which means arriving with tickets in hand up to an hour before opening. If you are visiting during a slow season you can probably afford to arrive 15 minutes early.

Arriving crowds peak at about 11:00 a.m. and then level off. Many families and the faint of heart start leaving at about 4:00 p.m. Thus, your best shot at the more popular rides is before 11 and after 4. During the heat of the day you can catch the shows in the large theaters that offer posted starting times and shorter lines. You may also find that in the hour before closing many rides have no lines at all.

Of course, CityWalk is another matter. Things don't start hopping there until 8:00 or 9:00 p.m. and the place stays open until 2:00 a.m. Factor that into your planning. You might find that a day that starts at 7 and ends at 2 the next morning isn't much of a vacation.

Orlando's Weather

Orlando's average annual temperature is a lovely 72.4 degrees. But as already noted, averages are deceptive. Here are the generally cited "average" figures for temperature and rainfall throughout the year:

	High (°F)	Low (°F)	Rain (in.)
January	71	49	2.3
February	73	50	3.0
March	78	55	3.2
April	83	59	1.8
May	88	66	3.6
June	91	72	7.3
July	92	73	7.3
August	92	73	6.8
September	90	72	6.0
October	85	66	2.4
November	79	58	2.3
December	73	51	2.2

(Source: Visit Orlando)

Use these figures as general guidelines rather than guarantees. While the average monthly rainfall in October might be 2.4 inches over the course of many years, in 2011 there were 7.4 inches of rain that month, with over 6 inches falling in one day alone. In June 2005, Orlando International Airport recorded 16.74 inches of rain, over twice the historic average. The same holds for temperatures, especially in the winter months. January 2010 saw lows dip into the twenties.

Orlando's weather is most predictable in the summer when "hot, humid, in the low nineties, with a chance of afternoon thunderstorms" becomes something of a mantra for the TV weather report. Winter weather tends to be more unpredictable with "killer" freezes a possibility. As to those summer thunderstorms, they have become more intense in recent years, beginning earlier and lasting longer. Also, June through September is hurricane season, with late August and early September the most likely time for severe weather.

Gathering Information

Universal Orlando maintains a number of phone lines that provide recorded information about prices, opening hours, and special events. Toll-free numbers that work in the United States and Canada are (800) 711-0080 and (888) 322-5537. Here you can get general park information, buy tickets, and make hotel reservations. Or call (407) 224-4233 and press 3. For the hearing impaired, there is a TDD line at (800) 447-0672. If you are interested in booking a package, get in touch with Universal Vacations at (877) 801-9720. If you are calling from other countries outside the U.S. or are already in Orlando, the number to call is (407) 363-8000, which is the main switchboard.

■ The Internet

There are a number of resources on the Internet you may want to check out before your trip. The main Universal Orlando site can be found at www.universalorlando.com, and has the most "official" information. It has sections on both parks, CityWalk, and the resort hotels, as well as information about upcoming special events. You can send a message to Universal's guest service coordinators at www.visitorsatisfaction.com/contactus. If you are interested in booking a package vacation that includes a hotel room and other add-ons, the website for Universal Vacations is www.universalorlandovacations.com.

An excellent source of pre-trip intelligence can be found at www.

DISboards.com. The "dis" in disboards stands for "Disney Information Station," but the site has a discussion board devoted exclusively to Universal Orlando. On the home page, scroll down and click on the link for "Universal Studios/Islands of Adventure Forums."

Getting There

Universal Orlando is located near the intersection of the Florida Turnpike and Interstate 4 (abbreviated I-4 and pronounced "Eye Four"). It is bounded by Kirkman Road on the east, Vineland Road on the north, Turkey Lake Road on the west, and I-4 on the south. Universal Boulevard runs through the park property from the International Drive tourist district to Vineland Road.

There are four entrances to the park complex. The main entrance is via the Universal Boulevard overpass from International Drive. There are also entrances from Kirkman, Vineland, and Turkey Lake. The Kirkman Road entrance sits on a main thoroughfare and is quite busy. The other entrances seem almost anonymous by comparison. Perhaps because of that, they tend to be the lesser used and, therefore, the quickest ways into the resort. All entrances feed cars down broad, palm-lined boulevards to a toll-plaza-like entrance between the two huge, multilevel parking garages sandwiched between Universal Boulevard and Kirkman Road.

Practically speaking, the entrance you wind up using will probably depend on the direction from which you approach.

■ From International Drive

If you are staying in one of the many hotels in the International Drive area, your obvious approach is up Universal Boulevard, crossing I-4 to the main entrance. This approach provides a nice view of the Royal Pacific Resort and Islands of Adventure as you cross the Interstate.

■ From the south on I-4

Note: This is the route you will be taking if you are coming from the airport via Route 528 ($2.25 toll), which joins I-4 south of Universal.

Coming from the south (that is, traveling "east" on I-4), the most direct route into the park is to take Exit 75A, International Drive, and turn left at the top of the ramp. This puts you on the Universal Boulevard approach. There are two other alternatives, however. On especially busy days, when the overpass at Exit 75A can be backed up, you might save a little time by getting off at Exit 74, Sand Lake Road. Turn left off the ramp, under the

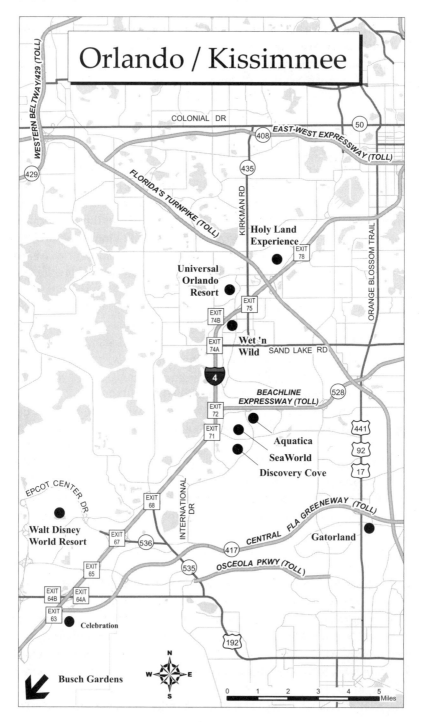

Orlando / Kissimmee

Interstate, and then right almost immediately onto Turkey Lake Road. You can't miss it; just follow the "Universal Orlando" signs. Just opposite Dr. Phillips High School, you will see the Universal sign on your right. Your third choice is to drive past Exit 75A and take the left hand Exit 75B, which feeds you onto Kirkman Road; the entrance to the park will be on your left at the first light.

■ From the north on I-4

Visitors approaching from the north (that is, traveling "west" on I-4) have a choice of using Exit 75B or, a little further along, Exit 74B. Of the two, Exit 74B offers the most direct route to parking. It takes you to Hollywood Way, where you turn right and head straight ahead to the parking garages. It is also the better choice if you are staying at Royal Pacific Resort or Cabana Bay Beach Resort. If you are heading to the Hard Rock Hotel, Portofino Bay Resort, or any of the hotels along Major Boulevard, use Exit 75B.

■ From Florida's Turnpike

Whether you are coming from the north or south, take Exit 259 and follow the signs to Tampa via I-4, then get off I-4 at either 75B or 74B.

Parking at Universal Orlando

Whichever entrance you use, you will arrive at the tollbooth entrance to the two huge parking structures; one is five levels high, the other six, and they hold a total of 20,000 cars. At the booth, an attendant will collect your daily parking fee of $17 ($22 for RVs, buses, and trailers). Preferred or Premier Annual Passholders can show their pass for free admission to the parking lots. Parking is $5 (or free for Florida residents) between 6:00 p.m. and 10:00 p.m., except during special events, and is free for all after 10:00 p.m.

Tip: The leftmost open tollbooth lanes usually have the shortest lines.

Once you have paid the parking fee, you will be directed to your parking space. The parking structures are ingeniously designed so that as one level fills up cars are routed directly to the next level, without having to corkscrew upwards as you do in most multistory parking lots. If you arrive early, you will be directed in such a way that the two parking structures are filled in the most efficient way possible. However, the structures are often understaffed later in the day, leaving drivers to fend for themselves, so drive cautiously if arriving after noon.

One of the great things about Universal Orlando's parking is that most of it is covered, thus protecting you and your car from the broiling Florida sun and those sudden afternoon downpours. If for any reason you find yourself directed to the open roof, ask the attendant to direct you to sheltered parking on one of the lower levels. It may take some polite persistence but it can be done.

The various sections in the two structures are named after movies or characters (Jaws, Jurassic Park, Cat in the Hat, and so forth); rows are indicated by numbers, with the first digit indicating the level. Thus "Jaws 305" would be on the third level. As always in these situations, it's a good idea to take a picture of your row number with your smartphone.

Once parked, you've got a healthy walk ahead of you to the attractions. Universal claims that the farthest parking space is just a nine-minute walk from CityWalk, but at the end of a long day it can feel like a million miles.

Handicapped Parking. Handicapped parking spaces are provided close to the main entrance on Level 3. Follow the signs for handicapped parking and you will be directed accordingly.

Preferred Parking. If you'd like to shave a few minutes off your walk, you can pay $25 ($5 for Preferred annual passholders, free for Premier) for a parking space that's almost as close to the main entrance as the handicapped spaces.

Valet Parking. Get in the Hollywood spirit by having an attendant park your car for you as you pull up right at CityWalk. Just follow the signs. The fee is $15 if you stay for less than two hours and $35 for over two hours ($25 if you arrive after 6:00 p.m.). "Red carpet" service, which guarantees you'll get your car in five minutes or less, is $45. Preferred Annual Pass holders pay a flat rate of $15 ($25 for Red Carpet) no matter how long they stay. Premier Passholders can valet for free (plus gratuity), or use Red Carpet for $15. If you are coming just for lunch Monday through Friday, between 11:00 a.m. and 2:00 p.m., you can have your parking stub validated at most full-service CityWalk restaurants. A stay of under two hours is **free** with validation and two to four hours is $15, but a stay of over four hours will cost you the full $35, even with validation. If you leave your car in valet past closing time (2:00 a.m. Sunday through Thursday, 3:00 a.m. Friday and Saturday) you'll face a $50 fee in the morning.

Passenger Drop-Off. If you're in a generous mood, you can drop your family off near CityWalk before you go off to park the car. Look for the signs directing you to the drop-off area, which is just across Universal Boulevard from the Valet Parking area.

Parking for Resort Guests. If you are staying at one of the on-property resort hotels, use any of the entrances and follow the signs to your hotel. All of the hotels have separate gates, with separate, paid parking facilities for guests. Non-guests can also use these lots but at rates higher than those charged to guests and considerably higher than the fee levied at the main theme park parking garages. In other words, the hotel parking does not provide an economical or more convenient alternative to regular parking, unless you are getting valet parking validated at a hotel restaurant.

Alternatives To Driving

If you are staying at an off-site hotel, look into the **Super Star Shuttle** bus service that ferries guests at area hotels to Universal Orlando, SeaWorld, and Wet 'n Wild. There are about eight separate routes and hotels as far afield as downtown Orlando and the Route 192 corridor in Kissimmee participate in this program. The service is typically free to guests, but some hotels may charge a small fee. In theory, you must be a guest of a participating hotel to use this service, but this is seldom if ever enforced. Hotels near a pickup point cheerfully send their guests next door to catch the shuttle.

Unfortunately, information on routes, schedules, and which hotels are currently participating is hard to come by. The best bet is to ask the hotel you are planning to book whether they participate in the program. Once at Universal Orlando, you can stop by the bus station under the Hub between the parking garages and CityWalk to see which routes service which hotels. The service runs from the hotels to Universal Orlando all day, with fewer departures in the afternoon. Return trips don't start until about 4:00 p.m. You should be able to pick up a printed schedule from your hotel or the driver.

If you are staying along the International Drive corridor, you can hop on the **I-Ride Trolley** to reach the corner of Kirkman Road and Major Boulevard (stop number four on the Green Line). From there, follow the walking directions given below. The trolley is $2.00 for those 10 and older, $1.00 for kids 3 to 9, and 25 cents for those 65 and older. Kids under 3 ride **free**. Exact change is required. All-day and multi-day passes, which are a good deal, are available at many hotels and retail shops along I-Drive, but not on the trolleys. For more information or to view a route map visit iridetrolley.com.

You can also reach the parks via public transportation; Orlando's **Lynx buses** cost $2, exact change required. A weekly bus pass costs $16. Route 21 links downtown Orlando with the I-Drive corridor, passes through the Major Boulevard hotel area (see *Chapter Seven: Staying Near the Parks*), and stops near the Hub in Universal Orlando. Getting from the Walt Disney

World area to Universal is tricky, but possible. Take Lynx Route 50 from Disney's Ticket & Transportation Center or Downtown Disney to SeaWorld and switch to the I-Ride Trolley. For more information, call (407) 841-5969 or visit www.golynx.com on the Internet. On the website you will be able to download maps of the routes that interest you.

It is actually possible to **walk to the parks** and quite a few people do it. If you are staying at one of the hotels located along Major Boulevard on the Kirkman Road side of the property (see *Chapter Seven*), you can reach CityWalk in 15 to 30 minutes, moving at a purposeful pace. From Major Boulevard, follow the signs for valet parking and you will find an escalator that takes you to CityWalk. If you are staying on the other side of I-4, at a hotel near Universal Boulevard and I-Drive, you are looking at a much, much longer walk. Coming from this direction, use the escalator leading up from the bus station.

If you are staying at a luxury resort (See *Chapter Five: The Luxury Resorts*), you can use the **free water taxis** to CityWalk or the **shuttle buses** that drop you near Universal Studios Florida. Cabana Bay has its own shuttle bus service to the bus station under the Hub.

You can neatly solve all your transportation problems by taking a **taxi, van, or limo** from the airport and staying at an onsite hotel for the duration of your stay. Quicksilver Tours (888-468-6939) provides town car and stretch limo services. They will stop en route to let you stock up on groceries and such for your room and they offer an innovative "three-way" option. They will take you from the airport to Universal, then a few days later from Universal to Walt Disney World, and finally back to the airport, all for $170. For a family of four, it's a bargain for the convenience and comfort. The website, www.quicksilver-tours.com, has a full price list.

Otherwise, Mears Transportation offers walk-up shuttle van service from the airport for $32 round trip per person, $24 for children 4 to 11. No reservation is necessary. Taxi fare from the airport runs $42 to $49.

Staying at one of Universal's resort hotels without the temptation of a car is a great way to maximize your vacation enjoyment. If you are staying on in Orlando, you can always rent a car in your hotel at the end of your stay.

Arriving at Universal Orlando

From your parking space, you will walk to the nearest of a series of escalators and moving sidewalks that will funnel you to "the Hub," a large circular space on the third level with access from both parking structures and from the bus station. In the Hub, you can rent a wheelchair ($12), but not strollers or electric convenience vehicles. For those, you'll have to wait until you reach the theme parks. The Hub also has restrooms and a few vending kiosks if you just can't wait to get that Universal T-shirt or hotdog.

Tip: You can rent a wheelchair here and then "upgrade" to an ECV once you reach the park.

From the Hub, after an efficient security check (have your bags open for inspection) it's a straight shot along more moving sidewalks to CityWalk, Universal's dining, shopping, and entertainment venue. In CityWalk, you can continue straight ahead to Islands of Adventure or hang a sharp right and head for Universal Studios Florida.

Whichever park you choose to visit, you will cross a bridge over the artificial canal system that links the resort hotels to the parks and arrive at an attractive entrance plaza where you will find a row of ticket windows and, nearby, a Guest Services window, of which more later.

Once inside the park gate, be sure to pick up a **2-Park Guide Map** from the racks just past the entrance. The large fold-out brochures contain maps of both parks and a listing of restaurants, shops, and helpful information such as the show times of many attractions.

On the front will be listed the parks' official opening and closing times and the dates for which the information is valid, which could be for just the day on which you receive it or for several days or weeks. If you forget to pick up a map at the entrance, you'll will find more near the cashier's desk in most shops throughout the parks.

Opening and Closing Times

Universal Orlando is open 365 days a year. In the slow seasons, the parks may open at 9:00 a.m. and close at 6:00 p.m. During the high season, the parks may open at 8:00 a.m. and close at 11:00 p.m. On-site hotel guests and those purchasing certain "partner hotel" vacation packages are granted "early park admission" into Islands of Adventure's Wizarding World of Harry Potter and (during certain seasons) select attractions at Universal Studios Florida one hour prior to the "official" opening time. If you can't enter early you can stay late. Typically, the last visitors aren't shooed out until an hour or more after closing time.

Again, opening and closing times can also be affected by special events. If the park will be closing early, there should be a large sign posted near the entrance gates informing you of this sad fact. You can also double-check today or tomorrow's official hours by calling (407) 224-4233 and pressing "1."

Tip: Take your time leaving the parks at night unless you're absolutely exhausted (a strong possibility). Strolling slowly through these magical streets under a moonlit sky (either alone or with a special someone) is an unforgettable experience when you are among just a handful of people in the park.

The Price of Admission

Universal Orlando has a variety of ticket options, with a variety of bells and whistles, that seem to change with astonishing regularity. So take this section with a grain of salt. If past experience is anything to go by, the information below will change before the next edition comes out. The number, variety, and configurations of passes offered may very well change and, of course, prices are subject to change without notice.

■ Buying Tickets

Your best bet is to buy tickets on the Universal website before you come to Orlando, as much for the time savings as the discounts offered, although the discounts and sweeteners are substantial. All online options allow you to print out your admission ticket at home, ready to take to the gate, or pick up at the parks using the electronic kiosks just outside the entrance. Swipe the same credit card you used to make the purchase, enter the confirmation code you received at the time of purchase, and you will receive a ticket you can take to the gate. It's simple and fast. The kiosks are only for the pick up of tickets purchased online and cannot be used to purchase tickets.

There is no charge to print tickets at home or use the kiosks. If you prefer to have your tickets sent to you, Fed-Ex shipping (domestic and international) is available for $14 to $19. If you use a travel agent, allow several weeks to receive your tickets. You can also visit your local AAA office if you are a member, or try the services of Ticketmania, described later.

If you must wait to purchase tickets until you are in Orlando and can't use the Internet, you can purchase tickets at the park when you arrive for your visit. Tickets can also be purchased at the Universal Studios store in the Orlando International Airport, where many tourists begin their Orlando adventure. You might also look around for an Internet cafe or borrow a computer to get those online-only offers and discounts.

Tickets can also be purchased at the resort hotels at the concierge desk. There is no extra charge for this service, and you will receive the discounted online rate for multi-day tickets. However, once you check in you will no doubt want to start using your front of the line privileges in the parks immediately (see below), so once again you are losing precious time. Better to have your tickets in hand before you arrive.

■ Ticket Options

Universal Orlando's tiered ticket pricing encourages purchasing longer passes by sharply reducing the premium when you add additional days and parks. All multi-day tickets must be fully utilized within 14 days after the first use, and include 14 nights of free admission to CityWalk's clubs. Whatever your choice, children under three are admitted **free**.

For the most recent information you should check www.universalorlando.com and click on the "Tickets" link, although as noted below, the website does not always list every type of ticket available. Another excellent source of intelligence about the latest prices and special admissions offers is www.mousesavers.com. If you'd prefer to get your information straight from the horse's mouth, you can try emailing Universal at guestservices@universalorlando.com or call (407) 224-7840.

All that being said, prices (including 6.5% sales tax) were as follows when this book went to press (the online prices are listed in parentheses):

Base Ticket: One-Park Access
(Universal Studios Florida **or** Islands of Adventure)

	Adults (age 10+)	Children (3-9)
1 Day	$102.24 ($102.24)	$95.85 ($95.85)
2 Days	$166.13 ($144.83)	$155.48 ($134.18)
3 Days	$176.78 ($155.48)	$165.06 ($143.76)
4 Days	$187.43 ($166.13)	$174.65 ($153.35)

Park-To-Park Ticket: Two-Park Access
(Universal Studios Florida **and** Islands of Adventure)

	Adults (age 10+)	Children (3-9)
1 Day	$144.84 ($144.84)	$138.45 ($138.45)
2 Days	$208.73 ($187.43)	$198.08 ($176.78)
3 Days	$219.38 ($198.08)	$207.66 ($186.36)
4 Days	$230.03 ($208.73)	$217.25 ($195.95)

You can usually add one visit to **Wet 'n Wild** to any adult multi-day ticket for about $38, about $11 less than a single day admission purchased directly from Wet 'n Wild. The trade-off is that you miss a day (or most of a day) of touring the theme parks. So consider carefully if that's worth it.

Two other ticket options, **Park-to-Park with Unlimited Express Tickets** and the **Orlando FlexTicket** are discussed a little later.

■ CityWalk Party Passes

CityWalk's entertainment venues levy a "cover charge" in the evenings. If you wish, you can purchase a CityWalk Party Pass for $12.77, including tax. It offers admission to all entertainment venues for the evening, so you don't have to pay a separate cover at each club or restaurant. Be aware that all multi-day tickets include 14 consecutive nights of admission to CityWalk's clubs. So be sure to check your pass before plunking down money for a Party Pass you don't need. For more on the CityWalk Party Pass, see *Chapter Four: CityWalk*.

■ Annual Passes

Universal Orlando offers three Annual Pass options.

Two-Park Annual Power Pass:
All ages: $228.96 ($202.34 for FL residents)
Two-Park Preferred Annual Pass:
All ages: $314.16 ($276.89 for FL residents)
Two-Park Premier Annual Pass
All ages: $463.26 ($410.01 for FL residents)

To sweeten the deal a little bit, Universal's "FlexPay" lets you pay for these in 11 interest-free payments, following a hefty down payment.

What's the difference? The **Annual Power Pass** comes with about 92 blackout dates (Christmas through New Year and Easter Break at both parks, plus mid-June through mid-August at USF only), does not include parking, and offers no additional discounts. The **Preferred Annual Pass** is valid 365 days a year, includes free standard self-parking, and entitles the holder to a host of attractive discounts on food, merchandise, and stays at the resort hotels. Since parking is $17 a day, you need only visit six days during the year before the additional cost of a Preferred Annual Pass pays for itself — and that doesn't take into account any shopping and dining discounts.

The **Premier Annual Pass** adds a few nifty perks not offered by the Preferred Annual Pass. These include free self-parking in the Preferred Parking area or free valet parking (gratuity excluded), Universal Express Plus access to rides and attractions after 4:00 p.m. daily, admission to all CityWalk clubs for the passholder and a guest (passholder only Friday and Saturday), one non-peak Halloween Horror Nights ticket, eight free bottles of water, and other benefits.

In addition to the freedom to come and go as you please, Preferred and

Premier Annual Passes confer a number of other benefits, including 10% to 20% discounts on tickets to the parks, Blue Man Group, AMC Cineplex, and CityWalk. Preferred passholders also receive a 10% discount on souvenir purchases and food (excluding alcohol and walk-up stands) in the parks, while Premier passholders receive 20% off merchandise and 15% off food. The Preferred Pass will get you a 10% discount on food in many of CityWalk's restaurants; Premier provides a 5% to 10% bump to that price break.

The special rates at the resort hotels, which can shave as much as 30% off the daily rate, are an especially attractive perk for annual passholders. Annual passholder rates are usually available during the slower times of year, so don't expect deep discounts at Christmas, Spring Break, or during the height of the summer rush. There are additional discounts and privileges (like early admission or private attraction previews) that change from time to time; they are outlined in the brochure you receive with your Annual Pass and changes will be announced in the annual passholders' newsletter, which is published quarterly, and via monthly ePassport emails.

For the very latest information on Universal's Annual Passes visit www.universalorlando.com/Theme-Park-Tickets/Annual-Passes.aspx.

■ Florida Resident Specials

Universal offers online-only ticket and annual pass prices designed to encourage those who live closest to the parks to visit more often. A typical Florida Resident Special involves a reduced price for admission to both parks during slower periods of the year. At press time, Universal offered Floridians two- and three-day tickets for $45 below gate price, with 180 days before expiration (instead of 14). To get these deals you must be able to show proof of Florida residence such as a Florida driver's license when you first use your pass. These tickets come with a long list of blackout dates at both parks, including Christmas, Easter, and June through August. The best way to find out what Florida Resident Specials are currently available is to visit www.universalorlando.com and click on the "Florida Residents" link in the top right corner.

■ The Star Treatment

If you've ever dreamed of being ushered around the crowds like a celebrity, consider a **VIP Experience**. For $230 per person, plus tax ($299 during peak attendance periods) — *in addition* to regular park admission — you can join a group of up to 11 other VIPs for a five-hour escorted behind-the-scenes tour of one park of your choice. Not only will you see things that ordinary visitors don't, you will be whisked to the head of the line for "at least eight" attractions and be guaranteed the best seats. After your tour, you'll have unlimited Universal Express Plus (see below) for the rest of the day. These tours start at 10:00 a.m. and noon. If you'd like to do a VIP Tour of both parks, that can be arranged, too. There is a seven-hour **One-Day, Two-Park VIP Experience** departing daily at 10:00 a.m. for $249 ($329 peak).

If you'd like to corral up to nine close friends, you can all take a private eight-hour **One-Day, One-Park Private VIP Experience** ($2,400; may be unavailable during peak periods). That gives you nearly 60% more time at a slightly higher per-person cost. What's more, this tour starts when you want it to and can be customized to your group's special interests. The group must be preformed; that is, you can't join another group. Nor does your group have to total 10. You can bring five friends or eight, or go all by yourself. The cost remains the same. A **One-Day, Two-Park Private VIP Experience** ($2,750), and even a **Two-Day, Two-Park Private VIP Experience** ($4,250) are also offered. Again, the VIP tours are for a group of up to 10 people.

You can get more information about both kinds of VIP tours, as well as additional options, by calling (866) 346-9350. You can also request a VIP tour reservation by email at viptours@universalorlando.com. Reservations must be made at least 72 hours in advance (two weeks prior during summer and holiday periods) and a credit card hold is required. If you must cancel your reservation, do so at least 72 hours prior to the tour; otherwise, your credit card will be charged.

If you can afford it, this is a terrific way to see the parks. The guides are personable and extremely knowledgeable. Becoming a guide is a lengthy and highly competitive process and only a few who apply make the cut.

■ The Orlando FlexTicket

Several of the non-Disney theme parks, namely Universal Orlando, Sea-World, Wet 'n Wild, Aquatica, and Busch Gardens Tampa, have banded to-gether to offer multi-day, multi-park passes at an extremely attractive price. This option is called the Orlando FlexTicket and it works like this:

Five-Park, Fourteen-Day Orlando FlexTicket:

(Universal Studios Florida, Islands of Adventure, SeaWorld, Wet 'n Wild, Aquatica)

Adults:	$340.75
Children (3 to 9):	$319.45

Six-Park, Fourteen-Day Orlando FlexTicket Plus:
(adds Busch Gardens Tampa)

Adults:	$383.35
Children (3 to 9):	$362.05

Once activated at the turnstiles of the first park you visit, these tickets offer unlimited visits to the parks they cover (including visiting multiple parks per day) for the next 14 consecutive days. As for parking, you pay at the first park you visit on any given day. Then show your parking ticket and Orlando FlexTicket at the other parks on the same day for complimentary parking. The six-park option includes free bus transportation from Sea-World to Busch Gardens. FlexTickets purchased at Universal Orlando also provide 14 days' admission to "select" CityWalk nightclubs.

Remember, these tickets expire. That is, if you use an Orlando FlexTicket for only five days, you can't return a month later and use the remaining nine days. These passes offer excellent value for the dollar; the five-park pass works out to about $23 a day! On top of that, they offer the come and go as you please convenience of Annual Passes, albeit for a much shorter time.

FlexTickets can be tricky to find on Universal's website, but they are also sold through wetnwild.com or visitorlando.com. Passes may also be purchased at any of the participating parks' ticket booths, or through your travel agent before coming. You cannot print these tickets at home, so online purchases will incur $14 to $19 in shipping charges. There are a number of attractive vacation packages now being offered that include the Orlando FlexTicket plus hotel accommodations in the International Drive area and other benefits. For more information, contact your nearest travel agent.

Which Price Is Right?

First, it is a good strategy to purchase your tickets online at the Universal Orlando website. This gets you a $20 discount on multi-day tickets. But mostly what the online option does is save you time.

If your schedule only allows one day at Universal Orlando, the choice is both simple and complicated. Simple because you'll only need a one-day pass, complicated because you must choose between two wonderful parks or try to do both parks in one day. If you will be visiting at a busy time of year, the best advice is to choose one park. The one-day, two-park option will pretty much give you a "Universal's Greatest Hits" sort of experience with many attractions missed for lack of time. However, if you are visiting during a slow period, are staying at an on-site hotel (which gives you preferred access to rides), or know you will be skipping kiddie attractions and "aggressive" rides like the roller coasters, then you can probably comfortably do two parks in a single day. Conversely, if you will only be doing the aggressive thrill rides, then the two-park option might also work for you, especially if you are staying on site.

But please, please, please don't try to cram both parks into a single day. Now that both Harry Potter areas, Diagon Alley and Hogsmeade, are open, a visit to Universal Orlando cries out to be — at the very minimum — a two-day experience. In fact, Universal's multi-day options are so reasonably priced that you really owe it to yourself to slow down and smell the roses. But if you only have one day available, please try to avoid the temptation to do both parks.

So let's say you have one day. Which park should you choose? The easy answer is that with the opening of Diagon Alley and the almost-as-new Transformers ride plus the Springfield U.S.A. area USF will be the one all your friends back home want to hear about. And yet, IOA has those roller coasters and what is arguably the superior Harry Potter ride.

On a practical level, if you like live shows and 3-D movies but hate upside-down roller coasters and soaking water rides, you might find Universal Studios Florida more to your liking. USF also features fewer outdoor attractions, making it a drier choice in inclement weather. Read the chapters that follow and make your own decision.

If you have two days, then the most sensible option is to purchase a Two-Day Base Ticket and visit each park on different days. If you can spend three or four days in the parks, additional discounts kick in that make the Park-to-Park Access option most attractive. Note that Two-Park tickets are mandatory to experience the *Hogwarts Express* train connecting the parks' Harry Potter areas.

At four days, however, the cost of parking (4 days times $17 is $68!) makes it more economical to purchase a Preferred Annual Pass (with its discounts) for one member of your party, and Park-to-Park tickets for the rest. And if you are considering a stay at one of the resort hotels, remember that an annual pass will entitle you to special rates if you come at the right time of year. For example, annual passholder rates at the Hard Rock Hotel can sometimes be $60 less than the best rate available. A four-day stay and the annual pass practically pays for itself!

Think twice before grabbing a Power Pass, however. This option makes sense only if you have figured a way around paying for parking. The dollar difference between a Preferred annual pass and the Power Pass is roughly five days of paid parking. Factor in the blackout dates and the money you lose by not getting a discount on meals and shopping and the Power Pass looks even less attractive. The Premier Annual Pass is only recommended for locals and frequent visitors who like late afternoon Express access, the added luxury of preferred or valet parking, CityWalk clubs, and Halloween Horror Nights. If you don't plan on taking advantage of those perks, it will be hard to make the additional investment pay off.

The Orlando FlexTicket is also an excellent buy for people whose main interest is Universal and who have two weeks to spend in central Florida. You can spend one day each at the other parks and the remaining 10 or 11 days coming and going as you please at the two Universal parks. The per-day cost is roughly $24 to $27, which is a lot of entertainment bang for the buck.

If you have any doubts about whether you will enjoy the theme park experience, you can hedge your bets. You can upgrade any pass to a more expensive pass while you are still in the park. The price you pay will be exactly what you would have paid if you'd purchased the more expensive pass when you first arrived.

Discounts

Discounts on Orlando theme park tickets in general are not what they used to be and Universal, with its discounted online multi-day ticket pricing and "best price guarantee," has done an excellent job of discouraging you from shopping around. If you insist, there are some options if you desperately need to save a few bucks. Be aware that any discounts you find will be off the so-called gate price, not the discounted price Universal offers online. Make sure you know Universal's online price for the tickets you need so you can make apples-to-apples comparisons.

AAA. Triple-A members receive a modest discount for up to six people, at the gate on the two-day Universal Orlando pass only. The policies on AAA discounts change frequently, so double-check by calling one of the toll-free numbers given earlier. AAA members can also buy their tickets through a local AAA club office, in which case the discount will no doubt be better and will vary from club to club.

Ticket Brokers. Ticket brokers are ubiquitous in Orlando; just about every hotel lobby has one, although they do not often have the best deals. It's easier to shop online before your visit. Two reputable online brokers are TicketMania.com and UndercoverTourist.com, both of which offer free shipping.

Timeshare Come-ons. Some ticket brokers advertise Universal tickets for an eye-popping $20 or even for free. The catch is, you must agree to sit through a presentation on timeshare properties. My advice: Don't.

Medical Discounts. Disabled guests receive a 15% discount on one- and two-day tickets. You must "request this discount at the front gate at the time of your ticket purchase." You will not be asked to prove you have a disability or other medical condition.

Active Military. Active members of the U.S. military receive a 10% discount on multi-day tickets at the front gates. For a 15% discount on "select advance purchase tickets" call (800) 407-4275.

Travel Agents. Bona-fide travel agents (there is a strict screening process) receive complimentary one-day admission to the parks. For more information on how to apply, visit www.universaltravelagents.com.

Vacation Packages. If you purchase a vacation package that includes airfare, hotel, and a rental car, as well as passes to Universal Orlando, you are probably getting a very good buy on the tickets. If you are making Universal Orlando the primary focus of your trip, these package deals offer excellent value and make a lot of sense. Packages purchased through universalorlandovacations.com may include free dining, early park admission, and other exclusive perks; there's even one that features a volunteer experience with ill children at Give Kids the World.

Best Price Guarantee. If you find a better deal online *after purchasing tickets from Universal*, let Universal know at (877) 589-4783 or email them via www.visitorsatisfaction.com/contactus/ and they will make up the difference in Universal Orlando Resort Gift Cards, which you can use for food or merchandise at the parks.

Discounts in the Parks. Once inside the parks, your AAA card will get you 10% off most food and merchandise. If you pay with an American Express card, you will receive 10% off food and non-alcoholic beverages, 10% off merchandise purchases over $50 and 15% off merchandise purchases over $75. Use your Amex card to pay for Photo Connect (see *Good Things to Know About* ... below) and receive a complimentary photo.

Universal Express

Long lines are the biggest complaint people have about theme parks. Wouldn't it be great if you could just get on every ride without having to cool your heels in line for an hour or more? Well, the **Universal Express Pass** system lets you do just that. Or you can purchase a hi-tech toy that trims your wait times more modestly.

Universal Express works like this: Most rides and attractions have an "Express queue" marked with the "Universal Express" logo. Show your Express Pass to an attendant, have it scanned, and you're in, bypassing the regular queue line. Read on for the fine print.

■ Universal Express for Resort Guests

Guests at the luxury resort hotels (but not Cabana Bay Beach Resort) get the best deal in the theme park industry — unlimited Express Pass access for the length of their stay. Upon check-in, you can use kiosks in the lobby that snap an image of every member of your party and spit out personalized Express passes, photo included. This system replaces the use of hotel room key cards as the open sesame to the Express queues in the parks, which presented a number of problems, not the least of which was people sharing their cards with friends who weren't hotel guests. Because each pass is embedded with a photo of the user, the passes are much more secure.

Note: These personalized Universal Express Unlimited passes are used *only* for Express access to rides and attractions within the parks. You will still use your room key to get early access to the parks and, thus, the Wizarding World of Harry Potter (see *Chapter Five* for details).

Once in the parks, these passes grant immediate access to the Universal Express Pass queues. Simply show your card to the attendant at the Express queue and you are in. Best of all, you can use this perk all day and ride each ride as many times as you wish.

Everyone staying in the same room can take advantage of this perk at his or her own discretion, but even if your family tours the parks as a group, the official policy is to check every card. Cards will be examined carefully by an attendant to make sure that your pass is still valid, so make sure everyone has theirs, just in case.

Tip: Your pass gives you Express access on the day you check in and all day the day you check out. So you can check in very early and, even though your room isn't ready, get a pass to use at the parks. When you check out, hang on to your card and use it at the parks for the rest of the day.

■ Universal Express for Everyone Else

If you are not staying at one of the luxury resorts, you can buy your way to the front of the line by purchasing — in addition to your park admission — an Express Pass with a bar code that grants you entry into the Express queues. These passes come in two flavors — the basic Universal Express Pass, which gives you Express access to each ride or attraction once per day, and the Universal Express Unlimited Pass, which as the name suggests lets you ride every ride as many times as you like on each day. The passes can be utilized whenever you choose; you don't have to make a reservation or pick up a ticket and return later at an assigned time.

These passes can be purchased for one park (Universal Studios Florida **or** Islands of Adventure) or for two parks (Universal Studios Florida **and** Islands of Adventure). If you purchase a pass at the parks, it will be a one-day pass and can be used on the date of purchase only. If you purchase passes in advance online, which is your better choice, you can buy one-, two-, three-, or four-day passes, which are date specific. That is, they can be used only on the day or days you choose when you purchase them in advance online, which is the preferred method.

These passes are not particularly cheap and they are priced and sold on a per-day basis, so the cost can mount up quickly. To find out how much you will pay for the privilege of Express access, go to the "Tickets" drop-down menu on the UniversalOrlando.com website and look for the "Express Passes" link.

Note: Universal occasionally changes the navigation on their site, just to keep you on your toes.

At press time, one-park Universal Express Passes have been selling in advance online for between $35 and $110 (plus tax) per day depending on the date. One-park Universal Express Unlimited Passes were $50 to $140. Two-park passes were $40 to $120 per day for the basic one-use-per-ride version and $60 to $150 for the unlimited option. The same passes bought at the park will cost about $10 more. In the past, a one-park Express Pass pass only valid after 4:00 p.m. was occasionally sold on peak days for $36. If this option is offered again (never a sure bet) it will undoubtedly cost more.

Quantities of all types of passes are limited (the exact number issued is a closely guarded secret) and once they're gone for a given day, they're gone. Like airlines that try to squeeze every last cent out of the available seats on a flight, Universal reserves the right to bump prices up without notice if they think the demand is great enough. At each ride, your card will be scanned by an attendant using a hand-held device, so you will not be able to use the basic Universal Express Pass more than once per ride.

When you purchase in advance online you will be presented with a calendar stretching out a year; each day has been assigned a dollar amount. This, by the way, is a great way of gauging the relative number of guests in the parks on a given date, or at least Universal's best guess as to attendance. You may decide that, if the dates of your visit will be a slow time (as indicated by the lowest price for passes), paying for Express access is a luxury you don't need. (See *Notes and Comments* below.)

■ Notes and Comments on Universal Express

Before you spend a small fortune on Universal Express Passes, think carefully about the Passes and minuses.

Most importantly, none of the insanely popular Harry Potter rides offer Express access. That means you'll wait like everybody else for *Escape From Gringotts*, *Hogwarts Express*, the Ollivanders wand experience, and *Forbidden Journey*. (*Flight of the Hippogriff* and *Dragon Challenge* have Express access, but they are reworkings of earlier rides.) Apparently, J. K. Rowling decreed that Universal couldn't separate the haves from the have-nots on her rides. Bully for her! And Universal Express does not give you priority access into the Wizarding World areas when entrances are limited due to capacity.

In addition to the Harry Potter rides, Universal Express is not accepted at the low-capacity attractions *Pteranodon Flyers* and *Kang & Kodos' Twirl 'n' Hurl*. The rides and attractions that do accept it will be indicated by the yellow Universal Express logo on the map you pick up when you enter the theme parks.

There is actually a downside to Universal Express on some rides like *Revenge of the Mummy*, *Transformers*, *Men In Black*, and *Spider-Man*. Because you miss the queue line, you miss the setup for the ride's story line. Consequently, you don't experience the ride at its fullest. The best advice is to try using the Universal Express Pass system only after you have experienced these rides at least once through the regular line. Also, Universal Express Passes are not the only way to jump to the front of the line. A few rides in each park offer "single rider lines" that can cut your waiting time dramatically. These are indicated in the *Good Things To Know About...* sections of *Chapters Two* and *Three*.

I will go out on a limb and suggest that at slow times (days when Express Passes are cheapest) they are probably not necessary, especially if you are willing to get to the park at opening and stay the entire day. The exception might be a case in which you have just one day and there is an Express-eligible ride (or two) you absolutely don't want to miss. In that case, it might be worth hedging your bets with a basic Universal Express Pass.

At the other end of the spectrum are busy periods like Christmas, when an Express pass may be the only way to guarantee you'll experience all your favorite rides. But consider this: If there are three people in your party and two-day Universal Express Unlimited passes are $150, that's $450! That could be more than the difference between a night's stay at an on-site luxury resort and what you're already paying to stay elsewhere. Remember that a one-night stay at an on-site resort gives you two days of free front of the line access! So sharpen your pencil and think this decision through.

Note: You may sometimes hear Universal Express referred to as "Front of the Line" or FOTL. Some people mistakenly take this to mean that they will quite literally be placed on the ride ahead of everybody else who is waiting. Not so. In effect, you are placed on a separate, shorter queue. You will experience a short wait, at least at peak times. The official word is that it will be no more than 15 minutes although at peak times it can be longer. Usually it is much less. On the other hand, there will be situations (I'm looking at you *Poseidon's Fury*) when an Express pass will save you no time at all.

Of course, rules and policies may change, so check with Guest Services or your resort hotel concierge for exceptions and restrictions at the time of your visit.

■ U-Bot Ride Reservation System

Universal offers another way to beat those long waits in line. It's called the U-Bot Ride Reservation System and it operates alongside (but does not replace) the existing Express options. U-Bot is an egg-shaped electronic gizmo resembling the 1990's Tamagotchi toys. Use the buttons to select the ride you want a reservation for on the black and white screen, and the U-Bot will give you a time after which your party is allowed to enter through the Express entrance. You can use your reservation at any time after the time given, but you will not be able to get another reservation until that one is used. Like Universal Express, U-Bot is not valid at *Escape From Gringotts, Forbidden Journey, Kang and Kodos',* or *Pteranodon Flyers.*

The cost is $40 per person for unlimited reservations and $30 per person for one reservation per ride, although these prices could rise in busier periods. Up to six people can share one but all are charged the same fee. Pricing is subject to change and the system may not be available at the time of your visit. The system can only be used in one park at a time, and requires a credit card deposit to ensure you return the gadget.

Universal's Prepaid Dining Plans

Universal offers a number of prepaid dining and drink offers of varying value. The various plans are not so much about saving money (it's unlikely that you will save much) as they are about the convenience of knowing you have your meals paid for before entering the parks. Here are the details; all prices include tax.

■ Universal Dining Plan

Universal has introduced a "Universal Dining Plan" (UDP) similar to the one popularized by Walt Disney World. This is not an "all-you-can-eat" deal, but a credit system where guests prepay for a set number of meals. The plan costs $55.37 per day for adults, $19.16 per child (3 to 9), and can only be purchased with a hotel and park ticket package booked through Universal Parks & Resorts Vacations (universalorlandovacations.com); it is not available for purchase at the parks. You don't have to buy it for every day of your vacation, but you must purchase it for every member of your party over age two staying in your hotel room.

Using the plan is cumbersome and comes with some fine print that may not be to your liking. If you have purchased the plan, when you arrive at your on-site hotel you will receive a voucher that can be exchanged for a Dining Card at any on-site hotel ticket desk, or at dining reservation carts, or Guest Services inside the parks. The UDP card tracks your dining credits. For every plan day purchased, each guest gets:

- One table service meal (entree, dining plan dessert, soft drink)
- One counter service meal (entree, soft drink)
- One snack (from food cart or counter service)
- One beverage (from food cart or counter service)

The good news is that over 100 locations in the parks and CityWalk participate in the plan, including such popular sit-down restaurants as Mythos and Leaky Cauldron. The bad news is that not every dining venue is represented, including Three Broomsticks. The vast majority of venues listed as participating in the plan are in the "snacks" category and include seasonal carts that come and go. The fine print notes that venues can be added and deleted without notice, so what will be on offer when you visit is hard to predict.

The Dining Card does not allow you to order just anything. Table service restaurants give you free rein, but at quick service and snack venues only those menu items called out with the UDP symbol are fair game. Only the small size of beverages qualify for the plan, for example; more expensive desserts tend to be excluded. Kids must order from the kids' menu only. No substitutions are allowed, which means that you can't opt for a salad in lieu of a dessert for example. Gratuities are not included, so to tip your server at a table service restaurant you will have to use cash or credit card.

Personally, when the virtually non-existent cost savings are added to the minor inconveniences and the restricted choices, the Universal Dining Plan does not strike me as a particularly good deal. Your mileage may differ, of course.

■ Universal Dining Plan — Quick Service

This could be called the "Universal Dining Plan for the Rest of Us." Unlike its big brother, it is available to everyone visiting the parks, but it cuts out the table service restaurants and limits you to:

- One counter service meal (entree, soft drink)
- One snack (from food cart or counter service)
- One beverage (from food cart or counter service)

The cost is $21.29 for adults and $13.83 for kids (3 to 9). You have a better chance of saving money with this plan than you do with the full Universal Dining Plan. If you order the most expensive item in each category, an adult might save about $10 to $12.

This plan can be purchased at any dining venue or shop in the parks.

■ Coca-Cola Freestyle Souvenir Cup

If you have a deep thirst or a desire to taste the bewildering variety of Coca-Cola "freestyle" flavors, this offer might appeal to you. Purchasing a "Coca-Cola Freestyle Souvenir Cup" for $12.77 entitles you to unlimited soft drink refills from the parks' newfangled Freestyle machines, which dispense over 100 exotic varieties of sugar water. You can add another day of refills for $6.38; computer chips inside the cups keep you from cheating. Confusingly, a variety of souvenir cups is sold inside the parks for $9.57 to $15.98 that can be refilled for $0.99 anywhere *except* at Freestyle fountains.

Good Things To Know About...

Here are some general notes that apply to both of the theme parks at Universal Orlando. Notes that are specific to the individual parks are included in the appropriate chapter.

■ Access for the Disabled

Universal Orlando makes a special effort for its disabled guests. (In fact, you are likely to see disabled people among the staff at the parks.) Special viewing areas are set aside at most shows; there are even kennels for guide dogs that cannot accompany their masters on some rides.

Guests with prosthetic limbs must be able to grasp the ride restraints; for safety, certain attractions may require limb removal before riding, or have additional restrictions. Visit Universal's website and search for "ADA Information" in the search field to download their "Rider's Guide" with detailed accessibility information.

Wheelchairs can be rented in the Hub between the parking lots, as well as inside the parks, for $12 per day. Electric convenience vehicles (ECV) can be rented just inside the entrances to both parks; the rate is $50 per day. For either, you must provide a $50 cash deposit or credit card information, and a signed rental contract. A one-week advance reservation is recommended for ECVs, which tend to sell out quickly. Call (407) 224-4233 to make reservations at either park.

Tip: You can rent a wheelchair at the Hub (near the parking garages) and then "upgrade" to an ECV once you reach the park. When you return the ECV, you will have a wheelchair waiting for the trip back to the Hub.

Even if a disability doesn't require a wheelchair, stop by Guest Services with the disabled person and request a free "Attraction Assistance Pass" (AAP). It allows those incapable of waiting in the standard queue to use an alternate entrance. No medical proof should be required, but if your disability (or your child's) isn't obvious you may want to bring a letter from your doctor. Note that this does not entitle you to "skip the line" on busy days; if the standby wait is over 30 minutes, you will be instructed to return later for your ride.

■ Auditions

If you think being a performer at Universal Orlando would be a lot of fun, you are not alone. To whet your appetite, visit universalauditions.com, where they announce upcoming tryouts and give details on exactly what they're looking for. Who knows? This could be your big break.

■ Babies

Little ones under three are admitted free and strollers are available for rent if you don't have your own. There are also diaper changing stations in all the major restrooms (men's and women's) and nursing facilities at First Aid. But that's as far as it goes. Make sure you have an adequate supply of diapers, formula, and baby food before you head for the park. Strollers and "kiddie cars" can be rented just inside the entrances of both parks. Single strollers are $15 per day and doubles are $25; single kiddie cars are $18, doubles are $28.

■ Baby "Swaps"

All rides can accommodate parents whose little ones are too small to ride. One parent rides, while the other waits in a holding area with the child. Then the parents switch off and the second parent rides without a second wait in line. It's a great system, and works just as well for timid older children.

■ Breakdowns

Rides break down. They are highly complex mechanical wonders and are subjected to a great deal of stress. Some mechanical failure is inevitable. If you are on a ride when it breaks down, you may receive a pass that will give you priority access to the ride once it's working again.

■ Car Trouble

If you return to your car and find the battery dead, Universal will give you a free jump start. Raise the hood to alert the attendants. If the problem is more serious, they will help you get assistance.

■ Drinking

Universal Orlando provides beer at outdoor stands, in all sit-down restaurants, and at many fast-food outlets as well. Wine is also available. Hard liquor is served at many restaurants and at walk-up windows in CityWalk, and booze flows freely inside the parks during Halloween and Mardi Gras events. The legal drinking age in Florida is 21 and photo IDs will be requested of anyone appearing 30 or younger. Try to feel flattered rather than annoyed. Although you can drink as you stroll about, taking alcoholic beverages through the turnstiles as you leave the parks is not allowed.

■ Emergencies

As a general rule, the moment something goes amiss, speak with the nearest Universal employee (and one won't be far away). They will contact security or medical assistance.

First Aid. Each park has two first aid stations. See the chapters on the individual parks for information on locations.

Lost Children. It happens all the time, and there's a good chance an alert employee will have spotted your wandering child before you notice he or she is gone. Rather than frantically search on your own, contact an employee. Found kids are escorted to Guest Services and entertained until their parents can be located.

Lost Property. Go to Lost & Found on the Front Lot at Universal Studios Florida or in the Port of Entry at Islands of Adventure — or dial (407) 224-4233 and press "2" — and report any loss as soon as you notice it. The Guest Services window in CityWalk also has a lost and found section. Be prepared to provide as accurate a description as possible. Universal has an excellent track record for recovering the seemingly unrecoverable.

■ Guest Services

The friendly folks at Guest Services can answer just about any question you have. If you have a problem or complaint while in the parks, seek out the Guest Services office at the front of the park (in the Front Lot at USF and in Port of Entry at IOA). If you have a question you can call (407) 224-4233 and press "3," to speak with a Guest Services representative.

■ Happy Hour

Boozers despair! The once generous and expansive happy hours inside Universal Orlando's parks are a thing of the past. Only Backwater Bar in Islands of Adventure continues the tradition. At press time, only three places in CityWalk were cutting drink prices — NBA City (4:00 to 7:00 p.m.), Emeril's (4:00 to 8:00 p.m.), and Red Coconut (4:00 to 9:00 p.m.).

■ Height Restrictions and Other Warnings

Due to a variety of considerations, such as sudden movements and the configuration of lap restraints, some rides will be off-limits to shorter (typically younger) guests. The following rides have minimum height requirements:

E.T. Adventure (USF)	34 in. (86.4 cm.)
Woody Woodpecker's Nuthouse Coaster (USF)	36 in. (91.4 cm.)
Flight of the Hippogriff (IOA)	36 in. (91.4 cm.)
Pteranodon Flyers (IOA)	36 in. (91.4 cm.)
Despicable Me (USF)	40 in. (101.6 cm.)
The Simpsons Ride (USF)	40 in. (101.6 cm.)
Transformers (USF)	40 in. (101.6 cm.)
High in Sky Seuss Ride (IOA)	40 in. (101.6 cm.)
Spider-Man (IOA)	40 in. (101.6 cm.)
Men In Black (USF)	42 in. (106.7 cm.)
Escape From Gringotts (USF)	42 in. (106.7 cm.)
Jurassic Park River Adventure (IOA)	42 in. (106.7 cm.)
Popeye & Bluto's Bilge-Rat Barges (IOA)	42 in. (106.7 cm.)
Dudley Do-Right's Ripsaw Falls (IOA)	44 in. (111.8 cm.)
Revenge of the Mummy (USF)	48 in. (121.9 cm.)
Forbidden Journey (IOA)	48 in. (121.9 cm.)
Hollywood Rip Ride Rockit (USF)	51 in. (130 cm.)
Doctor Doom's Fearfall (IOA)	52 in. (131.1 cm.)
Incredible Hulk & *Dragon Challenge* (IOA)	54 in. (137.2 cm.)

In addition, any child under 48 inches must be accompanied by an adult on all rides and must be able to sit upright without help. Stationary seating is available at *Despicable Me, Shrek 4-D, Terminator 2:3-D,* and *Twister* for guests who don't meet the height requirement, or anyone who doesn't want to be shaken, bumped, or dropped. Parents of small kids trying to decide between the two parks should note that IOA has 12 height-restricted rides to USF's 9, and has higher average minimums, although IOA also has more playgrounds. Height requirements will also be noted in the following chapters at the start of each applicable attraction's description.

Another problem may be encountered by taller and heavier guests. *Forbidden Journey*, the roller coasters, and *Doctor Doom's Fearfall* employ state-of-the-art harness-like contraptions to make sure that you don't go flying off into space. Unfortunately, not everyone fits into them. Anyone with a chest measurement over 50 inches may have difficulty fitting into the harness and at 54 inches (137.2 cm.) you can pretty much forget about it. Height is less of a problem (they say basketball players have ridden) but some extremely tall individuals may also be out of luck, especially at *Rip Ride Rockit,* which has a 79-inch height limit. Some attractions have designated seats designed to accommodate larger riders; ask an attendant for details. All rides with restrictive restraints provide a sample seat outside so you can check to see if you'll fit. These, by the way, also offer great **photo ops**.

■ Internet Access

Universal has made major strides in providing free Wi-Fi in the parks and in CityWalk, although it can still be spotty in places. If you're having problems getting Wi-Fi on your smartphone, try moving to a different location. The lobbies of the on-site hotels are a reliable place to find free Wi-Fi. If all else fails, use 3G (rather spotty) or LTE (quite strong) service on your smartphone inside the parks.

Universal has released a free smartphone app for iPhone and Android that offers park and hotel information along with real-time wait times for rides and attractions. Unfortunately, it can be hard to find on the app stores amid the welter of copycat apps from third party vendors, so poke about until you see the official Universal logo.

■ Kids' Menus

All table service restaurants and most quick service venues offer a $7 kids' menu.

■ Leaving the Parks

You can leave either park at any time and be readmitted free the same day. Just have your hand stamped on the way out. You will also have to show your ticket again when you return, since some tickets only allow admittance to one park. Those with annual passes can skip this formality.

Most people use this system when they visit the restaurants in CityWalk or go back to the hotel for a quick afternoon nap, but it's a good idea for Mom and Dad to have their hands stamped when leaving the park for the day, just in case you need to check back with Lost & Found.

■ Lockers

Electronically controlled lockers are available at both parks and allow un-limited in-and-out all-day access. They cost $8 or $10 a day, depending on size, and accept both bills and credit cards. The more "aggressive" rides re-strict what you can carry with you, so lockers are provided and their use is mandatory. They are usually free for a short period of time, which varies with the length of the lines. After that, $3 is charged for each half hour of use, to a daily maximum of $20. Should you overstay your welcome, you will have to pay to retrieve your stuff. Water-related rides also provide lock-ers, but charge $4 for the first 90 minutes and $3 for each additional hour, up to a $20 daily maximum.

■ Pets

If you have pets, inform the attendant when you pay for your parking and you will be directed to the Universal Studios kennels. Pet boarding is $15 a day for each animal (50% off the first pet for Premier annual passholders). The accommodations are comfortable, if not precisely luxurious. You sup-ply the food, they supply the bowl and water. However, Universal's staff will not feed or care for your pet; they won't even touch it. If your pet needs to be walked or fed at specific times, you must return to the kennel and take care of it yourself.

Kennels close two hours after park closing; after that, you'll have to ap-peal to Security to spring your pet. Pets are not only welcomed but pam-pered at the luxury resort hotels (but not at Cabana Bay).

■ Phone Numbers

Although most are mentioned elsewhere, here is a handy list of important phone numbers:

General Info:	(407) 363-8000
TDD Line:	(407) 224-4414 or (800) 447-0672
Guest Services:	(407) 224-4233 - Press 3
Lost and Found:	(407) 224-4233 - Press 2
Park Hours:	(407) 224-4233 - Press 1

Ticket Sales: (407) 224-7840
Universal Vacations: (407) 224-7000 or (877) 801-9720
Jobs: (407) 363-8080
Event Hotline: (407) 224-5500
Merchandise: (407) 224-5800 or (888) 762-0820
Dining: (407) 224-4233
Hotel Reservations: (888) 273-1311
Portofino Bay: (407) 503-1000
Hard Rock Hotel: (407) 503-2000
Royal Pacific: (407) 503-3000
Cabana Bay: (407) 503-4000

■ Photos, Photo Connect, and Star Card

Guests are welcome to take their own snapshots in the parks, but you'll never want for opportunities to purchase photographic proof of your Universal adventures. Grab a free **Photo Connect** card from any street photographer, character meet-and-greet, or on-ride photo counter. Have it scanned by any further paparazzi you pose for and load it with as many shots as you like. Then buy prints at ride exits, meet-and-greets, and the photo shops near each park's entrance. Prices start around $20 each ($30 for *Forbidden Journey*) with online digital copies offered for $5 extra; a few (like *Rockit* and *Hulk*) sell videos as well. Any unpurchased pics go poof when the parks close.

You can download and share photos you've purchased through Universal's Photo Connect service by registering the number under your Photo Connect card's barcode at photoconnect.amazingpictures.com. To do so, however, you have to buy a "package" that lets you view all your digital purchases in an online gallery and then turn them into (pricey) prints, posters, pillows, and plates.

If you want to buy more than a picture or two, a likely scenario, the most cost-effective option may be purchasing an online **Star Card package**, which offers unlimited digital downloads of all your photos for three consecutive days as well as a CD full of your chosen photos for $59.95. Other options include a one-day package (without the photo CD) for $39.95 and a fourteen-day package for $89.95.

There's an annual passholder plan, also for $89.95, with unlimited photo downloads for a full year. All online photos expire 90 days after purchase (except for passholders) so don't forget to download them. Note that prices and package elements change frequently, both upward and downward, but you'll always save by buying online.

■ Priority Seating

Some restaurants in the parks and most in CityWalk offer "priority seating," which is subtly different from a reservation. It means that the restaurant will give you the first table that will accommodate your party that becomes available at or after the time you requested. To arrange a table, call (407) 224-3613 or visit OpenTable.com.

■ Shopping from Home

Forgot to buy a replica Allspark for your favorite uncle, or Slytherin robes for your least-favorite cousin? You can take care of both through Universal's online merchandise shop at www.universalorlando.com/Merchandise/MerchandiseHome.aspx. Domestic shipping starts at $6.95; international orders run $30 to $70. If you need assistance, call (888) 762-0820 or (407) 224-5800 and they will help you shop.

■ Smoking

Florida state law prohibits smoking in all restaurants. Smoking is not permitted in lines to the rides and attractions either. In fact, Universal has tried to take things a step further by limiting outdoor smoking to specified areas, marked on the maps with purple signs bearing a lit cigarette symbol. This system has met with only partial success and complaints about smoking in non-designated areas are frequently heard.

■ Visiting the Resort Hotels

The resort hotels offer plenty of atmosphere along with good restaurants and bars. You don't have to be a hotel guest to enjoy them. Feel free to stroll over from CityWalk or the theme parks for a meal or drinks or just to look around. Or take the complimentary water taxis from the dock in CityWalk or the shuttle bus to Cabana Bay; some people don't realize that they are open to all and not exclusively for hotel guests. Hotel pools are reserved for registered guests, of course, but if you are staying on-site you can pool-hop anywhere in the resort.

Beware of paid parking at the hotels; unless you get validation from one of the hotel restaurants, you may get sticker shock.

A Note on Costs

Let's face it, visiting a theme park resort destination is not precisely a budget vacation, and Universal Orlando is no exception. A three-day visit by a typical family of four will cost over $650 in admissions alone. Of course, compared to other forms of entertainment, Universal Orlando offers excellent value for the dollar, as most people will agree.

Nonetheless, most of us must keep an eye on how much money we are spending, so throughout the book you will be given a quick idea of how much things like restaurants and hotels cost using dollar signs. Unless otherwise noted, all listed prices from here on in are *before* tax (except alcohol, which is always priced tax-inclusive).

For restaurants, estimates are for an average meal, without alcoholic beverages. In the case of full-service restaurants, estimates are based on a "full" meal consisting of an appetizer or salad, an entree, and dessert. At the end of the book, in *Chapter Seven*, you will find a list of hotels that are off Universal's property but convenient to the parks. Hotel estimates are based on one night's stay in a double room. The cost rankings are as follows:

	Restaurants	**Hotels**
$	Under $15	Under $100
$$	$15 - $25	$100 - $150
$$$	$25 - $40	$150 - $200
$$$$	Over $40	Over $200

As for fast-food prices, you don't have to worry about comparison shopping within the parks; a soda or popcorn should cost the same no matter which cart or window you buy from. (The exceptions are higher prices at some third-party franchises like Starbucks, and at specialty eateries in the Harry Potter and Simpsons areas). Rather than repeat prices in the following chapters, here is a sampling of standard costs for quick-service comestibles before tax:

Cheeseburger & fries: $7.99/ +bacon $0.75   Chicken Caesar Salad: $8.99
Hot dog & chips: $8.49/chili dog & fries $8.99   Turkey Leg & Chips: $12.99
Deli Sandwich: $8.99/Soup & sandwich $9.99   Meatball Sub: $7.99
Pasta: $6.99/ with meatballs: $8.49   French Fries: $2.99
Chicken Fingers or Wrap w/ fries: $8.79   Chili Cheese Fries: $4.99
Fried Chicken platter or Fish & Chips: $13.99   Onion Rings: $3.89
Pizza: $7.49 to $8.49 personal/ $32 pie   Side Salad: $3.69

Rib Meal: $15.99/Rotisserie Chicken: $10.99   Corn on the Cob: $3.49
Soda: $2.99 22 oz/ $3.19 32 oz/ $8.99 souvenir   Bottled Water: $2.75
Hot Tea/ Coffee/ Hot Chocolate: $2.39   Bottled Juice: $2.29
Milkshake: $3.99 to $6.29   Pretzel or Churro: $3.99
Popcorn: $3.49 reg/ $5.99 souvenir/ $1.29 refill   Novelty Ice Cream: $3.99
Frozen Slush: $3.75 virgin/ $7.75 alcoholic   Fruit Cup: $3.79
Soft Serve: $3.49 cup/ $4.49 waffle cone   Bag of Chips: $2.99
Draft Domestic Beer: $6.25 / $8.75 pilsner   Wine: $6 glass
Pastries and Cakes: $3.99 to $4.89   Brownie: $3.49
Dippin' Dots: $4.99 reg/ $5.99 large   Brookie: $2.79
Root Beer Float: $3.59 to $5.79   Soup: $3.49

Accuracy and Other Impossible Dreams

While this book strives to be as accurate, comprehensive, and up-to-date as possible, these are all unattainable goals. Any theme park worth its salt is constantly changing and upgrading its attractions. Restaurants change their menus; shops revamp their choice of merchandise with the seasons and even the theme of the shop itself. On top of that, some attractions are seasonal; that is, they operate only when the crowds come.

What are most likely to change, alas, are prices. Like any business, Universal reserves the right to change its prices at any time without notice, so it's possible that prices will be revised after the deadline for this book. If you do run into price increases, they will typically be modest.

The Intrepid Traveler, the publisher of this book, maintains an entire website with updated information about Universal Orlando and other non-Disney attractions in the Orlando area. Log on to the blog for the latest on prices and new rides and attractions:

■ **http://www.TheOtherOrlando.com/tooblog**

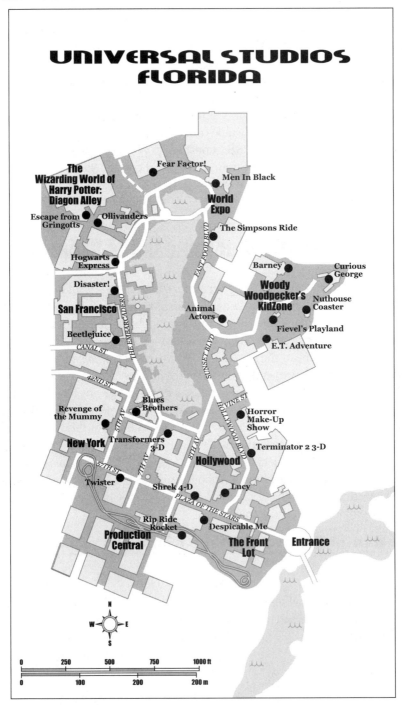

UNIVERSAL STUDIOS FLORIDA

The Wizarding World of Harry Potter: Diagon Alley

Escape from Gringotts

Ollivanders

Fear Factor!

Men In Black

World Expo

The Simpsons Ride

Hogwarts Express

Barney

Curious George

Disaster!

Woody Woodpecker's KidZone

Nuthouse Coaster

San Francisco

Animal Actors

Fievel's Playland

Beetlejuice

E.T. Adventure

CANAL ST

THE EMBARCADERO

FAST FOOD BLVD

SUNSET BLVD

42ND ST

Blues Brothers

Revenge of the Mummy

HOLLYWOOD BLVD

VINE ST

Horror Make-Up Show

New York

Transformers 3-D

Terminator 2 3-D

5TH AV

8TH AV

7TH AV

57TH ST

Hollywood

Twister

Shrek 4-D

Lucy

PLAZA OF THE STARS

Rip Ride Rocket

Despicable Me

Entrance

Production Central

The Front Lot

N W E S

| 0 | 250 | 500 | 750 | 1000 ft |
| 0 | 100 | 200 | 200 m |

CHAPTER TWO:

UNIVERSAL STUDIOS FLORIDA

R ide The Movies! The brilliant opening-day ad slogan coined by Steven Spielberg, though sadly no longer in circulation, still says it all. In creating its first Florida theme park, Universal Studios built on the lessons learned over three decades at their original Hollywood movie-themed attraction and injected a giant jolt of high-tech thrills. In the years since, most of the park's filmmaking "edutainment" has given way to some of the world's greatest thrill rides. But the cinematic spirit still thrives here among meticulously detailed, movie-like sets that can make the simple act of sitting down to eat a hot dog seem like an adventure.

In the past decade or so, Universal Studios Florida has gone through an amazing evolution. Former headliners have been replaced or radically revamped from their original incarnations, and numerous new adventures have been added. Only the *E.T. Adventure* remains essentially unchanged. So if your last visit here was in the late nineties, it's a whole new park to you.

The process accelerated when Comcast acquired NBC-Universal and started pumping money into revamping old attractions and creating new ones. With the recent additions of *Transformers*, Springfield U.S.A., and the spectacular Wizarding World of Harry Potter: Diagon Alley with its *Hogwarts Express* link to Islands of Adventure, twenty-something Universal Studios Florida is starting to outshine its younger sibling next door.

Eating in Universal Studios Florida

Universal is unlikely to draw plaudits from die-hard gourmets. But Universal's culinary wizards have demonstrated a flair for witty and tasty themed food, starting with the Simpsons area and extending into Diagon Alley. And if you want a step up from the standard carnival fare, Finnegan's and Lombard's Seafood Grille, the two full-service restaurants in the park, have at least a dish or two that's better than average. Try the Fresh Fish at Lombard's or one of the Irish specialties at Finnegan's, for example, and you will feel very well fed indeed.

For most families, however, the fare will be of the standard fast-food variety — most of it edible and not too outrageously priced. The prices of modest choices in the full-service restaurants are roughly equivalent to the prices at the fast food joints. So for about the same amount or just a few dollars more, you can enjoy the luxury of table service and constant refills of your iced tea. It's an option worth considering.

In addition to the standard eateries, which are described in detail later, there are innumerable street-side kiosks, offering a wide variety of drinks and snacks, that appear and disappear as the crowds and weather dictate.

Shopping in Universal Studios Florida

It's easy to spend more on gifts and souvenirs than on admission. The standard, all-American souvenirs (T-shirts and the like) are priced slightly higher than their off-park equivalents, though some of them are very nicely designed. More upscale clothing, with the Universal logo displayed very discreetly, is sometimes available. When it is, it tends to be expensive but well made.

Rather than lug purchases with you, take advantage of Universal's package pickup service. Most shops will be happy to send your purchases to the It's A Wrap shop, near the front entrance, where you can pick them up on the way out. Or you can simply save all your shopping for the end of your visit and stop into the Universal Studios Store while the rest of the crowd is rushing to the gate at closing time. This shop has a good, although not complete, selection of merchandise from virtually every other shop in the park. You can also shop online at . . .

www.universalorlando.com/Merchandise/MerchandiseHome.aspx

All of USF's shops will be touched on later.

Good Things To Know About...

Here are some notes that apply specifically to Universal Studios Florida. General notes that apply to both parks will be found in *Chapter One.*

■ American Express Lounge

If you used your Amex card to purchase your park ticket or annual pass, you are entitled to enter the **American Express Passholder Lounge**, located in Production Central and open daily from noon to 5:00 p.m. Behind an easily overlooked door across from the Shrek shop lies a simple but air-conditioned oasis offering free phone charging stations, bottled water, and light snacks. You'll need your ticket receipt and credit card to get in, though simply showing your admission and Amex will usually suffice; ask at the ticket booths for details.

■ First Aid

There is a first aid station and nursing facility on Canal Street, across from *Beetlejuice's Graveyard Revue* and just beside Louie's Italian Restaurant. You'll also find first aid on the Front Lot near the Studio Audience Center.

■ Getting Wet

The *Curious George* play area in Woody Woodpecker's KidZone is straight out of a water park, and kids who visit there will not be able to resist the temptation to get absolutely drenched. On cooler days when a wet child could catch a chill, bring a towel and a change of clothes. On hot days, the park also opens a hydrant in the New York area for impromptu splashing.

■ PG-13 Ratings

Universal issues a "parental advisory" for kids under 13 on the following rides and attractions:

> *Beetlejuice's Graveyard Revue*
> *Terminator 2: 3-D*
> *Twister*
> *Universal Orlando's Horror Make-Up Show*

Most parents seem to ignore the warnings. In this day and age (sadly, perhaps), it's hard to imagine a child being shocked by anything.

■ Reservations

Both Lombard's Seafood Grille and Finnegan's accept dining reservations. They are highly recommended at any time and especially if you are visiting during the busy season, although a reservation is not an absolute guarantee of avoiding a short wait. You can make your reservations first thing in the morning when you arrive or by phone up to 24 hours in advance. The number to call is (407) 224-3613, or you can book a table online through OpenTable.com.

■ Single Rider Lines

At busy times, "Single Rider" lines can cut you to the front of the queue provided you are willing to be separated from your party. *Men In Black, Revenge of the Mummy, Transformers*, and *Hollywood Rip Ride Rockit* have single rider lines. Single rider entrances may shutter if there is too much demand (or not enough), so you can't always count on this option.

■ Special Diets

Lombard's Seafood Grille and Finnegan's can provide kosher meals with about an hour's advance notice and offer dishes with gluten-free and peanut-free ingredients; ask for the chef to make your meal. Call Food Services at (407) 363-8340 to make arrangements. Louie's Italian Restaurant also serves gluten-free pasta upon request. On vendor carts, turkey legs, fruit, and slush are gluten-free, hot dogs and churros are peanut-free, and turkey legs are both.

The 2-Park Guide Map's list of dining spots calls out restaurants offering "healthy choices," which usually means vegetarians can be accommodated; Lisa's Teahouse in Springfield's Fast Food Boulevard has the widest meat-free menu. Universal eliminated trans-fat oil from its menus in 2007; foods are fried in a canola/soy blend. Still, if you're on a low-fat regimen, sticking with salads and fruit plates is probably the best strategy. Lombard's has a nice selection of seafood and salads.

■ Special Events

The year is sprinkled with special events tied to the holiday calendar. The events listed here, with the notable exceptions of Rock The Universe and Halloween Horror Nights, are usually included in regular admission, but separate admission is sometimes charged for evening events.

Among the seasonal events Universal Studios puts on are:

Mardi Gras. New Orleans' pre-Lenten bacchanalia comes to Florida in the form of a nighttime parade, complete with garish and gaudy floats, plenty of baubles and beads that are flung into the outstretched hands of the crowd, and concerts by classic and current musical artists. The event typically runs Saturdays and select Fridays from early February until mid-April.

Christmas. Ho, ho, ho! It's a Hollywood version of a heartwarming family holiday, complete with a scaled-down version of New York's famous Macy's Thanksgiving Day Parade, giant balloons included.

Rock The Universe. For one weekend in early September, Universal Studios shoos out the normal paying guests at about 5:00 p.m. and turns the park over to Christian teens saving souls with the Devil's music. Top religious rockers like Switchfoot and Third Day have appeared at what is billed as "Florida's Biggest Christian Music Festival." Admission to this "hard ticket," after-hours event is not included in any pass, and runs $58 (plus tax) for one night, $96 for both nights.

Halloween Horror Nights. Universal's wildly popular after-hours frightfest is held on selected nights from late September through Halloween. As the daytime guests depart, the park is turned into an elaborately themed bacchanalia of the bizarre, featuring famous Hollywood monsters alongside original horrors from the fiendish minds of Universal's fearmasters. The heart of the award-winning event is the half-dozen-plus haunted mazes in which visitors shuffle, scream, and sometimes crawl past movie-quality tableaus of terror. Rock musicals, gory magic acts, and bawdy comedy shows (like the long-running "Bill & Ted" pop-culture satire) are staged, and most of the major rides are open. The park's thoroughfares are filled with fog and lurching "scareactors," but relax: they observe a strict "no-touching" policy.

Event details are announced in the summer, so keep an eye on HalloweenHorrorNights.com/orlando for official info. In the meantime, check ParkRumors.com, HHNrumors.com, and BehindTheThrills.com for lurid speculation. A separate admission of roughly $96 (plus tax) is required, with various discounts and "frequent fear" season passes available ($76 to $255). If you already have a park ticket you can get a HHN add-on for $42, $57, or $73 depending on the night.

The event is intense in every sense: loud, claustrophobic, violent, suggestive, scatological, and alcohol-saturated. It is not appropriate for children, nor for many adults. If you intend to attend, do so on a "non-peak" night (Sunday or Wednesday) or brace yourself for overwhelming crowds. Purchase tickets in advance and arrive well before the event start time.

Lines for the mazes build within an hour of opening, so see as many as you can early; then see shows and explore the open-air "scare zones" until the crowds thin out in the final hour of the night. Express Passes are sold (for $60 to $110) though on busy nights you may face long waits even with them. An "RIP" guided tour ($110 and up, plus admission) is your only prayer for seeing everything on peak nights. For a real scare, check the price tag for a private RIP tour ($1,299 and up).

The Shooting Script:
Your Day at Universal Studios Florida

Universal Studios Florida (like its sister park) is best experienced in small bites over several days. That being said, it is perfectly possible see more or less everything at Universal Studios Florida in one very full day. This is especially true if you are staying in one of the on-site hotels, which will give you early entry and preferred access to virtually all the rides and attractions. It is also true if you have heeded the advice in *Chapter One* and arrived during one of the less hectic times of year.

If circumstances or perversity have led you to ignore this sage advice, you will have to plan carefully and perhaps purchase a Universal Express Pass (see *Chapter One: Planning Your Escape*) if you are intent on seeing as much of the park as possible in a one-day time span. Even at less busy times, you might want to consider following some of the strategies set forth in this section. Lines for more popular rides can grow long enough to make the wait seem tedious even in slack periods.

A little later, you'll get detailed descriptions of every attraction, eatery, and shop in the park. This section provides an overview, some general guidance, and a step-by-step plan for seeing the park during busier periods.

Doing Your Homework

You can arrive at Universal Studios knowing nothing about any of the films or TV shows on which its attractions are based (although it's hard to imagine that being possible) and have a perfectly good time. Indeed, you don't need to understand a word of English to be entertained here, as the happy hordes of foreign tourists prove.

Nonetheless, there are a few attractions that will benefit from a bit of research prior to your visit. *E.T. Adventure* will make a lot more sense to those who have seen the film. This is especially true for younger kids who might find E.T.'s odd appearance a bit off-putting if they haven't seen the film. Fortunately, this is the kind of homework that's easy and fun to do. Netflix will have all the research material you need. While you're at it, you might want to add *Shrek* and *Despicable Me* to your queue, if only to whet the kids' appetites for their visit. Finally, Diagon Alley, Universal Studio's new Harry Potter area is largely inspired by the later books, so be sure to catch up on films five through eight. Oh heck, see them all!

What To Expect

Universal Studios Florida uses the "back lot" as its organizing metaphor. The back lot is where a studio keeps permanent and semi-permanent outdoor sets that can be "dressed" to stand in for multiple locations. USF consists of seven such "sets" — Hollywood, Woody Woodpecker's KidZone, World Expo, The Wizarding World of Harry Potter: Diagon Alley, San Francisco, New York, and Production Central — in addition to the Front Lot. You will find a helpful map of the layout of the sets in the **2-Park Guide Map** brochure that you can pick up at the entrance gates or in many shops throughout the park. Each set will be discussed in detail in the sections that follow.

It will also help to have a basic idea of the different types of rides, shows, and attractions Universal Studios Florida has to offer. Each type of attraction has its own peculiarities and dictates a different viewing pattern.

Rides. As the term indicates, these attractions involve getting into a vehicle and going somewhere. Some, like *E.T. Adventure*, are the descendants of the so-called "dark rides" of old-fashioned amusement parks; you ride through a darkened tunnel environment lined with things to look at. *Men In Black* adds exciting elements of interactivity to the old formula, while *Escape From Gringotts* blends this concept with roller coaster thrills.

Rides are the first major attractions to open in the morning and should be your first priority. Rides have a limited seating capacity, at least compared to the theater shows. They don't last long either; most at Universal are no longer than five minutes. They tend to be the most popular attractions because of the thrills they promise (and deliver). The result: Lines form early and grow longer as the day wears on and more people pack the park.

Theater Shows. Whereas the rides offer thrills, theater shows offer entertainment and, occasionally, education as well. Theater shows can be live (*Horror Make-Up* show), on film (*Shrek*), or a combination of both (*Terminator*). They occur indoors, out of the heat and sun, in comfortable theaters. They last about 25 minutes on average. Most film shows start running soon after opening time and run continuously. Live shows start about midday and have their show times listed in the 2-Park Guide Map.

Because they seat 250 to 700 people at a time, a long line outside a theater show can be deceptive. Many times you can get in line as the next group is entering and still make the show. This is not always true during the busier times, however. Ask an attendant if getting in line now will guarantee a seat at the next show.

Amphitheater Shows. These shows differ from theater shows in that they take place in larger semi-open auditoriums that do not offer the luxury of air conditioning. They start about midday, with show times listed in the 2-Park Guide Map brochure.

Outdoor Shows. These are small-scale shows involving a few entertainers. They occur on the streets at times that may or may not be announced in the 2-Park Guide Map.

Displays and Interactive Areas. These two different types of attractions are similar in that you can simply walk into them at will and stay as long as you wish. That's not to say you won't find a line, but, with the exception of *Fievel's Playland*, lines are rare at these attractions.

All the Rest. There's a great deal of enjoyment to be derived from simply walking around in Universal Studios Florida. The imaginative and beautifully executed sets make wonderful photo backdrops and, when things get too hectic, you can even find a grassy knoll on which to stretch out, rest, and survey the passing scene.

Academy Awards

If you have a limited time at Universal Studios Florida, you probably won't be able to see everything. However, it would be a shame if you missed the very best the park has to offer.

Here, then, is my list of Academy Awards:

Escape From Gringotts. Another Potter magic spell.

Transformers: The Ride-3D. Totally incoherent and who cares?

Despicable Me Minion Mayhem. Funny, family-friendly, and 3-D!

The Simpsons. Simulator thrills and Simpsons satire! What a combo.

Revenge of the Mummy. Eternal torment has never been such fun.

Universal Orlando's Horror Make-Up Show. Fun and games with dead bodies and strange critters.

Runners-Up

These aren't on the list of the best of the best but they make many other people's lists and they are very, very good.

Terminator 2: 3-D Battle Across Time. With this show, the award for "best 3-D show in Orlando" moved from Disney to Universal.

Shrek 4-D. Another boffo 3-D entertainment that solidifies Universal's preeminence in the genre.

Curious George Goes To Town. Just for kids and just wonderful.

Hollywood Rip Ride Rockit. A one-of-a-kind coaster for thrill ride junkies and music fans alike.

Men In Black: Alien Attack. A ride-through video game pits you against the universe.

E.T. Adventure. A bicycle ride to E.T.'s home planet is like *it's a small world* on acid.

The One-Day Stay

If you are staying at an on-site hotel and thus have preferred access or have purchased a Universal Express Pass (see *Chapter One*), then you can largely ignore the following advice and proceed as you wish. At certain times, on-site hotel guests may get to enter the park an hour before the public to experience select attractions (usually Diagon Alley). If you can take advantage of this perk, do so.

Expect The Wizarding World of Harry Potter: Diagon Alley to be mobbed from minute one; unless you have early access, your best bet is to follow the plan below until afternoon, and save Potter for late in the day.

1. Get up early. You want to arrive at the park before the official opening time. Allow at least half an hour to park your car and get to the main entrance.

2. Since you were smart enough to get your tickets the day before, you don't have to wait in line again, at least not for tickets. Position yourself for the opening of the gates and go over your plan one more time.

3. As soon as the gates open, move briskly to *Despicable Me*.

4. Make a left after exiting *Despicable Me* and ride *Hollywood Rip Ride Rockit*, using the single rider line if available.

5. Ride *Transformers*, using the single rider line if standby exceeds 30 minutes.

6. Head past Mel's Drive-In, around the lagoon, to *The Simpsons Ride*.

7. Continue next door to *Men In Black*. Use the regular queue if this is your first time on *MIB*; otherwise use the single rider line.

8. Continue counter-clockwise past the London waterfront to *Disaster!*

Option: If *E.T. Adventure* is high on your list, go there first and then head for *Disaster!*; if not, save *E.T.* for late in the day when many of the kiddies and their exhausted parents will have left.

9. Ride *Revenge of the Mummy*. If the wait is over 30 minutes, use the single rider line.

10. At this point, you will have been on the most popular rides. The

crowds are beginning to get noticeably larger and the sun is high in the sky. Take a break, maybe eat lunch. If the park is particularly crowded and you feel you are "running late" you may want to limit your lunch to quick snacks you can carry with you as you move from line to line. There are plenty of outdoor kiosks dispensing this kind of portable "finger food."

11. Now the time has come to start checking out the theater and amphitheater shows. *Terminator 2:3-D* and the *Horror Make-Up Show* are both must-sees. Check your park map for *Beetlejuice, Animal Actors,* and *Blues Brothers* show times.

12. Experience *Twister* if the wait isn't too long, then see *Shrek 4-D*.

13. Continue your rounds of the shows you want to see and check in periodically at any rides you missed (or would like to try again). Don't forget *Universal's Superstar Parade,* held daily in late afternoon.

14. As the crowd thins toward closing time, visit Diagon Alley (which is even more enchanting at night) and ride *Escape From Gringotts,* or circle back to the rides you missed. Great times to find shorter lines to even the most popular rides are during the parade and about an hour before the official closing time.

15. If *Universal's Cinematic Spectacular* is running, find a viewing location near the water about ten minutes before the performance.

16. The park doesn't lock the gates at the scheduled closing time. So this is a good time to buy your souvenirs; you'll have saved some prime touring time and won't have to lug them around for so long. Many of the smaller eateries will be open as well, so feel free to grab a well-earned dessert. And you'll still have plenty of time to visit *Lucy: A Tribute* before heading to your car.

The One-Day Stay for Kids

For selfless parents who are willing to place their child's agenda ahead of their own, here is an alternative one-day plan that will serve the needs of younger children — age 11 and below, maybe 7 or 8 and below. Often it happens that young children are better equipped to handle the more intense rides than their elders. Presumably, you know your own child or grandchild and will be able to adapt the following outline as needed.

1. Get to the park bright and early. As soon as you are in, ride *Despicable Me*. (If your kids are under 40 inches tall, ask for stationary seating.)

2. Head to see *Shrek 4-D*. Afterwards, visit *E.T. Adventure*.

3. Try *Kang & Kodos' Twirl 'n' Hurl* near *The Simpsons Ride*.

4. Depending on your kids' tolerance, check out *Men In Black* and *Dis-*

aster!, in that order. (Take note of height restrictions.)

5. Check show times for *Barney* and *Animal Actors on Location!* Try to steer your little ones away from *Barney's Backyard*, *Fievel's Playland*, and *Curious George*, explaining that you'll return later.

6. Break for lunch. Try Finnegan's if the kids will sit for table service, otherwise try the Springfield U.S.A. fast food court.

7. Let the kids burn off steam at *Fievel's Playland* and *Barney's Backyard*. The heat of the day is the best time to get soaked at *Curious George*.

8. Check the map for character "party zones" and parade show times.

9. Save Diagon Alley for as late in the day as possible. (Note that kids under 42 inches tall can't ride *Gringotts*.)

The One-Day Stay for Potterphiles

Note: This itinerary, keyed to the chronology of the books, requires a two-park pass and works best during slow periods and with early entry. If you are visiting during one of the busiest periods, all bets are off.

1. Get to Diagon Alley as early as possible and relive Harry's experience as he got kitted out for Hogwarts. Visit Ollivanders, enjoy the "wand experience," and buy your interactive wand.

2. Skip *Gringotts* for now and head out of Diagon Alley and into King's Cross Station for your ride to Hogsmeade on the *Hogwarts Express*.

3. Ride *Forbidden Journey*. Because so much of the queue is an attraction in itself, you might not mind the wait. If the crowds are thin and you're not queasy, ride again.

4. Stroll Hogsmeade and test out your wand at the interactive stations.

5. Ride *Flight of the Hippogriff* and *Dragon Challenge* as your taste dictates. Pop into the Three Broomsticks for a butterbeer or for a meal if you're hungry, but do savour the ambiance.

6. Take the *Hogwarts Express* back to London and continue your exploration of Diagon Alley and Knockturn Alley and further hone your wand skills.

7. Do some shopping, put a Colloportus spell on your wallet if you don't want to go broke! Dine or snack at The Leaky Cauldron, but do visit it.

8. Ride *Escape From Gringotts*. Twice.

9. If there's time left over, ride some of the top Muggle rides elsewhere in the two parks.

■ THE FRONT LOT ■

In movie studio parlance, the front lot is where all the soundstages, as well as the administrative and creative offices, are located — as opposed to the back lot, which contains the outdoor sets. Here at Universal Studios Florida, the Front Lot is a small antechamber of sorts to the theme park proper, which can be looked on as one huge back lot. You will find the following services on the Front Lot:

■ To your left as you enter the park are . . .

Restrooms. These flank the lockers.

Lockers. There are two small bays of electronically controlled lockers. The rental fee is $8 for the day with in-and-out access, and the machines accept both bills and credit cards. If these are full, you can find more lockers (including some larger and more expensive ones that are handy if you have a lot of stuff) on the other side of the plaza.

Mail. You'll find a small U.S. Postal Service drop box to the right of the lockers. Stamps are available at the Universal Studios Store (see below).

Phone Cards. Also near the lockers is a phone-card vending machine.

Stroller & Wheelchair Rentals. Wheelchairs are $12 a day and strollers $15. Double strollers are $25. Slightly more elaborate strollers, called "kiddie cars," feature a kid's steering wheel and cup holders and rent for $18 and $28 respectively (when available).

A motorized "electric convenience vehicle" (ECV) is yours for $50 for the day, $65 if you want a canopy to shield you from the sun. ECVs and wheelchairs require either a $50 cash deposit or a record of your credit card; ECVs can be reserved in advance with at least 24 hours notice and this is highly recommended. You must be over 18 to rent an ECV. Both ECVs and wheelchairs can be transferred from park to park, including via *Hogwarts Express.* If you left a cash deposit, however, you must return the ECV where you rented it.

■ To your right as you enter the park are . . .

Guest Services. This office performs a wide variety of functions. You can pick up information and brochures about special services and special events. If you have a complaint about anything in the park, make your feelings known here. They also field compliments. So if some Universal employee has made a positive difference to your experience in the park, make a note of their name and take a moment to share your experience here. It really does make a difference for those outstanding employees.

Guest Services will also exchange some (but not all) foreign currency, to a maximum of $500, for a flat fee of $5. If you exchange the limit, that works out to a one percent fee, a better deal than you'll get elsewhere.

If you've come to Universal Studios Florida for the day and like what you see, Guest Services can upgrade your one-day pass to any of Universal Orlando's multi-day pass options. The price you paid for your one-day pass will be deducted from the price of the multi-day pass. In other words, you will pay exactly what you would have paid had you purchased the multi-day ticket in the first place.

There are some simple rules: Upgrades must be purchased before you leave the park. Everyone in your party who wants one must show up with their original ticket in hand. Free or complimentary passes are not eligible for upgrades. Upgrades are non-transferable and Universal enforces this feature by requiring your signature on the pass and requesting photo ID. If you really liked your visit, you can also sign up for an Annual Pass here.

ATM. Next to the Studio Audience Center is an outdoor ATM, where you can get a cash advance on your Visa, MasterCard, Amex, or Discover. The machine is also hooked into 12 bank systems, including Cirrus, Plus, NYCE, AFFN, and Maestro for those who would like to withdraw money from their bank account back home. A $2.95 fee may be charged for use, in addition to any fee levied by your institution.

Studio Audience Center. There is far less television production at Universal than there used to be, especially since *TNA Wrestling* ceased filming here. If anything is being taped on the nearby soundstages during your visit to Universal Studios, this is the best place to get information and tickets. A show can have an audience of 50 to 300 and tape one to six episodes on a single day.

Each show will have a minimum age requirement, which can vary greatly. Tickets are free and distributed on a first-come, first-served basis. Show up early, but try not to be disappointed if you come up empty.

First Aid. Nursing aid is available here, under the Studio Audience Center marquee, should you need it. There is also a "family bathroom" if, for example, you need to assist a disabled spouse. A special room is set aside for nursing mothers. If you just need to change a diaper, you will find diaper-changing facilities in restrooms located throughout the park.

Lost & Found. The Studio Audience Center window does double duty as Lost & Found. Items that if lost elsewhere would probably be gone forever have a surprising way of turning up at theme parks. Universal personnel always check the rides for forgotten belongings. Items are kept for 30 to 90 days, but credit cards are destroyed after four days. You can call (407) 224-4233.

Lockers. Here are more of those electronic lockers, with still more lockers just around the corner in a narrow, easy to overlook passageway that leads to Hollywood Boulevard and the *T2* theater. Daily rental is $8 or $10, depending on size, and allows unlimited in-and-out access.

Shopping on the Front Lot

In the Front Lot, Universal has shrewdly located a number of shops that cater to the needs of both the arriving and departing guest.

If you left the camera at the hotel or find yourself short of batteries, your first stop should be **On Location**. They can also help with sunscreen, sunglasses, and tote bags. In addition you will find a constantly rotating inventory of T-shirts, baseball caps, and the like. If you have your photo taken by a roving photographer in the park, there's no obligation to buy a print, but if you just can't resist, you can view and claim your pictures here. There are also computer kiosks where you can register your email address with **Universal's Photo Connect** service if you've purchased a **Star Card** package; see *Chapter One* for details on Universal's photo packages.

Studio Sweets, a small shop on your left as you enter the park, sells scoop-your-own bulk candy at caviar prices. There is also a wide assortment of cookies, cupcakes, chocolate- and caramel-dipped apples, and fudge.

By far the largest shop in the park, the **Universal Studios Store** is located just next to (in fact, it surrounds) Studio Sweets. Here you will find a representative sampling of the wares to be found in the various smaller shops scattered about the park. There are plenty of T-shirts and toys, magnets and mugs, all emblazoned with various film faces and logos. If you want to save all your souvenir shopping until the end of your visit, you should be able to get something appropriate here. There is even a section devoted to Harry Potter paraphernalia and memorabilia. Just be aware that the selection is not exhaustive and that the special item you admired elsewhere might not be for sale here.

It's A Wrap (studio lingo for "we've finished shooting the movie") is a nifty name for this vest-pocket souvenir stand that straddles the exit to the park. The selection centers on "last chance" souvenirs and styles from last season, so you can often get serious discounts of 30% to 50% here.

■ HOLLYWOOD ■

Hollywood is one of the smaller "sets" at Universal Studios Florida. It is about two city blocks long, stretching from *Lucy: A Tribute* near the park entrance to The Gardens of Allah motel near the lagoon. Along the way is an imaginative and loving recreation of the Hollywood of our collective subconscious.

Terminator 2: 3-D Battle Across Time

Rating:	★ ★ ★ ★
Type:	A "3-D Virtual Adventure"
Time:	About 20 minutes
Short Take:	The most exciting 3-D theater attraction in Orlando

When the Governator swore "I'll be back," he wasn't kidding! Most attractions based on movies are developed without input from the films' creators. With *T2:3-D*, "King of the World" James Cameron (director of box-office behemoths *Titanic* and *Avatar*) and his *Terminator* star Arnold Schwarzenegger set out to prove they could do it better themselves. And, boy, did they ever! Reports are that $60 million was spent to create this show. You'll get their money's worth.

You step off Hollywood Boulevard into the rebuilt headquarters of Cyberdyne, the not-so-nice corporate giant of the *Terminator* flicks, which is out to refurbish its image and show off its latest technology. The pre-show warm-up, which takes place in a large anteroom to the theater itself, features a delicious parody of the "Vision of the Future" corporate videos and television commercials that were all the rage in the early Aughts. The pre-show also gets the plot rolling: Sarah Connor and her son John have invaded Cyberdyne and commandeered the video screen to warn us against the new SkyNet project (which sounds remarkably like the Bush-era National Missile Defense system). According to Sarah and John, SkyNet will enslave us all. The Cyberdyne flack who is our host glosses over this "unfortunate interruption" and ushers us into the large auditorium. There we settle into deceptively normal looking theater seats, don our "protective glasses," and the show begins.

And what a show it is. Without giving too much away, suffice it to say that it involves a spectacular three-screen 3-D movie starring Ah-nold himself, along with Linda Hamilton and Eddie Furlong (the kid from *Terminator 2*). In one of the more inspired touches, the on-screen actors move from screen to stage and back again, Arnold aboard a roaring motorcycle.

Tip: If you have a sensitive spine, ask an attendant for the stationary seats to avoid a short, sharp drop at the end.

While the Terminator franchise has moved on, with two more films and a TV show released since *T2:3-D* premiered, this attraction preserves the series at its peak popularity. The special effects remain spectacular, and the slam-bang, smoke-filled finale still has people screaming and shrieking in their seats.

Note that the huge interior queue can hold over 1,100 people, while the theater holds 700 people; with shows starting every 20 to 30 minutes, the line moves fairly quickly.

Universal Orlando's Horror Make-Up Show

Rating: ★ ★ ★ ★ ★
Type: Theater show
Time: 25 minutes
Short Take: Hilarious! Universal's best-kept secret

How to take something gory, gruesome, and downright disgusting and turn it into wholesome, funny family fare? Universal has solved the problem with this enjoyable (not to mention educational) foray into the ghastly art of make-up and special effects for the horror genre. The key is a horror make-up "expert" with a bizarre and goofy sense of humor who is interviewed in a studio make-up lab by an on-stage host and straight-man. During a laugh-filled 25 minutes, our expert leads us through a grisly show-and-tell of basic horror movie tricks and gimmicks. It's a roaring success that many call "Universal Studios' best-kept secret."

Tip: The subject matter is undeniably gross and the performers are given fairly wide latitude to ad-lib. The easily offended may find either the subject matter or the humor (or both) beyond the bounds of good taste. Universal warns "parental guidance suggested," whatever that means.

Using the inevitable volunteer from the audience (to very amusing effect), we learn how harmlessly dull knives can be made to leave bloody trails on bare human flesh and, thanks to video projected onto two screens, we get a brief history of extreme make-up from Lon Chaney and Jack Pierce to modern masters Tom Savini and Rick Baker. Also on hand are mechanical werewolf heads like those used for the still stunning transformation scene in *An American Werewolf in London*. The show ends with a preview of a new, remotely controlled monster and yet another dirty trick played on a "volunteer." The performers, all skilled improvisers, play off the audience, making every show slightly different and rewarding repeat visits.

This show actually instructs while it entertains. Everyone will have a keener understanding of basic horror effects, and young children will be sternly warned about the importance of safety at all times. ("Don't do this at home . . . Do it at a friend's house!")

The waiting area for this show is the lobby of the Pantages Theater, where you can peruse memorabilia displays from Universal's horror-movie history while waiting for the show to begin.

The best seats in the house. If all you want to do is enjoy the show, the oft-repeated Universal refrain is absolutely true — every seat's a good seat. Exhibitionists hoping to be selected as a volunteer should be aware that the performers have a predilection for young women seated in the middle, close to the stage.

Lucy: A Tribute

Rating:	★ ★ ½
Type:	Museum-style display, with video
Time:	Continuous viewing
Short Take:	Best for adults with a sense of history

Lucy: A Tribute is a walk-in display honoring the immortal Lucille Desiree Ball. It's hard to miss, since you bump into it almost as soon as you enter the park. There's hardly ever a crowd, so feel free to breeze on by and take it in later. If you run out of time . . . well, truth to tell, you haven't missed much. Still, fans of the great redhead (and who isn't?) will find at least something of interest here, even if it's just a reminder to pull down those Lucy videos at home and take a four hundredth look.

The "tribute" is simply a large open room ringed with glassed-in display cases, like shop windows, crammed with Lucy memorabilia — photos, letters, scripts, costumes, and Lucy's six Emmys. One of the more interesting windows contains a model of the studio in which the ground-breaking *I Love Lucy* show was shot. It was the first show shot with the three-camera method still used today. A fascinating footnote: The sets in those days of black-and-white TV were actually painted in shades of gray (furniture, too) to provide optimum contrast on the home screen.

Continuously running videos feature Bob Hope and Gale Gordon reminiscing about Lucy, while brief clips remind us of just how much we really did love Lucy. You'll hear the people next to you saying, "Oh, I remember that one," or "I lo-o-o-ved that one."

There's some interesting material here about Lucy's career before she became a television icon and an interactive *I Love Lucy* trivia quiz. And if you think the 3-D movie craze is something new, check out Lucy's stereographic family snapshots from the 1950s.

Tip: This attraction often opens an hour after the rest of the park.

Selected Short Subjects

■ Hollywood Celebrities

Hollywood Boulevard is a great place for star spotting. **Stars of yesteryear,** like Marilyn Monroe and Lucy, as well as famous **cartoon characters** like Woody Woodpecker and Scooby Doo have been known to put in appearances, and the Simpsons have been showing up in a large RV to mix and mingle with the crowds along the Boulevard. Characters from *Universal's Superstar Parade* appear at scheduled times for a "party zone" near Mel's Drive-In. You can have your photo taken with them or even get an autograph.

■ Preview Center

The Preview Center, hidden behind the Darkroom facade, is the only storefront at Universal where you can make money instead of spending it. The center operates sporadically (usually only weekdays), but when it's open you can be recruited to give your opinion on upcoming TV pilots, film trailers, and commercials. As remuneration, you may receive a gift or modest amount of cash. If you're on a single-day pass, the per-hour pay isn't worth it, but try stopping by during an extended stay.

■ Musical Entertainment

The **Studio Brass Band** appears most mornings in front of *Lucy: A Tribute*, playing energetic versions of classic movie and TV themes, from *Barney Miller* to *Men in Black*. From time to time, usually during the park's busier periods, you may find a fifties-style rock & roll group holding forth on a small stage outside Mel's Drive-In. The groups vary in size and composition, but the nostalgic set list is virtually guaranteed to please.

Eating in Hollywood

■ Beverly Hills Boulangerie

What:	Sandwiches, sweets, and coffee
Where:	At the corner of Rodeo Drive
	and Plaza of the Stars
Price Range:	$

This faux-bistro blends the current craze for coffee bars with a tasty array of breakfast and dessert baked goods. It's an unbeatable combination. If you're visiting during one of the less crowded times of year (so you don't have to dash right off to *Despicable Me*), you might want to pause here for a fortifying if calorie-laden breakfast. Sit outside on sunny days to entertain yourself with the passing people-watcher's parade.

If you subscribe to the when-on-vacation-start-with-dessert philosophy, why not start the day off right with an eclair or a slice of cheesecake (made daily)? Choices range from basic pastries and muffins to lavish cupcakes and fancy cappuccinos. Later in the day, you can stop in for an Italian melt panini on ciabatta bread or a smoked turkey, roast beef, or ham and Swiss sandwich on your choice of baguette or croissant. Or soothe your conscience with a Tuna Salad, or a Health Sandwich of Swiss cheese, sprouts, cucumbers, and avocados. Sandwiches come with a tasty side of potato salad and fresh fruit. You can also get combinations with salad or soup.

■ Mel's Drive-In

What:	Fast-food burger joint
Where:	At the end of Hollywood Boulevard,
	across from the lagoon
Price Range:	$

Remember the nostalgia-drenched drive-in restaurant from *American Graffiti*? Well here it is in some of its splendor. No curvy car hops, alas, but you will see a few vintage cars parked outside.

Inside, you will find a fairly typical fast-food emporium with fifties decor. Place and pay for your burger or hot dog order at the cashier, then step forward to pick it up. If the food and non-service won't bring back memories of those great cheeseburgers and real-milk shakes you had way back when, at least there are jukeboxes (non-functional, alas) to flip through at the tables. An outdoor seating area looks out to the park's central lagoon.

The menu is limited, but grilled chicken in a sandwich or over a salad widens your choices. You can upgrade from fries to crunchy onion rings for a few cents more, although the chili-cheese fries are kinda yummy. Soft drinks, shakes, and root beer floats are the beverage choices here. Mel's is a good spot for a quick bite with kids who like no surprises with their meals.

■ Schwab's Pharmacy

What:	Ice-cream parlor
Where:	In the middle of Hollywood Boulevard
Price Range:	$

Schwab's is famous in Hollywood lore as the place where a sharp-eyed talent scout discovered a sweater-clad, teenaged Lana Turner sipping soda at the counter. At Universal Studios, Schwab's lends its name to a small, black-and-white tiled, vaguely forties-ish ice-cream parlor featuring Ben & Jerry's cones, milk shakes, sundaes, and ice cream floats, as well as double scoop sundaes and banana splits. Although there are a few tables, Schwab's is primarily aimed at those looking for a quick take-out snack.

In keeping with its namesake's primary business, Schwab's also has a small supply of over-the-counter cough drops and headache remedies.

■ Cafe La Bamba

What:	Character breakfast; cafeteria-style Cali-Mex lunch
Where:	Across from Mel's and the lagoon in the Hollywood Hotel
Price Range:	$$+

Cafe La Bamba is a lovely hacienda-style eatery whose ambiance is a cut above your average fast-food restaurant, evoking a Spanish mission courtyard with adobe walls and tiled floors.

The Cafe hosts a daily character breakfast featuring the stars of *Universal's Superstar Parade*. For $26 ($13 ages 3 to 9) you get a plated sit-down starter of eggs and pancakes in the presence of SpongeBob, Dora, Hop, and Gru's Minions. Reservations are required (call 407-224-7554 at least 24 hours in advance) and grant diners reserved viewing for the afternoon parade (park admission required).

After breakfast, Cafe La Bamba switches over to serving California-style Mexican standards (burritos, tacos, tostada salads) alongside chipotle BBQ ribs, mojo roasted chicken, and chimichurri skirt steak platters. Portions are substantial, ingredients and seasonings are a step above Taco Bell, and the menu makes a nice change of pace from the usual burgers and pizza.

During slower periods, the building is reserved after breakfast for special events. Thankfully, **Carmen's Veranda** in front of the restaurant is still in operation all year. There, you can get a frozen drink (with or without liquor), draft beer, or hard lemonade, as well as turkey legs and hot pretzels.

Shopping in Hollywood

Hollywood Boulevard is an imaginative recreation of major Hollywood facades, some of which still exist and others of which have vanished into the realm of cherished memories. It makes for a pleasant stroll and a fitting introduction to the movie-themed fun that awaits you in the rest of the park.

The Brown Derby is hard to miss: it's the big hat across from *T2:3-D*. Unlike the Hollywood original, this one isn't a restaurant but a hat shop, befitting its shape. A variety of belts, bags, and sandals are also sold here.

Tip: A small collection of goofy novelty hats near the shop entrance contains all the ingredients for an irresistible **photo-op**. Don't be bashful, because you won't be alone.

Silver Screen Collectibles opens onto the Plaza of the Stars, just across the street from the Universal Studios Store. At the other end, it merges with *Lucy: A Tribute*. Expect to find T-shirts and other merchandise featuring cartoon characters. Betty Boop merchandise is prominently featured. The tiny Lucy section, strategically located at the entrance/exit to *Lucy: A Tribute* stocks a slim selection of DVDs and a smattering of books and T-shirts in homage to the great redhead.

You can't miss **Cyber Image** if you see *Terminator 2: 3-D Battle Across Time* (and you should); you walk right through it when you leave the theater. Here's your chance to take home a lifesized endoskeleton to adorn your family room. For the less well-heeled there are sci-fi and superhero toys, T-shirts, and comic books, although DVDs of *The Terminator* films are oddly unavailable.

Studio Styles is the small store sandwiched between Schwab's Pharmacy and the now-defunct Darkroom photo developers (remember film?). It sells sunglasses, watches, casual clothing, and accessories by fancy designers like Gucci, Prada, Nixon, and Dolce & Gabbana. If you're itching to drop a couple of Benjamins on a pair of Oakleys or Ray Bans, this is the spot. There is also a selection of Skullcandy headphones, in case you left your earbuds at the hotel.

Next to Mel's Drive-In, under the sign that says "Williams of Hollywood," you'll find **Theatre Magic Shop**, a fascinating boutique that gives away (well, *sells*) the secrets of the magician's trade. The target audience is the absolute beginner and most of the magic kits sold here come with an instructional DVD to help bring you up to speed quickly. The big seller is "The Levitator," a trick that lets you magically spin cards in mid-air. There are frequent 12-minute magic shows timed to attract the crowds pouring out of the nearby *T2* and *Horror Make-Up* shows.

WOODY WOODPECKERS KIDZONE

Although its intense thrill rides have brought Universal Studios Florida a reputation as an "adult" theme park, it hasn't forgotten the kiddies. Woody Woodpecker's KidZone, located along a winding avenue off the central lagoon, is a perfect case in point. If you have children under ten, you could very easily spend an entire day here, with only an occasional foray to sample other kid-friendly attractions in the park. There's a nice balance here, too, from stage shows to play areas to kiddie-scale "thrill" rides. They will be described in roughly the order you encounter them as you wend your way deeper into Woody's KidZone.

Tip: At the end of the Hollywood set, past Cafe La Bamba, look for the Gardens of Allah Villas on your right. Cut through here for a shortcut to Woody's KidZone and the *E.T. Adventure.*

Animal Actors On Location!

Rating:	★ ★ ★ ½
Type:	Amphitheater show
Time:	About 20 minutes
Short Take:	Fun for just about everybody

This awww-inspiring spectacle shows off the handiwork of Universal's animal trainers and their furry and feathery charges. Volunteers are pulled from the audience to serve as foils for several amusing routines. In one especially fascinating segment, we learn how birds can be filmed in flight using a large fan and some trick camera work. In another, we learn how a dog's on-screen behavior can be guided by an off-screen trainer.

Just which animals you see will depend to some extent on which "stars" are available when you visit. But you can probably count on a display by a well-trained if slightly mercenary bird and a bit that uses a child volunteer from the audience.

In between the fun and games, the show sneaks in a few points about the serious business of producing "behaviors" that can be put to use in films. When an animal balks at performing a trick, as they do with amusing frequency, the trainer will work patiently with the animal until the behavior is performed correctly. We learn that what for us is light entertainment is serious business for the folks (both two- and four-legged) on the stage.

The best seats in the house. There really are no bad seats for this one. However, if you'd like a shot at serving as a landing strip for that mercenary bird, try sitting in the middle of the middle section.

E.T. Adventure

Rating:	★ ★ ★ ★
Type:	Gondola ride
Time:	5 minutes
Height Req.:	34 in. (86.4 cm.)
Short Take:	Kids love this one (some adults do, too)

Based on the blockbuster movie, the *E.T. Adventure* takes us where the movie didn't — back to E.T.'s home planet. In a filmed introduction, Steven Spielberg, who directed the film, sets up the premise: E.T.'s home, the Green Planet, is in some unspecified trouble, although it looks like an advanced case of ozone hole that is turning the place a none-too-healthy-looking orange. You have to return with E.T. to help save the old folks at home. How to get there? Aboard the flying bicycles from the film's final sequence, of course — a tipoff that this ride is aimed at the very young. After this brief setup, the doors ahead open and we line up to tell a staffer our first names and get the "passports" we will need for the journey.

Passports firmly in hand, we walk through a cave-like tunnel into the misty, nighttime redwood forests of the Northwest. This set is a minor masterpiece of scenic design and some people think it's the best part of the adventure. As we wend our way along a winding "nature trail" among the towering trees, we make out the animated figure of Botanicus, a wise elder from E.T.'s planet, urging us to hurry back. Here, too, we glimpse the jury-rigged contraption E.T. used to communicate in the film.

At the staging area, we hand in our passports and collect our "bikes" (look for E.T. to pop his head out of the basket on the front), which are actually 12-passenger, open-sided gondolas hanging from a ceiling track. They have bicycle-like seats, each with its own set of handlebars.

The best seats in the house. On the whole, the left side of the gondola provides better views than the right, especially of the city. Best of all is the far left seat in the first row.

This ride might be likened to a bike with training wheels. It has many of the aspects of more thrilling rides — sudden acceleration, swoops, and turns — but toned down so as not to be truly frightening. In the first phase of the ride, we are zipping through the redwoods, dodging the unenlightened grown-ups who want to capture E.T. for study and analysis. This section can be a little scary for small kids and a little loud for older adults. Soon, however, we are soaring high above the city in the ride's most enchanting interlude. We rise higher until we are in the stars themselves and are then shot down a hyperspace tunnel before we decelerate abruptly and find ourselves in the steamy world of E.T.'s home planet.

It's an odd cave-like environment but soon, apparently buoyed by our arrival, the place perks up and we are flying through a psychedelic world of huge multicolored flowers in wondrous shapes, past talking mushrooms and plants (or are they creatures?) with dozens of eyes. All around are little E.T.s, peeping from under plants, climbing over them, and playing them like percussion instruments. It's all rather like Disney's *it's a small world* on acid.

All too soon, E.T. is sending us back to our home, but not before a final farewell when those passports pay off cleverly. Listen carefully!

Some are captivated by this ride, but it has a few flaws. Spielberg authorized a whole new cast of characters for it (culled from the obscure paperback sequel *E.T. and the Book of the Green Planet*) but, other than Botanicus, they are hard to identify, much less get to know. Also, the humans in the woods look a bit like department store mannequins. Still, the ride will appeal to younger children and their timid elders, who can get a taste of a "thrill" ride without putting the contents of their stomachs at risk.

This is also one of the few rides at Universal where seeing the film on which it is based will definitely add to the appreciation of the experience. Without this background, much of the ride may seem merely odd. This will be especially true for younger children who will be better able to empathize with E.T. and his plight if they've seen the movie.

E.T. is one of Universal's most popular rides for people of all ages, so the lines can become dauntingly long. On busy days, there can be another wait of 30 or more minutes once inside before you reach the ride itself.

Tip: When the *Animal Actors* show lets out (about 25 minutes after the posted show time), the crowds stream over to get on line for *E.T.* Time your visit accordingly.

Note: There are two Universal Express entrances in this ride, one outside and a second shortly after you enter the forest inside the building.

Fievel's Playland

Rating:	★ ★ ★
Type:	Interactive play area
Time:	As long as you want
Short Take:	For young and very active kids

Based on Steven Spielberg's charming animated film, *An American Tail*, about a shtetl mouse making his way in the New World, *Fievel's Playland* is a convoluted maze of climb-up, run-through, slide-down activities that will keep kids amused while their exhausted parents take a well-deserved break.

Don't forget to bring your camera for great **photo ops** of the kids amid the larger-than-life cowboy hats, victrolas, water barrels, playing cards, and cattle skeletons that make up this maze of exploration.

The highlight is a Mouse Climb — a rope tunnel that spirals upwards. At the top, kids can climb into two-man (well, two-kid) rubber rafts to slide down through yet another tunnel to arrive at ground level with enormous grins and wet bottoms. Don't worry, there's also a set of stairs to the top of this water slide.

Photo op: A shot of your kid hitting the bottom of the slide makes a great souvenir and a ground-level video monitor of the top of the slide lets you know when your little darling is about to descend.

This is a place you can safely let the kids explore on their own. The ground is padded. There's seldom a wait to get in to *Fievel's Playland* but long lines do form for the water slide. If time is a factor and if you will be visiting one of the water-themed parks on another day, you can tell the kids that there are bigger, better water slides awaiting them tomorrow.

Note: Even though this attraction is aimed squarely at the kiddie set, don't be surprised if your young teens get in the spirit and momentarily forget that romping through a kid's playground is not the "cool" thing to do.

A Day in the Park with Barney

Rating:	★ ★ ★
Type:	Theater show with singing
Time:	About 20 minutes
Short Take:	For toddlers and their long-suffering parents

According to the publicity, Universal's *Barney* attraction is the only place in the United States where you can see Barney "live." For some people, that may be one place too many. But for his legions of adoring wee fans and the parents who love them, this show will prove an irresistible draw. Even old curmudgeons will grudgingly have to admit that the show's pretty sweet.

This was the first attraction at Universal to have its own stroller parking lot and it's usually full. After the young guests have availed themselves of Mom and Dad's valet parking service, they enter through a gate into Barney's park, complete with a bronze Barney cavorting in an Italianate fountain.

In a brief pre-show, Mr. Peekaboo and his gaudy bird friend Bartholomew put on a singing, dancing warm-up act that wouldn't be complete unless the audience got splashed. Then, using our imaginations, we pass through a misty cave entrance sprinkled with star dust to the main theater.

Inside is a completely circular space cheerfully decorated as a forest park at dusk. Low benches surround the raised central stage, with more comfortable park benches against the walls. The sight lines are excellent no matter where you sit, although Mr. Peekaboo reminds us that once we've chosen a seat we must stay there for the entire show.

The show is brief and cheery and almost entirely given over to sing-alongs that are already familiar to Barney's little fans. Barney is soon joined by Baby Bop and B.J. and the merriment proceeds apace, complete with falling autumn leaves, a brief snowfall, and shooting streamers.

The theater audience empties out into **Barney's Backyard**, which is the day-care center of your dreams. Here, beautifully executed by Universal scenic artists, is a collection of imaginative and involving activities for the very young, from making music to splashing in water, to drawing on the walls. For parents who are a bit on the slow side, there are signs to explain the significance of what their kids are up to.

True star that he is, Barney stays behind after the show for a well-organized meet and greet session with his young admirers that lets each tyke have a special moment and a photo with the lovable guy. A few of the kids seem overawed to be so close to this giant vision in purple.

Barney's Backyard is where little kids get their revenge. Whereas many rides in the park bar younger children on the basis of height, here there are activities that are off limits to those over 48 inches or even 36 inches. Kids will love it. Grown-ups will wish there were more of it.

Tip: This wonderful space has a separate entrance and you don't have to sit through the show to get in here. Keep this in mind if the family's youngest member needs some special attention or a chance to unwind from the frustrations of being a little person in a big person's amusement park.

Woody Woodpecker's Nuthouse Coaster

Rating:	★ ★
Type:	A kiddie roller coaster
Time:	About 1 minute
Height Req.:	36 in. (91.4 cm.)
Short Take:	A thrill ride for the younger set

Woody Woodpecker's Nuthouse Coaster is described as a "gentle" children's roller coaster, knocked together by Woody from bits of this and that, running through a nut factory. The eight cars on the "Knothead Express" are modeled after nut crates; they run along 800 feet of red tubular steel track supported by bright blue steel poles that are in turn held together with knotty boards and rope.

The ride features some mild drops and tilted turns but it shouldn't prove frightening to any child who meets the 36-inch minimum height requirement, although there have perhaps been some none-too-happy grandparents. You can see the entirety of the very brief ride from outside the queue. The line moves very slowly, and the trip is over before it starts, so try to dissuade your kids from riding if the wait is posted at more than 15 minutes.

Curious George Goes To Town

Rating:	★ ★ ★ ★
Type:	A water-filled play area
Time:	Unlimited
Short Take:	It will be hard to drag kids away

Woody's KidZone turns into a water park in this elaborate play area themed after the illustrated books about George, the playful monkey, and his friend The Man in the Yellow Hat. Expect your kids to get sopping wet here and enjoy every minute of it.

The fun begins innocently enough with a small tent housing a play area for very young children. Nearby is one of those padded play areas with jets of water shooting up from the ground in random patterns. Little ones still in diapers love it. But the main attraction lies a few steps farther along, in the town square. On opposite sides stand the Fire Department and the City Waterworks, dubbed "City H2O." On the second floor balcony, five water cannons let kids squirt those below, and high above is a huge water bucket that fills inexorably with water and, with the clanging of a warning bell, tips over, sending a cascade of water into the square below as kids scramble to position themselves under it for a thorough and thoroughly delightful soaking.

Behind the facades of this cartoonish town square lies a two-level, kid-powered, waterlogged obstacle course. All sorts of cranks, levers, and other ingenious devices give kids a great deal of control over who gets how wet. Most kids take to it with fiendish glee. The concept isn't unique to USF, but the version here is one of the best in recent memory.

When your kids are ready for a change of pace, they can repair to the **Ball Factory**, behind the town square. This cheerfully noisy two-level metal structure is filled with thousands of colored soft foam balls. The noise comes from the industrial strength vacuum machines that suck balls from the floor and send them to aimable ball cannons mounted on tall poles or to large bins high overhead. Some vacuums send balls to stations where kids can fill up mesh bags with balls they then take to the second level balcony to feed into the ten "Auto Blasters" that let them shoot balls at the kids down below. It's a scene of merry anarchy and many adults quickly get in touch with their inner child and become active participants in the chaotic battle raging all about. Those ball bins, like the water buckets outside, tip over periodically, pummeling eager victims below and replenishing the supply of balls.

Curious George is one attraction that can keep kids happily occupied for hours on end. It will also appeal to the older kids in your family who might find some of the other offerings in Woody Woodpecker's KidZone too "babyish." It's not unusual to see ever-so-hip young teens thoroughly enjoying themselves as they splash about with their younger siblings.

Tip: Bring a towel and a change of clothes for the kids if the weather's cool. If you want to avoid getting wet, follow the marked "dry path" to the Ball Factory. This is also a good activity to schedule just before you leave the park, either for the day or for a nap-time break.

Selected Short Subjects

■ Character Meet and Greet

SpongeBob SquarePants holds court during popular daily meet and greets in a window of his namesake store (see below). Don't be deceived by a seemingly short queue inside the shop; the line starts outside around the building. Appearances take place on a fairly continuous basis till 4:00 p.m.

Eating in KidZone

■ KidZone Pizza Company

What: Food stand with outdoor seating
Where: On Exposition Plaza, next to SpongeBob StorePants
Price Range: $

This walk-up fast-food counter serves up a restricted menu of quick eats. Personal-sized cheese and pepperoni pizzas, chicken fingers with fries, a chef salad, and assorted tropical coolers are available. This stand is generally open from about midday to 4:00 p.m.

If you're looking for something a bit more substantial, or a place to eat in air-conditioned comfort, take the short stroll to Springfield's Fast Food Boulevard in World Expo (see below).

Shopping in KidZone

KidZone was transformed into a significant shopping destination with the arrival of **SpongeBob StorePants**, one of the most eye-popping emporiums you're likely to encounter. Inside a ship-like hull (complete with a giant anchor outside) you'll find a vast selection of yellow shirts, caps, and cups emblazoned with the iconic cartoon cleaning implement. There's SpongeBob's trademark pineapple for the kids to crawl into, and an area for meet and greets with Mr. SquarePants himself. Adults will enjoy the off-kilter wit of the Nickelodeon cartoon, evident in the snarky signage ("Souvenirs make great souvenirs!" and "Free Receipt with Purchase.").

E.T.'s Toy Closet is the small shop you must pass through as you decompress from your visit to E.T.'s home planet. There are plenty of E.T. toys and such, but perhaps your best bet is a souvenir photo of your child on a bike with E.T. in the basket and a huge silver moon as backdrop. Don't forget the Reese's Pieces!

The Barney Shop is just what it says, a small stock of Barney-related clothing, toys, games, books, and DVDs.

Tip: Parents can avoid exposing their children to the temptations of this shop by exiting through one of the side doors of Barney's Backyard.

■ WORLD EXPO ■

The theme of World Expo began as a typical World's Fair Exposition park. The result is a display of contemporary architecture and design that manages to be at once very attractive and rather characterless, although the buildings look quite zippy at night. With the addition of **Springfield U.S.A.** — hometown to the Simpsons family — this area's aesthetics became much more animated.

The Simpsons Ride

Rating:	★ ★ ★ ★ ½
Type:	Simulator thrill ride
Time:	4.5 minute ride, with 10 minutes of preshows
Height Req.:	40 in. (101.6 cm.)
Short Take:	A wild and witty spin through Springfield

Welcome to Krustyland, the Krustiest Place on Earth™! Krusty the Clown is opening his theme park's "All-New Thrilltacular Upsy-Downsy Spins-Aroundsy Teen-Operated Thrill Ride," and you can join the Simpson family as the first suckers — um, lucky winners — to try it. Krusty's criminal nemesis, Sideshow Bob, has been spotted in the vicinity, but not to worry: as Homer says "they won't kill you in a theme park as long as you've got a dime in your pocket."

Over the past quarter century, Matt Groening's *The Simpsons* has grown from crudely animated interstitials on FOX's *Tracy Ullman Show* to the world's most popular animated family. Thankfully, their translation to the theme-park world hasn't come at the expense of their satirical edge. From the queue video (featuring classic clips of "Itchy and Scratchy Land" and "Duff Gardens," along with sharp new skits) to the cliche-skewering signage ("Captain Dinosaur's Pirate Rip-off: A Ride So Old, It Should Be Extinct"), this attraction pulls no punches in biting the corporate hand that feeds it.

Once inside the carnival-colorful building, you'll wait among midway booths staffed by Apu ("$100 Tacos for $100"), Patty and Selma ("Finders Keepers, Losers Weepers"), and other characters. You'll be separated into groups of eight and directed to a "funhouse" holding room, where you'll see a gruesomely hilarious safety warning before boarding the ride.

The Simpsons Ride retains much of the basic flight-simulator infrastructure of *Back to the Future: The Ride (BTTF)*, the attraction it replaced. The vehicles face a mammoth, curved movie screen that completely fills your line of vision and represents the true genius of this ride concept. Other simulator-based rides (like the *Star Tours* ride at Disney) use a movie screen that serves as a window to the outside of your spaceship or other vehicle. With this concept, however, you are outside and the environment wraps around you. The illusion is startling, not to mention sometimes terrifying. (Look up as the ride starts for a vertigo-inducing effect.)

In reality, the movement of the simulator's stilts is surprisingly modest. You never actually move more than two feet in any direction. But try telling that to your brain. The kinetic signals sent by your body combine with the visual signals received from the screen to convince you that you are zooming along at supersonic speeds, making white-knuckle turns at dizzying angles.

The new ride improves on its predecessor with high-resolution digital projectors and new tactile and olfactory effects. Though still very turbulent, *Simpsons* is noticeably less jarring than *BTTF*, which had a reputation as a neck-wrecker in its later years. Best of all, the writing and voice acting (with nearly the entire original cast except Harry Shearer's Burns and Smithers) are worthy of an episode from the TV show's best seasons. Die-hard fans of the ground-breaking *BTTF* can take solace in a Doc Brown cameo in the queue video, and the knowledge that USF is still home to Orlando's best simulator-based ride.

The best seats in the house. The best way to experience this attraction is from the front row of the middle car in the middle level of the dome. At the point where the line splits, ask the attendant for Level 2, then ask the next attendant for Room 6. You may need to wait longer, but it's worth it: you'll experience less distortion of the image, and reduce any tendency toward motion sickness. Sit in the front row of the car for comfort, especially if you are tall.

Kang & Kodos' Twirl 'n' Hurl

Rating: ★ ★ ★
Type: Spinning flying saucer ride
Time: 2 minutes
Short Take: Clever reimagining of a carnival classic

Kang & Kodos' Twirl 'n' Hurl is inspired by the drooling space-cyclopses featured in the Simpsons' "Treehouse of Horror" episodes. Here, the homicidal aliens have been harnessed for a family-friendly spinner similar to

Disney's *Dumbo* or IOA's *One Fish, Two Fish.* "Help attack your fellow humans" by controlling the elevation of your saucer-styled vehicle (held aloft on supports ensnared by Kodos' green limbs) with a joystick; flying at the correct altitude triggers cries and quips from the spinning character targets positioned around the ride's perimeter. Remember, "this will be a pleasant ride without anything evil or nefarious, so enjoy...and suspect nothing!"

Kang & Kodos' adds kinetic interest to the World Expo waterfront (especially when its colorful nighttime lighting is flashing), and offers a much-needed option for tykes too tiny for *The Simpsons Ride.* But at its heart, it's a very slow-loading kiddie ride that can easily be skipped on a tight schedule.

Note: This ride does not accept Universal Express.

Men In Black: Alien Attack

Rating:	★ ★ ★ ★
Type:	Interactive ride with laser weapons
Time:	4 minutes
Height Req.:	42 in. (106.7 cm.)
Short Take:	This one gets addictive

Men In Black may be back in fashion, thanks to 2012's 3-D theatrical sequel, but here at Universal skinny ties and sunglasses never went out of style. *Men In Black*, the ride, is a bit like stepping inside a life-size video arcade game, with the element of competition thrown in just to make things interesting. The experience begins when you visit "The Universe and You," a science exhibit left over from the New York World's Fair of 1964. Soon you discover that it's just a cover to enable you to apply for admission to the elite corps of MIB. You are not alone and the wait can get lengthy. Fortunately, snaking your way through the MIB building is an entertaining experience and devotees of the films will find much familiar here. A lengthy and amusing orientation video featuring Rip Torn and Will Smith is worth watching even when there's no line. Farther along, a training film starring two amusingly retro cartoon characters, Doofus and Do-Right, provides safety instructions for the testing vehicles that await you.

Tip: If you don't mind having your party split up, look for the single rider line after your first trip through. It is invariably much shorter than the main line and a real time saver.

Eventually, you are assigned to a vehicle with five other recruits. At each seat is a laser gun and a personal scoreboard that keeps track of hits. You are cruising through a target range, testing your marksmanship, when an urgent bulletin announces that a Prison Transport full of nasty space bugs has crash landed in the middle of Manhattan. At once, you are reassigned to a dangerous but exciting mission. You and another team are dispatched, side by side, to do battle with the aliens through the dark and gritty streets of a cartoon New York.

What follows is a few minutes of chaotic fun. Aliens in every imaginable buggy shape pop up from garbage cans and taxi hoods, from around corners and in shop windows. It's a super-sized sci-fi version of those old shooting galleries down at the boardwalk. Your job is to zap them before they zap you. When the bugs score a hit, your vehicle is sent into a tailspin.

Tip: The guns auto-fire, so hold down the trigger the entire time; you'll score higher and avoid finger cramps. Aim for aliens on the upper stories and hit the same target multiple times to boost your score.

At one point, you discover that aliens have infiltrated the vehicle of the other team and you must fire at your own comrades. Finally, your MIB trainer (Will Smith's Agent J from the movies) appears on a giant screen to warn you that a particularly nasty bug is bearing down on you. Suffice it to say that it's big enough to swallow two MIB training vehicles. Gulp!

Tip: To score a bonus 100,000 points, press the flashing light in front of you as soon as you hear Rip Torn say the "b" in "Hit the red button!"

The vehicles are not simulators but they do allow for sudden swoops and 360-degree spins that are both thrilling and discombobulating. And while the two vehicles depart at the same time and cruise along side by side for most of the ride, their progress can be affected by the direct hits scored by the aliens. As the battle progresses, every rider builds an individual score based on their success in targeting the enemy (you will see the tiny red dots of the laser guns dancing on the alien targets); the individual scores contribute to the overall team score. There is a sneaky way to significantly increase your score that you'll have to discover on your own.

Tip: The maximum possible score is 999,999 and, yes, it can be done.

At ride's end, both vehicles are once again cruising side by side as Will Smith appears on another screen to announce which team came out ahead. The averaged scores of each vehicle are posted for all to see. Then, Smith breaks the news on how your team did: Galaxy Defender, Cosmically Average, or Bug Bait.

In a final clever touch, Smith uses his neuralizer to erase your memory of the whole experience and you emerge to discover that you have just completed your visit to "The Universe and You," which turns out to be about the possibility of life in outer space. "Are we alone?" the sign asks. "Of course we are," is the reassuring answer.

MIB is a lot of fun and it's hard to imagine anyone having serious complaints. Video game addicts will probably want to ride again and again to improve their scores. Obviously there is at least some skill involved in wielding the laser guns because individual scores in a vehicle can vary by as much as several hundred thousand points. On the other hand, the experience is so chaotic that it is hard to know how well you are doing or get the kind of visual feedback that would help you fine tune your aim.

The best seats in the house. Riders on the outside of the vehicles (i.e., in the seats that are the farthest from the loading platform) have the first view of targets and greater freedom of motion for aiming.

On the way out, you can pause to purchase a photo of your laser-gun-wielding team in the training vehicle.

Note: This ride requires that you stow all your belongings in nearby electronic lockers that are free for a short period of time but charge a hefty fee if you overstay your welcome. For more information, see *Good Things To Know About...Lockers* in *Chapter One*.

Fear Factor Live

Rating: ★ ★ ½
Type: Amphitheater show
Time: 30 minutes
Short Take: The TV show comes to life

For big fans of gross-out reality television shows, this live version of the repeatedly canceled NBC show may make for great live entertainment. Six contestants, who have been preselected prior to each show, compete in three events. Contestants are ruthlessly eliminated and forced to take the "Walk of Shame" until the two finalists square off in a multipart test of nerves, climbing ability, and guts. The stunts are not for sissies, involving considerable height, or "carnivorous" eels, or other nastiness. Most impressive is the final challenge, which features two tilted convertibles raised to the rafters; contestants must climb onto the water-slicked hoods to retrieve flags attached to the grilles.

Note: If you'd like to be a contestant, you must present yourself in front of the attraction 70 minutes prior to the show. You must be 18 or older (with photo ID), and your chances seem to be enhanced if you are reasonably good looking and in better than average physical shape.

For those of us who don't meet any of these qualifications, there's still hope. Volunteers are drawn from the audience to fill a variety of roles.

Some (kids, mostly) fire water cannons (remember those water-slicked car hoods?) and other fiendish devices designed to make the main contestants' jobs even harder. Others are given challenges (like confronting creepy-crawlies and drinking yucky concoctions) that might make them wish they'd thought twice about volunteering.

Note: This show has at times performed "seasonally," which means at times of peak attendance. It may be closed during the time you visit.

Selected Short Subjects

■ Back to the Future Props

On the border of Springfield U.S.A. and KidZone, you'll find a couple of reminders of one of USF's former headliner attractions. The Jules Verne-esque steam train and DeLorean time machine parked near the taco truck are authentic artifacts used in the *Back to the Future* film trilogy that inspired the ride that originally occupied the Simpsons simulator. Doc Brown often stops by to take photos with *BTTF*'s still-faithful fans.

■ Krustyland Carnival Games

While up-charge sideshow games are generally the least attractive attraction in a theme park, the Krustyland facade is at least a thematically appropriate place for these carnie come-ons, which Universal had custom-designed to capitalize on various Simpsons characters. Here you can try your skill at tossing "radioactive" rings for Mr. Burns, tossing a softball into Duff beer cans, or playing Whac-a-Rat with Itchy and Scratchy. If you fancy yourself a superhuman, try ringing the bell with a mighty blow of your "sledgeHomer."

Games cost several dollars and, as with the boardwalk attractions they mimic, the odds are heavily weighted toward the house. Universal, however, makes it easier to win at least something, and some of the Simpsons-themed prizes (like skateboards) are surprisingly substantial.

■ RobOasis

In the *Men In Black* plaza, on the way to KidZone, is this clever advertisement for Coca Cola. A tiny alien who is something of a Coke fiend ("Take me to your liter!") sits in a tiny space ship and prattles on about his Earth mission. To either side are niches in the shape of old-fashioned glass Coke bottles. Step in and have your entire body suffused with a fine misting spray of cool water. A fun free refresher for a hot day.

Eating in World Expo

In addition to these Simpsons-themed food outlets, there are some permanent outdoor refreshment stands in the broad plaza outside *Men In Black*.

■ Fast Food Boulevard and Moe's Tavern

What:	Simpsons-themed cafeteria
Where:	Springfield U.S.A., near the *Animal Actors* stage
Price Range:	$ - $$

Simpsons fans rejoice! All of Homer's favorite munchies have been brought to life in the fast food court of your dreams, cleverly hidden behind a series of storefront facades stretching from the Android's Dungeon comic shop (actually a concealed restroom) to the Kwik-E-Mart store, and sporting six different Springfield-inspired serving stations.

Lisa's Teahouse stocks grab-and-go vegetarian delights. **Luigi's** personal pizzas (in cheese, veggie, or "meat likers") have an agreeable New York-style oiliness that outdoes the park's other pies. **The Frying Dutchman** serves baskets of fresh-caught fried fish, tender calamari, and coconut shrimp with hushpuppies and tater tots. **Cletus'** double-battered fried chicken and waffle sandwich has become an instant cult hit (ask for extra maple mayo on the side). **Krusty Burger** is the most popular window, with "The Clogger," two patties with bacon smothered in cheese sauce and served with "kurly fries," more than living up to its name. The boneless "Ribwich" is also drool-worthy. Finish your meal with a cupcake or giant donut, and wash it all down with a **Duff Beer** (in Yuengling-like regular, Coors-esque Lite, and porter-style Dry) or a non-alcoholic **Flaming Moe** (orange soda with dry ice "flames") or Buzz Cola (a no-cal cherry cola).

The main seating area sports huge murals depicting dozens of Simpsons characters, while video monitors scattered around show a too-short loop of memorable food-themed cartoon clips. You can also take your food into the adjoining **Moe's Tavern**, where you can sit at the bar or pool table, and snap a selfie with barfly Barney. Sharp-eyed TV viewers will recognize the Love Tester, red telephone (intermittently ringing with prank calls), and other iconic props. Additional seating is available at outdoor tables.

Tip: Draft Duff at Moe's bar costs less per-ounce than the bottled brew.

■ Duff Gardens

What:	Outdoor eating and drinking
Where:	Springfield U.S.A., across from Fast Food Boulevard
Price Range:	$ - $$

Once a bland concrete walkway, the waterfront near *The Simpsons Ride* is now graced by a beautiful brick beer garden featuring the **Duff Brewery**, serving signature Simpsons intoxicants, along with non-alcoholic beverages like banana Squishees and a brief menu of bites (foot-long hot dogs, chips, and pretzels) to munch on. Also sharing the area are **Lard Lad**, a walk-up window serving super-sized donuts and ice cream sundaes, and **Bumble-bee Man's Taco Truck** (featuring carne asada, fish, chicken, and Korean braised beef tacos). Once you've got your snacks, explore Springfield's sights, including the Seven Duffs topiaries; statues of Jebediah Springfield, Duffman, and Milhouse; and Chief Wiggum's crashed cop cruiser.

The lower level along the water behind Duff Gardens is open for seating and strolling during the day and reserved for VIP viewing of *Universal's Cinematic Spectacular* starting two hours before the show. VIP seating costs $15 (or is included with special dining packages available at all in-park sit-down restaurants except Lombard's; $30 adults, $18 kids) and can be secured (limited availability) 45 minutes prior to show time at the Duff Brewery bar. VIP seating includes one cupcake, one non-alcoholic beverage (except the Flaming Moe), and gratuity, so the view itself costs about $8; if you do the dining deal and order an entree over $16 the seating is "free."

Shopping in World Expo

The **Kwik-E-Mart,** Homer's favorite convenience store, stands outside the exit of *The Simpsons Ride*. On sale are all the expected souvenirs from Springfield, from T-shirts and DVDs to "Flaming Moe" energy drinks. The tongue-in-cheek signage plastered inside and outside the store ("Today's Merchandise at Tomorrow's Prices!") is an attraction in itself. If you get thirsty for an ice-cold "Squishee," a stand outside sells the sweetened slush. Be sure to answer the ringing pay phone outside the shop for a special Simpsons message.

The **MIB Gear Shop** is a spacious, high-ceilinged shop that sells necessaries for MIB agents. Everything from T-shirts to sweatshirts to customized caps and jewelry is available, most emblazoned with oozy alien imagery. You will also find some Frank the Pug plush dolls and a selection of action figures, sunglasses, watch bands, and toys tied into the latest movie. In the back you'll find a black-light corner with glowing garb and geegaws. For an "out of this world" experiment, try the freeze-dried "alien" ice cream or bug-filled lollipops (better yet, don't).

THE WIZARDING WORLD OF HARRY POTTER:
■ DIAGON ALLEY ■

A big tip of the wizard's peaked hat to the design geniuses at Universal! Their *honourable labours* let us *savour* the *flavour*, *colour*, and *humour* of the *neighbourhoods* in Harry Potter's wizarding world that were stripped from J. K. Rowling's books by her U.S. editors, apparently afraid that exposure to British spelling and slang would corrupt America's youth. (Sorry. A pet peeve. I feel better now.)

Diagon Alley is the second installment in Universal's Wizarding World of Harry Potter, the first being Hogsmeade in Islands of Adventure (see *Chapter Three*). Not to put too fine a point on it, this new "land" is a masterpiece of imagination and the design and engineering skills that bring fantasy to life.

Those familiar with the Potter books know that the wizard world exists alongside our workaday world but is largely invisible to Muggles, as non-wizards are called. And so it is that Diagon Alley is concealed behind what has come to be known as the "London Waterfront," a facade of London landmarks that are nowhere near the water.

Near the Lagoon, a crescent-shaped park contains the Eros fountain from Picadilly Circus and the high-speed, purple, triple-decker **Knight Bus** that picks up wizards stranded in the Muggle world. Don't miss the **photo op** with Stan, the bus conductor and his talkative shrunken head.

The facade itself is a mashup of London streetscapes. From left to right, you will see King's Cross Station, gateway to *Hogwarts Express*, the Leicester Square tube station, the Haymarket Theatre, and a row of Edwardian townhouses along Grimmaud Place. That slightly discolored one at number 12 is the ancestral home of Sirius Black, rendered invisible to Muggle eyes by a Fidelius curse. Look for the **house elf** peeking out at the curtains.

The actual entrance to Diagon Alley is an anonymous break in the brick wall at the Leicester Square tube stop. Indeed, anonymity is something of a leitmotif here. Important spots within, like The Leaky Cauldron restaurant, Knockturn Alley, and the Ollivanders wand experience are called out subtly, if at all. Only Gringotts Bank, with the huge dragon draped on its roof is obvious. Once inside, Diagon Alley stretches before you in all its glory, a seeming carbon copy of the set used in the films, and one that is especially enchanting at night. There is just one major attraction here, but it can take hours to savor the richness of the theming. Enjoy!

Escape From Gringotts

Rating:	★ ★ ★ ★ ★
Type:	Indoor roller coaster with 3-D effects
Time:	4.5 minutes
Height Req.:	42 in. (106.7 cm.)
Short Take:	Another Universal smash hit

Imagine that *Revenge of the Mummy* and *Transformers* got together and mated; the resulting offspring might look a lot like the experience in *Escape From Gringotts*. And as anyone who has seen them in the Potter films knows, the roller coaster-like transports through the vaults of Gringotts Bank are tailor-made for a theme-park attraction. Universal's ride designers pulled out all the stops in bringing this goblin-run savings and loan to life, integrating an indoor coaster track (*Mummy*) with simulator technology and 3-D projections (*Transformers*), then upping the ante with massive sets and an ingenious queue line guaranteed to keep you entertained.

As we enter the attraction, we glimpse the richly appointed lobby of the bank to the right, but if the park is crowded on your visit don't get your hopes up. The queue moves quickly to an outdoor area and reportedly stretched to one and a half miles on opening day. Whether the wait proves lengthy or nonexistent, the real adventure begins when you enter Gringotts' lobby with its marble columns, vaulted ceiling, and magnificent chandeliers, past rows of goblins hard at work on their books. It appears, from what the no-nonsense head goblin overseeing this beehive of activity says, that we are here to open an account. Unbeknownst to us we have arrived on the fateful day that Harry and company have arrived to liberate a certain horcrux from the vault of so-sexy-we-hate-to-hate-her Bellatrix Lestrange.

The first stop on our journey is a "security" station where our pictures are taken for our bank ID, which is actually a souvenir photo ($20) to be retrieved at ride's end. Then we walk down a corridor where, as we pass reading tables strewn with copies of the *Daily Prophet* and its moving photos, we overhear Harry and his cohorts plotting their heist.

Next stop is an office even messier than mine where Blordak, a Gringotts banker, briefs us on the introductory tour of the vaults to which we will be treated. He is soon joined by Bill Weasley, Ron's eldest brother, who works at Gringotts as a "curse breaker," a job that apparently involves neutralizing curses on ancient tombs so that they can be stripped of their valuables — banking at its finest. Bill thoughtfully (does he know something?) offers to accompany us on our tour.

Then it's off to the old-fashioned elevators that will take us nine miles down into the bowels of Gringotts. The obligatory safety warning is cleverly delivered by a magical portrait of a goblin who lists in excruciating detail all the medical problems that should prevent you from riding, finishing up with "and any other condition" (gotta love those lawyers!). The ride itself is great fun; ventilation grills at the top of the car let us monitor our progress and glimpse the "security trolls" who pull the levers to send us ever downwards. All the while the floor bounces and the car jostles.

When we reach the bottom, we're almost there. We have just to pick up our 3-D safety goggles and climb a spiral staircase to the loading platform, which is atmospherically located in a stalactite-studded vaulted chamber.

The wonderfully steampunk ride vehicles appear to be two identical 12-person cars linked together. Seating is four abreast in three rows, with each row a little higher than the one in front. Ride attendants efficiently guide you to a row.

The best seats in the house. For reasons that I choose not to reveal, but which will become obvious when the ride begins in earnest, the first row of the first vehicle is the thrill seekers' choice. That being said, the old cliche, "there are no bad seats," is pretty much true. At various points in the ride, the linked vehicles separate and turn to give everyone an excellent view of the action. Note that riders in the outside seats can get their elbows bunged up a bit with the sharp turns and sudden acceleration during the ride.

Tip: If you'd like to ride in that front row, ask a ride attendant politely. No guarantees, but they can often make it happen.

And this is where the story really begins. No sooner has the tour begun than Bellatrix appears to mess it up. She casts a particularly nasty spell and off we go. As harrowing as the experience is, it has a number of saving graces: we have a close encounter with a fire-breathing dragon, we meet Lord Voldemort and live to tell the tale, and we are rescued by Harry and his friends aboard that same dragon.

The effects are spectacular, as the ride vehicles careen through enormous and realistic cavern sets to pause at 3-D screens where the story unfolds. It is over all too soon.

Bill Weasley (played by Domhnall Gleeson) is the star of this show. Harry, Ron, and Hermione appear, but in the distance, in CGI form, their voices provided by voice doubles. Some Potter nerds grouse about the quality of the voice talent. Ungrateful wretches!

This ride is not terribly intense as these things go. The roller coaster elements may be startling to some but they are brief. I recommend that the coaster averse give it a try. There's a bar in Carkitt Market to help calm your post-ride nerves.

Hogwarts Express

Rating: ★ ★ ★
Type: Train ride with special effects
Time: About 4 minutes
Short Take: Clever idea but a bit of a letdown

When this ride was announced it was hailed as a "game changer," the first ever attraction-cum-transportation to take visitors from one theme park to another. Board in USF's King's Cross Station, hard by Diagon Alley, and disembark in Hogsmeade or vice versa. And yes, it is just that. It was, in fact, a brilliant idea. So it saddens me to have to report that the final result is only so-so. I suspect your enjoyment of the experience will depend on the length of your wait to ride. Breeze right on and you'll probably say, "That was fun!" Wait an hour and you might say, "That was it?"

And yet, what the design wizards have achieved is quite impressive — a train journey between two parks that passes through a utilitarian (and completely unseen) backstage area while mimicking the journey to Hogwarts so familiar to those who've seen the movies or, even better, read the books.

Note: This ride requires that you have a two-park pass or an annual pass. Universal has thoughtfully provided kiosks at either end where you can upgrade your one-park pass.

Your journey from USF begins with an intensely boring queue line that represents a vast, featureless King's Cross Station. There is nothing to create a story line for your journey and little to divert your attention, although the queue does dip into an alcove where you can buy food and drink. What theming there is consists of piles of very old suitcases and valises; apparently no one in England has purchased luggage in 60 or 70 years.

If you're wondering how you'll manage the magical passage through the wall to Platform Nine and Three-Quarters, I won't spoil the surprise. Suffice it to say, you'll see your fellow travelers pass through solid brick and they'll see you do the same even though you don't actually get to do it. It's a clever effect.

Things brighten up considerably once you climb a narrow staircase to the actual platform. Up here, they've done an excellent job of evoking King's Cross, for those who know it. Even more impressive is the train, a red and black behemoth that is wonderfully detailed. You'll also get to see Harry's luggage (more of those old bags) piled up and ready for loading, complete with an unconvincing animatronic Hedwig.

The loading process is a masterpiece of efficiency. Trains depart every eight minutes, so the line moves quickly. Two trains ply the tracks between destinations, passing each other somewhere backstage, which speeds things up quite nicely.

The cars you board are the same old-fashioned vehicles you saw in the films, featuring an exterior corridor and a series of compartments with facing, bench-like seats accommodating eight passengers. Once everyone is seated, the doors close and you realize you can't see through the frosted glass to the corridor, while on the other side all you can see is the stone wall of King's Cross Station, not the actual wall but one depicted on a screen that becomes your window to Harry's world.

As the train pulls out of the station, you pass by London streets and get a glimpse of "the gherkin," as London wags have dubbed a pickle-shaped office building. Take note, too, of the black trails in the sky that can only be Dementors after Harry. The train passes by Malfoy Manor through sleeting rain as a flock of ominous black birds swirls about. As the train nears Hogwarts, Hagrid makes an appearance and then the castle itself looms into view. While you don't get to see Harry and friends, you see their shadows on the frosted glass and overhear their conversation. You also feel the chill of the Dementors as their bony hands touch the glass pane of your compartment. The effects used on both the frosted glass and the exterior window are clever while never quite managing to be convincingly realistic.

All too soon you arrive at Hogsmeade Station, nestled among the tracks of *Dragon Challenge* (see *Chapter Three*), and the ride is over. The saving grace is that you can pack the whole clan on this ride, no need to leave granny and the toddlers to cool their heels as you had to do at *Escape From Gringotts*.

Tip: If crowds are low, it is often possible to get in line immediately for the return trip to London. Ask a ride attendant, or just hop into an under-populated row of people waiting to board.

Ollivanders

Rating: ★ ★ ★ ★
Type: Small-scale show
Time: About 5 minutes
Short Take: A charmingly magical moment

Yes, Ollivanders is a shop, the "maker of fine wands since 382 BC" as they never tire of telling you. But Ollivanders is also an attraction thanks to a "wand experience," the entrance to which is wonderfully inconspicuous. Just to the left of the shop is a door marked only by a wand symbol over the entrance. Step in and you are in a small holding area.

Groups of only 20-odd guests at a time are ushered down a narrow corridor lined with shelf after shelf of boxed wands and into a tiny shop, its towering shelves also stocked with dusty boxes. Actually, there are three separate but identical shops here, all the better to accommodate the eager lines of wand enthusiasts, but you'd never know it.

Once in the shop, a kindly proprietor greets you and selects one or two lucky customers (almost always children or young teens) to test out a wand. As Potter devotees know, wands have embedded in their cores various magic substances like unicorn hair or a phoenix feather, and each wand must choose its own master. As the volunteers test the "wrong" wands, a range of disastrous special effects are triggered. Flowers wilt and shelving collapses, requiring the shopkeep to magically repair the damage. Finally, the destined wand is found, as signified by a swirl of light and wind straight out of the cinema.

Afterwards, the volunteers are sent into the adjoining shop to pay for their new wand (or another of their choosing), and the next group is ushered in. There is no charge to attend or participate in the show, but if you want to take your wand home it will run about $45 (see *Shopping* below).

The entire show lasts about five minutes and the effects are sweetly simple. But the actors involved are so engagingly "in character" (all with exhaustive knowledge of wand arcana and credible accents) that it's worth the wait, especially if your child is the one selected.

Tip: There are multiple "spells" rigged throughout the shop, so repeat visitors will experience slightly different shows.

Selected Short Subjects

■ Interactive Wands

Remember those wands running amok in Ollivanders? Well, if you care to shell out $45, you can have one of your very own to take out into the Wizarding World and cast spells of your very own.

The new interactive wands are slightly thicker than the "replica" wands that were on sale (and still are) in Hogsmeade prior to the debut of Diagon Alley. The extra bulk accommodates a small glass bead at the tip; it is backed by a reflective material that sensors at various spell-casting spots can detect. Wave your wand just so and — voila! — magic happens.

There are 14 locations listed on the map, as well as some that are left for you to discover on your own. Golden medallions on the pavement tell you where to stand and the direction in which to point your wand, the spell to utter, and the path your wand should describe to work your magic. Attendants are often nearby in case you need coaching.

■ Knockturn Alley

Knockturn Alley, the "dodgy area" that Hagrid warned Harry away from, is a dark L-shaped tunnel that begins next to the entrance to The Leaky Cauldron. It is so dark, in fact, that it may be difficult to fully appreciate the clever theming.

By all means take the time to read all the signage and peek into shop windows like **Markus Scarrs Indelible Tattoos** ("Ornate Designs To Impress or Menace"), but the real fun is testing out your newfound wand skills. At the huge shop window of **Dystyl Phalanges**, you can conjure a large drawing of a gorilla skeleton to mirror your every move and at **Noggin and Bonce** you can conduct a choir of shrunken heads.

The star attraction in Knockturn Alley, however, is **Borgin and Burkes**, the antique shop where "evil-looking masks stared down from the walls, an assortment of human bones lay upon the counter, and rusty, spiked instruments hung from the ceiling." It was, of course, a notorious front for sales of dark-magic paraphernalia. The theming here is quite wonderful and you could spend an hour looking at all the weird and wonderful stuff on display, most of it tantalizingly out of reach or in glass display cases. Don't miss the **Vanishing Cabinet**, in which you can still hear a certain ill-fated bird chirping away. It's a shop, too, where you can buy crystal skulls, enchanted necklaces, and nasty looking T-shirts. But as a shopkeeper confessed "the super interesting stuff is not for sale."

Tip: Invisible writing on the maps that come with your interactive wand becomes magically visible in Knockturn Alley.

■ Carkitt Market

This relatively spacious area just to the right of Diagon Alley is never mentioned in the Harry Potter books. It was created by the ever-inventive Ms. Rowling specifically for the Wizarding World. Reminiscent of London covered markets like that at Covent Garden, its main function seems to be to provide some breathing room for the crowds that will flock to Diagon Alley. It also serves as a venue for live performances, yet another way it echoes Covent Garden and similar London tourist attractions.

Needless to say it is themed to within an inch of its life, from the Victorian glass roof high overhead to the shopfronts of the House-Elf Placement

Agency, the Jellied Eel Shop, Dr. Filibuster's Fireworks, and the Museum of Muggle Curiosities, none of which you can actually visit unfortunately. For the shops you can visit, see *Shopping* below.

The headline live attraction is **Celestina Warbeck and the Banshees**. The "singing sorceress," who is mentioned only briefly in the Potter canon and appears only via the wireless, comes into her own in this highly enjoyable 12-minute musical entertainment, which plays several times a day on a raised stage in a corner of the market.

Backed by an attractive girl group (not real banshees, alas) Celestina, who in Rowling's imagination looks a lot like Shirley Bassey, belts out favourites like "You Charmed the Heart Right Out of Me," "You Stole My Cauldron But You Can't Have My Heart," and "Beat Back Those Bludgers, Boys."

A charming quartet of puppeteers presents **Tales of Beedle The Bard**, based on the book mentioned in *Harry Potter and the Deathly Hallows* and then published by J. K. Rowling in 2008. Using spindly hand-held puppets and some impressive stage effects and props, they bring to life *The Fountain of Fair Fortune* and the *Tale of the Three Brothers*. Each story teaches a simple moral and will, hopefully, encourage your young ones to read the book.

■ Gringotts Money Exchange

Carkitt Market also plays host to this amusing diversion. Ostensibly you can step in here to have your worthless Muggle money exchanged into the Gringotts Notes that shops catering to wizards prefer. The exchange rate is at par in denominations of $10 and $20. These notes can be used just like Muggle money here and at Hogsmeade, but my guess is that Universal hopes you won't be able to resist hanging onto them as souvenirs.

The real reason to drop by is to chat with the same gruff, stern-faced, animatronic goblin who greeted you in Gringotts lobby — although he denies he's the same guy. He asks if you have any questions and replies with a limited number of canned responses that are presumably chosen by the nearby attendant who overhears your questions. It's pretty easy to stump him, but the encounter makes for a nice **photo op**.

Eating in Diagon Alley

The dining in Diagon Alley follows the template set when Universal opened the first Wizarding World installment a few years back over at Islands of

Adventure (see *Chapter Three*): A large sit-down buffeteria restaurant and a series of small shops and stands offering sweet snacks and beverages. In an attempt (largely unsuccessful) to match the breakaway success of butterbeer, a bunch of new drinks have been created based on concoctions mentioned in the Potter books. GillyWater, which here is actually just plain old water without the slightest hint of gillyweed, and more adventurous thirst slakers like Fishy Green Ale, Otter's Fizzy Orange Juice, Peachtree Fizzing Tea, and Tongue-Tying Lemon Squash (all about $5) can be found at various places around Diagon Alley. The area's flagship restaurant, The Leaky Cauldron, features eight dishes that are new to the wizarding world.

■ The Leaky Cauldron

What: British fare in an enchanted setting
Where: On your left as you enter Diagon Alley
Price Range: $$

It's a little easier to get into The Leaky Cauldron here than it seemed to be in the films, but once inside Harry would find the place familiar. It's a bit less visually dense and a lot brighter than in the films, but it has the same high ceilings and refectory-style seating. The food is rather like the ambiance — close but not exact.

Breakfast ($16) is served from park opening to 10:30 a.m. and includes a "traditional" English breakfast, although I'm not sure many Brits would recognize the croissant. Two breakfast dishes were conjured specially for Diagon Alley, an egg, leek, and mushroom pasty and apple oatmeal flan, which rather magically doesn't actually contain any oatmeal.

For the remainder of the day, The Leaky Cauldron dishes up theme park versions of traditional British pub grub ($12 to $16) like bangers and mash, toad in the hole (sausage in pastry), cottage pie, and the like; most of it is pretty good considering. The beef, lamb, and Guinness stew is served in a bread bowl, while everything else is served on black plastic plates. The Ploughman's Lunch ($20) consists of English cheeses, bread, cornichons, and Branston pickle (a sort of A-1 Sauce alternative) and is shareable.

In addition to butterbeer ($5), you can sample Fishy Green Ale, Otter's Fizzy Orange Juice, and Peachtree Fizzing Tea, all non-alcoholic. But the Wizard's Brew and the Dragon Scale Ale ($8.50) are the real deal.

Service is buffeteria style. Order and pay at the walk-up counter and you will receive a tray with your drinks and a heavy numbered candlestick. A host or hostess will show you to a seat and the candlestick will guide a kitchen scullion to your table with your entree. If you have coffee or tea, you'll have to stir your own cardboard cup — unless you're a wizard, of course.

The Leaky Cauldron may not be a gastro pub, let alone a gourmet delight, but its hearty fare will keep you going as you explore Diagon Alley.

■ Florian Fortescue's Ice Cream Parlour

What: Ice cream, soft serve, and cakes
Where: At the corner of Diagon and Horizont Alleys
Price Range: $

Aside from the cute hats of the servers there's precious little theming in this no nonsense shop that serves up soft and hard ice cream, along with a few baked goods and other sweets. Ice cream is served in cups ($5) or waffle cones ($6); sundaes are $7. In addition to the usual flavours there are some exotic choices, such as Earl Grey and Lavender and Chocolate Chili, which packs a noticeable bite. And who will be able to resist trying Butterbeer ice cream? Still, simple combos like soft serve strawberries and cream seem to work best for most Muggles.

If you really want to splurge, try the **Eton Mess** ($13), a version of a traditional English pudding (that's dessert to you Yank Muggles) created at the famous boarding school of royalty. Here it's vanilla soft serve with a strawberry topping and meringue bits served in a souvenir sundae glass.

■ The Hopping Pot

What: Walk-up drinks and snacks stand
Where: Carkitt Market
Price Range: $

The huge wooden tun that marks this watering hole is almost bigger than the stand it advertises. Here you can sample the Wizarding World's own Wizard's Brew (a creamy stout) or Dragon Scale Ale (an amber ale) ($8). The Tongue Tying Lemon Squash ($5), made to order, is nicely tart. Of course, butterbeer's also on offer. Not much in the way of food. Three tiny Cornish pasties are ($7); there are also crisps ($4), imported from England no less.

■ Eternelle's Elixir of Refreshment

What: Walk-up drink stand
Where: Carkitt Market
Price Range: $

Located near the Gringotts end of Carkitt Market, this small round stand dispenses bottles of GillyWater, plain old water (okay, it's filtered), that you can flavour with small vials of "elixirs" — Babbling Beverage Mixture (watermelon), Fire Protection Potion (fruit punch), Draught of Peace

93

(berry), and Elixir to Induce Euphoria (pineapple). I suspect the real euphoria is experienced by the Barnum-like genius who figured out how to get tourists to pay $8.25 for flavoured water that they have to mix themselves.

■ The Fountain of Fair Fortune

What: The name says it all
Where: In Horizont Alley, near Gringotts
Price Range: $

The name is a shameless ripoff of a beloved children's story from *The Tales of Beedle the Bard* used for crass commercial purposes to sell an intoxicating, or at least enchanting beverage. Here, at an old-fashioned bar behind which stand large silver kegs, you can drink your fill of butterbeer or its frozen slushie cousin. Yum. They also serve up the stronger stuff available at the Hopping Pot, but no food.

The joint is immediately next door to Florian Fortescue's. DIY Butterbeer floats, anyone?

Shopping in Diagon Alley

Diagon Alley is the Mall of America of Harry Potter's wizarding world and in this faithful reproduction it is crammed with colorful shops that Potter nerds will recognize from the books. Unfortunately (or maybe fortunately for the family exchequer), many of them are merely facades. Even so, there are more than enough actual shops to keep Potter fans deliriously happy.

First, a friendly word of warning: If you or your kids are diehard Harry Potter fans who enjoy dressing up to enter this fantasy world, you can spend an awful lot of money here. If you are not a gazillionaire, you might want to set a strict limit for your brood and try mightily to stick to it. Here then are the shops you will encounter as you proceed up Diagon Alley from the main entrance:

Clothing for the well-dressed Quidditch fan is available at **Quality Quidditch Supplies**, everything from shirts, scarves, and felt pendants, all themed to your favorite Hogwart's house ($33 to $109). The big seller seems to be the Gryffindor '07 rugby shirt ($33). Full-size Quidditch brooms are available for $35, but desktop models are $65. For the more cerebral, check out the magnificent Quidditch-themed chess set ($300).

Weasley's Wizard Wheezes, as you may recall, is three stories high, but here you only have access to the ground floor. Don't forget to look up to check out the fireworks seen through the skylight. Then you can turn your attention to the plethora of joke toys, magic tricks, games, and other novelties. There's candy, too, and malingering scholars will want to stock up on Puking Pastilles ($7) and Skiving Snackboxes ($40). Me, I'll settle for the chocolate frogs with their wizard trading cards ($10). A T-shirt advertising the store is $27.

Across the street is **Madam Malkin's Robes for All Occasions**, where you can kit yourself out for your next term at Hogwarts. Academic robes ($109) in all sizes, house scarves ($35), silk ties ($32), and some very handsome, high-quality sweaters ($85) are all available along with less expensive T-shirts. The shop thoughtfully provides a full-length mirror that comments on your appearance when you consult it.

Ollivanders, of course, sells the wands you will not be able to resist. There are 62 different wand styles available, 22 of which are interactive (see above under Selected Short Subjects). The interactive wands cost $45 while all others, sometimes referred to as "replica" wands are $35. Of special note are Ollivanders 13 "original" wands, all interactive, each made of a different type of wood, based on the ancient 13-month Celtic tree calendar, which associated different trees to dates, much as the more familiar astrological calendar does. The easy way to choose a wand is by your birthday, but you may hear teenagers earnestly discussing each other's personality traits in an attempt to pick the perfect wand.

Located in Horizont Alley, across from Fortescue's, **Magical Menagerie** offers one-stop shopping for stuffed animals ($15 to $33), including some of your favorite pets from the books such as Crookshanks, Fluffy, Fang, and Scabbers. *Scabbers*?? Needless to say, many plush owls are on offer as well, with Hedwig a best seller.

The following shops are located in the Carkitt Market area.

Wiseacre's Wizarding Equipment is the "dump store" for *Escape From Gringotts*, which means you can't miss it. The T-shirts, mugs, and smartphone cases that make up most of the stock hardly seem like wizarding equipment but there you have it. The decor, however, is worth spending some time with. The astronomical and astrological paraphernalia are real jaw droppers. None are for sale, alas. Connected to Wiseacre's is the next door shop, **Scribbulus Writing Implements**, where you will find colorful quill pens ($10 to $30), some of which use actual bottled ink. Hogwarts stationery supplies include sheets of parchment ($11 to $13), wax seals, and notebooks in various sizes. If Ollivanders is packed, you can pick up a wand at **Wands by Gregorovich**, a vest pocket shop across from the Owl Post. Just be aware that Gregorovich does not stock the 13 "original" wands that only Ollivanders carries.

One of the cleverest shops in Carkitt Market is **Shutterbuttons**, near the Owl Post, where through the Muggle-world magic of green screen technology you can have yourself and your family inserted into various scenes from the Wizarding World, which are then collected into a sort of living scrapbook. There's no cost to try it out and preview the result, but if you fall in love with the finished product (a likely scenario), you can purchase a DVD and have a digital version sent to your email address for $70.

The darkest shop, in all senses of the phrase, is **Borgin and Burkes,** already mentioned in the review of Knockturn Alley above. Despite the high price tags, the most popular items actually for sale here are the Death Eater masks ($100), made of the same rigid material as hockey masks and wall-mountable, and replicas of Lucius Malfoy's walking cane, complete with concealed wand ($100). Also available are Bellatrix Lestrange's gown ($240) and faux leather bustier ($110). You can even pick up Lord Voldemort's gown ($295) and become He-Who-Might-Go-Broke. The less well heeled can make do with mugs and T-shirts.

Play like a kid . . . live like a 'King.'

Top: Seuss Trolley Ride in Islands of Adventure
Bottom: Hard Rock Hotel lobby

Above: Welcome to
Universal Studios Florida.

Right: Mel's Diner, just
like you remember it.
(Hollywood)

Below left: Meet the stars.
(Hollywood)

Below right: I need mouth-
to-mouth. (Hollywood)

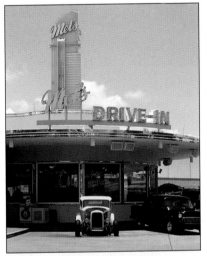

Above: Getting discovered at Schwab's. (Hollywood)

Left: Absolutely Gru-some. [Production Central]

Below: It's the Krustiest Place on Earth.™ (World Expo)

Above: A coaster just for kids. [KidZone]

Right: The mummy's minion beckons. (New York)

Below left: She loves you! [Universal Studios]

Below right: The Superstar Parade. [Universal Studios]

Above: Optimus wants YOU! [Production Central]

Left: Rip Ride Rockit will take you to new heights. (Production Central)

Below left: Climb aboard, puny earthlings. (World Expo)

Below right: Men in Black. (World Expo)

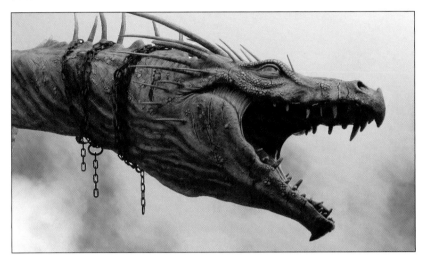

Above: Not just another pretty face.

Right: Do you have a question?

Below: Carkitt Market shops

[All photos from Diagon Alley, USF]

Above: Celestina Warbeck entertains.

Left: Weasley's Wizard Wheezes.

Below: The London 'Waterfront.'

[All photos from Diagon Alley, USF]

Above: Welcome to Islands of Adventure. (Port of Entry)

Right: Yes, it's a restaurant — Mythos. (Lost Continent)

Below left: Here be griffins. (Lost Continent)

Below right: Gourmet eats at Mythos. (Lost Continent)

■ SAN FRANCISCO ■

With the closing of *Jaws*, the "set" that used to be called San Francisco/ Amity became simply San Francisco, making this the smallest themed land in the park. With that, rumors began to swirl that this tiny "City by the Bay" will be swallowed up earthquake-like and replaced by ... well, opinions vary. In the meantime, let's enjoy what's here — a pretty decent thrill ride from the park's early days (albeit one that's been substantially altered) and a love-ly seafood restaurant.

Disaster!

Rating:	★ ★ ★ ½
Type:	Show and ride
Time:	25 minutes, ride portion is 3 minutes
Short Take:	Best for the ride

Disaster! takes the "Ride the Movies" slogan to its logical extreme. Here, the ride *is* the movie and everyone who rides it is a star. Well, okay, everyone who rides it is an extra. There are chills and thrills in store, but first you have to go through some mildly amusing silliness to put you in the mood.

The experience begins with a visit to Disaster Studios, an "independent, boutique" studio, the creation of disaster flick genius, Frank Kincaid. Kincaid is quite the Renaissance man, writing, directing, and producing shoe-string-budget disaster epics like *Baboom*, *Fungus*, and *300 Knots Landing*, which is about a plane crash apparently.

Once inside, you discover you have stumbled into a casting call. One of Mr. Kincaid's lackeys is looking for a few willing victims... er, *volunteers* to serve as actors and stunt people for Kincaid's next blockbuster. There are parts for a young child, 10 to 12, a "gardening grandma," a "hunky" guy (who usually winds up being anything but), and assorted other types, so if you're interested in being part of the action, you probably have as much of a chance of being selected as the next guy.

Then it's on to the next room, for the best part of the pre-ride show. Here we meet Mr. Kincaid himself, played by a subdued, but still bizarro, Christopher Walken. Through a bit of technological magic called "Musion" that will have you scratching your head and asking, "How'd they do that?" Kincaid (or at least a holographic simulation of him) strides on stage and

97

interacts with his assistant.

Kincaid treats us to a brief lecture on his "secret" rules of disaster films ("The annoying guy always dies") and announces his next magnum opus, *Mutha Nature*, a global warming eco-disaster flick starring Duane "The Rock" Johnson as a heroic park ranger battling evil corporate villains.

In the third room, the volunteers picked earlier are put to work filming bits and pieces that will later be edited into the final film. "Time is money," Mr. Kincaid points out, so these bits are shot in an ultra-fast-paced illustration of "green screen" techniques, but minus any explanation of the what and why, it may seem a bit confusing. Perhaps in the age of DVD special features, it's assumed there's no mystery left to movie-making. The big news, however, is that Mr. Kincaid has decided to cast all of us in the grand finale to his film. With that, the audience is ushered in to the final phase of the *Disaster!* experience.

This is the part most people come for, a simulated earthquake aboard San Francisco's BART (Bay Area Rapid Transit). The train (with open sides and clear plastic roof) pulls out of the Oakland station, enters the tunnel under the Bay, and soon emerges in the Embarcadero station. A voice over the train's P. A. system instructs you to scream for the camera as the earthquake reaches eight on the Richter scale and the Embarcadero station begins to artfully fall apart. Floors buckle and ceilings shatter. The car you're in jerks upward, while the car in front of you drops and tilts perilously. Then the entire roof caves in on one side, exposing the street above. A propane tanker truck, caught in the quake, slides into the hole directly toward us. The only thing that prevents it from slamming into the train is a steel beam that impales the truck and causes it to burst into flames. Next, an oncoming train barrels into the station directly at us, but the buckled track sets it on a trajectory that narrowly misses us. And it's still not over. What looks like the entire contents of San Francisco Bay comes pouring down the stairs on the other side.

All too soon, the terror is over and the train backs out of the station, returning us to "Oakland." As it backs out, we are treated to a trailer for *Mutha Nature*, into which have been inserted the scenes shot earlier, to humorous effect. *Disaster!* has retained the most exciting elements of the former *Earthquake* attraction and refreshed the tired preshow portions with fun, if somewhat frantic, results.

Tip: The exuberant performance of the sign-language interpreter, presented at selected shows, is a treat whether or not you are hearing-impaired.

The best seats in the house. The train holds about 200 people and is divided into three sections. The first section (that is, the car to the far left as you enter the BART station), has its seats facing backwards. The other two sections have seats facing forward. This arrangement assures that people in the first section won't have to turn around to see most of the special effects the ride holds in store. The front of each section has a clear plastic panel but the view is somewhat obstructed. Avoid the first two rows of a section, if possible. Probably the best view is to be had in the middle of the second car. The major attraction for those sitting on the right (as the train enters the tunnel) is the flood, which can get a few people wet. The more spectacular explosion of the propane tanker and the wreck of the oncoming train are best viewed from the left. As always, the outside seats are the primo location.

Beetlejuice's Graveyard Mash-Up

Rating: ★ ★
Type: Amphitheater show
Time: 20 minutes
Short Take: Best for teens and waking the dead

Beetlejuice began his career at Universal as a street performer on the New York set. The show was simple, sweet, and a lot of fun. Then he was "discovered," given his own amphitheater show with a big set and a ton of amps and pyrotechnics. Since then he has been headlining a series of shows that have grown ever louder, ever bigger, and ever dumber.

The most recent incarnation (or should I say reanimation?) has your "host with the most" throwing a Graveyard Mash-Up with the Universal Classic Monsters Frankenstein, his bride, Dracula, and Wolfman, abetted by a quartet of androgynous dancers in black tights and white fright wigs. New in this version are Phantasia, a pretty Phantom of the Opera, and Cleopatra, who bumps and grinds ... I mean *walks* like an Egyptian.

There is no plot, just a non-stop medley of pop songs, including memorable hits from the eighties and forgettable songs of more recent vintage. Every once in a while the match up of the song and the character singing it makes sense, but more often not. The singing ranges from competent to cringe-worthy. The choreography sometimes seems like it was cribbed from a high school musical and not a very good one at that. Most distressingly, Beetlejuice, who used to be the undeniable star of the show and quite funny, seems almost an afterthought. I left the show humming the pyrotechnics and making a mental note to watch *Beetlejuice* (Tim Burton's hit movie of 1988 starring Michael Keaton) one more time.

Tip: The latest version of the show has toned down the raunchiness and Universal now recommends it as "Best for Family" on its website, although the parental warning symbol remains on the 2-Park Map.

The best seats in the house. There are really no bad seats for this one. An interesting seating choice would be next to the pit in the center of the house, where the sound and light techies run the show. If your kid has dragged you to the show for the fifth time, you can amuse yourself watching these wizards ply their high-tech trade. Seating is pretty much first-come, first-served, although at peak periods attendants may direct you to a seat to speed the flow.

Eating in San Francisco

The San Francisco area enjoys the distinction of playing host to Universal Studios Florida's best sit-down restaurant. Here, in the order you encounter them as you proceed from Diagon Alley on your way to New York, are your choices:

■ San Francisco Pastry Company

What:	Small pastry and coffee shop
Where:	Across from *Disaster!*
Price Range:	$

Right at the entrance to Lombard's stands this tempting alternative. It features most of the pastries and sandwiches you found at the Beverly Hills Boulangerie in Hollywood as well as coffee, cappuccino, bottled beer, and soft drinks. There are no tables inside and only a small outside seating area, so many customers will have to take their snacks to one of the scenic spots along the nearby waterfront.

■ Lombard's Seafood Grille

What:	Elegant restaurant evoking Fisherman's Wharf
Where:	On the lagoon, across from *Disaster!*
Price Range:	$$ - $$$

Lombard's is a full-service restaurant boasting the most elegant decor at Universal Studios — and the best food. The main dining room exudes an industrial-Victorian aura, with brick walls, filigreed iron arches, and tapestry-covered dining chairs. The room is dominated by a huge, square, centrally located saltwater fish tank like something Captain Nemo might have imagined. Windows on three sides look out over the lagoon.

The seafood here is a cut above your local Red Lobster and beautifully presented. Appetizers cost $5 to $9 and range from creamy bisques and chunky chowders to balsamic-glazed fried calamari and chicken wings. For the main course, the grilled, blackened, or baked Fresh Fish and Seafood listed on a separate menu ($18 to $20) is a good bet. Other entrees ($13 to $20) reflect the diverse cuisine of San Francisco and include fish and chips, a San Francisco Stir Fry, beef medallions, and shrimp mac & cheese. There are also gluten-free salads ($9 to $16), and sandwiches ($11 to $18), including a Boursin steak sandwich, a lobster roll, and a decent burger.

The wine and cocktail menu is short and to the point. Wines by the bottle are in the $20 to $32 range, with a blah champagne at $38. Wines by the glass ($5 to $8) are serviceable, as are the martinis and specialty cocktails ($7 to $12).

Mini-desserts served in tall skinny shot glasses are $1.75. By the way, these desserts-in-a-glass are served at the parks' other full service restaurants. A better choice is the key lime pie ($5).

There is a children's menu offering kid-friendly fare (including fish & chips and linguini with marinara) for about $7 per entree. Reservations can be made by calling (407) 224-3613 or online at OpenTable.com.

A special *Universal's Cinematic Spectacular* package meal is available for $44.99 adults, $12.99 ages 3 to 9 (plus tax and gratuity). Diners first order an appetizer and entree off a special menu that is nearly identical to Lombard's standard fare, minus some top-dollar items like lobster. After the main course, they retire to watch the day-ending lagoon show from the rear waterfront patio, while sampling from a dessert bar; after-dinner drinks are available for an additional charge. The location provides an excellent, intimate, in-your-face view of the spectacle. In fact, you may get soaked by the dancing fountains if the wind is blowing your way. See the show's description later in this chapter and call (407) 224-7554 to reserve a package.

■ Chez Alcatraz

> ***What:*** Outdoor drink stand
> ***Where:*** On the lagoon, across from *Disaster!*
> ***Price Range:*** $

This seasonal stand is a great little bar in warm weather, serving up a variety of mixed and frozen drinks. A short snack menu featuring house-made potato chips, hummus dip, and a fruit and cheese plate, is available seasonally.

Tip: Look behind the bar for "Bruce the Shark." The iconic ichthyological **photo-op** was relocated here when the *Jaws* ride was bulldozed.

■ Richter's Burger Co.

What: Fast-food burger joint
Where: On the lagoon, across from *Disaster!*
Price Range: $

That's Richter as in scale, and just in case you didn't get it the first time, one glance at the damaged interior of this warehouse-like structure will let you know that the theme here is pure earthquake. It's a fun environment in which to chow down on standard burger fare.

The Big One is a burger or cheeseburger served with "a landslide of fries," while the San Andreas is a chicken sandwich. The Fault Line is an "all-natural gardenburger" with cheese, and The Richter Scale salad comes with chicken breast. Frisco shakes, chocolate and vanilla, are offered. Richter's also features a Coca-Cola "Freestyle" dispenser, capable of mixing over 100 soda varieties, including the deliciously obscure Orange Coke.

The food is serviceable at best and the self-service toppings bar (unlimited tomatoes, lettuce, onion, and pickles) is a great bonus. The decor is fun and imaginative, and worth more than a passing glance. At the back, you'll find tables with a lagoon view and a balcony offering a bird's-eye view of the ordering area.

Shopping in San Francisco

The shopping scene here has diminished considerably with the disappearance of the Amity section. In fact, there's hardly any shopping at all! The **San Francisco Candy Factory** is another place selling scoop-it-yourself candy at inflated prices along with other goodies like coated apples and fudge. **Salty's Sketches** offers much better value in the form of Universal's expert caricaturists, who will immortalize your goofy grin for posterity. These artists must all have studied under the same master because their styles are almost identical and the quality of the renderings excellent. And the cost is also surprisingly moderate given the high quality of the finished product.

NEW YORK

Compared to some others on the lot, the New York set seems downright underpopulated — with attractions, eateries, and shops, that is. Whole streets in New York are given over entirely to film backdrops. Gramercy Park, Park Avenue, the dead end Fifty-Seventh Street that incongruously ends at the New York Public Library, and the narrow alleys behind Delancey Street contain nary a ride or shop. These sets, however, provide some wonderfully evocative backgrounds for street shows and family portraits, especially the library facade, with a collection of familiar skyscrapers looming behind it. They also include some clever inside jokes for those familiar with the movie industry. Check out the names painted on the windows of upper story offices along Fifth Avenue and see if you can spot them.

Of course, New York does have attractions, including the blockbuster *Revenge of the Mummy* and *Twister* (although oddly enough, neither of the films involved is set in the Big Apple).

Tip: Look down the dead end streets on either side of Louie's Italian Restaurant, for a backstage glimpse of the *Hogwarts Express* making its way between Diagon Alley and Hogsmeade. Why Universal chose to spoil the illusion this way is a bit of a mystery.

Revenge of the Mummy

Rating:	★ ★ ★ ★ ½
Type:	Indoor roller coaster and dark ride
Time:	About 4 minutes
Height Req.:	48 in. (121.9 cm.)
Short Take:	A brilliant blend of thrills and chills

The *Revenge of the Mummy* starts innocently enough. It seems Universal is in need of more extras for this new film and you are lucky enough to be passing by as they solicit volunteers. (Don't get your hopes up. *Revenge of the Mummy* is not a real film, it's just a polite fiction for the sake of the ride.)

As you enter the queue line, it looks like one of those "The Making Of..." displays that Universal mounts from time to time. Props and set pieces are scattered about, all carefully labeled. On video monitors, director Steven Sommers, star Brendan Fraser, and others on the crew give chatty interviews about the making of the film, dropping ominous references to ancient curses and strange happenings. A recurring character in these vignettes is Reggie, a hapless gofer who keeps losing his anti-Mummy amulet to Hollywood big wigs.

Then the queue line takes a sharp turn through a narrow passageway and things become truly strange. It appears you are in the tomb of Imhotep where the usually cheerful ride attendants have started acting strangely.

There's no more video and the queue line now looks remarkably like a real Egyptian tomb in the Valley of the Kings at Thebes and something in the air seems to bring out the evil in your fellow tourists. Press a glowing scarab and you can startle folks elsewhere in line with a frightening blast of air and watch the result on a video monitor. Oddly, there's nothing to indicate whether this is supposed to be a movie set or the real thing, whether you're still in twenty-first century Orlando or back in the 1930s.

Tip: The single riders line will usually have you riding with little or no wait, but you'll miss all the interactive queue effects.

Up a rickety wooden staircase, past a massive sculpture of Anubis, the god of the Underworld, you finally reach the loading platform for the ride. Once again, there's no explanation of why you are being asked to board the 16-passenger, four-abreast cars, or what lies ahead. The ride vehicles appear to have been built by U.C. & Sons of London, England, back in 1925 to make tomb exploration easier (could "U.C." stand for Universal Creative?).

The best seats in the house. The front row provides the best view of the dark ride elements, and they're worth checking out. Coaster fans, however, will find that the far left seat in the back row offers the most "air" (that feeling of being lifted out of your seat on the ride's drops).

Like the queue line, the ride itself starts deceptively. It's not too far removed from those gentle "dark rides" at a certain family park complex down the Interstate. But you're still in that nasty Imhotep's retirement home and before long things get dicey. You turn a corner and there's Reggie again, all wrapped up for Mummy take-out, warning you to turn back.

Imhotep himself appears rather dramatically and looking decidedly the worse for wear after several millennia of entombment. "With your souls, I shall rule for all eternity," he bellows, which sounds like a great slogan for a modern-day political campaign.

Around the next bend, you are given a stark choice: Get with the program and receive riches beyond imagination or resist and die a hideous death. Your cries of "I'll take the gold! I'll take the gold!" go unheeded and the ride begins in earnest.

Tip: Check the early scenes of the ride for some subtle references to *Kongfrontation*, the ride the *Mummy* replaced.

At this point, the curse of the Mummy takes hold, and this description stops so as not to reveal too much about what follows. Suffice it to say that the ride morphs into a supercharged roller coaster experience that takes place largely in near darkness. And, of course, what would a Universal ride be like without a little pyrotechnics? In short, if you think this will be just another indoor roller coaster ride, think again. The Mummy himself puts it nicely: "Death is only the beginning."

Thanks to linear induction technology, you will go from zero to 45 miles per hour in less than two seconds, pulling a full G, and for much of the ride you will be at or above that speed as you zip up and down through a series of sharp turns past visual effects that remind you that the Mummy and his unholy minions are still breathing hotly down your neck.

Tip: Those who balk at mega-coasters like *The Hulk* and *Dragon Challenge* over at Islands of Adventure are still encouraged to give *Revenge of the Mummy* a try. Because the ride is so smooth, it is only slightly more intense than *Spider-Man* at IOA.

Note: This ride requires that you stow all your belongings in nearby electronic lockers that are free for a short period of time but charge a hefty fee if you overstay your welcome. For more information, see *Good Things To Know About...Lockers* in *Chapter One*.

As you exit, check the souvenir ride photos to see the clever way in which the ride vehicles have been articulated (split in two) so they'll hug the track better and enhance the thrills.

All in all, this ride is a major success that further cements Universal's reputation for being on the cutting edge of ride technology. The roller coaster elements certainly deserve the highest marks. However, connoisseurs, who look on theme park rides as an art form, will note some narrative lapses and anticlimactic effects that keep the ride from full five-star status.

Twister . . . Ride It Out

Rating:	★ ★ ★
Type:	Stand-up theater show
Time:	15 minutes
Short Take:	A slow start, but amazing in-your-face special effects

Here is an attraction that will almost literally blow you away. Based on the hit film of the same name, *Twister* is a theater show without seats that leads you through three sets for a payoff that lasts all of two minutes. But what a two minutes it is!

The journey begins as you snake though a waiting line in Wakita, Oklahoma, around large props from the film. You are entertained by two disk jockeys ("the storm chasers of rock and roll") from WNDY ("windy") who spin peppy rock songs with appropriately stormy titles. You will be kept cool by large fans that blow a fine water mist over the crowds. As you draw closer to the Soundstage on which the real adventure unfolds, the entertainment gives way to videos of actual tornadoes, some of which are really scary.

The line may seem formidable, but don't despair. This show can handle 2,400 people each hour, so the line moves fairly quickly. Once inside, the show follows a familiar three-part format. In the first chamber, themed as the prop room for the film, you watch a video in which the vivacious Helen Hunt and an oddly wooden Bill Paxton set the scene. If you missed the movie, this segment gives you the information you need to understand what the film and this attraction are all about.

The second chamber is themed as the ruined interior of Aunt Meg's house from the movie. Trees and the front end of an automobile protrude through the ceiling, where a string of video monitors continue the introduction process. There is barely any "edutainment" in this attraction, but what little there is happens here. We get a brief explanation from Bill and Helen of how "dangerous" it was to act in front of the film's niftier effects.

Finally, it's on to the final chamber where the "real" show happens — live, in-person, and right before your eyes. You enter a set where you stand on a three-level viewing area under the deceptive protection of a tin roof. In front of you is the Wakita street that runs past the Galaxy outdoor movie theater where a "Horror Night" double feature of *The Shining* and *Psycho* is being shown. The street is deserted, but no sooner is everyone in place than all heck breaks loose and the inanimate objects before you take on a scary life of their own.

The best seats in the house. You will have a great experience here no matter where you stand. However, die-hard thrill seekers will want to be as close to the action as possible. Stay to the right as you are ushered into this final chamber if you want to stand in the front row. Most people hug the railing, but you can form a second row and make your way to dead center if you wish. Ask an attendant for the stationary section if you want avoid a shock at the finale.

You've probably already figured out that you'll be living through the vortex of a twister. Some of the effects are versions of what you may already have seen while riding *Disaster!*, and the final funnel effect sometimes fizzles. But first-time viewers always get a big kick out of the explosive ending.

Tip: This is a wet, if not precisely soaking, experience. A poncho might be in order if you're really fussy. Otherwise, you probably will find the sprinkling fun, even refreshing. Interestingly enough, one seems to get wetter in the back row than in the front.

Selected Short Subjects

■ Arcade

Why would anyone pay good money to get into Universal Studios Florida and then waste their time in a video arcade? The Arcade at the exit of *Revenge of the Mummy* never seems to lack for customers, so some people seem to have an answer to that question.

■ The Blues Brothers

The Dan Ackroyd/John Belushi routine that made a better *Saturday Night Live* sketch than it ever did a movie is immortalized in this peppy street show, which holds forth from a makeshift stage on Delancey Street.

The warm-up comes courtesy of a belting blues singer whose gospel-tinged renditions of blues standards are a show in and of themselves. Then, backed by a live sax player and a recorded sound track, Jake and Elwood goof and strut their way through a selection of rock and blues standards, winding up with a rousing, extremely high-decibel version of "Soul Man."

The genial performers, who are look-alikes only to the extent that one is tall and lanky and the other short and stout, do the material justice, and Jake's hyperkinetic dance steps are a highlight of the show. If you like your rhythm and blues straight and unadulterated, you should enjoy it. During the holiday season a special Christmas version is performed, featuring "Snow Man" and "Santa Claus is Coming to Town."

Eating in New York

■ Finnegan's

What:	Irish pub and sit-down restaurant
Where:	Across from *Revenge of the Mummy*
Price Range:	$$

Finnegan's has two parts and two personalities. The first is a full-fledged

Irish pub complete with live entertainment and walls crowded with beer and liquor ads and offbeat memorabilia. Cozy up to the antique bar and order a yard of ale if that's your pleasure, or choose from a classy selection of domestic and imported beers. Guinness stout, Harp lager, and Bass ale are available on draught; try a five-beer sampler if you're feeling adventurous. Hard cider and wine are also available. Cementing the "neighborhood bar" feel are first-rate bartenders who'll remember your name.

The other half of Finnegan's is a full-service restaurant hidden behind the false facades of the New York lot. The decor here is pared down and perfunctory, reflecting the room's other identity as a movie set. Fortunately, the food is anything but pared down or perfunctory. The theme is Irish and British Isles, with generously sized entrees to match. Appetizers (in the $7 to $9 range) include "Irish Chicken Stingers," Cornish pasties, and Scotch eggs. The potato leek soup makes a great starter.

Among the entrees ($12 to $17, with sirloin steak at $22), Irish fish and chips is traditional, right down to the newspaper it's served in. The shepherd's pie is a juicy souvenir from the Emerald Isle, topped with perfectly browned mashed potatoes. There's also bangers and mash (sausage and mashed potatoes), Irish stew, and (of course) corned beef and cabbage. All entrees are accompanied by steamed vegetables in a nutmeg-tinged sauce.

For lighter appetites, there are sandwiches ($10 to $13), soups ($5), and salads ($12 to $13). Kids can pick from "Isle of Grilled Cheese," "Cloves of Chicken Fingers," or three other entrees ($5 to $8). For dessert, the same miniature sweets served at Lombard's and IOA's Mythos are also offered here, at $1.75 for each sugar-stuffed "shot." Reservations can be made by calling (407) 224-3613 or online at OpenTable.com.

■ Louie's Italian Restaurant

What: Cafeteria-style Italian restaurant
Where: At the corner of Fifth and Canal, near the lagoon
Price Range: $

Louie's is a remarkably successful re-creation of the ambiance of New York's Little Italy section — tiled floors, plain tables, and cafe chairs. The only hint you're at Universal Studios is the cafeteria style serving area and the odd ceiling with its jagged edges and movie lights that remind you the restaurant can do double duty as a film set.

The fare is standard Italian and just the basics. Cheese, pepperoni, and vegetable pizza is served by the slice or whole pie ($32 to $34). Entrees include spaghetti and meatballs and fettuccine alfredo with chicken. Meatball and chicken parmesan subs and a Caesar salad round out the menu. There is imported Italian beer and wine as well as Miller Lite and Yuengling. In one corner of the restaurant, there is a counter selling gelato and Italian ice. The quality is generally above average, as well, making Louie's one of USF's better cafeterias. Louie's is quite large and makes a good place to duck in out of the sun or rain for a rest.

Across from Louie's, under the "Games and Amusements" marquee, is a **Starbucks** serving coffee, cappuccino, and pastries, as well as a **Ben & Jerry's** serving ice cream sundaes and smoothies.

Shopping in New York

New York is an international city and the shopping here reflects that. Recalling Gotham's heyday as a largely Irish city, **Rosie's Irish Shop** sells a variety of genuine Irish imports, along with much less expensive souvenirs, many bearing pithy Irish sayings. Discriminating shoppers will want to grab a mug emblazoned with the coat of arms of the author of this book. Across the street, a tiny storefront next to the Blues Brothers stage offers **Psychic Readings** and temporary henna tattoos.

The Film Vault, located across the street from the *Transformers* ride, is not the place to look for DVDs of your favorite films (although there is a *very* small selection). Nor does it sell, as the sign would have you believe, "motion picture memorabilia." Instead, it is packed with movie-themed tchotchkes that range from the kinda fun to the downright tacky, like the tiny Oscar statuettes that say "World's Best Mom" and the like.

Sahara Traders is the shop you pass through after your escape from *Revenge of the Mummy*. Here you can pause to pick up your candid Mummy ride photos. In the shop itself, you will find the requisite Mummy T-shirts and knickknacks. More attractive are figurines based on ancient Egyptian originals and some nice books on Egyptology. On the other hand, you can also get a perfectly silly shiny gold and black pharaoh's hat.

The cleverly named **Aftermath** forms the exit to *Twister*. There are plenty of *Twister* souvenirs here, including more shot glasses than in most shops. Reflecting the film's farmland setting, many of the items for sale are cow-themed. There's also a wall of kitschy knickknacks inspired by that other twister movie, *The Wizard of Oz*. Other than that, you'll find an eclectic variety of Universal Studios souvenirs.

■ PRODUCTION CENTRAL ■

Production Central is modeled on a typical film studio front lot. Essentially, it is a collection of soundstages and has a resolutely industrial feel to it. But with recent additions injecting some architectural pizzazz, this area now has visual interest to match its entertainment value.

Hollywood Rip Ride Rockit

Rating:	★ ★ ★ ★
Type:	Music-themed steel coaster
Time:	About 2 minutes
Height Req:	51 in. (130 cm.) min.; 79 in. (200.7 cm.) max.
Short Take:	A ground-breaking (but also back-breaking) ride

Towering over the soundstages, smashing through the New York firehouse facade, and snaking its way toward CityWalk, the *Hollywood Rip Ride Rockit* literally changed the face of Universal Studios Florida forever. Billed as "the most technologically advanced coaster in the world," this first Floridian installation from innovative European designer Maurer Söhne boasts statistics to make any speed freak salivate. It's the tallest (167 feet) and one of the fastest (65 mph) coasters in Orlando, and features a number of unique, newly engineered elements.

The experience begins in a flatscreen-festooned queue near the Blue Man Group theater, where "edgy" animated characters introduce themselves as the camera crew for your new music video. The seven 12-passenger trains are just as high-tech, with on-board video and sound systems, and color-changing LEDs that put on a carnival light show as they swoop overhead. Even the boarding process has been upgraded: a moving walkway keeps cars continuously loading, minimizing wait times.

Once in the car, you'll use a seat-mounted display to select a soundtrack from one of five musical genres, including "Classic Rock/Metal" (ZZ Top, Limp Bizkit), "Country" (Dwight Yoakam, Kenny Chesney) and "Rap/Hip-Hop" (Black Eyed Peas, Kanye West). With 30 songs to choose from, everyone should be able to find something they'll like screaming along to.

Tip: If you press the *Rip Ride Rockit* logo for 10 seconds a hidden menu of "bonus tracks" will appear. Type in any three-digit number. A "Pocket Rockit" iPhone app is available to tell you all the codes!

Once your music selection is made, you begin the ride by ascending a "record-breaking" vertical lift (lying flat on your back!) in only 17 seconds, then dive into a 103-foot "non-inverting" twisted loop dubbed a "Double-Take" above the plaza stage. Other maneuvers take you spiraling through the *Twister* queue facade, "crowd surfing" over waiting guests, and skirting the edge of CityWalk. The twisty track is deceptively disorienting (and surprisingly silent); you'll be back in the station before you know what hit you.

During the ride, while your chosen song is delivered to your eardrums at up to 90 decibels courtesy of custom in-seat speakers, 14 digital cameras along the track (plus 6 in each train) capture your every shriek. You may purchase packages with still photos ($20 and up) and personalized music videos ($30 to $40) in a freely web-sharable format after you return to earth. (Bonus tracks do not appear on souvenir videos due to licensing restrictions.)

Rockit isn't as intense an experience as the *Incredible Hulk*, but delivers more kick than *Revenge of the Mummy*. It's too wild to be considered a "family coaster" (especially in the bumpy back seats) but the lack of upside-down inversions makes it a good bet for tweens ready to graduate to grown-up thrills. The best news for coaster purists (or worst for the weak-kneed) is that there are no over-the-shoulder restraints, only a large curved lap bar to hold you firmly in place while allowing bursts of out-of-your-seat airtime.

Tip: Rockit offers a single rider line, but check the posted wait time before using it. Sometimes it can be the same or longer than the standard line!

Despicable Me Minion Mayhem

Rating: ★ ★ ★ ★ ½
Type: 3-D simulator ride
Time: About 5 minutes
Height Req.:   40 in. (101.6 cm.)
Short Take: A funny, family-friendly thrill

If you thought only clean-cut, law abiding families attend amusement parks, think again. Nefarious super-villians take vacations too! Gru, the adorably evil antihero of Universal's 2010 animated hit *Despicable Me*, has relocated his home to visit Universal Studios Florida with his adopted daughters in tow, and you're invited to an open house. Take a trip to Gru's secret laboratory, where he'll transform you into one of his mischievous Minions and let his girls train you to endure hilarious indignities in a Rube Goldberg obstacle course. You probably have nothing to fear, unless your fellow Minions catch sight of a beloved banana, in which case all bets are off!

Despicable Me is based on the same sort of simulator hardware as the former *Jimmy Neutron* and *Hanna-Barbera* attractions. This latest incarnation adds cutting-edge "4K" digital 3-D projectors for ultra-sharp, in-your-face visual effects, and a oversized new screen. The room containing your vehicle is actually a movie theater divided into twelve eight-seat sections. Each section is a simulator car, a cousin of the high-tech simulators used to train airline pilots. It hovers a few feet off the ground, like a box on stilts, and moves and tilts in sync with the on-screen action. It may only move a foot or so in any direction, but try telling that to your mind. Still, the gyrations are gentler than those of the similar *Simpsons* ride, making this a perfect starter thrill for those building up their courage.

Minion Mayhem was made with the participation of the original film's talent, including comedian Steve Carell. Accordingly, the movie's successful blend of humor and heart is well-represented in the ride, from the funny pre-show safety instructions ("Your 3-D goggles will last five times longer than the person wearing them") to the heartstring-tugging finale. In an inspired touch, disembarking riders are dumped in an interactive disco party, where they can catch "boogie fever" with a costumed dancing Minion.

Tip: There is a row of stationary benches in the front for little ones and those who wish to forego the thrill ride aspect of the show. You are very close to the screen here, however, making for somewhat distorted viewing, which might induce the queasiness you are trying to avoid. If you choose this option, try to sit as close to the center aisle as possible.

The best seats in the house. The most advantageous spot is in the middle of the house in the last or next-to-last row. From there, you get the best, least distorted view of the screen.

Transformers: The Ride - 3D

Rating:	★ ★ ★ ★ ★
Type:	3-D motion simulator ride
Time:	5 minutes
Height Req.:	40 in. (101.6 cm.)
Short Take:	An exhilarating blur of mechanical mayhem

The Transformers began in the 1980s as devilishly clever children's toys, little cars and trucks that unfolded into nifty sci-fi robots. There was a loose story line behind the toys, involving good and evil alien robots from a distant planet that, for reasons best known to their creators, chose to model themselves on twentieth century Earth vehicles. They quickly burst the bonds of their toy boxes to become a Marvel comic book, an animated TV series, and finally one of Hollywood's most successful (and perhaps most inane) action movie franchises.

There have been so many iterations of the Transformers story line that it would take a Talmudic scholar to unravel them. Fortunately, *Transformers: The Ride* restricts itself to the wildly successful four-film (soon to be five-film) series directed by action wunderkind Michael Bay.

Here at USF, we enter the headquarters of NEST (Non-biological Extraterrestrial Species Treaty) as recruits in training for the human forces that, allied with the heroic Autobots and their leader Optimus Prime, battle the evil Decepticons, led by Megatron, whose battle-to-the-death has destroyed their native planet of Cybertron and has now spilled over to Earth. (Who writes this stuff?)

It's hard to miss NEST headquarters. While the building itself is pure industrial-anonymous, the entrance is topped by a humongous statue of Optimus Prime himself. They say it's 28 feet tall, but it seems much, much larger. If they wanted to hide their HQ from the Decepticons, Optimus' pride squelched that idea!

At any rate, the NEST building houses and protects the last fragment of the All-Spark. The AllSpark is a... well, it's the.... Let's just say it's what Alfred Hitchcock used to call a McGuffin, a meaningless something or other that drives the plot. It's important, the Decepticons want it, and if they get it we can all kiss our asteroids goodbye. You'll actually get to see the AllSpark in the queue line, not that it will make you any the wiser.

If you haven't seen the films, not to worry. An extensive briefing by General Morshower (from *Transformers: Revenge of the Fallen*, the first sequel) and Autobot Ratchet (a better name for an alien we have yet to hear) will give you all this background and then some.

Tip: During slower periods it is possible to breeze through the queue so quickly that you miss the set up. So if you need that background (and it is sorta fun), you may want to slow down and watch the video briefings. Of course, during busy periods the line can be dauntingly long. In that case, especially if you've ridden once or twice, the single rider line can speed you to the loading platform. The singles queue tops out at about 30 minutes, at which point employees will close it off; hang around the entrance for 10 minutes or so and it should reopen.

As we progress through the queue, we learn that things on the battlefront are getting a bit dicey, so much so that raw recruits must be used as cannon fodder (should that be robot fodder?) in a last ditch attempt to save Earth from those nasty Decepticons.

With that scary news we board ride vehicles that seat 12 passengers four abreast in three rows. One point that many riders miss is that their vehicle is actually an Autobot named Evac, which becomes very important in a matter of seconds. Then it's off to find and destroy Decepticons.

The best seats in the house. The first of the three rows in the vehicle provides the most immersive view — almost too immersive. Surprisingly, the middle and rear rows receive better 3-D images with less disorientation.

As your ill-fated journey proceeds, it is your bad luck to interrupt the Decepticon, Ravage, as he seizes the AllSpark. Before you know it, Evac, your Autobot vehicle, has retrieved the AllSpark and from then on you become Target Number One for every Decepticon in town. Suffice it to say that you careen from near disaster to near disaster as Megatron takes personal interest in you and Optimus Prime comes to your defense. You narrowly escape becoming collateral damage each time, as your vehicle is flung from one perilous Decepticon face-off to another.

One of the most amazing elements in this ride is completely invisible to riders. At one point, your ride vehicle enters an elevator and rises up a floor only to descend again later in the ride. We defy you to figure out when these moves happen.

Note: If you have ridden the *Spider-Man* ride at Islands of Adventure, you will notice some intriguing similarities. The ride technology is the same, although the theming of the ride vehicles is different, and the basic plot line of the ride follows the same template, right down to that amazing plunge at the finale.

Shrek 4-D

Rating: ★ ★ ★ ★
Type: Theater show
Time: 25 minutes
Short Take: Another boffo 3-D extravaganza

Welcome back to Duloc, that magical kingdom where everything is perfect — or would be if it weren't for all those pesky fairy tale characters that Lord Farquaad tried to do away with. If you remember the film (and if you don't, don't worry), Shrek sent Lord Farquaad to his eternal rest while rescuing and falling love with the beautiful Princess Fiona.

But it's hard to keep a good villain down, it seems, and as we enter Duloc we find ourselves in a dungeon antechamber where Pinocchio and the Three Little Pigs are being tortured under the direction of the ghost of Lord Farquaad. On the "Dungeon Cam" we see the gingerbread man tacked down to a torture table awaiting an even worse fate. Apparently, we're next.

In a very funny preshow we learn, courtesy of the Magic Mirror from the old Snow White tale, that the evil Lord still carries a considerable torch for the lovely Fiona, who is now off on her honeymoon with Shrek and Donkey. (Not most people's idea of the perfect honeymoon perhaps, but there you have it.) The preshow also does an excellent job of reprising the plot of the film for those who were foolish enough to miss it.

The ghost of Farquaad vows to steal Fiona and make her his spirit bride and, just to cover all the bases, decides to torture us for information as to her whereabouts.

Tip: Sidle to the right as you wait in the first chamber and take the time to read the instructions for "Duloc Express," a witty send-up of the Universal Express Pass system.

The next stop is a spacious, 300-seat 3-D theater where the story continues on film. The 15-minute film that follows would be a minor masterpiece of 3-D animation just by itself. But the clever designers of this show have added so many little extras that *Shrek 4-D* ends up in a virtual dead heat with *T2* as the top 3-D theater attraction in all of Orlando.

Best of all are the seats. They aren't quite simulators, but let's just say they make the tale unfolding on the screen a truly moving experience.

Tip: The moving seats can buck quite violently, so ask an attendant for a non-moving chair if you have a bad back.

We see Shrek and Donkey trying to plot a course to the Honeymoon Hotel when Farquaad's henchman, Thelonius, appears and kidnaps Fiona. The chase that follows packs enough thrills and cliffhangers (literally) for a full-length action film and involves not one but two fire-breathing dragons. Good prevails, Fiona is saved from a watery death, and in true fairy tale fashion everyone lives happily ever after. Except Farquaad.

Both the preshow introduction and the film do a wonderful job of poking fun at the conventions of films based on fairy tales, theme park attractions, and theme parks themselves, making *Shrek 4-D* Orlando's most subversive attraction. And it must be therapeutic for theme park employees to be able to visit an attraction where guests are actually warned, "Cell phone users will be flogged. Flash photographers will be burned at the stake. Enjoy the show!"

Selected Short Subjects

■ Music Plaza

The Hollywood Bowl-styled stage that sits at the foot of *Hollywood Rip Ride Rockit's* signature loop is home to Universal's seasonal concert series. The 2,400-square-foot performance space features eco-friendly lighting equipment and a bone-shaking sound system. Performers range from today's Top 40 to oldies acts. Recent guests have included Adam Lambert, The Steve Miller Band, Big Time Rush, and Earth, Wind & Fire. Some concerts, like those during Mardi Gras and the Summer Concert Series, are included in your regular admission. Others, including the "Rock The Universe" Christian music events, require a separate ticket. Popular artists can fill up the 15,000-square-foot astroturf viewing lawn hours early, so unless you're a die-hard fan, just wait until showtime and find a spot in the New York area in sight of the 20-foot-high projection screens.

■ Donkey's Photo Finish and Transformers Meet & Greet

Along the street connecting *Shrek* and *Transformers*, you'll find a pair of unusual **photo ops.** Just across the street from the *Shrek 4-D* exit, you will find a rustic stable facade where you can get your picture taken with everybody's favorite noble steed, Donkey. Shrek shows up too, as does Princess Fiona from time to time. While Shrek is the usual theme park costumed character, Donkey is a clever animatronic who sticks his head out of his stable door and, thanks to an unseen performer doing an uncanny Eddie Murphy imitation, ad libs to hilarious effect with guests and passersby. Just eavesdropping is a great way to kill time.

On the opposite side of the street from the Supply Vault store, a high-security military bunker serves as backdrop for meet and greets with *Transformers'* cybertronic stars, as embodied by stilt-walking performers wearing astonishingly elaborate robot costumes. Optimus Prime, Bumblebee, and Megatron rotate posing duties throughout the day. Interactive versions that can converse with guests are reportedly on the way.

You can snap photos with your own camera, but if you've left yours back at the hotel, there is a Photo Connect photographer on hand to oblige. You can pick up (and pay for) prints and digital copies at an adjacent stand.

Eating in Production Central

■ Classic Monsters Cafe

What:	Buffeteria restaurant
Where:	Across from *Twister*
Price Range:	$-$$

Those glamorous ghouls of our collective black-and white subconscious take center stage in an eatery filled with souvenirs from zany sci-fi movies like *Abbott and Costello Go To Mars* and chillers like *Frankenstein, The Mummy,* and *Dracula.* The Creature from the Black Lagoon even floats in a big tank in the "Swamp Dining" room. Amazingly enough, they have resisted the seemingly irresistible temptation to use terms like Monster Meals, FrankenFries, and Mummy's Pasta on the menu.

Chief on the better-than-average bill of fare are comfort foods like four-layer lasagna, rotisserie chicken, and ribs. Cheeseburgers and giant slices of cheese or pepperoni pizza are available. Nathan's chili-cheese hot dogs and wedge salads with bleu cheese round out the menu. Draft light beer is available in addition to the usual assortment of soft drinks and desserts.

Outside, a kiosk dubbed **Bone Chillin' Beverages** serves up harder stuff, including mixed drinks and slushies. There's nothing stopping you from bringing these more potent potables inside to enjoy with your meal.

The food is served "buffeteria" style in Frankenstein's laboratory, which makes you wonder if eye of newt is among the condiments. You can take your pick of several dining areas — Space, Crypt, Swamp, and Mansion Dining — each with a different theme and all packed with life-sized statues, props, and photographs. Universal Studios' early success was fueled by its inventive horror movies, and this gleefully ghastly gastronomic goulash is a fitting celebration of that bygone era.

Shopping in Production Central

Super Silly Stuff is the unavoidable gift shop at the exit of *Despicable Me Minion Mayhem,* but at least it's been adorably decorated after the fluorescent amusement park featured in the film. You'll find tons of T-shirts and toys featuring Gru, Margo, Edith, Agnes... and, of course, lots and lots of Minions. The plush selection is especially notable; it's hard to pick which is cuter, the stuffed Minion or the bug-eyed unicorn.

Survivors of *Transformers: The Ride-3D* stumble out into NEST's

Supply Vault, which is festooned with as many video screens and control panels as the ride's queue. The Vault stocks an exhaustive array of Transformers T-shirts and toys, including Evac action figures, and chocolate Allsparks exclusive to Universal's parks. Hang onto your wallet and check out the high-end collectibles inside the clear circular case.

You will enter **Shrek's Ye Olde Souvenir Shoppe** in a good mood because you will be exiting from the immensely entertaining *Shrek 4-D* attraction. It houses the usual assortment of Shrek-ified souvenir fare, from T-shirts to plush dolls of all the principal characters. Petite green "ogre ears" like the ones sometimes worn by the ride attendants make a nice fashion statement (so much nicer than those large clunky round black ears worn by the fashion-challenged) and they're cheap, too. There is also a line of princess apparel, and accessories including tiaras, cone-shaped hats, purses, and (for the casual princess) T-shirts.

Tip: Check out the mirror behind the cashier.

EXTRA ADDED ATTRACTIONS

Universal offers a pair of live daily spectaculars designed to keep you in the park (and spending money) until the end of the operating day, and to send you off into the evening toward CityWalk in a good mood. On both accounts, they succeed pretty well.

Universal's Superstar Parade

Rating: ★ ★ ★ ½
Type: Character parade
Time: 15 minutes
Short Take: Colorful fun, especially if you know the characters

This is Universal's first attempt at a genre that Disney has perfected — the daytime character parade aimed at kids. It's an entertaining, if somewhat abbreviated, effort.

Nickelodeon's *Dora the Explorer* and *SpongeBob SquarePants*, Universal's *Despicable Me*, and *Hop* (a computer-generated cartoon about the Easter Bunny), provide the characters for this rolling street party. Four elaborate floats, each featuring a different kidtoon franchise, are festooned with kinetic elements, including a giant video screen on Gru's super-villain SUV, and acrobatic monkeys swinging on Dora and Diego's rolling jungle. Accompanying the large set pieces are a platoon of smaller themed vehicles and dozens of hard-working dancers.

The pageant traverses the New York, Production Central, and Hollywood areas of the park once a day in late afternoon, stepping off near *Beetlejuice's Graveyard Review* and exiting at Cafe LaBamba (check the park map for details). The entire production pauses twice for five-minute high-energy dance performances set to disco-fied Top 40 tunes. The first stop is in New York, near *Revenge of the Mummy* and *Twister*; the second is along Hollywood Boulevard, from the park entrance up to Mel's. If you want to see the dance numbers, position yourself somewhere between these points; if you only want to see the passing floats, find an uncrowded spot elsewhere.

The Dora and Hop floats pause near the New York arcade and *T2*, while

Despicable Me and SpongeBob stop by Macy's and the *Horror Makeup Show*. It's hard to predict exactly which characters will stop in front of the viewing spot you've picked out. So if your kids are hell-bent on greeting Gru, or meeting one of the other parade stars in particular, consult your park map for the **Character Party Zone** times and locations. Each clan of characters makes two daily pre-parade appearances near Mel's between late morning and mid-afternoon. This is an ideal time to get photos or autographs, since there's no time to get up close during the parade.

Universal's Cinematic Spectacular

Rating: ★ ★ ★ ★
Type: Multimedia extravaganza
Time: 17 minutes
Short Take: A fitting finale to your day

Those large barges emblazoned with Universal marquees that you saw floating in the lagoon all day come to life at night, just before park closing, for a fitting grand finale. When the show begins, the scaffolds extending upwards from the waterborne platforms become high-tech waterfall screens, generating liquid canvases on which a kaleidoscopic survey of Universal film history is projected. Subtitled "100 Years of Movie Memories," this celebration of the company's cinematic centenary contains clips ranging from silent classics like *The Hunchback of Notre Dame* (that's Lon Chaney under all that hideous makeup) to more recent studio releases like *Frost/Nixon* (that's Frank Langella under all that hideous makeup). There are a few howlers among the century of classics spotlighted (*Battleship*, anyone?), and the bulk are of relatively recent vintage, but by and large this show is a swell love-letter to Universal's legacy.

The film clips are arranged in a series of thematic montages: horror, humor, good vs. evil, tragedy and triumph. Since many found it hard to discern a throughline in its predecessor, for this show Universal brought in Oscar-winner Morgan Freeman to lend his legendary voice to the linking narration, giving the proceedings welcome warmth and gravitas. The rapid-fire selections range from Hellboy to Hitchcock and from The Duke to Vin Diesel. The screens (all show exactly the same clips, and are equally legible from either side) are filled with monsters and mobsters, aliens and astronauts, comedy and carnage, heroes and the Holocaust. Fireworks punctuate key screen moments, and a few dozen colorful fountains hidden throughout the lagoon sway to the emotion-packed soundtrack like an aquatic ballet.

Since its debut, Universal has continued to enhance the show with additional laser-light effects and new film clips featuring recent hits like *Ted* and *Les Miserables*.

It's unlikely you'll be able to identify every movie and every star represented, but you'll probably come away with a renewed appreciation of just how many films Universal has produced over the years and how many of them were first-rate. And if the movie memories don't move you, the razzle-dazzle, slam-bang finale that fills the sky overhead with fireworks will. If you come expecting an epic spectacle on the scale of Epcot's *IllumiNations* or Disney California Adventure's *World of Color*, you're likely to go home somewhat let down. But considering that Universal sits in the middle of a residential neighborhood, it's a pretty amazing display.

The best seats in the house. First, understand that you will probably be standing for this show, although some people find places to sit, especially on the rocks on the World Expo side of the lagoon. Stand in the waterside terraced park near Mel's for a clear, if narrow, view of the film and fountains; Central Park (across from Gardens of Allah) provides a panoramic "surround sound" experience. There are also good views along the London waterfront and near Richter's. Lombard's Seafood Grille and Duff Gardens offer reserved viewing for a price (see above).

Note: This show is presented nightly during busy seasons, and irregularly during slower periods. See Universal's website for performance dates.

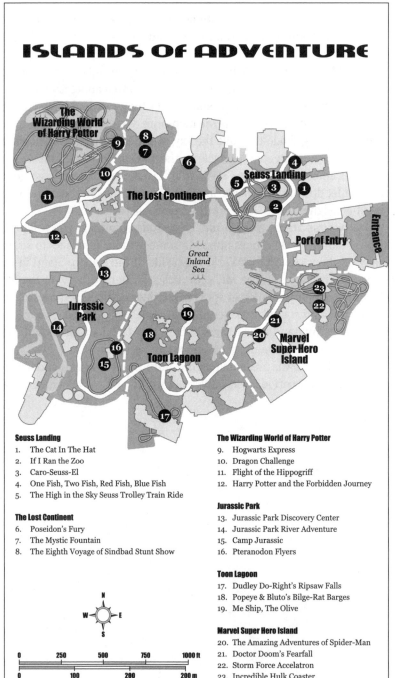

ISLANDS OF ADVENTURE

Seuss Landing
1. The Cat In The Hat
2. If I Ran the Zoo
3. Caro-Seuss-El
4. One Fish, Two Fish, Red Fish, Blue Fish
5. The High in the Sky Seuss Trolley Train Ride

The Lost Continent
6. Poseidon's Fury
7. The Mystic Fountain
8. The Eighth Voyage of Sindbad Stunt Show

The Wizarding World of Harry Potter
9. Hogwarts Express
10. Dragon Challenge
11. Flight of the Hippogriff
12. Harry Potter and the Forbidden Journey

Jurassic Park
13. Jurassic Park Discovery Center
14. Jurassic Park River Adventure
15. Camp Jurassic
16. Pteranodon Flyers

Toon Lagoon
17. Dudley Do-Right's Ripsaw Falls
18. Popeye & Bluto's Bilge-Rat Barges
19. Me Ship, The Olive

Marvel Super Hero Island
20. The Amazing Adventures of Spider-Man
21. Doctor Doom's Fearfall
22. Storm Force Accelatron
23. Incredible Hulk Coaster

CHAPTER THREE:

ISLANDS OF ADVENTURE

Billed as "Orlando's next-generation theme park," Islands of Adventure certainly raised the competitive bar with its assortment of cutting edge attractions, thrill rides, and illusions. And thanks to a certain boy wizard, Orlando's "next big thing" is now even bigger.

Islands of Adventure (IOA) is located right next door to Universal Studios Florida (USF), less than a ten-minute stroll away. You can get there even faster aboard the *Hogwarts Express* from Diagon Alley. Despite the proximity, Islands of Adventure is not just more of Universal Studios. It has a separate identity and, with some notable exceptions, its attractions draw their inspiration from very different sources than those in its sister park.

Islands of Adventure also kick-started Universal's push to stay at the cutting edge of ride technology and it has remained there ever since. And while parts of USF can look downright utilitarian, every nook and cranny in IOA has been themed to within an inch of its life; there's even a soundtrack that changes from island to island and from area to area within islands. In fact, this may be the most themed theme park you've ever visited. And whereas USF seemed to pride itself on being the "adult" alternative in Orlando's theme park sweepstakes, IOA created an abundance of rides and activities for younger visitors.

Guests reach Islands of Adventure through the Port of Entry, a separate themed area that serves much the same function as the Front Lot at Universal Studios Florida. Through the Port of Entry lies a spacious lake, dubbed the Great Inland Sea. Artfully arranged around it are six decidedly different "themed areas" — Seuss Landing, The Lost Continent, The Wizarding World of Harry Potter: Hogsmeade, Jurassic Park, Toon Lagoon, and Marvel Super Hero Island. The "islands" of Islands of Adventure are not true islands, of course; but the Great Inland Sea's fingerlike bays set off one area from the next and the bridges you cross to move from one to another do a remarkably good job of creating the island illusion. The flow of visitors is strictly controlled by the circular layout. If you follow the line of least resistance (and it's hard not to), you will move through the park in a circle, visiting every island in turn.

Eating in Islands of Adventure

Islands of Adventure's best-kept secret is the food. Those who truly care about the taste and quality of what they put in their stomachs and who despair of eating well in a theme park will find much to celebrate here.

Mythos, the full-service restaurant in The Lost Continent, is an award-winning dining experience that is exceptional by theme park standards. The food at Islands of Adventure's other full-service restaurant, Confisco Grille, is also very good.

The fast food in the park is a cut above the norm, too. Best of all, given the obvious quality of the food, the prices are no more than you would expect to pay for far less adventuresome cooking at other theme parks.

Shopping in Islands of Adventure

Much of what can be said about the shopping in Universal Studios Florida can be repeated for the shopping experiences offered in Islands of Adventure. However, several things are worth noting.

The Middle Eastern bazaar section of The Lost Continent offers a number of shops run by some very talented artisans. Look here for the kind of gifts that won't scream "bought in a theme park!" Look, too, in Port of Entry for unusual folk sculptures and decorative items.

For the child in us all, there's a satisfying selection of classic kids books for sale in Seuss Landing, and the treasure trove of comic books to be found in Marvel Super Hero Island is nothing to look down your nose at. Finally, the Wizarding World sets a new standard for theme park shopping with unique merchandise sure to have Potter fans panting.

Again, keep in mind the wisdom of saving your shopping for the end of the day. The Islands of Adventure Trading Company in Port of Entry has a good selection of souvenirs representing all of the park's islands, including a sampling of Potter products. There's even a Universal Store in CityWalk, which means you can shop for souvenirs days after your tickets to the parks have expired. You can also shop online at . . .

www.universalorlando.com/Merchandise/MerchandiseHome.aspx
. . . or by phone by calling (888) 762-0820.

Good Things To Know About . . .

Here are some notes that apply specifically to Islands of Adventure. General notes that apply to both parks will be found in *Chapter One: Planning Your Escape*.

■ First Aid

There is a first aid station with nursing facilities in Port of Entry, just past the turnstiles, in the Open Arms Hotel building. A second first aid station will be found tucked away in the bazaar area near the Sindbad theater in The Lost Continent.

■ Getting Away From It All

Each of the islands has a park-like, attraction-free section tucked away near the shores of the Great Inland Sea. They were designed as venues for private parties and corporate events. They are little visited by most guests and offer a terrific opportunity to escape the madding crowd. They also boast excellent views across the Sea to other islands. On days when the park is open past sunset, they are surprisingly private and quite romantic places to snuggle up with that special someone.

■ Getting Wet

Islands of Adventure has some great water-themed rides. They offer plenty of thrills but they pose some problems for the unprepared. Kids probably won't care, but adults can get positively cranky when wandering around sopping wet.

The three water rides, in increasing order of wetness, are *Jurassic Park River Adventure, Dudley Do-Right's Ripsaw Falls,* and the absolutely soaking *Popeye & Bluto's Bilge-Rat Barges.* Fortunately, these three wonderful rides are within a short distance of each other, allowing you to implement the following strategy:

First, dress appropriately. Wear a bathing suit and T-shirt under a dressier outer layer. Wear shoes you don't mind getting wet; sports sandals are ideal. Bring a tote bag in which you can put things, like cameras, that shouldn't get wet. You can also pack a towel, and it might be a good idea to bring the plastic laundry bag from your hotel room.

Plan to do the rides in sequence. When you're ready to start, peel off the outer layer, put it in the tote bag along with your other belongings, and stash everything in a convenient locker. You can use the all-day lockers in Port of Entry, but more convenient choices are the banks of small lockers at the entrances to *Ripsaw Falls, Bilge-Rat Barges,* or the *Jurassic Park River Adventure.* These lockers cost $4 for 90 minutes, plus $3 each additional hour, up to $20 per day. The all-day lockers are more spacious but will cost you a flat $8. You decide.

Once you've completed the circuit of rides, you will be very, very wet, especially if you have gone on some of the rides more than once. You now have a choice: If it's a hot summer day, you may want to let your clothes dry as you see the rest of the park. Don't worry about feeling foolish; you'll see plenty of other folks in the same boat, and your damp clothes will feel just great in the Florida heat. In cooler weather, it's a good idea to return to the locker, grab your stuff, head to a nearby restroom, and change into dry clothes. Use the plastic laundry bag for the wet stuff.

Another option is the "Haystack" full-body dryers outside *Bilge-Rat Barges* and *Ripsaw Falls.* A family of four can fit inside the big outhouse-like closets and be blasted with hot air for $5. Expect to get warm, not dry.

The alternative is to buy an Islands of Adventure rain poncho (they make nice souvenirs and are usually available at most shops) and hope for the best. This is far less fun and you'll probably get pretty wet anyway.

■ Reservations

Mythos and Confisco Grille both accept priority seating reservations. During busier periods you may spot a small kiosk in Port of Entry where you can make reservations. You can book online through OpenTable.com. If you're really planning ahead, the central reservations number is (407) 224-4012. They will take reservations up to 30 days in advance.

■ Single Rider Lines

To help shrink long lines, some rides open single rider lines when things get busy. You will frequently find single rider lines at *Doctor Doom's Fearfall* and *Spider-Man. Forbidden Journey, Incredible Hulk, Ripsaw Falls, Bilge-Rat Barges*, and *Jurassic Park River Adventure* offer them sporadically. Operation of single rider lines is solely at the discretion of the lead ride attendant, so don't count on this time-saving ploy.

■ Special Diets

The map in the 2-Park Guide Map has a special symbol for restaurants serving vegetarian meals. Confisco and Mythos can provide kosher meals with 24 to 48 hours advance notice. Call Food Services at (407) 363-8340 to make arrangements. These restaurants are also able to accommodate other special dietary needs, such as gluten-free or low-carb regimens. Consult the menu and discuss your needs with the server.

■ Special Events

Islands of Adventure has fewer special events than Universal Studios Florida next door, but its lone holiday celebration is a Christmas crowd-pleaser.

Grinchmas. December sees Seuss Landing transformed into a winter wonderland, complete with Seussian holiday decor and a *Mannheim Steamroller*-scored musical show starring the Grinch himself, who proves to be a delightful (if parentally incorrect) host.

Treasure Hunt: Your Day at Islands of Adventure

The initial excitement over Harry Potter has subsided slightly, but Hogsmeade still draws huge crowds that are expected to increase now that the *Hogwarts Express* is ferrying passengers there from Universal Studios Florida's Diagon Alley. That makes seeing all of Islands of Adventure in one day a lot harder than it used to be. Of course, the definition of "all" will be different for everyone. For example, many people will have no interest in subjecting themselves to the intense thrills of the roller coasters, *Doctor Doom*, or *Forbidden Journey*. Teenagers, young singles, and those without children can probably skip the interactive play areas (although they're pretty nifty and worth a peek).

Those who want to see literally everything Islands of Adventure has to offer can still probably come pretty close in a single day, especially if they are willing to arrive early and step lively. If you pay for Universal Express Passes or enjoy the front-of-the-line privileges of staying at one of the luxury resorts (see *Chapter Five*), then seeing it all is much more manageable.

Doing Your Homework

This assignment is not mandatory, but those who have not seen the original *Jurassic Park* (or the 2013 3-D re-release) should really rent the DVD before visiting Islands of Adventure. This easy-to-handle research project will add to your enjoyment of what the designers have achieved in IOA's Jurassic Park.

If you have not yet introduced your small children to the magical world of Dr. Seuss, this is an excellent excuse to do so. A knowledge of *The Cat in the Hat*, *If I Ran the Zoo*, and other Seuss books will make their visit to Seuss Landing a whole lot richer, and reading from the books is a great way to pass the time on those long car trips to Florida.

And of course, reading the seven-volume Harry Potter series and seeing the eight accompanying movies is mandatory to get the absolute most out of IOA's Wizarding World: Hogsmeade, which is based on the first four books. You can certainly enjoy the rides and shops without any prior Potter knowledge, but at a minimum you'll enjoy the wealth of detail much more if you've at least seen the first film.

What To Expect

Islands of Adventure has many of the same kinds of attractions as Universal Studios Florida, with some notable exceptions. As at Universal Studios Florida, your first step is to consult the **2-Park Guide Map** brochure, which you can pick up as you enter the park or in many shops throughout the park. It has a great map of the six "islands," each of which will be discussed in detail in the sections that follow. Here are some general observations about what's in store for you:

Rides. The rides here come in all shapes and sizes, from relatively tame kiddie rides to slam bang simulators and coasters. They also vary widely in terms of "throughput" — the number of people they can accommodate per hour. *Pteranodon Flyers*, for example, has a minimal throughput, while *Cat in the Hat* processes a surprising number of riders each hour.

Roller Coasters. Coasters spawn long lines, although the ones at Islands of Adventure are so intense that sometimes the wait to ride is surprisingly brief. Both coasters have separate lines for the daring few who want to ride in the front row; for these folks the wait is often lengthy.

Amphitheater Shows. These operate on a fixed schedule listed in the 2-Park Guide Map. Generally, seating is not a problem.

Theater Shows. Only *Poseidon's Fury* and *Ollivanders* could fall into this category and neither is an exact fit. Wait times for these attractions can be lengthy.

Displays and Interactive Areas. There are three separate interactive play areas for children; all of them can captivate your kids for hours on end. Keep that in mind when planning your touring schedule. The displays in the *Discovery Center* in Jurassic Park, while also enthralling for many children, are less likely to eat up considerable chunks of time.

All the Rest. Islands of Adventure has many more places to get away from the crowds than does its sister park. In fact, if you have a multi-day pass, you might want to bring a good book one day and just chill out along the shore of the Great Inland Sea.

Not-So-Buried Treasure

If you have limited time to spend in Islands of Adventure, or if you simply choose not to run yourself ragged attempting to see it all, here is the best the park has to offer:

Harry Potter and the Forbidden Journey. The current state-of-the-art in thrill ride technology, and quite simply the best ride in Orlando.

Spider-Man. Orlando's former top ride, narrowly dethroned by *Forbidden Journey*, still packs a wallop with its high-definition 3-D visuals.

The Hulk. Those who can tolerate the cutting-edge coaster experience (and you know who you are) will want to ride *The Hulk* several times. Absolutely awesome. (*Dragon Challenge*, once on this list, has unfortunately been neutered; see the review of the ride for the sad details.)

Popeye & Bluto's Bilge-Rat Barges. Soaked to the skin fun.

■ Runners-Up

Here are a few more suggestions that aren't at the very top of the list but are well worth considering:

Cat in the Hat. This kiddie ride manages to be both traditional and cutting edge.

Jurassic Park River Adventure. River boats, raptors, and a hair-raising splashdown.

Dudley Do-Right's Ripsaw Falls. IOA's take on the themed flume ride is a cut above most in this genre.

Seuss Landing and *Camp Jurassic.* Even if you don't go on the kiddie rides, you should at least take a slow stroll through these over-the-top wonderlands to marvel at the design.

Mythos. This is a restaurant, not a ride, but the eye-popping interior design makes even a cheeseburger a special experience.

The One-Day Stay

If you have time, you should avoid trying to cram this wonderful park into a single day; multi-day passes and the Orlando FlexTicket offer excellent value and the luxury of a more leisurely pace. Realistically, however, one day is all many visitors have. In this case, if you are staying at one of the luxury resort hotels, your personal Unlimited Express Pass and the early admission to the Wizarding World your room key may afford (at press time, early entry was for Diagon Alley only) means that you won't have to plan your visit to the park like a military campaign. The same can be said (although to a lesser extent) for the paid Universal Express Passes.

If you are a die-hard Potter partisan who has traveled to Orlando primarily to visit his world, and assuming you have a two-park ticket, I refer you to the *One-Day Stay for Potterphiles* in *Chapter Two*. Here, I assume you are visiting only Islands of Adventure.

In peak seasons, it's strongly advised that you stay at one of the on-site hotels and get to the park gates at least 15 minutes before opening time. The same applies if early entry is on offer. After entering, exit Port of Entry to the right through Seuss Landing, bearing left past Green Eggs and Ham, and cross the bridge to Lost Continent. Continue on to the Wizarding World: Hogsmeade. Once inside, head straight for *Ollivanders Wand Shop*, followed by *Forbidden Journey*, the roller coasters, and the remaining shops. After you've slaked your thirst for Butterbeer, explore the rest of the park counter-clockwise from Jurassic Park to Lost Continent, using your Express Pass (if you have one) to bypass the normal lines.

Potter fans staying off-site can try arriving at the park as early as humanly possible, heading straight to Hogsmeade as soon as possible, and following the plan above. However, since there are no Universal Express queues in Hogsmeade, a much better idea is to follow the steps below, leaving Hogsmeade for last. Note that this plan works best when the park is open past sunset (ideally 9:00 p.m. or later).

1. Arrive at the park at least 30 minutes prior to the official opening time. As soon as the gates open, proceed straight to the end of Port of Entry and turn left.

2. Cross into Marvel Super Hero Island and enjoy the *Spider-Man* ride.

3. Hard-core thrill seekers should ride *Hulk* and *Doctor Doom*, preferably in that order. If lines are short, you may want to take the opportunity to ride *Hulk* twice. Using single rider lines can speed things up considerably.

4. Now head through Toon Lagoon to ride *Dudley Do-Right's Ripsaw Falls* followed by *Popeye & Bluto's Bilge-Rat Barges*, assuming you don't mind getting wet. It's enticing to leave these soakers until later in the day, but in hot weather you'll face a long wait by early afternoon.

5. Ride the *Jurassic Park River Adventure.*

6. Consult the park map or ask an employee if timed entry tickets to Hogsmeade are being distributed. If so, retrieve one from the kiosks in Jurassic Park (across from Pizza Predattoria) or Lost Continent (near *Sindbad*).

7. Check out the *Discovery Center* in Jurassic Park.

8. At this point, it may be close to noon and time to take stock. Take the bridge near the *Jurassic Park Discovery Center* to the Lost Continent. *Poseidon's Fury* is a good choice for midday since the queue is indoors and mercifully air-conditioned if rather boring. Also, check the schedule for the *Sindbad* show, and consider lunch at Mythos.

9. Afternoon is also a good time to explore Seuss Landing. Don't skip *The Cat in the Hat*, and enjoy any other rides if the wait is short.

10. About three hours before closing time (or once your entry ticket becomes valid), walk through Lost Continent into The Wizarding World of Harry Potter: Hogsmeade. By now the early-morning Potter fans have pooped out and crowds should be much more manageable.

11. Stroll through the village and then ride *Dragon Challenge.*

12. Ride *Flight of the Hippogriff* if you have kids or the line is short.

13. Ride *Forbidden Journey*. If the posted wait is over 30 minutes, ask an attendant for the "castle tour," followed by the single rider line. Use the storage lockers near *Dragon Challenge* if the line extends outside the castle.

14. Visit *Ollivanders* if the line ahead of you is under 45 minutes.

15. Save your shopping for closing time, since the stores stay open later.

Again, those who are temperamentally averse to the giant coasters and intense thrills like *Doctor Doom* will find it much easier to take in all of Islands of Adventure in a day. But as noted earlier, coaster lovers may be pleasantly surprised at how short the lines are, especially at slower times of the year, because these giants scare off a lot of people. The exception is the line for the first row, which is often lengthy.

The One-Day Stay With Kids

Many kids, especially those who are tall enough to avoid the height restrictions listed in *Chapter One*, will be perfectly happy going on all the rides, in which case the strategy outlined above will work just fine. However, if you have children who are too short or too timid to tackle the thrill rides, you can adopt a much different strategy.

1. If your Potter-crazy child won't pay attention to anything else in the park once they've spotted Hogwarts' spires, bite the bullet and get there at the crack of dawn. If you have park-to-park tickets, use the plan in *Chapter Two* and start your Potter adventure in Diagon Alley.

If you decide to pass on the early-morning Potter patrol, you should make *Pteranodon Flyers* your first priority — assuming your kid is between 36 and 56 inches tall and you feel your child will enjoy it. This ride takes only two people at a time per vehicle and does not accept Universal Express, so the line gets very long very quickly.

Otherwise (and if your child is over 40 inches tall), do *Spider-Man* first. Most kids will have no problem with this one, although some of their adult guardians may. After that, you can relax and take your time.

2. Take a trip to Seuss Landing for those who won't find it too "babyish." However, even kids who consider themselves too "sophisticated" for most of Seuss will get a kick out of *The Cat in the Hat* ride. Your first ride in Seuss Landing should be the *High in the Sky Seuss Trolley Train Ride*, because of its slow loading time.

3. You can pretty much pick and choose after that, using the height restrictions listed earlier and your child's preferences to guide you. Despite the cartoon violence, *Sindbad* is a fun show for kids; and don't miss the *Mystic Fountain* in front of the stadium entrance.

4. When you need a break, steer your kids to an age-appropriate play area — *If I Ran the Zoo* and *Me Ship, The Olive* for younger children, *Camp Jurassic* for older ones.

5. Save the Wizarding World for late in the day when the thickest crowds have dissipated. Visit *Ollivanders* and ride *Flight of the Hippogriff* (ask for a seat near the front). Then ask for a "castle tour" to walk through the *Forbidden Journey* queue, but bypass the ride if your kid is under 48 inches tall or spooked by spiders and skeletons.

Note: Whichever plan you follow, be sure to pick up a copy of the 2-Park Guide Map as you enter the park.

■ PORT OF ENTRY ■

The towering lighthouse with the blazing fire at the top, modeled after the ancient lighthouse of Pharos in Alexandria, Egypt, marks the gates to Islands of Adventure and the beginning of your adventure. This striking structure is only the most obvious of the metaphors used in an eclectic blend of architecture and decor that evokes the spirit of wanderlust and exploration. At the base of the lighthouse, a series of sails like those on ancient Chinese junks shade the ticket booths for the park.

Through these gates lies Port of Entry, a sort of storytelling experience that combines evocative architectural motifs and haunting music to build your anticipation as you enter more fully into the spirit of discovery. Universal's scenic designers have outdone themselves on this one. To centuries-old Venice, they've added images of Istanbul, a soupçon of Samarkand, a touch of Timbuktu, and a dash of Denpassar to create a ravishingly beautiful example of fantasy architecture. Hurry through in the morning if you must, but if you are among the last to leave the park, you should really linger in Port of Entry and drink in the atmosphere.

As you marvel at the architectural details and the exquisite care with which the designers have "dressed" this sensuous streetscape, pay attention to the sounds that swirl around you. In addition to the chatter of your fellow adventurers, you will experience one of IOA's "next level" touches. Like all the other islands in the park, Port of Entry has its own specially composed soundtrack that unfolds as you walk along, drawing ever closer to the Great Inland Sea. But there are other inspired aural touches as well, like the muffled conversations from dimly lit upper-story windows hinting at intrigue and adventures unknown. It's a very special place.

Tip: See if you can find the gambling hall, dance studio, "Lost Explorers Hall," former fire department, and jail-broken prison.

Port of Entry serves some more mundane purposes as well. Before you pass through the gates you will find, on your left, a pale green building that houses Group Sales. If you are the leader of a group of 20 or more, this is the place to pick up your tickets. To the right of the ticket booths, you will find a Guest Services walk-up window marked "Will Call." Stop here if you have arranged to have tickets waiting for you. There is also a covered pavilion filled with touchscreen kiosks where you can pick up passes pre-ordered online; on busy days, there is sometimes an employee selling passes here. Nearby is the only **ATM** in Port of Entry, so if you are in need of ready cash, make sure to stop here before you enter the park. Other ATMs are found in The Lost Continent, The Wizarding World of Harry Potter: Hogsmeade, Jurassic Park, and Marvel Super Hero Island.

Once past the ticket booths and the entrance turnstiles, you will find a spacious semicircular plaza. Directly ahead of you is a large stone archway. The fantastic facades of the buildings to either side hide a variety of Guest Services functions.

■ To the left of the archway are . . .

Restrooms. Because there are some things you don't need to carry on your adventures. Nearby are phones and a phone card vending machine.

Lockers. There are four bays of electronically controlled lockers here. Rental fees are $8 for the day for smaller lockers and $10 for family size, both with in-and-out access. The machines accept bills and credit cards.

Stroller & Wheelchair Rentals. "Reliable Rentals" has a large sign outside informing you that all the jinrickshaws, gliders, submersibles, and tuk tuks are either out of service, decommissioned, hired, or, in the case of the time machine, "stuck in the 6th century." Fortunately they still have strollers ($15 for singles, $25 for doubles) and wheelchairs ($12). Slightly more elaborate strollers, called "kiddie cars," feature a kid's steering wheel and cup holders and rent for $18 and $28 respectively.

A motorized "electric convenience vehicle" (ECV) is yours for $50 for the day, $65 if you want a canopy to shield you from the sun. ECVs and wheelchairs require either a $50 cash deposit or a record of your credit card; ECVs can be reserved in advance with at least 24 hours notice and this is highly recommended. You must be over 18 to rent an ECV. Both ECVs and wheelchairs can be transferred from park to park. If you left a cash deposit, you must return the ECV where you rented it.

■ To the right of the archway are . . .

Guest Services. Questions or complaints? The cheerful folks here can help you out. Annual passes can also be obtained here.

Lost & Found. Don't give up on that lost item. There's a very good chance a fellow tourist or a park staffer will find it and turn it in. Check back the next day, too, just in case.

First Aid. This is one of two first aid stations in the park. The other is in The Lost Continent, near the Sindbad Theater.

Now that you have replenished your wallet, stowed your excess gear, and rented your strollers, you step through that crumbling stone archway incised with the thrilling words "The Adventure Begins" and start your journey toward the Great Inland Sea and the magical islands that ring it.

Port of Entry's main (and only) street is given over to a variety of shopping and eating establishments. As you stroll along, don't be surprised if someone tries to talk you into a photographic souvenir of your visit; this is, after all, an exotic marketplace bustling with hawkers. There's no charge to have your photo snapped; at the end of the day, you can stop into DeFoto's (see below), survey the results, and make your decision.

At the far end of this market street, under another crumbling archway that's being propped up by a jury-rigged contraption of giant planks and chains, the street opens out into another broad plaza on the shore of the Great Inland Sea. Amid the souvenir kiosks that dot the plaza, look for a large electronic signboard that can help you plan your itinerary. The board is updated regularly with the current waiting times for the all the attractions. If no wait time is posted, the ride may be temporarily out of commission.

Tip: Roughly opposite the Backwater Bar (see *Eating in Port of Entry,* below), is a secluded park-like snarl of rock-shielded walkways along the edge of the Inland Sea. At the end, on a point of land jutting into the water, you will find a little-visited hideaway that is wonderfully romantic at night.

Eating in Port of Entry

Whether you're on the way in, on the way out, or just breaking for lunch, there's both good food and fast food to be had in Port of Entry.

■ Croissant Moon Bakery

What:	Sandwiches, pastries, and coffee
Where:	On your right as you enter, under the second archway
Price Range:	$

Every theme park needs a place near the entrance to serve those who saved some time by skipping breakfast only to arrive at the park starving to death. Croissant Moon Bakery opens when the park does and its popularity tends to overwhelm its minuscule indoor seating area and the small number of outdoor tables. There are two separate lines here, starting from opposite ends of the deli-like counter, and both serve exactly the same fare.

For breakfast, there are muffins and such along with Lavazza coffee. Better yet, treat yourself to one of the pastries, pies, or cakes that are served here. Many of them are exceptional. Or pick up an "On the Run Continental Breakfast" (coffee, fruit cup, and your choice of muffin or Danish).

Later in the day, try the Port of Call sandwich platters. Peppered roast beef, smoked turkey, and honey-glazed ham are served with potato salad and fresh fruit, while hot, pressed paninis come with pasta salad. Soup and a salad are also available.

■ Confisco Grille

What:	Full-service restaurant with flair
Where:	On the waterfront plaza
Price Range:	$$ - $$$

The simple wooden chairs are painted green and blue and there are no tablecloths. But don't let the casual atmosphere fool you. Confisco Grille is a full-service sit-down restaurant that serves up a limited but imaginative menu that draws on far-flung culinary influences.

Part of the fun is the decor, vaguely Mediterranean with Turkish accents, that asks you to imagine you are in the Port of Entry Customs House. The place is lit by hanging lamps in a variety of styles and decorated with bizarre items, like a stegosaurus skull, confiscated from would-be smugglers. There is at least one item representing each "island" of IOA; see if you can spot them all.

But the real fun is the food. Appetizers ($5 to $10) include loaded nachos, peach-chipotle chicken wings, or "shrimp-scargot" (scampi with cheese and rosemary flatbread).

Burgers are done well here, with the bacon cheddar version a standout. Other sandwich choices ($10 to $13) include a "fork and knife" meatball sandwich, a Tex Mex wrap, and a turkey club sandwich. Entrees and pastas ($9 to $17) are a mixed bag, with the House Specialty Pad Thai noodles a bit on the bland side but the Penne Puttanesca worth trying. Entree-sized salads ($11) get high marks, too. Wines are served by the glass and the bottle. Kids can order from a separate menu ($7 to $8) featuring penne, pizza, burgers, and grilled cheese. The dessert selection includes Universal's $1.75 shot glasses served at other sit-downs, but you can order a "brookie," a cookie inside a brownie, with ice cream for $5.

Perfect for lunch, Confisco might make a good choice for a light dinner on days when the park is open late. (Check Confisco's closing time on your way in. It closes earlier than the park itself on slower days.)

The adjacent **Backwater Bar** is too upscale to be a perfect replica of the kind of tropical dive where lonely adventurers come to drink away their memories of that low-down cheap saloon singer they loved and lost in Rangoon, but it will do in a pinch. And if Confisco is crowded, they serve the full menu at the bar. While the bar itself is small, there's a large outdoor seating area, a great place to survey the passing scene while getting a buzz on.

Backwater Bar is also the sole remaining watering hole in the parks to have a happy hour (4:00 p.m. to 7:00 p.m.).

■ Starbucks

What:	You have to ask?
Where:	Across from Confisco, on the waterfront
Price Range:	$

There's nothing unusual about this Starbucks except perhaps for the fact that with only six seats it's a lot smaller than the ones back home.

■ Cinnabon

What:	Gooey pastries and coffee
Where:	Right next to Starbucks
Price Range:	$

Another outpost of the well-known national chain (the other is in City-Walk), this walk-up stand sells classic Cinnabon pastries in a variety of styles and quantities. Drinks range from plain milk to a fancy mochalatta chill. All seating is outdoors. Unlike the CityWalk Cinnabon, this one offers soft serve ice cream.

Tip: Take your food from these two stands and eat it on a bench in the park by the water. It's a bit hidden, but keep looking. It's worth it.

Shopping in Port of Entry

As you would expect of any great city along the ancient Silk Road, the main street of Port of Entry is lined with shops and bazaars filled with traders offering trinkets and treasures from near and far. Most of these emporiums have one or more entrances opening onto the street but be aware that they form one continuous space inside, so they offer a cool and convenient refuge from the broiling sun or driving rain to those entering or leaving the park.

Islands of Adventure Trading Company is the largest of the shops in Port of Entry and it occupies most of the left-hand side of the street as you walk toward the Great Inland Sea. As the name suggests, you will find here a broad selection of souvenirs representing all the islands in the park. It's the usual array of logo-ed T-shirts and trinkets, everything from key chains, to mugs, to jackets and sweaters (in season), most with IOA logos or characters. This store stocks the best selection of Harry Potter merchandise outside of the Wizarding World, so do your shopping here if the Potter shops are too crowded.

Past the Islands of Adventure Trading Company is **Ocean Trader Market**, a bazaar reminiscent of a Middle Eastern souk, its sides open to the street and shaded with tent-like canopies. Inside is a selection of lightweight, brightly colored summer clothing and accessories for the ladies and a few shirts for the guys. Also on offer here are a smattering of offbeat handicrafts, including wooden decorative items from Indonesia.

Across the street is a string of shops that open one onto the other. The nearest to the park entrance is **DeFoto's Expedition Photography**, the place to stop for a variety of photo supplies and disposable cameras. You can replace the batteries or charger you forgot at home and pick up some nice photo frames or film posters while you're at it. De Foto's also offers sunscreen and suntan lotion, just in case you forgot those too. This is where you can view and purchase any Photo Connect photos of you and your family taken by those strolling photographers in the park, or purchase a Star Card package (see *Chapter One* for details).

Island Market and Export is a sweets shop selling overpriced candy and other goodies, while at the **Port of Entry Christmas Shoppe**, which sells tasteful hand-painted ornaments for the tree and the yuletide hearth, it's Christmas in July, or any other month for that matter. This is also Grinch central, with a section dedicated to Dr. Seuss's green Christmas-kidnapper.

Near the park exit sits **Port Provisions.** This tiny open-air shop straddles the exit and provides a last chance to pick up something small. It also offers a limited selection, but the sale merchandise (often 30% to 50% off original prices) is worth checking out by those in search of a bargain.

■ SEUSS LANDING ■

Probably best described as a 12-acre, walk-through sculpture, Seuss Landing adds a third dimension and giddy Technicolor to the wonderfully wacky world of Theodor Geisel, a.k.a. Dr. Seuss, whose dozens of illustrated books of inspired poetry have enchanted millions of children.

Universal designers have gone to great lengths to evoke the out-of-kilter world of the Seuss books, avoiding straight lines and square corners wherever possible. Bushes are trimmed into droll topiary creatures. Buildings curve and swoop and sometimes seem to be on the verge of toppling over. Much of the architectural detail looks as though it was sculpted out of some especially thick cake icing (actually cement-covered Styrofoam) and is now gently melting in the Florida sun. Even the foliage is goofy. Many of the wacky, twisted palm trees that you will see on the *Seuss Trolley Train Ride* were created by the fierce winds of Hurricane Andrew and loving transplanted here by Universal's grounds staff. The rest had to be painstakingly trained to create that Seussian look.

In its own cheerful, candy-colored way, the fantasy architecture here is just as successful and just as impressive as that in Port of Entry. Even if you have no interest in sampling the kiddie rides on offer here, you will have a great deal of fun just passing through.

If I Ran The Zoo

Rating:	★ ★ ★ ½
Type:	Interactive play area
Time:	Unlimited
Short Take:	Fabulous fun for toddlers

This interactive play area is based on the charming tale of young Gerald McGrew who had some very definite ideas of what it takes to create a really interesting zoo.

There are three distinct areas, each of which allows little ones a slightly different interactive experience. The first is filled with peculiar animals that appear over the hedges when you turn a crank or laugh when you tickle their feet. Little adventurers can also slide down the tunnels of Zamba-matant and crawl through the cave in Kartoom in search of the Natch before reaching a small island surrounded by a wading pool. There they'll be able to control bouncing globs of water and trap their playmates in cages made out of falling water. In the final area, kids can stand over a grate where the Snaggle Foot Mulligatawny will sneeze up their shorts. Then they can squirt a creature taking a bubble bath, only to get sprinkled themselves when the critter spins dry.

All told, there are 19 different interactive elements to keep your child giggling all the way through this attraction. Kids will dart about eager to try them all, which may be one reason the "Zoo Keeper Code of Conduct" at the entrance warns, "Keep track of adults, they get lost all the time."

The Cat In The Hat

Rating: ★ ★ ★ ★
Type: "Dark ride"
Time: 3.5 minutes
Short Take: Classic storybook dark ride with a little zip

Dr. Seuss's most popular book tells the tale of what happens when two kids, home alone, allow the cat of the title to come in for a visit. Step through the doors beneath that giant red and white striped top hat and you will get your chance to relive the adventure.

This is a "dark" ride but perhaps one of the brightest and most colorful you'll ever encounter. You and your kids climb into cars that are designed like miniature six-passenger sofas and set off through a series of 18 show scenes that re-create the story line of the book. Just don't expect the static tableaux of the older generation dark rides. Brace yourself for a few quick swoops, sudden turns, and maybe a 360-degree spin or three.

Along the way, the ride does a remarkably good job of telling the story of the book. The fantastic animated sculptures of the cat and his playmates, Thing 1 and Thing 2, spin and twirl while furniture teeters and topples. The wise fish, who is the tale's voice of reason, cries out warnings and ignored advice until, miraculously, all is set to rights before Mom gets home. Kids familiar with the book will be delighted and those who aren't will doubtless want to learn more.

This is a must-do for little ones, although a few very timid tykes still may find the swoops and spins of the ride vehicles (which have been toned down somewhat in recent years, but still pack some punch) a bit startling.

One Fish, Two Fish, Red Fish, Blue Fish

Rating:	★ ★ ★
Type:	Flying, steerable fish
Time:	2 minutes
Short Take:	Good, wet fun

Here's an interesting twist on an old carnival ride. You know, the one where you sit in a little airplane (or flying Dumbo) and spin round in a circle while your plane goes up and down. On this ride, based on the Seuss book of the same name, you pilot a little fishy. While you can't escape the circular route of the ride, you can steer your fish up or down.

Supposedly, if you follow the directions encoded in the little song that plays during the ride ("red fish, red fish up, up, up; blue fish, blue fish down, down, down"), you can avoid being doused by the water coming from a series of "squirt posts" that ring the perimeter. There are three verses to the song and, it seems it actually is possible to stay dry for the first two by following directions. The third verse, however, tells you that all bets are off and that your guess is as good as the next fellow's. It is the rare rider who gets through the ride without getting spritzed. Not that most people care. In fact, it looks like some kids do just the opposite of what the song counsels in the hope of getting Mom and Dad soaked.

Note: On cold days, and sometimes in the cooler morning hours, the ride does not spray water on the riders, which will probably come as a relief to parents and a disappointment to little ones.

This ride is very nicely designed, with perfectly adorable little fish cars and an array of Seussian characters serving as the squirt posts. Presiding over the center of the circle is an 18-foot-tall sculpture of the Star Belly Fish from the book.

Caro-Seuss-El

Rating:	★ ★ ★ ½
Type:	Old-fashioned carousel with Seuss figures
Time:	About 1.5 minutes
Short Take:	For carousel lovers and little kids

This ride marks yet another design triumph. The old-fashioned carousel has been put through the Seuss looking glass and has emerged as a towering, multicolored confection. In place of old-fashioned horses are marvelously imaginative Seuss critters with serene smiles plastered across their goofy faces. Even if you have no interest in actually riding the thing, it's worth the time it takes to stop and admire this imaginative whirligig in full motion.

The *Caro-Seuss-El* is billed as the world's first interactive carousel. Here kids can ride on the back of a beautifully sculpted Seussian animal like Cowfish from *McElligott's Pool* or the Twin Camels from *One Fish, Two Fish*. There are seven different characters and a total of 54 mounts on the 47-foot diameter ride. The interactive part comes when you pull back on the reins and watch your steed's head shake, his eyes blink, his tail wag. A special loading mechanism for wheelchairs allows the disabled to experience the ride from their own rocking chariots.

High in the Sky Seuss Trolley Train Ride

Rating:	★ ★ ★
Type:	Aerial train ride
Time:	3 minutes
Height Req.:	40 in. (101.6 cm.)
Short Take:	A pleasant new perspective on Seuss Landing

Based loosely on Dr. Seuss's anti-discrimination parable about Sylvester McMonkey McBean and the Sneetches, this brief excursion over Seuss Landing is designed for the kiddies but offers rewards for their adult companions.

Cute and colorful five-car, 20-passenger trolleys tootle along two separate tracks, each traveling a slightly different aerial route. In addition, each train has two different audio tracks, which adds up to four different experiences. This is definitely one your child will want to ride multiple times. Mom and Dad won't mind the repetition because there's plenty to see. Unfortunately, the slow-moving line may make that difficult unless you have Universal Express Passes, so head here early in the day.

The train to your right as you enter the platform has the more interesting route, as it passes though the Circus McGurkus restaurant before heading out over Seuss Landing. Most of the trip is in the open air on loopy swirling tracks that take you on a bird's eye tour of this magical land. If you weren't impressed by the design of Seuss Landing after strolling through, this ride will change your mind.

Note: This is a gentle ride, but it is "high in the sky," so those with a fear of heights might want to give it a pass.

And all the rest...

There are nooks and crannies of Seuss Landing that are easy to miss. These are not major attractions, to be sure, but if you take a fancy to this whimsical land, or if you have a young Dr. Seuss fan in tow, they might be worth seeking out.

Just through the woozy archway that marks the entrance to Seuss Landing from Port of Entry you will find, on your right, **McElligott's Pool**, a pretty little pond with a waterfall, some charming statuary, and some interloping ducks who have made it home. Just past this area, next to the Cats, Hats & Things shop, in a private courtyard with its own kid-sized entrance arch, lies **Horton's Egg**. Climb atop the spotted egg (a sign invites volunteers to do so) for a great **photo op**.

The **Street of the Lifted Lorax** is a small walk-through area next to the *Caro-Seuss-El*. It retells the story from Dr. Seuss's book, *The Lorax*, the moral of which is "Protect the environment!"

Oh! The Stories You'll Hear combines a little song and dance, a brief bit of storytelling, and a meet and greet with a few Seuss characters. You'll find it several times daily (see the 2-Park Guide Map for details) either outside in the courtyard between *Cat in the Hat* and *One Fish, Two Fish*, or inside Circus McGurkus Cafe in inclement weather. From time to time, a separate **Seuss Character Meet and Greet** is also held; times and locations will be listed in the 2-Park Guide Map.

A **How the Grinch Stole Christmas** musical show, featuring a soundtrack recorded by Mannheim Steamroller, is staged in the soundstage behind *One Fish, Two Fish* during the "Grinchmas" holiday season. The set and lighting are terrific, and the actors are all talented, but the tone is closer to the vulgar Jim Carrey film than the sweet storybook and sixties cartoon.

Note: If you are hurrying through Seuss Landing, you can save a few seconds by turning left at Green Eggs and Ham and following the path that circles behind the shops. This takes you through a broad open area next to the Inland Sea, which was apparently designed as a venue for corporate events, and beneath the tracks of the *Trolley Train Ride* and lets you out a few paces from the bridge that leads to The Lost Continent, thereby avoiding the crowds that throng Seuss Landing's colorful main drag. Stop and see the beach-going **Sneeches** and stubborn **Zax** along the way.

Eating in Seuss Landing

The eateries in Seuss Landing give new meaning to the term "fun food." The exteriors and interiors of the restaurants and outdoor stands here are every bit as ingeniously designed as the rides, with the same loopy, drooping, and dizzy details. And the small building that houses the Green Eggs and Ham Cafe is one of the best **photo ops** in the park. Dining here is strictly casual, with brightly colored plastic utensils.

■ Circus McGurkus Cafe Stoo-pendous

What: Large indoor cafeteria
Where: Across from the *Caro-Seuss-El*
Price Range: $

Under that enormous droopy big top is this humongous fast food emporium themed to a fare-thee-well with circus imagery a la Dr. Seuss. This is one of the most visually delightful restaurants in all of Islands of Adventure — clever, colorful, comfortable, and imaginative as all get-out.

To one side are two complete cafeteria lines; to the other a series of booths disguised as a circus train transporting a weird variety of Seuss creatures, like the Spotted Atrocious, "a beast most ferocious." In between is a spacious seating area under the twin big tops from which swing a nutty trapeze artist and a spinning mobile of Seuss characters. Periodically, a train from the *High in the Sky Seuss Trolley Train Ride* chugs by overhead bearing a load of happy passengers.

The food is designed with kids in mind, which means personal-size pizzas (both pepperoni and cheese), pasta with meatballs, and cheeseburgers. Grown-ups might prefer the Chicken Caesar Salad or the Fried Chicken Platter. A kids' menu features pasta and chicken meals, and desserts feature Dippin' Dots ice cream.

At one end of the room you'll see a zany pipe organ that is seldom played. There is limited seating just outside the doors if you'd prefer to dine al fresco.

■ Green Eggs and Ham Cafe

What: Walk-up fast food stand
Where: Near *If I Ran the Zoo*
Price Range: $

This unmistakable eatery — it's a giant green piece of pork — serves a standard selection of cheeseburgers and chicken fingers, but the namesake sandwich is the real reason to stop by. The Green Eggs and Ham Sandwich platter features a folded omelette, colored green with chopped herbs, and a slice of non-green ham and cheese on a sesame bun. As Sam I Am insisted, it tastes much better than it looks.

Note: Unfortunately, this stand only operates during peak periods.

■ Hop on Pop

What:	Ice-cream stand
Where:	Across from All the Books You Can Read
Price Range:	$

The enormous ice cream cone that decorates this walk-up stand says it all. Most delicious is the Brownie Sundae in a waffle bowl. The promisingly named Sundae On A Stick turns out to be a standard, chocolate-covered ice cream bar studded with sprinkles or nuts. Plain old waffle cones are also available with various toppings. Best of all is the root beer float.

There is no seating but you can take your goodies around the corner to the Green Eggs and Ham outdoor seating area or even head across the street and into Circus McGurkus to eat in air-conditioned comfort.

■ Moose Juice Goose Juice

What:	Frosted smoothies at an outdoor stand
Where:	On your left as you exit to Lost Continent
Price Range:	$

On closer examination, Moose Juice turns out to be frozen orange juice and Goose Juice is sour green apple. Cookies, churros, pretzels, and soft beverages are also available.

Shopping in Seuss Landing

It is impossible to miss the cheerful **Cats, Hats & Things** if you take the *Cat in the Hat* ride, but even if you don't, you might want to pop in for a quick look. Here you'll find plenty of souvenirs and clothing commemorating the famous cat, as well as Things 1 and 2. You'll also find the actual book that inspired the ride. A perennial favorite is the Cat's trademark striped stovepipe hat.

Tip: If you visit the shop, don't forget to take a peek into the quiet back courtyard that houses Horton's Egg (see above).

The **Mulberry Street Store** is the megastore of Seuss Landing, with its very own kid-sized entrance, and the tag line "Gizmos, Gadgets, Goodies Galore" pretty much sums it up. Here you'll find a large selection of Seuss wear for everyone in the family from the littlest tykes all the way to the grown-ups, who will find cotton p.j.s in their sizes. There are toys, T-shirts, and nightwear decorated with Seuss characters, and lots of infants' clothing, as well as games and books. Well-heeled Seussaphiles can salivate over the collectible artwork and statues, which start at several hundred dollars.

Photo Op: Outside, you can pose as part of a police escort that's whizzing by a reviewing stand filled with Seuss Landing dignitaries. One of them looks suspiciously like Dr. Geisel himself!

Even though it's called **Dr. Seuss's All the Books You Can Read**, much of the space here is given over to clothing, mugs, and plastic glasses. Fortunately, there are books and this happy, kid-scaled place is a great way to introduce your little ones to the magic of Seuss and reading in general. Books range from baby board books and small single volumes to fairly expensive collections. The shop offers some kid-sized places to sit down and read.

Finally, **Snookers & Snookers Sweet Candy Cookers** is yet another overpriced candy emporium redeemed by the presence of some wonderfully whimsical candy apples and gourmet cupcakes.

THE LOST CONTINENT

From the color and fantasy of Seuss Landing, the intrepid adventurer plunges into the mystery of The Lost Continent. Cross a wooden bridge to the sound of mystical wind chimes, and enter a land of ancient myth and legendary tales.

Photo Op: The first thing you see, when you enter from Seuss Landing, is a statue of an armor-clad griffin. This grim guardian is a favorite spot for tourists to pose for that "I was at Islands of Adventure" shot.

As you approach the Lost City, you glimpse over a craggy boulder an enormous hand holding an equally enormous trident. Only when you have walked a little farther do you realize that the boulder is an enormous head of the god Poseidon and what you are seeing are the remnants of a very large and very ancient statue that fell down eons ago. Just opposite is a brooding extinct volcano, with cascading waterfalls and the faces of titans carved in its flanks. It hides Mythos, perhaps the most eye-popping restaurant in any Orlando theme park.

The grand scale and attention to detail in the architecture of The Lost Continent is exceeded only by the adjoining Wizarding World. It's rare that theme park visitors pause just to take pictures of buildings but it happens here all the time. Add to the visual splendor what many people consider to be one of the finest restaurants in any theme park in the world and The Lost Continent becomes a small but special island indeed.

Poseidon's Fury

Rating:	★ ★ ½
Type:	Special effects extravaganza
Time:	About 20 minutes
Short Take:	Chaotic fun, but not everyone's cup of tea

Behind the ruins of Poseidon's statue lies his enormous temple, now cracked and crumbled by earthquakes, where his devotees once worshipped. Before entering, take a moment to drink in the scene. This is yet another of the park's triumphs of fantasy architecture. The scale alone is awe-inspiring. Check out the huge feet of Poseidon's now-tumbled statue and the towering trident that stands nearby. Marvel at the once-gorgeous mosaic floors now running with water diverted from its ancient course by long-ago earthquakes. Stare up at the towering facade, its massive columns seemingly ready to topple at any moment. The art direction that has created not just the iconography of an ancient and imaginary religious cult but its language as well is truly impressive.

With understandable trepidation, we step inside to a major disappointment — a cool, dimly lit, snaking passageway. Other than the flickering lights, some hard-to-read signage from "Global Discovery Group," and the ominous music, there's nothing here to hint at what lies ahead, certainly no advancing "plot line" to keep visitors informed and entertained as the line inches forward. It's one of Universal's most boring queues and when the line is long you'll be in it for a seeming eternity.

Tip: Visit *Poseidon* when the wait is five minutes. Not even Universal Express will let you escape a lengthy wait at busy times.

When we reach the front of the queue line, we are greeted by Taylor, a very young and very nervous volunteer assistant to ace archaeologist, Professor Baxter. The prof seems to have disappeared along with everyone else on the dig while Taylor was on a lunch break. Too bad, because the professor had announced the discovery of a "secret message" but disappeared before he could tell anyone what it was. Taylor, played by a young guy or gal, gamely carries on with our tour of recent temple excavations.

The first chamber contains an altar and ancient wall paintings documenting an epic struggle. Legend has it that a high priest of the temple, the dumbly named Lord Darkenon, seized power from Poseidon, sparking a battle in which all perished, and that the spirits of those combatants still haunt the ruined temple. There is another terrified transmission from Professor Baxter, and then all the lights go out.

Taylor grabs an ultraviolet lamp for illumination and in so doing reveals a hidden message written on the frieze that circles the chamber. Fortunately, the ancient Greeks had the foresight to write the message in English so Taylor can read it aloud. This turns out to be a big mistake because reading the message aloud awakens the spirit of Darkenon, who is no one's idea of a gracious host.

Without spoiling it for you, suffice to say that your journey will take you into an even spookier chamber and finally into the middle of a pitched battle between Poseidon, who uses water as his weapon, and Lord Darkenon, who responds with fire. The highlight is a "water vortex" that lets you walk underneath a seemingly impossible wall of rushing water.

It should be noted that this attraction has its detractors, myself included. The story has been dumbed down and shortened over the years and Taylor now rushes through it with a campiness that undercuts any spooky tension that might have once existed. Some people find the story line confusing and, in the heat of the battle, some of the dialogue does get hard to hear. Others just don't seem that impressed with the effects, which never seem to be firing on all cylinders. For many people, their enjoyment of the show will depend on how long they have waited to see it.

The best seats in the house. The entire show is experienced standing up. In the first two chambers, it really doesn't matter where you stand For the final battle scene, however, you will have a good deal more fun if you are in the very first row. It seems like most people instinctively climb the steps, not realizing that you can actually stand in front of the first guardrail, on ground level so to speak. That means that you can simply walk to the front as you enter and enjoy the best view.

The Eighth Voyage of Sindbad

Rating:	★ ★ ★
Type:	Amphitheater show
Time:	About 20 minutes
Short Take:	Slapstick stunts and dumb dialogue

In a 1,750-seat theater we get to witness the eighth voyage of the legendary Sindbad (seven just weren't enough). This is a live-action stunt show that attempts to rival the Indiana Jones show over at that other movie studio park (no, not Universal) but is betrayed by a clunky script.

Here Sindbad sets off on yet another search for riches untold, encountering along the way the inevitable life-threatening perils. Sindbad and his trusty but talkative sidekick Kabob (as in "Shush, Kabob!") have traveled to a mysterious cavern filled with treasure and the bones of earlier adventurers. Here the evil sorceress Miseria holds the beautiful Princess Amora in thrall and only the Sultan's Heart, an enormous ruby with magical powers, can free her. It's Sindbad to the rescue, but first he must battle Miseria for the Sultan's Heart and the ultimate power that goes with it.

Sindbad fights valiantly on the Princess's behalf. But this is no wimpy maiden in distress. Amora is a princess for the postmodern age, with hair of gold and buns of steel, who can hold her own against evil monsters, thank you very much. Together, the three heroes battle the forces of evil in its many grisly guises and (spoiler alert) eventually triumph.

It's an action-packed spectacular that features six "water explosions" and supposedly 50 — count 'em, 50 — of Universal's trademark pyrotechnic effects, including a 10-foot-tall circle of flames and a 22-foot-high fall by a stunt person engulfed in flames. However, there seem to be fewer and fewer effects with each visit.

Sindbad's set alone, with its dripping stalactites and crumbling pirate vessels, is stupendous. The show takes advantage of every inch of it, including the wrecked prow of an ancient ship that seems to have run aground in the very middle of the audience, and the stunts are all energetically executed by the athletic cast. Unfortunately, the dialogue is packed with clumsy one-liners and pop-culture anachronisms that drag the production down. The result is an occasionally dazzling but depressingly dumb display best enjoyed by children and non-English speakers.

The best seats in the house. If you enjoy getting wet, there are two "splash zones" in this show, one toward the front to the right of the audience and the other in the middle, to the left of the wrecked prow that juts into the seating area. Otherwise, every seat gives a good view of the action, which has very thoughtfully been spread all over the enormous set. Sitting a few rows back, just to the right of the wrecked prow, offers a particularly good perspective on the action, including some bone-crunching fights that happen almost on top of you.

Another good choice is the last row in front of either of the two arched entrances on the left and right. These seats give you a great panoramic view of the action, have a back rest, and offer a quick getaway at show's end. Another bonus, if you're sensitive to sound: the open archways behind you let the sound out instead of bouncing it back at you.

And all the rest ...

A mysteriously smoking and bubbling **Mystic Fountain** sits in front of the central entrance to the Sindbad show's amphitheater. Once just an interesting added touch to the fun of The Lost Continent, the fountain has been elevated to the rank of a full-fledged attraction on the park map. It would appear to be dedicated to some ancient and mysterious oracle, to judge by the open-mouthed face sculpted into it. Indeed, this fountain even talks to you. Although it seems friendly enough, beware. Its hidden agenda seems to be to get you very, very wet.

Tip: If the fountain is snoring when you stop by, it's "on break." Try coming back in 15 or 20 minutes.

Eating in The Lost Continent

The Lost Continent boasts the best dining value inside Universal Orlando's two theme parks — Mythos, which is among the better restaurants to be found in the theme parks of the world. For those who take a strictly utilitarian approach to food, there are walk-up stands offering a quick and filling bite.

■ Mythos Restaurant

What: Family-friendly fine dining
Where: Opposite *Poseidon's Fury*
Price Range: $$ - $$$

In keeping with the unspeakably ancient theme of the island, this restaurant is housed (if that's the right word) in an extinct volcano with water cascading down its weathered slopes. Step inside and you've entered a sea cavern whose sinuous walls have been carved out and smoothed by centuries of surging waves. Eerie yet soothing music tinkles through the air. In the main dining room, the cavern's roof vaults skyward and a large windowed opening gives out onto the lagoon and a spacious outdoor seating area. Subterranean streams run between the handsome seating areas, with seats upholstered in regal purple. The walls take on the shapes of long-vanished gods and their spirit minions. You can check the drinks menu for a guide to the symbolism; extra credit if you spot the errors. The effect is only a step or two this side of awesome.

Decor like this is a hard act to follow, and you find yourself wondering if the food can rise to the level of your heightened expectations. Well, the answer is "almost." The menu offers a wide variety of comfort food with a contemporary twist at surprisingly reasonable prices — and still manages to taste, well, just plain yummy. Unfortunately, in recent years more adventurous items have been replaced with middle-of-the-road alternatives, and repeat visitors will notice a significant falling off from the venue's original gourmet aspirations. Still, if you order wisely, Mythos serves up some of the best food to be had inside any Orlando theme park, without breaking your bank. The menu changes regularly (sometimes spotlighting a seasonal ingredient like wild mushrooms) so this description won't be exhaustive but will hopefully whet your appetite.

Soups and Appetizers ($5 to $10) always include the Chef's Signature Pizza of the Day. These are thin-crusted masterpieces that blend traditional cooking methods (there is a spectacular wood-fired pizza oven in clear view of the dining area) and eclectic ingredients that change with the seasons.

The creamy wild mushroom cassoulet is large and rich enough to share — with leftovers. One appetizer that has proven a perennial is the Tempura Shrimp Sushi, a miniature work of art served with a wasabi and soy drizzle. The soups (tomato or cream of mushroom) are nothing short of ambrosial.

Salads ($8 to $16) range from deceptively simple bowls of mixed baby greens to elaborate entree-sized extravaganzas featuring chicken, beef, shrimp, or salmon. Entrees ($11 to $20) range from a not so humble cheeseburger with smoked applewood bacon to some very well-executed specialty sandwiches and wraps. You can almost guarantee that the list of entrees will include pan-seared mahi-mahi and beef medallions with truffle butter, both good. The menu always includes a Risotto of the Day and a Pasta of the Day, which changes regularly and allows the chef to show off a bit. These are frequently the best things on offer.

You can add a small soup or salad to an entrée for $3. There is a kids' menu ($6 to $11) featuring simple dishes for the less sophisticated gourmet.

After one of these meals, desserts are generally a let down. Fortunately, there is the Warm Chocolate Banana Gooey Cake ($5.25), which is spectacular and probably the only dessert worth ordering. The others are "mini-desserts" ($1.75 each) served in skinny shot glasses; they are the same ones served at Confisco and are merely so-so.

The once impressive wine list is now a short list of what my vintner likes to call "entry-level wines" ($5 to $8 by the glass), but if you're feeling flush, you can still order a bottle of champagne ($144). For something more potent, try the specialty drink of the month ($6). They also serve draft ($6.25 to $7.50) and bottled beer ($5 to $6.50).

The restaurant seats 180 with an additional 50 seats outdoors, many of them sheltered by the overhanging volcano. An outdoor seat provides beautiful views on balmy nights, but the roar of the roller coaster across the water may obliterate quiet conversation.

Reservations are taken at (407) 224-4012 or via OpenTable.com, but try the restaurant's direct line at (407) 224-4534 to feel like a regular. Mythos is only open from 11:00 a.m. to 3:00 p.m., although hours are extended during busy periods (Spring Break, mid-July through August, and the Christmas season).

Tip: Check out the trippy checkerboard tile in the restrooms!

And after you've finished dining, it's just a short stroll to either the *Incredible Hulk* or *Dragon Challenge* roller coasters. This could be the best meal you'll ever lose!

◼ Fire Eaters Grill

What:	Walk-up fast food stand
Where:	Near *Poseidon's Fury*
Price Range:	$

This stand offers "walking sandwiches," which is good because the nearby outdoor seating is limited and not very well shaded. The fare is vaguely Middle Eastern and on the spicy side, featuring grilled lamb gyros and both chicken fingers and spicy chicken stingers. Chili cheese fries and chili cheese dogs round out the menu, but inexplicably cost more here than anywhere else in the parks. There are cookies and "brookies" (cookie filled brownies) for dessert, and soda and bottled beer to wash it all down.

◼ Doc Sugrue's Desert Kebab House

What:	Walk-up fast food stand
Where:	Near the *Mystic Fountain*
Price Range:	$

This circular stand at the entrance to Sindbad's stadium claims to serve "exotic cuisine from around the world," but the skewered meats on the menu are mostly Mediterranean. The grilled beef and chicken are surprisingly tender and well-seasoned (if not supersized) and are accompanied by pita bread and marinated veggies. For herbivores, hummus, yogurt, Greek salad, and a vegetable kebab fill out the flavorful bill of fare. Draft beer and a Coke Freestyle machine make up the drink choices. There are ordering windows on two sides of the building, so look for the shorter line.

Shopping in The Lost Continent

Some of the best shopping at Islands of Adventure is to be found in The Lost Continent, especially if your taste runs to one-of-a-kind craft items.

The **Treasures of Poseidon**, near the exit of *Poseidon's Fury*, sells a grab bag of T-shirts, flip-flops, costume jewelry, hats, and (oddly enough) a variety of live plants. It shares space with **The Pearl Factory**, which sells Japanese cultured pearls in a variety of settings at prices that start at about $29 and go up to $5,000 for a black Tahitian pearl necklace. For $16 you can pick an oyster and, if you like the pearl you find inside, have it set in a variety of gold settings for a modest fee

In the Sindbad area, the **Coin Mint** features hand-minted medallions of bronze, silver, or "gold layered silver," made to order while you watch by an artisan who's garbed in Renaissance clothing and speaks in a simulation of a British regional accent. The master minter uses a heavily weighted guillotine-like device to slam the designs onto discs. The tented shop also sells chains in sterling silver and crystal pendants.

Nearby, **Historic Families** offers classy coats of arms and accessories for the serious family historian. Especially nice are the elaborate hand-embroidered versions with two coats of arms designed to commemorate a marriage. And in case the marriage doesn't work out, the shop sells daggers and swords, too. Things can get pricey here.

Too timid for tattoos? The new-agey designs at **Mystic Henna Body Art** are painted on with henna and last anywhere from a few days to a few weeks before fading into memory. You'll sometimes also find a fortune-teller here (similar to the one in USF's New York) offering psychic card readings or practicing palmistry. Apparently they foresaw that many women would need some more clothing, so they offer it.

The Middle Eastern bazaar section of The Lost Continent has other specialty shops that change from time to time, including one offering "Free Magic Shows" similar to the ones on Hollywood Boulevard in Universal Studios.

THE WIZARDING WORLD OF HARRY POTTER:

■ # HOGSMEADE ■

The best way to arrive at Hogsmeade is via the *Hogwarts Express*, fresh from the stimulating environs of Diagon Alley. That way your ongoing experience in Harry's wonderful world will not be interrupted by having to traipse through less magical realms. But whether you take the train or approach the stone archway into Hogsmeade Village from Lost Continent (beneath a sign reading "Please Respect the Spell Limits"), you will be completely enveloped in the fictional world of Harry Potter's school days. It's a remarkable continuation of the 360-degree illusion created in Diagon Alley and, even though IOA's installment of the Wizarding World antedates Diagon Alley by some four years, they are both part of a seamless whole

With your arrival in Hogsmeade, you've seemingly been transported to the charming Scottish hamlet where Harry and his friends relax on winter holidays, down to the worn cobblestone streets and sparkling snow-capped eaves. Everywhere you look, from the looming hulk of Hogwarts Castle to the exquisitely detailed village storefronts, you'll find the same overabundance of exacting detail that made your visit to Diagon Alley so enthralling.

Universal may have initially oversold this first installment of the Wizarding World by referring to it as a "park within a park." At about 20 acres, the area is similar in size to the other "islands" and no separate admission is required. Return visitors to IOA will remember the area's re-purposed roller coasters, which may explain why they always have less of a wait than the other Potter attractions. Still, the area is enormously popular, although for the most part, the days when dedicated Potter devotees had to wait hours in the hot sun just to enter their hero's schoolday haunts are a thing of the past.

Hogsmeade's greatest asset, however, is also its Achilles' heel: the authentically intimate scale of the streets and stores. Unlike many other epic fantasies, the Potter books and films depict a more human-scaled world of congested markets and narrow alleyways. Confines here are just as cramped as Rowling imagined, which is great for preserving the illusion but poor for pedestrian management, a problem somewhat solved in Diagon Alley.

Tip: While the massive crowds of Hogsmeade's early days have subsided, it can still get crowded at busy times, in which case Universal may deploy kiosks in Lost Continent and Jurassic Park that issue timed entry tickets to Hogsmeade. The best advice is to avoid the busiest times of the year, stay at an on-site hotel to take advantage of early entry, and/or get an early start. At press time, early entry was offered only to Diagon Alley, which is the best place to begin your adventure with Harry and friends in any case.

If you aren't already a Potter-head, you'll want to pick up at least the first few novels or films to better appreciate the area, which is focused on the first four "years" in the seven-book series. Even if you're merely a Muggle with no prior Potter interest, the beauty and wit you'll find here may inspire you to start reading once you return home.

Harry Potter and the Forbidden Journey

Rating: ★ ★ ★ ★ ★
Type: Next-generation dark thrill ride
Time: About 30 minutes for the tour, 4 minutes for the ride
Height Req.: 48 in. (121.9 cm)
Short Take: A thrilling flight into Potter's magical world

As you emerge from Hogsmeade and round the corner, you'll catch sight of an awe-inspiring vision: the majestic spires of Hogwarts Castle, home to the ancient school where Harry and his schoolmates learn the ways of wizardry. Perched high atop a craggy cliff face, the edifice is actually an empty shell perched atop a massive camouflaged show building, but thanks to clever use of forced perspective it appears even larger and more imposing, if less colorful, than Cinderella's digs down the road. Pass between the school's stone gates (which mystically glow with the attraction's name at night) and enter the castle dungeon to begin your adventure.

Tip: Duck into the first left-hand cliff crevice for a glimpse behind the scenes.

Forbidden Journey is actually comprised of two attractions in one. The first is the queue, cleverly disguised as an elaborate walking tour of Hogwarts, which has opened its doors to non-magical Muggles like yourself for the first time in its ten-century history. (For serious continuity nerds, your visit occurs on a day "frozen in time" outside of the Potter canon, sometime between the events of *Goblet of Fire* and *Half-Blood Prince*.) Waiting in line is rarely considered entertainment, but here is the exception; with more details and effects than most entire attractions, this surpasses Disneyland's *Indiana Jones Adventure* as America's most impressive holding pen. If you were to walk slowly through the queue with no one ahead of you, examining the artifacts and watching all the effects, it would take almost 30 minutes. The production values are high enough that even those uninterested in the ride should still experience the castle tour; you'll be able to exit before the ride itself.

Tip: Universal Express is not valid on this attraction, but there is an unpublicized alternative queue line intended for non-riders that includes almost all of the normal line's magical effects, including a private portrait gallery (see below), with little or no wait. Unfortunately, it is often closed on extremely crowded days, just when it is most needed. Ask the first attendant you encounter outside the castle gates if the "castle tour" is open. Take it if available; at the end, ask how to transfer to the single rider line that starts in the final chambers. You'll experience most of the castle queue plus the ride for only about one-third to one-fourth of the standard wait time!

The tour begins in the dungeon, where you'll see screen-accurate reproductions of artifacts like the "One-Eyed Witch" and "Mirror of Erised," and pass by the "Potions Classroom." Emerge from the dark dungeon into the sunny greenhouse, where Professor Sprout's magical herbs, like hanging pitcher plants and mandrakes (thankfully silent), are raised.

Note: If the extended queue outside the greenhouse is in use, anticipate at least an hour wait before entering the air-conditioned interior.

Once inside the castle corridors, you will spend 20 to 30 minutes exploring some of Hogwarts' most iconic locations. Begin by passing a series of ancient-looking statues, including one of the school's architect, and the regal stone griffin that guards the Headmaster's office. Next you'll encounter a portrait gallery, featuring one of Universal's most startling effects: paintings that move and speak, appearing even up close to be oil on canvas instead of video projections. The four founders of Hogwarts (Godric Gryffindor, Rowena Ravenclaw, Helga Hufflepuff, and the never-before-seen Salazar Slytherin) greet you and bicker about the presence of Muggles inside their school. (This is where the "castle tour" begins.)

Next, you'll enter the spectacular set of Headmaster Dumbledore's office, exactingly reproduced from the films, right down to the Pensieve in the corner. Dumbledore (played by actor Michael Gambon in a startlingly real upgrade of *Disaster!*'s "Musion" hologram effect) welcomes you, warning that "there comes a time when all of us must choose between what is right, and what is easy." Oh, and look out for Hagrid's pet dragon, which has apparently gotten loose again.

Exiting the office, you encounter the Defense Against the Dark Arts classroom, festooned with skeletal beasts and other occult artifacts, where you are promised a multi-hour lecture on Hogwarts history. Luckily, Harry Potter himself (played by Daniel Radcliffe), along with his friends Ron (Rupert Grint) and Hermione (Emma Watson), materialize on a balcony above you from beneath their Invisibility Cloak (another amazing Musion). They invite you to play hooky with them, skipping the boring lecture in favor of a game of Quidditch (the series' flying-broom-based sport). Soon you are swept past the "Fat Lady" portrait (a delightful Dawn French) that guards the Gryffindor Common Room into the lounge's tapestry-hung confines, where a quartet of new paintings prepare you to board the "enchanted benches" that will take you on your adventure.

Tip: Check the cabinet on the left just past the Fat Lady for some hard to see props and costume accessories actually used in the Potter films.

The final step in your preparation comes courtesy of an animatronic Sorting Hat that delivers the inevitable safety spiel in rhyming verse. Finally, you enter the floating candlestick-filled Room of Requirement, which doubles as the boarding area. Four guests at a time step onto a two-stage moving sidewalk and are fastened side-by-side into one of 40-odd golden, high-backed benches that flow by in a constantly moving stream. The purple seats feature overhead restraints with a curved handlebar to grip and partitions that prevent you from looking at other riders.

With John Williams' theme music twinkling in your seat-mounted speakers, you glide sedately sideways until Hermione scatters some "Floo powder" over you. All at once your feet lift off the ground as you lean backwards, flying up through a glowing green vortex and floating into the castle's towering Observatory. Next, you are summoned by Harry and Ron, riding by on their broomsticks, and you plunge through the window after them, skimming precariously along Hogwarts' rocky foundations. Catching up with the boys, who assure you they haven't lost anyone on these "dodgy" devices yet ("this week, anyway"), you are confronted with Hagrid's missing dragon. Putting your Quidditch match on hold, you hide from the creature inside the creaky old Covered Bridge; you can spot his massive wing beating against the windows, and scorch-marks appear on the walls. Suddenly the floor collapses, dropping you eye-to-eye with the fire-breather, who delivers a warm blast of steam in your face. That sends you spiraling down into the Forbidden Forest below, lair of Aragog the enormous Acromantula and his web-spitting kin.

Before you say I've given it all away, that's barely the first third of the adventure! Before you're done, you'll be whacked by the Whomping Willow, watch a Quidditch play close-up, and see a Dementor suck your soul right out of your body. It's a dark, discombobulating, and often startling experience that will leave you breathless (and moist). Naturally, all ends well, with cheering throngs in the Great Hall, a wizardly admonishment to "tuck your elbows in," and a final flight through the Floo Network back to the room where you began.

After your journey, all that remains is to tumble downstairs into Filch's Emporium (see *Shopping* below), check out your souvenir photo, and sprint to rejoin the line for another flight.

Tip: For re-rides, use the single rider line, which starts in the dungeon across from the lockers. You'll skip the tour, going straight to the safety spiel room, and cut your wait considerably.

The best seats in the house. All four seats on each bench are excellent, but the middle two give the least distorted view of the curved screens. The "front" seat (far left when seated) gets the biggest "boo" scares, while the "back" seat (far right when seated) experiences the most motion.

How did Universal Creative create this masterpiece? By starting with the template they pioneered with *Spider-Man*: motion-simulator seats moving through a seamless blend of physical effects and projection screens. This time, they upgraded the sets from *Spider-Man's* comic-book stylization to fully sculpted environments that seem to extend in all directions, then stuffed them with animatronic monsters that aggressively lunge within a few feet of your face. As for the video, it ditches the 3-D (the glasses would go flying), but makes up for it with high-definition footage featuring the films' stars, projected onto vision-encompassing domes — think smaller-sized *Simpsons* screens, mounted on a clever carousel contraption that gives every car a sweet-spot perspective.

What elevates *Forbidden Journey* above those predecessors is the KUKA Robocoaster that mounts an industrial robotic arm on a moving track. The result is not a roller coaster. There are no sustained speeds, big drops, or upside-down moments. Nor is it a traditional simulator. With your legs dangling free, you have an unprecedented feeling of "floating" that will have you flat on your back and leaning dynamically from side to side. The motion is extraordinarily smooth, with little jerking or jarring, but its intensity will be disorienting to those prone to motion sickness. Universal owns exclusive rights to the technology so you won't see anything similar elsewhere.

Most amazing is the way that this next-generation underpinning is completely invisible to the rider. If you keep your head back in your seat as instructed, you'll never see the arm holding you aloft. Nor should you see any other ride vehicles, making it seem like a uniquely personal adventure.

Tip: After your first few times through, try sitting in an outside seat and leaning slightly forward for insight on how the magic happens.

Note: Some visitors with larger chest, tummy, or thigh dimensions may have difficulty with the ride's safety restraints. If you have any doubt, test out the sample seats outside the attraction entrance. If you pull down the harness and get a green light, you're golden, but if you get the yellow ask an attendant about special seating. You may be retested before boarding; don't take it personally, the attendants are only looking out for your safety.

An alternate stationary loading platform (complete with theming) is available for those needing to transfer from a wheelchair, or anyone physically unable to navigate the moving belt. Just ask an attendant for assistance, though it can get backed up on busy days.

Note: This ride requires that you stow all your belongings in electronic lockers located immediately inside the entrance. They are free for a period of time that varies with the queue length, but charge a hefty fee if you overstay your welcome. Be aware that long items like wizards' wands may not fit in the lockers, though you can use the "baby swap" as a "wand swap." Better yet, save your shopping until the end of the day, after your ride. For more information, see *Good Things To Know About...Lockers* in *Chapter One*.

Tip: On busy days, the line for the lockers will extend outside the castle. If you don't have any loose belongings, ask the employee at the front gate if you may proceed past the line. If you do have bags, consider using the lockers outside *Dragon Challenge* (you may be charged) or let a non-rider hold them. There is a also small compartment in the back of each rider's seat, just big enough for your keys, wallet, and cellphone or compact camera. Don't forget your belongings when your journey ends!

Dragon Challenge

Rating:	★ ★ ★
Type:	Twin roller coasters
Time:	1.5 minutes
Height Req.:	54 in. (137.2 cm.)
Short Take:	A shadow of its former self

An easily overlooked stone archway marks the entrance to this immense inverted steel roller coaster, hidden behind the stone wall through which the Hogwarts Express appears to emerge. Actually, two separate roller coasters lurk back there, travelling along separate but closely intertwined tracks that diverge and then converge to potentially terrifying effect.

Note: This ride requires that you stow all your belongings in electronic lockers located immediately outside the entrance, in a shelter disguised as a train station. They are free for a period of time that varies with the queue length, but charge a hefty fee if you overstay your welcome.

This coaster (formerly known as *Dueling Dragons*) is themed after the first of three tasks comprising the "Triwizard Tournament," the wizarding competition seen in the fourth Potter tale, *Goblet of Fire*. Begin by walking the meandering path toward the small (compared to Hogwarts) castle ahead. Along the way, you'll pass banners supporting Harry Potter and his competitors (Fleur Delacour, Victor Krum, and Cedric Diggory), as well as the Weasley's flying Ford Anglia, which has crashed into a nearby tree. Pass into the stone structure and you enter the Champions' Tent, where the Goblet of Fire stands spewing an otherworldly blue flame. Further ahead, you'll find the Triwizard Cup itself on a pedestal, a trio of golden dragon eggs, and a chamber filled with flickering floating candles. Those who remember the wonderfully macabre theming of the *Dueling Dragons* queue will be disappointed by the labyrinth of featureless stone walls that follows, but eventually you will be asked to turn left toward the red "Chinese Fireball" or right to the blue "Hungarian Horntail." While waiting for your coaster, look up at the shadowy dragons battling above the ruined ceiling.

This is an inverted coaster, which means that the cars, completely dressed to look like dragons, hang from a track over your head. Your feet dangle in the air below your seat. When the cars are fully loaded the passengers look as though they are hanging from the dragons' claws.

The two coasters share the same lift to the top of the first drop, but then the Chinese Fireball track peels off to the left as the Hungarian Horntail swoops to the right. Originally, pairs of trains were dispatched simultaneously, carefully synchronized so that, as they looped and swirled their way around, they met in mid air at three crucial moments. A computer actually weighed each coaster and then made the appropriate adjustments to get the timing just right. All told there were three near misses in the 50 seconds or so it takes to travel from the first drop to the point where the coasters slow down to reenter the castle.

Tragically, following a couple of unfortunate injuries involving flying objects during the near-misses, Universal permanently suspended synchronized operations of the dueling tracks in 2011. Instead, the formerly dueling dragons now fly solo, resulting in a solid, but no longer unique, suspended coaster experience. After over a decade of safe operations, it's a shame that current guests can't experience the dragons' most dramatic feature. On the plus side, the addition of the Hogwarts Express train station has introduced exciting new close encounters along both coaster tracks.

Tip: If you'd like to get a preview of this ride, look for the exit. It's to your left as you face the entrance. A short way up, you will find a viewing area behind a high metal fence; most likely a number of departing riders will have paused here for another look. This vantage point gives you a pretty good view of the twin coasters' routes. For those who have no intention of ever strapping themselves into this coaster, it's a pretty entertaining attraction in and of itself.

It's also possible to enter the queue line itself for a peek. Just a short way in is a spot where you can actually feel the wind rush through your hair as the coasters spiral past. If this dissuades you from venturing farther you can turn back.

The best seats in the house. The first row is the clear choice for the thrill seeker. Otherwise, the outside seats in each row give a better view (if you have your eyes open!) and are less likely to induce motion sickness. Seats farther back in the vehicle offer a different ride experience, partly because you can't see what's coming and partly because the back rows snap about with a bit more zip. Finally, the left hand track is more "aggressive" than the right one; that is, it has a few more spins to it and moves a bit faster at some points. Overall, the best seats are the first row inside on the Hungarian Horntail and the last row outside on the Chinese Fireball.

Flight of the Hippogriff

Rating:	★ ★ ★ ½
Type:	A junior roller coaster
Time:	About a minute
Height Req.:	36 in. (91.4 cm.)
Short Take:	Best for the view of Hogsmeade

Just past Hogsmeade Village and just before you enter Hogwarts Castle, you'll find a stone monolith marking the entrance to this cute coaster. Formerly known as *The Flying Unicorn*, the ride was re-themed around one of the favorite pets of Rubeus Hagrid, Hogwarts' "care of magical creatures" instructor. Eager riders-to-be wind around Hagrid's pumpkin patch and stone hut on the fringe of the Forbidden Forest, listening as the gentle giant instructs us on the proper way to approach the proud Hippogriff.

We board one of the two 16-rider trains, which appear to be made of woven wicker, and are urged to bow respectfully to the life-size animatronic eagle/horse that sits nodding in its track-side nest. After a slow climb to the first drop, which provides a spectacular view of the Wizarding World and beyond, the coaster glides briefly through a series of dips and swoops before returning to the wooden hut that serves as the station.

Smaller kids will delight in the gentle ride from the slower front seats, but even adults have been know to squeal when sitting in the surprisingly zippy back rows. Though the "Vekoma Junior" track is similar to Woody Woodpecker's coaster next door in USF, the *Hippogriff* is 400 feet longer, 15 feet taller, and 7 mph swifter. Striking vistas and rich theming make this a worthwhile spin even for childless grown-ups.

Ollivanders

Rating:	★ ★ ★ ★
Type:	Small-scale show
Time:	About 5 minutes
Short Take:	A charmingly magical moment

The Hogsmeade branch of Ollivanders is a virtual carbon copy of the Diagon Alley original and I refer you there for a fuller description.

Potter purists will tsk-tsk and tut-tut that there is no Ollivanders in Hogsmeade, but since Hogsmeade was the first element of the Wizarding World to open, Universal's designers made the wise decision to conjure up a branch. It has been packing them in (almost literally) since opening day.

Tip: If you have a two-park pass, experience the Ollivanders "wand experience" in Diagon Alley for faster throughput; otherwise, brave the lines here.

Hogwarts Express

Rating:	★ ★ ★
Type:	Train ride with special effects
Time:	About 4 minutes
Short Take:	Be a day-tripper

The best way to experience this attraction is to begin in Diagon Alley, so you may want to review the discussion of *Hogwarts Express* in *Chapter Two* before reading on. That being said, Potter fans shouldn't skip the return journey if time allows.

For starters, the queue experience is a step up from King's Cross Station, at least for a while. It begins along a sinuous, pine-scented pathway that affords a view of the clever way Hogsmeade Station nestles among the tracks of *Dragon Challenge*. Unfortunately, the queue turns away from the main entrance and snakes down to the station's basement. If you find yourself down here on a hot and sultry day, be prepared for some discomfort before you climb the stairs that take you to the platform and fresh air.

The boarding process is just as it was in Diagon Alley but the trip is far less portentous than the one from London and it starts out on a joyful note. As Hagrid waves you off, Buckbeak swoops past as if to say its own good-byes and a herd of centaurs gallops through the woods to see you off. Fred and George Weasley swoop by on brooms and, ever the jokers, unleash a fireworks display that turns into a clever advert for their Diagon Alley shop. You will once again see Harry and friends, or at least their shadows on the frosted window to the train's corridor. Of course you still have to pass by the Malfoy place, where it always seems to be a dark and stormy night. *Wait!* Was that Voldemort in that flash of lightning? No, couldn't be. Then, before you know it, you are back in London, where you see the Knight Bus zipping through narrow alleys and ducking under flyovers. And so to King's Cross. Time for a butterbeer!

And all the rest . . .

There are no formally scheduled theater shows within the Wizarding World. Nor are there any strolling actors portraying "Harry Potter" or any other named characters (you'll have to enter Hogwarts to see them in virtual form). But there are a number of interactive entertainments involving less-famous Potter characters that are worth seeking out.

The **Hogwarts Express Conductor** watching over the train just inside the Hogsmeade entrance archway is more than a living prop for **photo ops**. He's a veritable encyclopedia of Potter lore; just try to stump him.

Several times daily, two performances rotate presentations on a stage in front of the pseudo-Celtic, rune-covered monolith across from the friendly frozen snowman. Both are good fun, but operate on an unpublished schedule. No set show times are listed on the park map, but performances usually occur a couple times each hour, so hang around and see what pops up.

The **Frog Choir**, briefly seen in *Prisoner of Azkaban*, is an a cappella choir consisting of four Hogwarts students and two bass-singing frogs (psst, they're puppets). The group, led by an emphatically gesticulating conductor, performs beat-box versions of songs from the Potter scores, such as "Hedwig's Theme" and "Something Wicked This Way Comes."

At the **Triwizard Spirit Rally,** the visiting students from the Beaux-batons and Durmstrang show off their school pride. First the lovely French ladies demonstrate their ribbon dancing talents to a classical soundtrack. Then the Russian lads show off their martial arts skills with some fighting-stick acrobatics. Afterwards, everyone poses for pictures.

When you are exhausted from your adventures, seek refuge in **The Owlery**, a pleasantly shaded area beneath the innards of a rustic clockwork bell tower. Animatronic owls roost in the rafters, depositing realistic droppings on the beams below although not, it should be noted, on you.

The restrooms, located across from Ollivanders, are an attraction in and of themselves. If you listen over the flushing, you can hear the ghostly Moaning Myrtle sighing and weeping. Of course, if you're a parent you're probably already used to hearing a little child cry while you try to pee.

But the greatest Potter attraction is the one most likely to be overlooked in the rush to the headliner rides. Each street-facing window, including the ones that front inaccessible facades, contains delightfully detailed dressing and animated illusions. Hidden touches abound, from dueling chess pieces to rolling eyeballs. Here are a just few to keep an eye out for:

The goblin-run bank *Gringotts* has an ATM branch near the back patio. *Spintwitches* sporting goods sells quivering Quidditch equipment (but the Golden Snitch flying in their window has gone missing). *Tomes & Scrolls* displays living pictures of Gilderoy Lockhart (Kenneth Branagh), while *Scrivenshaft's* stocks quills and *Cerdiwens Cauldrons* offers pots that stir themselves. Inside *Dogweed & Deathcap Exotic Plants* you'll spot a potted Shrieking Mandrake and other freaky flora. *Gladrags Wizardwear* has Hermione's Yule Ball gown from the fourth film, with an animated kitty made of measuring tape pawing at its hem. In *Dominic Maestro's* second-story music shop, when the enchanted cello hits a bad note, sheet music flies.

Note: Some effects may not be working when you visit and others are reportedly being rejiggered to work with the interactive wands.

Eating in Hogsmeade

The Potter stories are filled with exotic foodstuffs and impossible beverages that have had readers salivating for years. In bringing to life the Wizarding World, J.K. Rowling was just as involved with the creation of comestibles as she was with the rides. Executive Chef Steven Jayson worked to ensure everything not only looked, smelled, and tasted as Rowling described, but also met her standards for nutrition. And ingredients for everything had to be shipped to Scotland for her personal approval. That's why you'll find Butterbeer and pumpkin juice to drink, but no corn syrup-based Coke products.

Speaking of **Butterbeer**, the phenomenally popular drink was introduced here in Hogsmeade and it's every bit as good as you've dreamed. It's a vanilla shortbread cookie-flavored soda, with a thick head of butterscotch non-dairy whipped topping. It's sweet but not overbearingly cloying and almost universally adored. The only debate is "cold" vs. slushie-style "frozen." Most vote for frozen, especially on a hot day. A disposable cup will cost about $4 cold and $5 frozen. A plastic "souvenir" tankard is $13 to $14, and can be refilled for the disposable price.

Tip: It's almost always quicker to get a Butterbeer inside the air-conditioned Hog's Head Pub or Three Broomsticks restaurant than at the scenic cart in the center of Hogsmeade's thoroughfare. Also, the carts don't honor Annual Pass discounts, but the inside vendors do.

Pumpkin Juice ($4) is more of an acquired taste. People either love its Thanksgiving pie spices and pulpy texture, or can't take more than a sip. Some say it's better at room temperature. The best part is the cute pumpkin-topped bottle. Other unusual drinks available in Three Broomsticks include pumpkin fizz (carbonated pumpkin juice) and non-alcoholic apple or pear cider ($3).

■ Three Broomsticks

What:	British fare in an enchanted setting
Where:	On your left as you enter from Lost Continent
Price Range:	$$

Grab a seat inside the tavern where Harry and his classmates unwind after a hard day of supernatural scholarship. The entrance, marked by the namesake trio of broomsticks, may appear deceptively brown and bland, as it is intended to blend in with the surrounding village. But look for subtle magical touches throughout its rough-hewn walls. The design of this wood-timbered restaurant actually inspired the look of *The Half-Blood Prince* film's set, instead of the other way around. So the elaborate catwalks and seemingly endless ceilings appear to have stepped straight off the screen. From time to time, shadows of house elves and delivery owls at work appear on the walls, surrounding you with wizardry while you dine.

The eating experience itself falls somewhere between counter-service and sit-down dining. You'll be directed by a greeter to a numbered cashier. Place your order, then pick up your food from an adjacent counter. At busy times, you will be shown to an empty table by a staff member who will bus your tray at the end and even refuse a tip. It's a far more civilized system than elbowing your way around similar quick-service eateries, but it can lead to lines out the door at peak mealtimes.

Tip: If it's not too hot outside, try a table on the back patio with a view of the lagoon.

Entree offerings ($9 to $16) are as authentically British as any you'll find in a theme park and tastier in some cases than in many an actual pub.

Shepherd's Pie is slightly spicy seasoned ground beef, lamb, and minced vegetables covered with a piped mashed potato crust; it's served with a blah iceberg salad and an un-magical selection of dressings. Cornish Pasties take a similar meat filling and stuff it into three small half-moon pastries, sort of like British empanadas. Finally, the Fish and Chips features three generous pieces of white fillets, dipped in an ale-infused batter, fried, and served with wedge-cut potatoes and tartar sauce. More American-oriented entrees include rotisserie-smoked chicken, chargrilled ribs, and combo platters, all served with roasted potatoes and corn on the cob, as well as smoked turkey legs with wedge fries. If you've a Hagrid-sized appetite, consider the "Great Feast" ($50 for four, $13 each additional serving), a giant-sized rib and chicken combo platter with salad. Other options include baked potato, split pea and ham or potato leek soup, or a rotisserie smoked chicken salad. Desserts ($4) usually include strawberry & peanut-butter ice cream, apple pie, and a chocolate trifle with cake and fresh berries. A "Children's Menu" ($7) includes mac and cheese, fish and chips, and chicken fingers.

In the mornings, breakfast ($15) is served from park opening to 10:30 a.m. Choose from the "traditional" British breakfast, Continental (with croissants and jam), American (scrambled eggs, bacon, sausage, potatoes), porridge, or pancakes. You can even start your day with a small serving of Butterbeer.

Attached to the side of the restaurant is the **Hog's Head Pub**, a gloriously grimy shrine to intoxication. In addition to virgin Butterbeers, there's a fine selection of European brews on tap, including Guinness, Bass, Stella Artois, Tennent's, Boddingtons, Yuengling Lager, and Strongbow. The featured potable is "Hog's Head Brew," a hoppy dark-amber Scottish ale brewed exclusively for the park. Sadly, the "Firewhiskey" on display isn't drinkable, but a full selection of hard liquor and wine is available behind the bar if you prefer. There is no happy hour here, so serious drinkers will want to continue to the Watering Hole in Jurassic Park.

Tip: Watch for the establishment's namesake (mounted behind the bar beside a brace of shrunken heads) come snorting to life.

Shopping in Hogsmeade

For many, shopping will be as much an attraction in the Wizarding World as the rides. There are no "Toys R Us" action figures or "I Survived" T-shirts here. Instead, everything for sale has been custom-designed down to the packaging to look like it was delivered direct from Harry's world. If you are any kind of fan, be prepared to drop a bundle.

Tip: These tiny shops are often packed during the day, so save your shopping for closing time. A smaller selection is also found in Port of Entry's Trading Company and CityWalk's Universal Studios Store, and most items (including wands) can be ordered online through UniversalOrlando.com.

Honeydukes Sweetshop is a pastel candyland that could give Willy Wonka a toothache. Popular items ($5 to $11) include the "Chocolate Frog," a solid milk chocolate amphibian that comes with a collectable "famous wizard" trading card, and "Bertie Bott's Every Flavour Beans" with tastes including Earth Worm, Black Pepper, and Vomit. The treacle fudge is too sugary to swallow, but the cauldron cakes, dark chocolate Peppermint Toads, and cinnamon Pepper Imps are all yummy.

Note: Honeydukes has incorporated the space formerly occupied by Zonko's Joke Shop, whose merchandise is now sold at Weasley's Wizard Wheezes in Diagon Alley.

Dervish and Banges specializes in wizarding school supplies, from neckties and scarves ($32 to $35) and class robes ($110, in sizes XXXS to XXXL) to Quidditch Bludgers and Golden Snitches. If you admire the hovering brooms tethered to the second-story balcony, you can take home a toy broom for $33, or a collectible Firebolt ($300) or Nimbus 2001 ($250) (non-flying models only, alas). Say hello to the Monster Book of Monsters snoozing in his cage, but watch out; he bites when woken.

Owl Post is a small annex of Dervish and Banges that serves as the exit for Ollivanders wand shop, so it quickly becomes claustrophobic. Here guests can purchase their own wand, selecting either an interactive model ($45) or settling for a "replica" ($35) without the magical properties. They carry the 13 "original" designs based on the 13-month Celtic tree zodiac. You can have your outgoing mail stamped with a Hogsmeade postmark in the covered area outside the entrance to Dervish and Banges (a postal box sits outside the shop). And you can't miss the holographic "Howlers" screaming at passersby from the window.

Filch's Emporium of Confiscated Goods, at the exit of the *Forbidden Journey* ride, is festooned with items reclaimed from rambunctious students, like copies of *Quibbler* magazine, Whammy Rockets, and bottles of Skele-Gro potion. While those props from the films aren't for sale, everything else is, including fold-out Marauder Maps ($50, or $70 in a handsome wood and glass case), Sorting Hats ($30), and copies of the books and films that started it all. Of course, you can also view and purchase souvenir photos of your *Journey* here ($25 to $43).

■ JURASSIC PARK ■

If you've seen the movie *Jurassic Park*, you will recognize the arches that greet you as you enter. If you haven't, you should stream the original film before coming. Knowing the film will help you understand a lot of the little details of Jurassic Park, including the frequent references to velociraptors. Here, Universal's design wizards have re-created the theme park that the movie's John Hammond was trying to create before all prehistoric heck broke loose, and the lush and steamy jungle landscape they have devised fits in perfectly with Florida's humid summers.

As in the movie, we are asked to believe that we are in a park containing actual living dinosaurs, some of which are quite dangerous. Periodically, roars are heard, and more than one child has been seen starting in terror when an unseen critter growled in the underbrush.

Unfortunately, the surprisingly realistic atmosphere has been somewhat disrupted by the boy wizard's arrival next door. It's understandably difficult to hide a huge honking castle, but it would be nice if they'd finally theme the bare building, or at least paint it "go-away-green."

Note: The Toon Lagoon end of the island has been somewhat disrupted by construction of a new attraction based on *Skull Island*, the upcoming movie reboot of the King Kong franchise. The new attraction is likely to be an expanded and technically updated version of the astonishing 3-D King Kong attraction in Universal Studios Hollywood's Backlot Tour in Los Angeles, in which case it should be a real gasper. No opening date has been announced, but since the film won't open until November of 2016, summer of 2016 is a good guess.

Discovery Center

Rating:	★ ★ ½
Type:	Interactive displays
Time:	Unlimited
Short Take:	Best for young dinosaur buffs

This is lifted almost straight from the film and houses a fast food restaurant, a shop and, on the ground floor, a children's "science center" that blends fantasy and reality in such a way that you might have to explain the difference to your more trusting kids. Kids will certainly recognize the huge

T-Rex skeleton that perches menacingly on a rock outcropping and pokes its head through to the circular railing on the upper level.

A nursery carefully incubates dinosaur eggs. Nearby, kids can handle "real" dino eggs and put them in a scanner to view the developing embryo inside. Periodically an attendant appears and conducts a deadpan scientific show-and-tell as you watch an adorable baby raptor emerge from its shell.

Closer to reality is an actual segment of rock face from the North Sea area containing real fossilized dinosaur bits from the Triassic, Jurassic, and Cretaceous eras. A series of clever "neutrino data scanners" let kids move along the rock face looking for dinosaurs. When a fragment is found, the scanner analyzes it and then identifies and reconstructs the dinosaur from which it came. In somewhat the same vein is an exhibit of life-sized dinosaurs that supposedly lets you see the world as the dinosaurs saw it by looking through high-tech viewfinders mounted periscope-style into the model dinosaurs' heads and necks and moving the creatures' heads around. Unfortunately, it rarely seems to work properly.

On the zany side is a DNA sequencing exhibit that explains the cloning premise on which the movie is based and then lets you combine your own DNA with that of a dinosaur to create a saurian you. And completely over the top (but a lot of fun) is a quiz show with the rather naughty name, "You Bet Jurassic." Here you and two other tourists compete in a game of dinosaur trivia. But don't get your hopes up; the grand prize is a lifetime supply of Raptor Chow, which is apparently manufactured from losing contestants!

On the back wall of the lower level you'll find a large mural depicting life in the Jurassic era. If you entered the *Discovery Center* from the upper level, you might want to take a peek through the massive double doors in the middle of this wall. They open out onto a spacious park-like terrace that descends to the shores of the Great Inland Sea. This is one of the loveliest open spaces in the park and offers a stunning view back to the Port of Entry and the lighthouse that welcomes arriving guests. With its tropical foliage, it's secluded and romantic at night. On very busy days, this area has been used as a standby queue for the Wizarding World: Hogsmeade.

Jurassic Park River Adventure

Rating:	★ ★ ★ ★
Type:	Water ride
Time:	5 minutes
Height Req.:	42 in. (106.7 cm.)

Short Take: A wild, wet dino-tour with teeth

This is the attraction that will draw people to Jurassic Park. The pre-ride warm-up plays it straight. Video monitors in the queue line emphasize proper boarding procedures and ride safety, just as you would expect in the "real" Jurassic Park.

River Adventure itself is an idyllic boat ride that gives you an opportunity to view from close range some of Jurassic Park's gentlest creatures. Unfortunately, on the trip you take with 25 other guests, things go very, very wrong. Your first stop is the upper lagoon, where you meet a 35-foot-tall mama ultrasaur and her baby. Then you cruise past the park's north forty where you glimpse stegosaurs and playful hydrosaurs. Too playful, alas.

Before you know it, you're off course in the raptor containment area and on the lunch menu. In a desperate attempt to save you, the boat is shunted into the environmental systems building, that huge 13-story structure at the back of Jurassic Park. It is in this vast, dark, and very scary setting that the ride reaches its climax. After narrowly escaping velociraptors and those nasty spitting dinosaurs, you come face to face, quite literally, with T-Rex himself. After that, the 85-foot plunge down a steep waterfall in pitch blackness will seem like a relief.

While still a solid blend of thrills and chills, the ride's robo-dinos show wear and tear, and there aren't as many of them here as in the Hollywood park's version. The huge show building promises more content than it delivers, since most of its volume is consumed by machinery. But if the effects are occasionally unpersuasive, the final drop never fails to please.

Tip: You can speed your way through this ride by asking the attendant to point you toward the single rider line (if available).

This is a great ride to experience at night, especially once you enter the main building. The bright Florida sun tends to give away the approach of the final breathtaking drop; at night it comes as a real surprise.

The best seats in the house. Clearly the first row of the boat is where you thrill seekers want to be; just be warned that you *will* get wet. Of course, you'll probably get wet no matter where you sit, although seats in the center of the craft are a little more protected. The ride attendants are more likely to accommodate a request for a seat that gives you some protection from a drenching than they are to put you in the front row. However, if you come early in the day or late in the evening, when the crowds are thinner, you may be able to pick any seat you want.

Camp Jurassic

Rating:	★ ★ ★ ★
Type:	Interactive play area
Time:	As long as it takes
Short Take:	Terrific fun for pre-teens

This 60,000-square-foot interactive kids' play and discovery area is about four times the size of *Fievel's Playland* over at Universal Studios Florida and will appeal to a slightly older age group, although kids of all ages will find plenty to keep them occupied. The place is a minor masterpiece of playground design and is highly recommended for kids who are getting antsy or who just need to burn off some excess energy. Even adults will enjoy sampling its pleasures.

Camp Jurassic transports you to a jungle on the slopes of an ancient active volcano. The roots of banyan trees snake around ancient rock outcroppings and an old abandoned amber mine offers exciting networks of rope ladders and tunnels, as well as subterranean passageways, to explore. There are corkscrew slides, cascading waterfalls, secret hideaways, and a place where kids can do battle with water cannons made up to look like the deadly spitting dinosaurs from the film.

Aside from the water cannons, all the fun here comes from kids burning off energy and exercising their imaginations as they run, climb, and slide their way through this intricate and imaginative maze of a prehistoric environment. Don't be surprised if your kid gets lost in here for an hour or so, and don't be surprised if you find yourself enjoying it just as much.

Pteranodon Flyers

Rating:	★ ★
Type:	A mild, hanging coaster
Time:	80 seconds
Height Req.:	36 in. (91.4 cm.) min.; 56 in. (142.2 cm.) max.
Short Take:	Not worth waiting for

Taking off from the back of *Camp Jurassic* is this "family" ride that glides gently around the camp's tropical perimeter for an enjoyable but all-too-brief soaring experience. The ride vehicle consists of a pair of swing-like seats, one behind the other, that dangle from a metal pteranodon. Pteranodons, you might remember, were flying dinosaurs with long mean-looking beak-like faces and hooks on their leathery wings. These pteranodons are not at all threatening. In fact, you hardly notice them once you are seated.

Your vehicle glides rather than rides along the overhead track, taking you on a journey that lets you survey *Camp Jurassic* below and the Great Inland Sea in the distance. This ride is a little more "aggressive" than the sky rides you may have encountered at other parks and offers a few mild "thrills" as the flyers bank and curve.

The main problem with this ride is that it accommodates so few riders. Universal has tried to remedy this situation by imposing a 36-inch minimum and 56-inch maximum height requirement; if you are taller than this, you must be accompanied by a child who falls within the range. This has helped somewhat, but compared to all the other rides in the park, its hourly "throughput" is still laughably low. The result is that the line forms early and lasts a long, long time. You won't be alone if you decide that an hour and a half wait for an 80-second ride is a tad on the absurd side. And Universal Express is not accepted at this attraction. So if you think this is the kind of thing your kid will demand to ride, plan on coming first thing in the morning. The wait also tends to be more reasonable shortly before the park closes.

Note: Be aware that some children, especially those with a fear of heights, might find this ride terrifying. And if they do, they won't have Mommy or Daddy to cling to since the two seats are quite separate.

Eating in Jurassic Park

Jurassic Park offers another stunningly beautiful restaurant, Thunder Falls Terrace, where the service is cafeteria style and the knives and forks are plastic but where the food is a cut above the average. And Burger Digs offers an often-overlooked rear balcony with a terrific view out over the Great Inland Sea. If (heaven forbid) you have work to do while you're in Orlando, this is a good place to do it; there are even outlets for your laptop. For the rest, there are a number of fast food options and an inviting outdoor bar that offers a perfect venue for people-watching.

■ Thunder Falls Terrace

What: Grilled cuisine with flair
Where: On your left as you enter from Toon Lagoon
Price Range: $$

This restaurant takes wonderful advantage of the *Jurassic Park River Adventure,* using it as both backdrop and entertainment. After you've taken your own harrowing journey on the ride, you can repair here, sit in air-conditioned comfort, and gaze through the picture windows at other happily terrified tourists as they emerge from the final 85-foot drop. There is an outdoor seating area that receives the cooling mist from the thundering waterfall next door. The luxurious jungle-lodge atmosphere also contributes to the experience. There are two spacious circular dining areas under soaring conical roofs held aloft by massive log beams and dominated by a large hanging black metal chandelier with amber glass panels and cutouts of dinosaurs.

The food is casual and it's served cafeteria style, but it is very good, with careful attention paid to both quality and presentation. The menu consists of unusually well-prepared backyard barbecue staples such as chicken, ribs, burgers, and wraps. The platters ($10 to $16) are served with a choice of two sides including roasted garlic herb potatoes, corn on the cob, yellow rice, and black beans. The corn on the cob is especially nice, roasted to perfection, with the peeled-back husks adding a festive touch to the platter. Thunder Falls also dishes up a couple of serviceable soups and a tasty entree-sized salad. The desserts include the cookie-in-a-brownie "brookie." All in all, this is the best "fast food" style restaurant in the park. With a very full meal running about $20, it's a real bargain for the quality. In addition to the usual soft drinks, beer and wine are available.

Note: This restaurant may be closed during the park's slower periods or for private events. There is also speculation that it may be demolished or re-themed as part of the next door Kong attraction now under construction.

■ The Burger Digs

What:	Walk-up indoor fast food counter
Where:	On the top level of the *Discovery Center*
Price Range:	$

This fast food eatery opened on an adventuresome note by putting alligator meat on the menu, but found few takers. Now you'll have to be content with cheeseburgers, double cheeseburgers, veggie burgers, and grilled chicken sandwiches. All are served with fries and a help-yourself fixin's bar laden with shredded lettuce, tomato, onions, and other burger enhancers. Beer is on tap, and milk shakes are for dessert. For an extra $3.50 you can add a shake to any platter.

You'll find plenty of indoor, air-conditioned seating just a few steps away from the serving windows, in a spacious dining room decorated with murals depicting life in the Jurassic age.

There is also a lovely balcony with a palm-fringed view of the Inland Sea — a great place to sit on a balmy day. Clearly the seating area here was designed with corporate events and private parties in mind. For the casual tourist, it means plenty of room to spread out, even to gain a modicum of privacy and peace on a hectic day.

■ Pizza Predattoria

What: Walk-up outdoor fast food stand
Where: Near *Jurassic Park River Adventure*
Price Range: $

Personal-sized pizza is the signature dish here. There is also a large meatball sub and a chicken Caesar salad. Sweets, soft drinks, and beer round out the menu choices. All seating is at nearby umbrella-shaded tables, but you could conceivably take a short stroll to The Burger Digs in the *Discovery Center* and eat your pizza in air-conditioned comfort.

■ The Watering Hole

What: Outdoor bar with snacks
Where: Near the *Discovery Center*
Price Range: $

Rather unusual for a theme park is this walk-up bar specializing in drinks that pack a prehistoric wallop. The main feature is specialty drinks like a frozen Strawberry Piña Colada and a Blue Raspberry. There's also beer, wine, and a small selection of liquor for those who prefer a more straightforward drink. Snacks served here include hot dogs with chips, pretzels, and nachos.

Shopping in Jurassic Park

Shopping is muted here, but the **Dinostore**, located on the top level of the *Discovery Center* opposite Burger Digs, is a small shop with a smidge of redeeming educational value. There are dinosaur model kits, books about dinosaurs aimed at the younger set, and dinosaur toys, as well as dinosaur and mineral collectibles. There is also a counter selling jewelry made from amber and other semi-precious stones.

Jurassic Outfitters is the gauntlet you run after splashing down on the *River Adventure* ride. As you might expect, you will find the Jurassic Park logo on every conceivable surface from T-shirts to mugs. Of particular interest are some Jurassic Park beach towels, which you actually might need. Best of all are the framed photos taken of you and your fellow tourists plunging screaming down the last drop of the ride.

■ TOON LAGOON ■

After the intensity of *Forbidden Journey* and Jurassic Park, the zany, colorful goofiness of Toon Lagoon is a welcome change of pace. Many of the characters you have come to know and love through the Sunday funnies in your hometown newspaper can be spotted here — some appear in blow-ups of their strips, some have been immortalized in giant sculptures, and some will actually be strolling the grounds and happy to pose for photos. A visit here offers a unique opportunity to live out a child's daydream of stepping into the pages of the comic strips and exploring a gaudy fantasy world filled with fun and laughter.

Toon Lagoon's main drag is **Comic Strip Lane,** a short street of shops and restaurants, including those described below. It is an attraction in itself. Nearly 80 comic strip characters call this colorful neighborhood home, including Beetle Bailey (on furlough from Camp Swampy no doubt), Hagar the Horrible, and Krazy Kat. The concept makes for all sorts of serendipitous juxtapositions. Hagar's boat hangs over a waterfall that falls into a big pipe that bubbles up across the way at a dog fountain where all the dogs from the various comic strips hang out.

Turning off Comic Strip Lane is the zany seaside town of **Sweet Haven**, a separate section of Toon Lagoon containing a variety of Popeye-inspired rides and attractions.

Water is a recurring theme in Toon Lagoon and you can get very wet here. See *Good Things To Know About...Getting Wet* in the introduction to this chapter for a strategy to follow.

Dudley Do-Right's Ripsaw Falls

Rating:	★ ★ ★ ★
Type:	Log flume ride
Time:	6 minutes
Height Req.:	44 in. (111.8 cm.)
Short Take:	Laughs, screams, and damp seats

In Dudley's hometown of Ripsaw Falls, as you might expect, Nell is once again in the clutches of the dastardly Snidely Whiplash. That's all the excuse you need to take off on a rip-roaring log flume ride that, like so many other attractions in this park, takes the genre to a whole new level.

The build-up takes us through a series of scenes in a "moving melo-drama" in which the much-loved characters unfold a typically wacky plot that includes not just Dudley, Nell, and Snidely but Inspector Fenwick and Horse, too, as our five-passenger log-boats rise inexorably to the mountain-ous heights where Snidely has his hideout.

Along the way we pass animated tableaux that advance the tie-her-to-the-railroad-tracks plot. The landscape is dotted with signs that echo the off-the-wall humor of the old cartoons. At one point the boat detours into the abandoned Wontyabe Mine, at another we pass a billboard advertising Whiplash Lager ("made with real logs"). Of course, Dudley triumphs almost in spite of himself. Anticipating victory a bit too soon, he strikes a heroic pose with his foot on a dynamite plunger, precipitating a plunge through the roof of a TNT storage shack as the riders are seemingly shot beneath the water surface only to pop back to the surface 100 feet downstream.

Another nice touch is that the final drop is curved rather than a straight angle; the result is that, as the angle steepens, you could swear you're hur-tling straight down. *Ripsaw Falls* isn't nearly as scenically elaborate as Dis-ney's similar *Splash Mountain*, but the sight gags are witty, and the dips are more thrilling.

Tip: You can speed your way through this ride by asking the attendant to point you toward the single rider line (if available).

This is one ride that just may be as entertaining to watch as to take. If you'd prefer not to take the plunge and actually go on the ride, you can stand and watch others take the steep 60-foot drop into the TNT shack. Or you can use the **Water Blasters** (25 cents) to spray the riders as they pass below you — good, clean, evil fun.

Note: The lap bar restraints on this ride can be extremely confining. Be prepared to suck in your stomach to get them secured.

Popeye & Bluto's Bilge-Rat Barges

Rating:	★ ★ ★ ★ ½
Type:	Raft ride
Time:	About 5 minutes
Height Req.:	42 in. (106.7 cm.)
Short Take:	Super soaking good fun

You may get spritzed a bit on the *Jurassic Park River Adventure* and on *Dudley Do-Right's Ripsaw Falls*, but for a really good soaking, you have to come to Sweet Haven, home to Popeye, Olive Oyl, and the gang. The barges of the name are actually circular, 12-passenger rubber rafts that twirl and dip along a twisting, rapids-strewn watercourse.

Just as Dudley has his Snidely, Popeye has Bluto. Their lifelong enmity and rivalry for the affection of Miss Olive form the basis for the theming on this ride, which involves Olive, Wimpy, Poopdeck Pappy, and all the rest. Water splashes into the sides of the raft in the rapids and pours in from above at crucial junctures. And at least one person in your raft is sure to get hosed by the little devils (actually someone else's kids) manning the water cannons on *Me Ship, The Olive* (see below) before the raft is swept into an octopus grotto where an eight-armed beast holds Popeye in its tentacled grip, preventing him from reaching his lifesaving spinach. Before it's all over, the hapless rafts have been spun into Bluto's fully operational boat wash, which is just like a car wash except it's for boats.

This is the spiffiest raft ride in town and the ride to take at the hottest, stickiest part of the day. Because the free-floating rafts spin and twist as they roar down the rapids, how wet you get is somewhat a matter of luck; you certainly will get damp and you may be drenched. The rafts have plastic covered bins in the center in which you can store things you'd rather not get wet. They do a pretty good job, too. Many people are smart enough to remove and stow their shoes and socks since plenty of water sloshes into the rafts along the way.

Tip: The heavier the raft, the faster the ride. So if you want a little extra oomph in your ride, get in line behind a bunch of weight lifters or opera stars.

Me Ship, The Olive

Rating:	★ ★ ★
Type:	Interactive play area
Time:	Unlimited
Short Take:	Nice, but can't beat *Camp Jurassic*

Resist the temptation to come here after the raft ride and throttle the little darlings who were squirting you with the water cannons. Instead, let your littlest kids loose in this three-story interactive play area representing the ship Popeye has named after his one true love. Older kids will find this spot of limited interest.

The ship theme is clever and well executed but makes for cramped spaces. Still there are some good reasons for at least a brief visit. The top level offers some excellent views of *Dragon Challenge*, all of Seuss Landing, and an especially good angle on the *Hulk* coaster. Videographers and photographers will definitely want to take advantage of these **photo ops**. Also on the top level is a tubular slide that will deposit little kids on the middle level where they will find, on the starboard side, four water cannons they can aim at hapless riders on the *Bilge-Rat Barges* ride — and they're free! Also on this level is a "Spinach Spinnet," a cartoon piano that little kids will enjoy banging on. Yet another corkscrew tubular slide takes your tykes to the bottom level, where they can play in Swee' Pea's Playpen. For those who cannot climb the many stairs of *Me Ship, The Olive*, a small elevator is thoughtfully provided.

And all the rest . . .

There are regular **Character Meet and Greet** sessions in Toon Lagoon, either along Comic Strip Lane or in front of the Toon Lagoon Amphitheater. The characters, naturally, are your funny paper favorites like Popeye and Olive Oyl, Beetle Bailey, and Woody Woodpecker. During busier periods, these events may be called out on the 2-Park Guide Map.

The **Toon Lagoon Amphitheater** near Marvel Super Hero Island once hosted television tapings and BMX stunt shows, but has sat unused for several seasons. If there is something showing inside during your visit, it's usually worth a look. Across from the amphitheater is a depressing strip of cheap-looking **carnival games**; just keep walking folks, there's nothing to see here.

Toon Lagoon's Comic Strip Lane offers some terrific **photo ops**. There are cut-outs that put you in the comic strip and many of the palm trees are mounted with comic strip speech balloons. You pose underneath and get a nice shot of you saying things like, "It must be Sunday...We're in color!" or "Don't have the mushroom pizza before you ride *Ripsaw Falls*."

Perhaps the best is a trick photo involving Marmaduke, that playful Great Dane. You'll find it on the facade of Blondie's restaurant (see below), and a nearby sign tells you exactly how to set up the shot.

If you turn to the right at *Me Ship, The Olive* and follow the path over the raging rapids of the *Bilge-Rat Barges* ride, you'll find yourself in a delightful snarl of walkways along the Great Inland Sea, another of the park's wonderful get-away-from-it-all spots.

Eating in Toon Lagoon

Don't look for a gourmet experience in Toon Lagoon, but don't expect to go hungry either. The food is aimed at kids and teens, which is to say it's fast and moderately priced. The eateries are colorful and full of fanciful fun, just like the funnies that inspired them.

■ Blondie's

What:	Overstuffed sandwich shop
Where:	On the plaza near the entrance to Sweet Haven
Price Range:	$

This one comes with a subtitle, "Home of the Dagwood." It's a sandwich of course, and for those who don't know, it's named after Blondie Bumstead's hapless hubby, who made comic strip history with his colossal, 20-slice, clear-out-the-fridge sandwich creations.

The sandwiches here don't quite live up to the gigantic depiction that graces the entrance to the joint, and they sprawl across the plate rather than tower above it as they do on the signage. But you'll likely find them pretty good nonetheless.

Pride of place among the "Made to Order Subs" ($9 to $12) goes to "Our Famous" Dagwood Sandwich, consisting of ham, turkey, roast beef, Swiss and American cheese on three slices of onion and poppy seed bread. Other choices are regular subs like ham, turkey, tuna, or roast beef, along with Nathan's hotdogs. Indoor seating is limited.

Note: This restaurant usually closes by 4:00 or 5:00 p.m.

■ Wimpy's

What:	Walk-up burger joint
Where:	In Sweet Haven across from *Bilge-Rat Barges*
Price Range:	$

Popeye's pal is as closely associated with hamburgers as it's possible to be, so it's good to see him here serving up the apotheosis of the all-American burger. Burger, chili dog, and chicken finger meals are served, with shakes, soft drinks, and desserts. Draft beer is available to slake that deeper thirst.

Service is from walk-up but shaded windows in a building that serves as a portside supply shack. All seating is outdoors, only some of it shaded. Perhaps the best spot to grab a table is in the shaded area overlooking the raging rapids of the *Bilge-Rat Barges* ride.

Note: This restaurant is open seasonally.

■ Comic Strip Cafe

What: Multicultural cafeteria
Where: On Comic Strip Lane
Price Range: $

This large, loud, and boisterous space serves four separate genres of fast food: Fish & Chicken; Chinese; Burgers & Dogs; and Pizza & Pasta. Each category has three to five entrees, and you can get any style of food at any open window. With so much variety, there's something to displease everyone, as this spot consistently serves the most uninspired menu in either park.

They won't win any awards from the healthy eating crowd, either. About the healthiest meal you'll find here is a grilled chicken sandwich. Desserts usually include brookies, cookies, and pie. Each counter has a separate line and cashier, but all offer the same menu choices.

The room itself is bright and garish in a self-consciously postmodern way. The high ceiling, with its exposed air-conditioning ducts and pipes, is painted a dark blue, but the walls are brightly striped and covered with blown-up panels and cutouts from a variety of Sunday funnies comic strips, providing a bit of light reading for those dining alone. There's plenty of table and booth seating indoors and a fair amount of al fresco seating as well.

■ Cathy's Ice Cream

What: Walk-up stand
Where: On Comic Strip Lane, near the Comic Strip Cafe
Price Range: $

In the comics, Cathy is constantly worrying about her weight. She must have taken leave of her senses, not to mention her scale, when she opened this place in partnership with Ben & Jerry's. The stand takes the form of a huge container brimming with a hot fudge sundae topped not by a cherry but by the disturbingly bikini-ed Cathy herself. Waffle sundaes are offered, as are milk shakes and ice cream floats.

Note: This window operates seasonally; the next closest ice cream is in Marvel Super Hero Island.

Shopping in Toon Lagoon

The shopping scene in Toon Lagoon is a little chaotic, with merchandise (and even entire shops) changing suddenly. The wares in **Gasoline Alley** seem to change more often than most, but usually include beach wear, towels, sandals, and custom-printed novelty signs. (And beware the oil cans stacked at the entrance!) Across the way, **Wossamotta U** offers cell phone charging ($5 for 30 minutes, $10 per hour) and other high-tech services as well as a small selection of merchandise.

Tucked away under Betty Boop's piano is the entrance to the **Betty Boop Store**, a shrine to the original boop-oop-a-doop girl. Collectible dolls and figurines are available in a variety of sizes and outfits not to mention price points. There are mugs, costume jewelry, and T-shirts, of course, but the sleepwear is a classier choice.

The biggest store in Toon Lagoon, **Toon Extra**, is not well marked, but you can enter it through Beetle Bailey's tent, under Flash Gordon's rocket, or through those huge rolled up Sunday funnies that serve as columns for the zany building in which it is housed. This is another Islands of Adventure shop that's worth popping into just to gawk at the decor. You will find a mix of clothing, most of it for kids, plush toys, and miscellaneous souvenirs.

MARVEL SUPER HERO ISLAND

Those from another planet may not know that Marvel is the name of a comic book company that revolutionized the industry way back in the sixties with a series of titles showcasing a bizarre array of super heroes whose psychological quirks were as intriguing as their ingeniously conceived superhuman powers. As might be expected, this cast of characters offers rich inspiration for some of the most intense thrill rides ever created.

Note: Even though Disney now owns Marvel, Universal still holds exclusive theme park rights to the characters "east of the Mississippi."

After the extensive theming of the other islands, Marvel Super Hero Island can seem a little, well, flat. But Universal was not cutting corners when it came to designing this island. Not at all. Marvel Super Hero Island is, in fact, a brilliant evocation of the visual style of the comic books that inspired it. Marvel used strong colors and simple geometric shapes to create a futuristic cityscape with an Art Deco flavor. Against this purposely flat backdrop, they arrayed their extravagantly muscled and lovingly sculpted heroes. Marvel Comics had a profound effect on American visual design, not to mention its effect on contemporary notions of the body beautiful.

But enough art history. What you've come here for are the thrill rides and Marvel Super Hero Island has some of the best examples of the genre you're likely to find in Central Florida.

The Amazing Adventures of Spider-Man

Rating:	★ ★ ★ ★ ★
Type:	3-D motion simulator ride
Time:	4.5 minutes
Height Req.:	40 in. (101.6 cm.)
Short Take:	An astounding spin into the comic pages

Until Harry Potter's arrival, *Spider-Man* was Universal's "next threshold attraction." It's still pretty darn impressive and a 2012 upgrade made it an even more mind-blowing experience.

Visitors step into the offices of the *Daily Bugle* only to discover that the evil villain Dr. Octopus and his Sinister Syndicate have used an antigravity gun to make off with the Statue of Liberty and other famous landmarks as part of a plot to bring New York City to its knees. Since cub reporter Peter Parker and all the rest of the staff are mysteriously absent, crusty editor J. Jonah Jameson drafts his hapless guests into a civilian force with the mission of tracking down the evildoers and getting the scoop on their nefarious doings.

Tip: About halfway through the queue, just after the newsroom, be alert for a **photo op** where you can have your picture taken. You can review the result at the Photo Connect desk in the Spider-Man Shop.

Guests board special 12-passenger vehicles and set off through the streets of the city, where they discover Spidey is already on the case. What ensues is a harrowing high-speed chase enhanced through a variety of heart-stopping special effects.

The vehicles are simulators, much like the ones in *The Simpsons* in Universal Studios Florida. Underneath they have six hydraulically operated stalks that can be used to simulate virtually any kind of motion. But these cars can also move through space, and they do, along tracks that allow for 360 degrees of rotation. The combination of forward motion, rotation, and simulator technology creates startling sensations never before possible.

Further heightening the experience is the environment through which the cars move. This is the world of Marvel comics sprung vividly to life and startlingly real. Intermixed with the solid set elements (that include enormous chunks of a cut up Statue of Liberty) are almost undetectable screens on which three-dimensional films add an extra measure of depth and excitement. Both villains and heroes seem to leap directly at you. At several points, various villains and Spidey himself drop onto the hood of the vehicle with a thud and a jolt. They are insubstantial three-dimensional cartoons, of course, but the effect is amazingly real.

As your ill-fated journey proceeds, it is your bad luck to keep interrupting the evildoers at awkward moments, and they do their utmost to destroy you, with deadly bursts of electricity, balls of flame, and deluges of water. They narrowly miss each time, sending your vehicle spinning and tumbling to its next close encounter with doom.

Finally you are caught in the irresistible force of an antigravity ray that sucks the vehicle ever upward as Spider-Man struggles valiantly to save you. The ride culminates with a 400-foot drop through the cartoon canyons of New York to almost certain death on the streets below. It's quite a ride.

Spidey's high-definition face-lift made a near-perfect attraction even better. The new "dichroic" glasses and Infitec 4K projectors produce the sharpest 3-D you've ever seen, and the computer-generated imagery was redesigned with realistic textures and hidden details to reward repeat riders.

Tip: Look for legendary Spider-Man co-creator Stan Lee in four virtual cameos amid the chaos; he's also the voice congratulating you as you exit.

The best seats in the house. Logically, the first row in the vehicle should be best, without fellow riders' heads in your view. But the other rows, because they are slightly farther from the screens, provide better 3-D effects.

Tip: Spider-Man usually offers a single rider line to speed your wait.

Doctor Doom's Fearfall

Rating:	★ ★ ★ ½
Type:	A free-fall ride with oomph
Time:	30 seconds
Height Req.:	52 in. (131.1 cm.)
Short Take:	A big buildup with a slow letdown, best for the view

Near the Bugle building is Doom Alley, a part of town that has been completely taken over by the bad guys of the Sinister Syndicate — Dr. Octopus, The Hobgoblin, and The Lizard. Here the archfiend Doctor Doom has secreted his Fear Sucking Machine, in which he uses innocent, unsuspecting victims (that's you in case you hadn't guessed) to create the Fear Juice with which he hopes to finally vanquish the Fantastic Four.

The payoff is a fiendish twist on the freefall rides that have long been a staple of amusement parks and that were artfully updated in Disney's *Tower of Terror*. But whereas those rides take you up slowly and drop you, *Doctor Doom*, in the true Universal spirit, turns convention in its head.

Sixteen victims, that is, passengers, are strapped into seats in small four-person chambers. Suddenly they are shot upward 150 feet at a force of four G's. There is a heart-flipping moment of weightlessness before the vehicles drop back, gently bouncing back upward a few times before all-too-quickly returning to terra firma.

Tip: You can speed your way through this ride by asking the attendant to point you toward the single rider entrance, inside the nearby arcade. It's usually open.

The best seats in the house. Chambers 3 and 4 look out over the park, while 1 and 2 give a less glamorous view of the interstate.

The Incredible Hulk Coaster

Rating:	★ ★ ★ ★ ★
Type:	Steel coaster
Time:	1.5 minutes
Height Req.:	54 in. (137.2 cm.)
Short Take:	Aaaargh!

In the scientific complex where Bruce Banner, a.k.a. the Incredible Hulk, has his laboratories, you can learn all about the nasty effects of over-exposure to gamma radiation. No, it's not more edutainment, it's the warm-up for another knock-your-socks-off roller coaster.

In a high-energy video pre-ride show, you learn that you can help Bruce reverse the unfortunate effects that have so complicated his life. All you have to do is climb into this little chamber, which is, in fact, a 32-seat roller coast-er. This is no ordinary roller coaster, however, where you have to wait ago-nizing seconds while the car climbs to the top of the first drop. It seems to get off to a fairly normal start, slowly climbing a steep incline, but thanks to an energizing burst of gamma rays you are shot 150 feet upward at one G, going from a near standstill to 42 mph. From there it's all downhill so to speak as you swing into a zero-G roll and speed toward the surface of the lagoon at 58 mph. This is no water ride though, so you whip into a cobra roll before being lofted upwards once more through the highest (109 feet) inversion ever built. After that it's under a bridge — on which earthbound (i.e. "sane") people are enjoying your terror — through a total of seven inversions and two subterra-nean trenches before you come to a rest, hoping desperately that your exer-tions have, indeed, helped Bruce out of his pickle.

Here's an interesting note for the technically minded. The initial thrust of this ride consumes so much power that, if the needed electricity were drawn directly from Orlando's electric supply, lights across town would dim every time a new coaster was launched. So Universal draws power at a steady rate from the city's power grid and stores it in a huge flywheel hid-den in the greenish building by the Inland Sea labeled "Power Supply." This enables them to get the power they need for that first heart-stopping effect without inconveniencing their neighbors.

Tip: This can be a very discombobulating experience. If you feel a bit weak in the knees at ride's end, look for the Baby Swap area on your right-where you can sit in air-conditioned comfort to regain your composure.

Note: This ride requires that you stow all your belongings in nearby electronic lockers that are free for a period of time that varies with the queue length, but charge a hefty fee if you overstay your welcome.

Tip: You may be able to speed your way through this ride by asking the attendant to point you toward the single rider line, if open.

And on your way out, don't forget to check out the evidence of your adventure. The high-speed cameras capture still photos and video of each of the eight rows of the coaster as it zooms past.

Storm Force Accelatron

Rating:	★ ★ ★
Type:	Spinning cup ride
Time:	1.5 minutes
Short Take:	A dressed-up standard carnival ride

Tucked behind the *Hulk* coaster and Cafe 4, under a futuristic purple and yellow dome, is this Marvelized version of a fairly standard amusement park ride. A large circular spinning platform contains four smaller circles that spin independently. Each of these small circles holds three cup-like cars that also spin independently. When the whole thing gets up to speed, there are three levels of spin. An added bit of oomph comes from the circular control in each car that allows the riders to control just how fast their car spins.

The cars are designed to hold four adults but with kids aboard the number can increase; apparently the record is eight passengers in a car. The spin control works quite well and with some vigorous turning you can add quite a bit of momentum to your brief spin cycle whirl. Even if you skip the ride, it's worth strolling back here to take a peek at the back end of *Hulk.*

Tip: To get the full effect of the strobe lights that represent Storm's lightning, ride this one at night.

And all the rest . . .

Kingpin's Arcade, admittedly, seems less out of place here than its equivalents elsewhere. That's because the world of video games is, after all, a comic book world and some of the machines in here represent the current state of the art in this genre. The games run on tokens that you can obtain from a vending machine. No refunds are given so you're forced to use them all, which might not be all that much of a challenge since some of the fancier games require six tokens. If you ride *Doctor Doom's Fearfall,* you will exit through this incredibly loud emporium. Look for the hole blasted in the wall that leads to Cafe 4.

Several times a day, according to a schedule listed in the 2-Park Guide Map, there is a **Character Meet and Greet** in the plaza opposite the entrance to the *Spider-Man* ride. Several characters from the X-Men comics — Rogue, Storm, Cyclops, and Wolverine — along with Spidey and Captain America, ride out in a parade of all-terrain three-wheelers to give autographs and pose photogenically with your kids. Unlike the costumed cartoon characters encountered elsewhere, these heroes will actually talk to you. However, if it's raining, they will be afraid to emerge from their backstage garage.

Eating in Marvel Super Hero Island

In keeping with the style of Marvel Comics, the food choices here are pared down and straightforward. Walk-up stands with names like **Ice Cream, Frozen Ice**, **Fruit**, and **Cotton Candy** sell exactly what their names suggest for a few bucks. Only slightly more elaborate are two cafeteria-like restaurants.

■ Cafe 4

What:	Italian food cafeteria style
Where:	Straight ahead as you come from Port of Entry
Price Range:	$

That huge gizmo that dominates the center of Cafe 4 and looks like a gigantic prop from a laboratory in a sci-fi movie beams colorful floating images of the Fantastic Four onto the curved ceiling above. The colorful mural behind the gizmo serves as a fitting welcome to this ultramodern cafeteria.

Judging by the menu, the Fantastic Four must be Italian food fans. Pizza is sold as nine-inch individual pies ($8 to $9, or $12 for a combo). The BBQ chicken pizza is especially tasty. You'll also find standard pasta dishes and a meatball sub. You can get a Caesar salad as a $4 side dish or with chicken as a $9 entree.

A spaghetti meal is offered for kids 11 and under. Breadsticks with marinara dipping sauce and entree-sized Caesar salads round out the Italian theme. Desserts and draft beer are served here along with the usual array of soft drinks.

There's plenty of indoor seating but it can get loud when it's filled with noisy kids. There's also a fair amount of outdoor seating that can get loud because of the screams from *Incredible Hulk* riders. A hole torn in the wall leads to the video game arcade (see above).

■ **Captain America Diner**

What: All-American diner fare
Where: Near *Spider-Man*
Price Range: $

The food here is perfectly themed: All-American Burgers and Super Hero Sides. The Whopper-like burgers on sesame seed buns are actually pretty good, as are the Steak 'n' Shake-worthy onion rings. Chicken fingers, chicken salad, and sandwiches are also served. Any diner worth its salt should serve milk shakes and this one does, chocolate and vanilla; they are also quite good. In keeping with the all-American theme, apple pie is served for dessert.

The decor is techno-modern, with steel seats and metal benches in the booths and huge mural-like depictions of characters from the Captain America comics looming overhead. There are two circular dining areas with tall walls of windows looking out to the Great Inland Sea. A small outdoor seating area is right on the Sea and makes a great place to eat, if you don't mind the occasional freeloading bird. These seats not only look out to The Lost Continent, but also offer one of the best vantage points for watching riders on *Hulk*.

Shopping in Marvel Super Hero Island

The shops here tend to mix and match their wares and styles come and go, so take the following notes with a grain of salt.

The **Comics Shop** is your chance to fill in that unfortunate gap in your literary education by immersing yourself in the Marvel universe. Colorful wall displays feature the last two or three issues of virtually every title in the Marvel comic line. You can also get large format paperback collections and novelizations based on popular characters. For collectors without the big bucks needed to acquire the real thing, there are hardbound, full-color volumes containing reprinted classic issues of titles such as *The Avengers*, *X-Men*, *Spider-Man*, and other Marvel properties. The selection of titles available is constantly changing so you might not find your favorites on the shelves when you visit.

Collectible — and high-priced — Marvel figurines and electric guitars (?!?) are also available. T-shirts, toys, and the standard Marvel souvenirs round out the offerings here.

The vest-pocket **Oakley** shop sells high-end sunglasses and watches bearing the Oakley logo and other ultra-hip brand names for $95 to $650.

They also stock backpacks, just in case you have any money left.

Amazing Pictures is a small kiosk next to the *Spider-Man* ride. Here you can get your portrait snapped and have your face artfully superimposed in a variety of scenes and magazine covers. Trying it out is free; if you love the results, it will cost $40 and up to have prints made.

You can't miss the **Spider-Man Shop** unless you're foolish enough to skip the *Spider-Man* ride. (If you're entering from the street, look for the "5 & Dime" sign.) T-shirts, mugs, and Spider-Man action figures form the bulk of the merchandise on display. Those who really identify with Spidey can also pick up Spider-Man figurines, toys, glasses, and key rings. Spidey lacks an on-ride **photo op** (odd, since the webslinger snaps your picture at the end) but if you took advantage of the photo op in the *Spider-Man* queue, you can stop by the Photo Connect desk at one end of the shop and get prints.

Across the street, the **Marvel Alterniverse Store** offers pretty much the same range of merchandise as the Spider-Man Shop, except it focuses on Thor, Iron Man, the Hulk, and other Avengers characters. In other words, this is Marvel T-shirt central, and if you're into this sort of thing, the assortment is fabulous. For the well-to-do kid, there are figurines and collectibles costing several hundred dollars. More affordable are videos, mugs, and action figures for younger kids. In the back of the store, you can have your photo taken with Spidey in front of a green screen that is replaced by an appropriately animated background in the purchased print.

CHAPTER FOUR:

(ITYWALK

Orlando's nightlife epicenter has shifted several times over the decades. In the 1970s and 1980s, downtown's historic Church Street Station was world-famous for its entertainment. It's gone now, put out of business, some say, by Disney's Pleasure Island in the 1990s. Pleasure Island is gone, too, put out of business, some say, by CityWalk. While Disney attempts to recapture the spotlight with its new Disney Springs area, the preferred place for post-attraction partying is at Universal Orlando's CityWalk, a happening enclave of heavily themed restaurants, nightclubs, shops, and movie theaters that rocks long after the nearby theme parks have closed up for the night. A 2014 expansion that introduced a number of new dining concepts, including some casual dining venues that combine exceptional food quality with bargain prices, has made the place more popular than ever.

Orientation

The layout and setting of CityWalk is ingenious. It is a 30-acre lozenge-shaped area plopped right down between Universal Studios Florida and Islands of Adventure. It is impossible to get from your car to either of the parks without passing through CityWalk and unless you take the *Hogwarts Express* (see *Chapter Two*) you will also have to traipse through CityWalk when switching parks. On top of that, a river runs through it — or rather a man-made waterway that separates most of CityWalk from the theme parks and links CityWalk to the Hard Rock and Portofino Bay Hotels and the Royal Pacific Resort.

Most of the buildings in CityWalk are arrayed along the perimeter closest to the parking structures, facing in toward the waterway. There are three

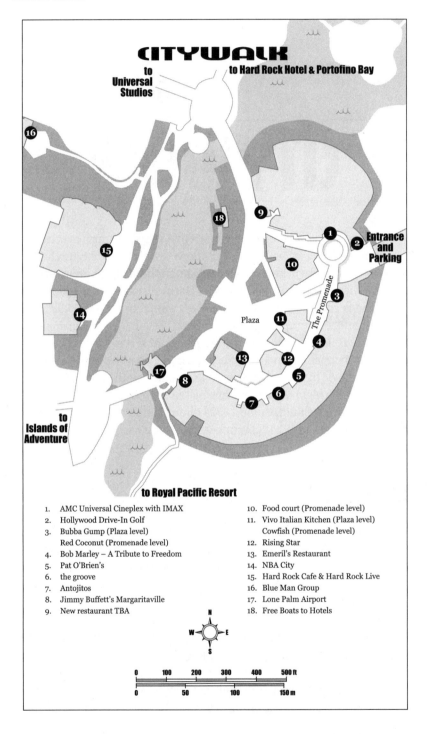

1. AMC Universal Cineplex with IMAX
2. Hollywood Drive-In Golf
3. Bubba Gump (Plaza level)
   Red Coconut (Promenade level)
4. Bob Marley – A Tribute to Freedom
5. Pat O'Brien's
6. the groove
7. Antojitos
8. Jimmy Buffett's Margaritaville
9. New restaurant TBA
10. Food court (Promenade level)
11. Vivo Italian Kitchen (Plaza level)
    Cowfish (Promenade level)
12. Rising Star
13. Emeril's Restaurant
14. NBA City
15. Hard Rock Cafe & Hard Rock Live
16. Blue Man Group
17. Lone Palm Airport
18. Free Boats to Hotels

major streets: a straight avenue that leads from the parking structures, a curving boulevard that leads from Universal Studios to Islands of Adventure near the waterway, and the Promenade that runs past the major nightclubs. Smaller streets wind between CityWalk's few freestanding buildings; one of these is a zigzag stairway that descends from the upper exit of the Cineplex to the waterway. It used to be called Lombard Street and that's how it will be referred to in this chapter because "Zigzag Stairway with No Name" is awkward. Along the waterway runs an esplanade in the middle of which is an outdoor performance space for special concerts and other events. Also along this esplanade is a dock where you can pick up a complimentary motor launch for the short trip to the resort hotels.

Smack dab in the middle of CityWalk is a large open space called simply the Plaza. On one side, a series of grass and stone platforms descends toward the water, forming a seating area for the performance space at water's edge. On the other, a stage sits over a sloping, waterfall-like fountain. At one of the two you are likely to find a D.J. or cover band entertaining the passing crowd with high-decibel tunes. From time to time you may see other off-the-wall entertainers — jugglers, stilt-walkers, and the like — roaming the grounds spreading smiles and good cheer.

Also in the Plaza is a street-level "fountain" consisting of several rows of hidden water jets that send up columns of water of various heights, at various times, in various patterns. It is seldom without a crowd of young kids and adults old enough to know better dodging and weaving through its liquid columns, getting thoroughly drenched.

With one exception, the nightclubs in CityWalk are located along the Promenade, which rises gradually from Plaza level, curving behind the Plaza, to the upper exit from the Cineplex. This clever arrangement makes the nightclub area a separate and easily policed enclave within an enclave. The exception is Hard Rock Live (a concert hall more than a nightclub), which is connected to the Hard Rock Cafe and lies across the waterway along a short walkway that connects Universal Studios Florida and Islands of Adventure.

Getting Information

It's not particularly easy to get information about what's going on at City-Walk prior to your visit. On the Internet, you can try visiting www.city-walkorlando.com, a poorly organized and hard to navigate site maintained by Universal Orlando. You'll be better off monitoring ads in the *Orlando*

Sentinel's Friday Calendar section and the free *Orlando Weekly*, which also carry listings of many CityWalk entertainment events. The main CityWalk number for "additional information" is (407) 363-8000. Press 1, then 5 and follow the automated prompts for an extensive inventory of recorded announcements about CityWalk's various restaurants and clubs. For dining reservations, dial (407) 224-3663 or surf to OpenTable.com.

Arriving at CityWalk

You arrive at CityWalk just as you would arrive for a visit to the theme parks. You park in the same parking structures and pay the same parking fee. Of course, you also have the option of valet parking, if you wish (see *Chapter One*).

If you arrive between 6:00 p.m. and 10:00 p.m., parking will be $5 (**free** for Florida residents). Parking after 10:00 p.m. is **free** for everyone. If you are arriving just for lunch and plan to stay for less than two hours, valet parking is free with restaurant validation (see below).

You enter CityWalk itself down a long broad avenue that passes by the Cineplex on your right (see map, above). That bridge you pass under is the Promenade and it leads from the upper exit of the Cineplex past CityWalk's string of nightclubs. An escalator to the bridge is available if you can't wait.

Note: If you are arriving by motor launch from one of the resort hotels, you will disembark at a dock near the bridge to Universal Studios.

Also by the bridge and the escalator is a kiosk called **Dining Reservations and CityWalk Information**. Here you can peruse menus of the various CityWalk restaurants, make dining reservations and priority seating requests (a process described below), and get pretty decent advice on how to plan your evening. Pick up here a brochure called **City Guide**, which is published monthly. It contains a colorful if hard-to-read map of the enclave and an extremely helpful list of events at the various clubs. You can also pick up a 2-Park Guide Map for the theme parks, although they sometimes run out.

Just past the bridge, on your left, you will see the **Guest Services** window; come here with questions and problems. A short walk will bring you to the Plaza, CityWalk's broad open center. From here you proceed straight ahead to Islands of Adventure, turn right to head to Universal Studios Florida, or turn left to make your way to the Promenade and the nightclubs.

The Price of Admission

Officially, there is no admission to CityWalk, but that's only partially true. First, if you are coming to Universal Orlando just to visit CityWalk, there's the parking fee to consider — unless, of course, you arrive after 10:00 p.m., which may be the perfect time to begin a visit to what is primarily a night-time attraction. More importantly, CityWalk's biggest draws, the nightclubs, all levy a $7 cover charge for the live evening entertainment starting at 9:00 p.m. Hard Rock Cafe never charges a cover, even when there's entertainment (which is rarely), and Hard Rock Live is not really a nightclub, so cover charges don't apply there. The Cineplex also charges admission.

If you are coming simply to enjoy the pleasures of CityWalk, you have a choice of paying each cover or admission charge individually or purchasing a one-day **CityWalk Party Pass**, which is sort of an "open sesame" to all the entertainment venues except Hard Rock Live, which always charges its own, separate admission. The Party Pass costs $12.77 (tax included); annual passholders receive a 20% discount; Premier passholders get **free** club admission. A Party Pass plus a movie at the AMC Cineplex is $15.88; if you want to see a 3D film, Imax, or IMAX 3D you will have to pay an upgrade fee at the box office.

If you have purchased a FlexTicket or any multi-day pass to the theme parks (a very likely scenario), then you already have 14 consecutive days of access to CityWalk's clubs, starting on the day you first use your ticket or pass. Be aware that the Party Pass will not be honored at clubs with special events and some clubs will occasionally levy an additional cover charge on Party Pass holders. To purchase your Party Pass, turn left at the Plaza and look for the box office windows outside the groove discotheque. If these windows are closed, check with the Guest Services window near the restrooms behind the information kiosk.

CityWalk also offers two "Deals" combining a meal at Fusion Sushi, Bob Marley, Pat O'Brien's, or Margaritaville and an entertainment activity. The **Meal & Movie Deal** ($21.95 including tax and gratuity) merges dinner with a standard Cineplex ticket (upgradable to 3-D or IMAX for an additional fee). The **Meal & Mini-Golf Deal** ($23.95 including tax and gratuity) gets you grub and 18 holes on the Hollywood Drive-In greens. The selection of entrees offered is limited to about a half-dozen options at each restaurant; a non-alcoholic beverage is included, but not appetizer or dessert. Standbys like Margaritaville's Cheeseburger in Paradise are on the menu, but so are more exciting options including Fusion sushi rolls, Bob Marley's curry chicken, and Pat O'Brien's jambalaya.

What's The Best Price?

If you purchased a multi-day theme park pass then price is not a consideration: 14 consecutive days of CityWalk club access is included. Go. Boogie. Enjoy. Otherwise, you may want to spend a few moments considering your options. If you plan on visiting most, if not all, of the clubs on a single night, the Party Pass is a fabulous deal. Of course, it's nearly impossible to visit all the clubs in one night, so you'll miss a lot. But even if you only visit two, the Party Pass pays for itself.

However, be aware that it is possible to visit two clubs and pay only one cover charge. It works like this: The cover charge clicks in at 9:00 p.m., but they don't go around from table to table to collect the cover from those already in the club. So you could arrive at, say, Marley's half an hour before the cover takes effect, grab a good seat, and catch the first show. Then you could move on to, say, Rising Star, paying the $7 cover there. If you call it a night then, you've only spent $7 in cover charges and saved a little money — $5.77 to be exact.

Since the additional cost of a Party Pass is so small, why not go for it? That way you can satisfy your morbid curiosity about clubs you otherwise wouldn't try. And who knows? You might discover a place you really love.

Good Things To Know About . . .

■ Discounts

Your Universal Orlando Annual Pass is good for a 20% discount for up to four people on the CityWalk Party Pass. At some times of the year (which seem to vary), your Annual Pass is good for a complimentary Party Pass from Sunday to Thursday. A Preferred Annual Pass will also get you a 10% discount on food and beverages (excluding alcohol) at many restaurants and clubs, and 2-for-1 beer at the groove; Premier passholders get an additional 5% (except at Bubba Gump) plus 2-for-1 well liquor at the groove and Rising Star.

Members of the American Automobile Association (AAA) are eligible for discounts at some restaurants (indicated in the City Guide brochure) and shops. However, which card gets what discount where is subject to constant change, so the best policy for the traveling tightwad is to ask about discounts every time you have to pay for something.

■ Drinking

The legal drinking age in Florida is 21 and the law is strictly enforced in City-Walk. The official policy is to "card" (i.e. ask for identification) anyone who appears under 30. So if you fall into this category make sure to bring along a photo ID such as a driver's license or passport to prove your age. Once you've passed muster, your server will attach a paper bracelet to your wrist, so you don't have to produce ID for the rest of the evening.

Alcoholic beverages are sold quite openly on the streets of CityWalk and from walk-up stands at the various clubs along the Promenade. To prevent those over 21 from purchasing drinks for underage friends, a standard policy is to sell one drink per person. Just to make sure, CityWalk maintains a very visible security presence (see below).

■ First Aid

And speaking of drinking, if you fall down and injure yourself, or have another health problem, there is a first aid station located near Guest Services. Just follow the passage to the restrooms and look for the door at the end of the passage.

■ Happy Hour

Happy hour ain't what it used to be. At press time, only three establishments were cutting drink prices — NBA City (4:00 to 7:00 p.m.), Emeril's (4:00 to 8:00 p.m.), and Red Coconut (4:00 to 9:00 p.m.). No word yet on happy hour at the new Cowfish restaurant.

■ Money

There is an ATM on your left as you enter CityWalk, near the Guest Services window. There are others just outside the upper exit from the Cineplex and near the groove.

■ Private Parties

Most of CityWalk's restaurants have facilities for private parties. The central number for information is (407) 224-CITY (2489) for groups of more than 20 and (407) 224-FOOD (3663) for smaller groups.

■ Reservations

All of the table-service restaurants except for Hard Rock Cafe and Bubba Gump accept reservations by phone at (407) 224-3663, or online through OpenTable.com. Emeril's accepts reservations up to six months in advance by calling (407) 224-2424.

Note: If you are a guest at one of Universal Orlando's luxury resort hotels, you can flash your room key card at the restaurant for priority seating at the first available table.

■ Restrooms

Most restrooms are inside the restaurants and nightclubs. You'll find "public" restrooms tucked away down corridors next to Guest Services, near Element, and near the groove on the Promenade.

■ Security

CityWalk's security is so pervasive and so visible that some people might wonder if there's something to be worried about. In addition to the in-house security staff with their white shirts emblazoned with the word "SECURITY," you will see armed members of the Orlando police force. What you won't see are the undercover security personnel who mingle with the crowds.

The primary mission of all these security elements is to prevent any abuse of state liquor laws. For example, while you can stroll around City-Walk with your beer or cocktail, you are not allowed to carry it back to your car or into the parks.

■ Valet Parking and Validation

Most restaurants will validate your valet parking ticket during lunch hour (11:00 a.m. to 2:00 p.m. Monday through Friday only). A two-hour stay is free. Emeril's validates anytime including Saturdays and dinner. The Cineplex does not validate parking.

The Talk of the Town

Just as the theme parks have their must-see attractions, there are some very special things in CityWalk. No star ratings are supplied for CityWalk, but here is a highly subjective list of personal favorites in a number of categories.

Best food. Emeril's has to be the choice here. Best wine list, too. There's really no serious competition.

Best for foodies. Those looking for the next hot culinary trend should head straight for The Cowfish and its "burgushi" menu.

Best bar. Now that Cigarz with its funky bar at the back has closed, the bar at Hard Rock Cafe with its spinning Caddy has no serious competition.

Best happy hour. Emeril's wins this one hands down. Fine wine and fabulous hors d'oeuvres at bargain prices.

Best food value. When you factor in what you pay for what you get, the modest Bread Box takes the prize, with Pat O'Brien's and Red Oven Pizza Bakery close behind.

Best place to take the kids. Hard Rock Cafe is the best, but NBA City and Margaritaville have kid-friendly aspects.

Friendliest service. Bubba Gump.

Best burgers. The Hard Rock Cafe. Have yours with one of their rich chocolate milk shakes.

Best dessert. Emeril's elaborate creations take the cake in this category.

Best for the midnight munchies. Finding food after midnight is not always possible. The Hot Dog Hall of Fame is open till one on weekends., but if Pat O'Brien's is serving late, that's the clear winner. Otherwise, check Margaritaville, or the food court upstairs.

Most romantic. If you're idea of "romantic" is letting your date know you're dropping a bundle on the meal, then Emeril's is the place for you. For free romance, take a moonlight cruise to the resort hotels on a shuttle boat.

Most fun. Jimmy Buffett's Margaritaville, with its wild and wacky decor and exploding volcano, wins the prize here.

Best decor. The retro styling (featuring a swimming pool-shaped dance floor) of the Red Coconut Club is marvelously mod. The Hard Rock Cafe's memorabilia collection is equally memorable.

Coolest. The hip and witty Red Coconut Club is one of the best clubs in Orlando.

AMC Universal Cineplex 20 with IMAX

This is the mall multiplex writ large with 4,800 seats in 20 theaters on two stories. The soaring lobby is decorated with giant black and white banners depicting cinema heartthrobs, and escalators whisk you past them to the nine theaters upstairs. The theaters range in size from an intimate 150 seats to nearly 600. Expect the usual assortment of first-run action, horror, and gross-out comedy flicks with the very latest releases playing in multiple theaters. Universal rarely screens "art films" or foreign cinema, and it's a shame it doesn't dedicate one screen to fare outside the modern Hollywood mainstream. On the other hand, the Cineplex has regular midnight performances of cult classics like *The Rocky Horror Picture Show*.

All the theaters here have stadium seating with plush high-backed seats that rock gently, and the screens are about twice the size of those you are probably used to. The Cineplex shows "RealD" digital 3-D films, and you can keep the glasses. Every theater is also equipped with digital video projectors and Sony Dynamic Digital Sound (SDDS), touted as "the most advanced digital cinema sound system in the marketplace today." So all in all, catching a movie here is a viable option for a rainy Florida afternoon.

The "IMAX" here is what film nerds sneeringly call LIE-max. It's an all-digital version of the real 70mm IMAX format that is supposed to create the illusion of a much larger picture, but it isn't worth the premium for normal films. IMAX 3-D, on the other hand, is more immersive than its RealD competition, and may be worth the two extra bucks. If you want the "real" giant-screen IMAX experience, you'll have to drive down Universal Boulevard to Pointe Orlando's Regal Cinema.

Admission (including tax) for adults is $11.50 for evening shows; bargain matinees (all shows that start before 3:55 p.m.) are $9.75. Children 2 to 12 pay $8.75 "A.M. Cinema" (shows that start before noon on weekends and holidays) are $6.50. Seniors (60+) pay $10.50 ($6.50 on Tuesdays), and students pay $8.75 on Thursdays. Add an additional $4 per ticket for RealD 3-D, $5 for IMAX, and $6 for IMAX 3-D. Annual Pass holders save $3 on up to two tickets for shows after 4:00 p.m.

In addition to the regular box office windows, there are vending machines to your right that allow you to skip the line and purchase tickets, at no extra charge, using your credit card. More detailed information can be downloaded at amctheatres.com/universal or obtained from a human being by calling (407) 354-3374. Or purchase tickets in advance online at www.fandango.com. Fandango charges a "convenience fee" of "up to" $2; tickets can be printed out at home or picked up at the box office.

Don't worry about going hungry while you watch. There is the usual array of soft drinks, popcorn, and candy, all at inflated prices. More interesting are the mini-pizzas, nachos, and chicken fingers. There's even a coffee bar if you crave a latte and a full liquor bar serving up exotic cocktails and draft beer.

AMC's "Distraction-Free Entertainment" policy states, "In order to provide the most enjoyable experience for adults attending R-rated features in the evenings, no children younger than 6 will be admitted to these features after 6 p.m." Bravo!

Tip: You may want to exit on the upper level, even if you are seeing a film on the Cineplex's bottom level. From there you can either descend Lombard Street, lined with shops, or stroll along the sloping Promenade, home to CityWalk's row of restaurants and nightclubs.

Hollywood Drive-In Miniature Golf

Hollywood Drive-In is a pair of elaborately themed 18-hole mini-golf courses that Universal has smartly shoehorned into the narrow area near valet parking. Featuring detailed outdoor and indoor environments created by Universal's theme-park designers, these 36 greens go beyond any putt-putt you're likely to have at home. The theme of this attraction is inspired by the cheesy classics of the drive-in movie era, as you'll probably guess from the 40-foot tall robot and haunted house set-pieces. As guests play through "The Haunting of Ghostly Greens" or "Invaders from Planet Putt" they'll encounter movie-style sets and interactive effects straight out of a sci-fi or horror B-movie. Even the pop-music soundtrack is appropriately themed, with "Thriller" heard on one side, and "Rocket Man" on the other. LED lighting lets you golf through graveyards or putt through a flying saucer after dark, and adds immensely to the attraction's visual interest in the evenings. In another high-tech twist, you can keep score on your smartphone (instead of using stubby pencils) with a free app available for iOS and Android.

Despite the detailed decor, the course layouts themselves won't pose much challenge for seasoned mini-golfers. The surroundings are superb, but the obstacles themselves aren't particularly advanced. Of the two, I slightly prefer the "Invaders" side for its tricky television and turntable holes, and cow-probing humor, though it does require navigating short flights of steps. The "Haunting" side is fully accessible, but (aside from a water-squirting merman and Rube Goldberg-like laboratory finale) the effects are a little less special, and the incessant meows from the "pet cemetery" quickly grow annoying.

Guests can get a preview of the greens by looking down over the side of the moving walkway as they approach CityWalk from the parking garages. The entrance to the course is to the right of the Cineplex box offices. The courses are open daily from 9:00 a.m. to 2:00 a.m. Playing through a single 18-hole course is $14.99 (plus tax) for adults, $12.99 for kids; if you'd like to play both, the prices are $26.98 and $22.98 respectively. That's a few bucks more expensive per head than its competitors along I-Drive, and much pricier if you factor in parking. Online advance tickets from HollywoodDriveInGolf.com cost about $1 less per course, but can't be purchased and used on the same day. Annual passholders, seniors, military, Florida residents, and AAA members save 10% (15% for Premier passholders).

This is a fun, if somewhat pricey, diversion for families staying on-site and looking for a way to keep the kids occupied for an hour or so after sunset.

■ RESTAURANTS ■
AT CITYWALK

Some of CityWalk's restaurants offer terrific entertainment (usually at night) and some nightclubs serve excellent food. The main distinction seems to be that "restaurants" open earlier in the day (11:00 a.m. to 5:00 p.m.) and serve full meals, while "nightclubs" open in the late afternoon or early evening and serve only a limited food menu. Among the restaurants, Jimmy Buffett's Margaritaville offers Buffett-esque entertainment in the evening, Antojitos has a mariachi band, and NBA City screens great moments in basketball history all day. All the others are strictly dining establishments. All restaurants (except Emeril's) serve the same menu at the same prices all day.

Note: At press time, NASCAR Sports Grille, which occupied a prime location just across the bridge from the entrance to Universal Studios Florida, had closed with no replacement announced.

Tip: You will find a key to the Price Range symbols used below in *Chapter One: Planning Your Escape* under *A Note On Costs* (page 43).

Hard Rock Cafe

What: American casual cuisine
Where: Across the waterway
Price Range: $$ - $$$
Hours: 11:00 a.m. to midnight (shop opens 9:00 a.m.)
Reservations: "Priority Seating" available at HardRock.com/px
Web: www.hardrock.com

The immense structure across the water, with the peculiar hodgepodge architecture, the giant guitar sticking out of the facade, and the huge electric signs, is the world's largest and busiest Hard Rock Cafe. Those who have visited other Hard Rocks will know what to expect — just expect more of it. For the uninitiated, the Hard Rock Cafe is a celebration of rock and roll history and lifestyle that has become an international marketing and merchandising phenomenon. From its auspicious beginnings in London's Mayfair section, Hard Rock has grown to a mega-chain, with restaurants in virtually any city that has pretensions to world-class status.

The Hard Rock's primary claim to fame is its extensive and ever-growing collection of rock memorabilia that is lovingly and lavishly displayed. As befits the largest Hard Rock in the world, the Orlando outpost has some spectacular mementos. After your meal, take the time to wander about and drink it all in. The staff won't mind; they're used to it. If you're lucky, they will be running free tours of the memorabilia collection. If not, the ginormous interactive touch-screen video wall near the bar can give you historical details on every artifact in Hard Rock's vast inventory.

There is dark paneling and deep carpeting on the floors and winding wooden staircases. There are rich gold frames on the photos, album covers, gold records, and other memorabilia that fill every inch of wall space. "Rock and roll is here to stay," they like to say. "We've got it screwed to the walls!" Upstairs, take note of the two circular rooms, one at each end, dedicated to the Roots of Rock and Woodstock 1969. There's also an elegant wood-paneled library dedicated to The King.

At the heart of the restaurant, downstairs, is a circular bar open to the second level. A magnificent 1961 pink Cadillac convertible spins lazily over the bar and above that is a splendid ceiling mural straight out of some domed chapel at the Vatican. Except that here the saints being serenaded by the angels are all dead rock stars, most of whom died from drug overdoses. To one side is a trio of towering stained glass windows paying homage to Chuck Berry, Elvis Presley, and Jerry Lee Lewis. All in all, this expansive Hard Rock has the look and feel of a very posh and very exclusive men's club — which is perhaps what rock and roll is, after all.

Tip: If your party is small, the bar is an excellent place to eat. The bar offers the full menu and quicker seating when the place is crowded. A seat here gives you an excellent vantage point from which to soak up the ambiance. If the downstairs bar is full, there is another upstairs.

The Hard Rock Cafe is also justly famous for its American roadhouse cuisine, which gives a nod to the black and southern roots of rock. Burgers, barbecue, and steak are the keynotes, with sweet and homey touches like milk shakes, root beer floats, and outrageous sundaes. It's no wonder the place was an instant hit when it opened in the midst of London's culinary desert. The menu also reminds us that, in its heyday, rock's superstars were scarcely more than kids. This is teenybopper comfort food prepared by expert cooks for people who can afford the best.

Probably the heart of the menu is the selection of barbecue dishes ($14 to $28), with the chicken and ribs combo a popular favorite. For those who prefer their barbecue Carolina-style, there's a pulled-pork sandwich. A big step up in sophistication are steaks like the succulent New York Strip.

Of course, if you're still a teenager at heart, you'll order a burger ($13 to $16). The best is the Hickory BBQ Bacon Cheeseburger, but there's also a Veggie Leggie to keep Sir Paul happy. If you want to return to your pre-cholesterol-crisis youth, you'll have a milk shake or a root beer float with your burger. The fries that go with them are very good, too.

Tip: Root beer floats aren't on the menu, but they'll whip one up if you ask nicely.

Lighter appetites can be satisfied with one of the appetizers ($11 to $21) or a salad ($14 to $20), while bigger appetites can order a small Caesar salad to go with their entree. But save room for dessert ($5 to $9) because the HRC Hot Fudge Brownie lives up to its fabled reputation.

Your meal comes complete with a soundtrack, of course, and the excellent choice of songs leans heavily to the glory days of rock in the late sixties and early seventies. Flat-screen monitors dotted around the restaurant identify the album from which the current track is taken. The volume has been turned up (this is rock and roll, after all) but not so high as to make conversation impossible.

No self-respecting Hard Rock Cafe would be complete without a shop hawking Hard Rock merchandise, and this one sports a sparkling floor embedded with guitar picks and a sculpture of musical instruments suspended from the ceiling. Believe it or not, the shop occasionally has lines just like the restaurant and they are handled the same way, with a roped-off queue filled with people who can't wait to add another Hard Rock shot glass to their growing collection.

NBA City

What:	American casual cuisine
Where:	Across the waterway
Price Range:	$$ - $$$
Hours:	Sunday through Thursday 11:00 a.m. to 10:30 p.m.; Friday and Saturday to 11:30 p.m. During busy times they will stay open later.
Reservations:	(407) 363-5919 or OpenTable.com
Web:	www.nbacity.com

This modern mélange of weathered brick, steel, glass, and concrete is almost dwarfed by the statue of a dribbling basketball player that graces its entrance. Both the building and its interior evoke the ambiance and mystique of a classic 1940s-era basketball arena, and devotees of the game will find much to enjoy here.

The two-level dining area, dubbed the CityWalk Cage, seems intimate but it holds nearly 375 people at capacity. The floor is that of a highly polished basketball court filled with tables. In fact, this is a regulation half court that can be cleared of tables and booths so that visiting NBA stars can hold clinics with eager youngsters, while fans watch from the upper level. Two massive projection screens flank the hoop and multiple monitors dot the walls. A constant stream of taped highlights from championship seasons past plays during your meal, with the volume thoughtfully turned up for the hard of hearing. There is the occasional nod toward women's professional basketball, but the emphasis is plainly on the guys.

This is hardly the place for a quiet business discussion or a romantic tête-à-tête. But if your idea of a good time is watching your hoop heroes' finest moments while you drop food into your lap, you'll love it here.

If you'd like some relief from the general din, try the **Skybox Lounge**, a bar and lounge on the second level, to the front of the building. Its decor is that of a posh sports club with cushy sofas and banquettes. If you wish, they will serve your meal here. The Skybox Lounge also has an extensive menu of pricey specialty drinks, with price breaks offered Monday to Friday from 4:00 to 7:00 p.m. and on game days. The drinks, as well as a modest wine list ($25 to $55), are available in the main restaurant. There is another quiet refuge on the second level, a glassed-in wedge of a dining area that is sometimes set aside for VIPs and private parties, but you can ask for it and see.

The cuisine might be described as upscale sports bar, and the portions seem to have been designed to fill up those eight-foot-tall basketball behemoths. Eating a starter and an entree may well force you to skip the scrumptious desserts. Many people will find a starter plenty big enough for a satisfying meal.

Appetizers ($9 to $16) include such standards as chicken wings, tomato and mozzarella salad, and quesadillas. The Parmesan Chicken Tenders could make a full meal, with a biting mustard sauce worthy of the name. For the lighter appetite, entree salads ($10 to $15) are offered, with side salads and soup ($5) also available.

The main entrees ($17 to $34) lean heavily to hearty meat and fish dishes like pork chops, steak, and salmon. Pastas ($15 to $18) tend to feature chicken and fish, with shrimp priced slightly higher. Sandwich offerings ($11 to $13) include burgers, a Philly Cheesesteak and a Cajun-spiced grilled mahi mahi. Ten-inch personal pizzas ($11 to $14) round out the menu. A "Rookie Menu" for kids features a small choice of entrees and a drink for $8.

Among the desserts ($6 to $10), the star is an NBA City original, the

Cinnamon Berries. Exquisitely ripe strawberries are dipped in batter, flash fried, coated in cinnamon sugar, and elegantly displayed in a circle on a bed of vanilla cream filigreed with strawberry sauce; a dollop of vanilla ice cream in a cinnamon tortilla cup topped with another fresh strawberry forms the centerpiece. It may sound a little weird but it's delicious.

Tip: The food and drink are only part of the fun here. In fact, you don't have to have a meal to enjoy NBA City. The entrance is flanked by a display of bronze basketballs bearing the handprints of basketball greats. If you've ever wondered why you're not in the NBA, losing your own hand in these massive prints will give you a hint. Inside, before you enter the dining room, you'll find the **NBA City Playground,** a place where you can test your free-throw skills and, if you're good enough, get some fleeting fame on the electronic scoreboard.

There is also a shop filled with NBA-branded clothing, personalized jerseys, and novelty items. This area stays open for about an hour after the restaurant stops serving.

Jimmy Buffett's Margaritaville

What:	Casual food with an island flair
Where:	Near the bridge to Islands of Adventure
Price Range:	$$ - $$$
Hours:	11:30 a.m. to 2:00 a.m. (full menu until 10:00 p.m., to 11:00 p.m. at busy times)
Reservations:	(407) 224-2155 or OpenTable.com
Web:	www.margaritavilleorlando.com

After crossing the bridge from Islands of Adventure and the NBA Restaurant, this is the first place you encounter in the main section of CityWalk, and a welcoming joint it is. Owned by singing star Jimmy Buffett and reflecting the easygoing themes of his popular songs, Margaritaville is a hymn to the laid-back life of the Parrot Head.

Probably the first thing you'll notice is the Hemisphere Dancer, the actual Grumman Albatross Jimmy immortalized in his book *A Pirate Looks At Fifty.* Today it serves as an over-the-top prop for **Lone Palm Airport,** a walk-up bar with a kids' play area and outdoor seating (see *Fast Food at CityWalk,* below).

After a fortifying drink, you'll be ready to step inside. The various sections of the bar-restaurant are decorated to reflect Jimmy's many interests and the songs he wrote about them. The **Volcano Bar** answers the question, "Where you gonna go when the volcano blows?" Every 45 minutes or so the volcano atop the bar rumbles ominously to life and spews out bubbling margarita mix that cascades down the slopes into a huge blender on the bar.

In the restaurant section, the booths are styled to evoke the back end of a fishing boat. Look up and you'll see a model of the Hemisphere Dancer. Huge whales and hammerheads "swimming" overhead decorate another bar section. Outside, facing Islands of Adventure, is the **Porch of Indecision**, a verandah seating area that features a live guitarist nightly. Buffett fans will enjoy spotting the insider references scattered through the decor while others will be having too much fun to care.

The "Floribbean" cuisine draws its inspiration from all aspects of Buffett's life story, from his Gulf Shore roots to his Caribbean island-hopping. The food also reflects the atmosphere of the ultra-casual, off-the-beaten-track island bars where Buffett used to perform, chow down, and waste away.

For starters or a light meal, check the Appetizers and the Bites sections ($6 to $16). Conch fritters were off the menu on a recent visit, but they'll still serve them up if you ask. The corn and crab chowder ($6) is also quite good. Regulars swear by the Volcano Nachos ($16), which can make a full meal. Of the entrees ($17 to $26), the jambalaya and the coconut shrimp are winners. At the high end are the New York Strip Steak and Black Grouper. Salads ($14 to $17) are, as the prices suggest, substantial and include a fried chicken Cobb salad (broiled chicken on request).

The Cheeseburger in Paradise ($12), alas, is merely a large but otherwise undistinguished example of the genre. Far better are choices like the Key West Fish Sandwich ($17). There's good news on the desserts. The Key Lime Pie ($8) is a winner and the Chocolate Hurricane at $16.50 might be the best bargain on the menu if you can round up five friends. The mammoth concoction of ice cream, brownies, Kit Kats, and Heath bars, along with healthy touches like bananas, whipped cream, and macadamia nuts, is served on a lazy susan and feeds up to six.

There are separate menus for kids, vegetarians, and the gluten free.

Those more interested in wasting away than in dining can peruse the lavish list of margaritas ($8.50 to $12.50) and other specialty drinks ($9 to $13), many of which are available in non-alcoholic versions for less. If you're having difficulty deciding, I'd recommend the Margarita Flight ($17), four different versions including Last Mango in Paris. There's less variety in the wine and beer categories, although Margaritaville's own Landshark Lager has gained a following.

A restaurant by day, Margaritaville transforms itself after the dinner crowd thins out into a cross between a nightclub and a full-fledged performance space showcasing bands and live performers that reflect in one way or another that certain indescribable Jimmy Buffett style. The house bands here are very good, alternating between Buffett standards and a mix of ca-lypso, easy-going rock, and country-western. Every great once in a while, Buffett himself drops by.

Jimmy Buffett has been very savvy in marketing himself, so it's no sur-prise that there's a very well stocked gift shop, the **Margaritaville Smug-gler's Hold**, attached to the restaurant with a second entrance from the Plaza. Here Parrot Heads can fill in the gaps in their Buffett CD collection or buy one of his books (he's a pretty good writer it turns out). In addition, there are plenty of T-shirts, gaudy Hawaiian shirts, and miscellaneous ac-cessories that the well-dressed beach bum simply can't afford to be without.

Emeril's Restaurant Orlando

What:	Gourmet dining
Where:	On the Plaza
Price Range:	$$$ - $$$$+
Hours:	Lunch 11:30 a.m. to 3:00 p.m.; dinner 5:00 p.m. to 10:00 p.m. Sunday through Thursday; to 10:30 p.m. Friday and Saturday; happy hour 4:00 p.m. to 8:00 p.m. daily
Reservations:	Recommended. Call (407) 224-2424, fax (407) 224-2525, or OpenTable.com
Web:	www.emerilsrestaurants.com/emerils-orlando/

Emeril Lagasse, the popular TV chef and cookbook author, brings his upscale New Orleans cuisine to Orlando in this lavish eatery decorated (if that's the word) with over 10,000 bottles of wine in climate-controlled glass-walled wine cases. This is an extremely handsome restaurant that evokes and improves upon Emeril's converted warehouse premises in the Big Easy. The main dining room soars to a curved wooden roof and the lavish use of glass on the walls facing the Plaza makes this a bright and sunny spot for lunch. The exposed steel support beams contrast with the stone walls and rich wood accents, while stark curved metal chandeliers arch gracefully overhead. It's a hip, modern look that matches the food and the clientele.

The cuisine is Creole-based, but the execution is sophisticated and the presentation elaborate. Many dishes are based on home-style comfort foods like barbecue, fried fish, or gumbos, and there's an unmistakable spiciness to much of it. Just about everything is elaborately garnished and served with a flourish. The result is a cuisine that is fun and festive with only the occasional tendency toward self-conscious seriousness, making Emeril's a great choice for a celebratory blowout.

Despite its noisy, bistro-like atmosphere, this is a first-class restaurant where dining is theater and a full meal can last two and a half hours, with the per-person cost, with drinks and wine, easily rising to over $100. In the European fashion, Emeril's closes after lunch to allow the kitchen a chance to catch its breath and ready itself for a different and more extensive dinner menu.

Lunch is far more casual than dinner — cheaper, too! — with most of the menu given over to appetizers ($6 to $13), salads ($10 to $11), burgers and sandwiches ($14 to $16), and pizzas ($10 to $12). Among the appetizers, the New Orleans barbecue shrimp is a standout and the daily gumbo is always worth asking about. Pizzas include variations you're unlikely to encounter elsewhere such as curried vegetable and confit mushroom.

There are only half a dozen or so entrees ($13 to $18) on the lunch menu but they include such winners as andouille-crusted trout, Brazilian seafood stew, and Emeril's take on spaghetti carbonara. At these price points they are real bargains. Occasionally, a buy-an-entree-get-a-free-appetizer-or-dessert deal is offered, making lunch virtually irresistible.

At dinner, the menu (and the prices) are "kicked up a notch," as Emeril might say, although the price points, especially for starters, are somewhat lower than they once were. Appetizers ($9 to $14) include New Orleans barbecue shrimp, fried green tomatoes, and smoked wild & exotic mushrooms. Soups and salads ($5 to $13) typically include a sturdy gumbo, chowder, and some artfully presented and deceptively simple green salads.

Entrees are pricier and more elaborate than at lunch. Fish and shellfish dishes ($25 to $32) include Florida black drum stew, roasted Atlantic swordfish, and sea scallops and jumbo shrimp served with gingered butternut squash. Meat dishes ($24 to $49) include a panko-gorgonzola crusted filet mignon, a chicken breast with an andouille-potato hash, duck confit spaghetti, and a 16-ounce ribeye with smoked paprika fries.

Desserts ($8 to $10) are equally elaborate, although it says something about the chef that his signature dessert is a homey banana cream pie served with chocolate shavings on a latticework of caramel sauce. There is a kids' menu, ranging from $7 tortellini to an $18 petite filet mignon for your budding gourmet.

Dining here is a special experience. Emeril's is not the kind of place where you will feel comfortable in full tourist regalia, even though the management officially draws the line only at tank tops and flip-flops. Stop back at your hotel to change and freshen up.

Tip: If you are dining alone or there are just two of you, you might want to try the "Food Bar," a short counter with stools that looks into the kitchen. The primo dining location is the L-shaped area by the windows; VIPs are seated here, so reserve well in advance if it's your preference.

Emeril's, by the way, is strictly a restaurant; there is no entertainment. For most people, the tongue-tingling food will be entertainment enough.

If you want to sample Emeril's but still stay within your budget, come for lunch or visit the bar for the daily happy hour (4:00 to 8:00 p.m.), when discount small plates and half-price beer, wine, and cocktails are available.

When Emeril's first opened it was the hottest table in town and tables were hard to come by. Those days have passed and it is often possible to walk in without a reservation and be seated at all but the busiest times. Still, if you know you want to dine here why risk disappointment? Make a reservation. If you can't plan ahead and can't get a same day reservation, try showing up early and asking for a seat at the bar; you can order from the whole menu there. It's always easier to get a table at lunch.

Antojitos

What:	Joyously loud Mexican eatery
Where:	Between the groove and Jimmy Buffett's
Price Range:	$$ - $$$
Hours:	5:00 p.m. to 11:00 p.m. (to midnight Friday and Saturday)

Reservations: (407) 224-2155 or OpenTable.com

Antojitos is the Mexican term for the kind of food you'd buy from a street vendor — tacos, enchiladas, tortas, gorditas, and the like — as opposed to what you'd eat at a sit down meal. Here the concept is stretched to encompass just about everything Americans have come to associate with Mexican food, from mammoth servings of sauce-smothered enchiladas to $90-a-shot premium tequila, making this more of a Tex-Mex joint than the "authentic" Mexican it claims to be. But who wants to quibble at a place this much fun?

The fun begins with the towering restaurant facade, which looks rather like a Spanish mission church after the next door paint factory has exploded. A painted VW minivan has been converted into a bar to serve patrons on the restaurant's patio. The first thing you notice on entering is the noise, followed by a riot of color and Mexican-street-style graffiti across the walls and ceilings. The ground floor dining area is wide open and bustling with a raised stage that hosts a mariachi band. There is a balcony with great views of the stage that is equally noisy. You can get some relief from the din (if you must) in private dining rooms upstairs or on the balcony overlooking the Promenade, an excellent choice in balmy weather.

If you're a regular Tex-Mex diner, very little on the menu will be new to you, although the churrasco steak with chimichurri sauce hails from Argentina and the tempura BBQ shrimp taco (quite good, actually) hails from who knows where. What might come as a pleasant surprise are the moderate prices. On the downside, the lighting in the main dining area tends to give your food a distinctly unappetizing hue.

You can start your meal with made-at-your-table guacamole (a restaurant affectation that may have already run its course) or choose from other "apertivos" ($8 to $16) such as Chicken Tinga Zarape, Tamales Hidalgo, or the mammoth Nachos Totopos. Enchiladas, tacos, and fajitas ($14 to $20) each enjoy their own section on the menu. The Enchilada Oaxaca with its rich mole sauce, the aforementioned BBQ Shrimp Taco, and the Grilled Skirt Steak Fajitas are all good bets.

The most expensive section of the menu is Comidas de la Casa ($14 to $27), which roughly translates as "home-cooked meals." The Combinacion Maya, a pork tamale, enchilada verde, and an ancho chili stuffed with carnitas, is perhaps the best choice, although the more expensive Churrasco Steak is nothing to sneer at. By the way, perhaps the most authentic item on the menu is the Coca-Cola imported from Mexico. It's made with real sugar rather than the corn syrup used Stateside and is much treasured by true Coke fiends.

Desserts ($4.50 to $5.50) are, alas, merely so-so. The Caramelized Banana Bread Pudding is a disappointment and the Mamey ice cream doesn't help. Coffee & Churros (actually, coffee creme bruleé and churros) may be the safest choice.

There is one area in which Antojitos shines — its selection of tequilas (and the drinks made therefrom). Tequila fanciers will feel like they've died and gone to heaven — and they probably will if they try to sample everything on offer on one visit! Of course, they might go broke first since many "ultra-premiums" are north of $50 a shot. Adventurous cocktail drinkers can sample margaritas made with sriracha hot sauce, agave nectar, miscellaneous fruits, and other ingredients ($10 to $13).

The mariachi band holds forth in the evenings and, if you like this sort of thing, they are a lot of fun, but if you linger over dinner you might hear duplicate sets. If mariachi music is not to your taste, ask for a table on the upstairs balcony.

The Cowfish Sushi Burger Bar

What: Burger-sushi mashup

Where: On the Promenade opposite Bob Marley's

Price Range: $$ - $$$

Hours: Not determined at press time

Reservations: None, but there's an app to get on the wait list

Web: www.thecowfish.com

Note: At press time, Cowfish was still under construction. What follows is based on the restaurant's existing locations and menus.

So you love sushi, but your boyfriend is a meat and potatoes kind of guy? Or is it the other way around? It's a common dining conundrum and a pair of restaurant entrepreneurs from North Carolina have come up with a solution designed to keep everyone happy — an inventive menu with separate sections for burgers, sushi (traditional and "fusion"), and a mashup of both called "burgushi."

The two-level Cowfish dominates the Plaza. There are two entrances. From the Plaza, an elevator takes guests to the second floor and the main dining room while an entrance on the Promenade gives access to three bars and a smaller dining area. Inside, the bright primary colors and a small fish-bowl-shaped aquarium filled with real cowfish set the tone for a fun dining experience. Adding to the fun are interactive screens inlaid into the main bar that let guests design their own fish and then release them into a virtual aquarium. At 500 seats, The Cowfish is the largest dining venue in City-Walk.

Sushi lovers can choose from sashimi, nigiri, honomaki, makimono, and cone-style hand rolls ($8 to $15). Combos are available for $15 to $28. These are all traditional sushi memes, guaranteed fresh, antibiotic free, and using locally sourced ingredients whenever possible. For the less traditional or more adventurous, there is a selection of Fusion Specialties, which are entree sized rolls, cut into nine pieces ($14 to $19). They include such tempting choices as the Two-Time Roll, slices of cucumber wrapped around yellowfin tuna, avocado, kani, and asparagus, topped with blackened tuna, spicy mayo, and tobiko, with ponzu sauce on the side. Then there's the Birkenstocky Shiitaki Maki with the eponymous mushroom, portabella, red pepper, and cucumber wrapped in brown rice and quinoa.

Burger lovers should be delighted with the hefty half-pound versions served up here ($10 to $16). There are some fairly standard burgers on offer, even a veggie burger, but most employ a medley of toppings that range from the intriguing to the bizarre. There's cheddar, boursin, feta, brie, chevre, and other cheeses; then there's applewood bacon, black forest ham, sauteed mushrooms and the like, along with sauces like chipotle aioli, tzatziki sauce, and avocado salsa. But nothing can match the Hunka Hunka — a burger topped with creamy peanut butter, fried bananas, and applewood bacon on a brioche bun. And if the versions on the menu don't do it for you, there is a bewildering array of Substitutions and Additions that will allow you to create your own over the top sensation. There are a few sandwiches other than burgers on the menu, including the Screamin' Korean Chicken, spiced with kimchi and sriracha ranch dressing.

But nothing will attract more attention or animated discussion than the Burgushi section. Here Cowfish chefs have attempted, like mad scientists, to combine disparate species into a whole new animal. Nature Boy's Wooooo-shi Buffalooooo-shi Roll [sic] combines chipotle bison, fried green tomatoes, grilled onions, and feta cheese, sprinkles it with tempura flakes, wraps it all in sushi rice and tops the resulting roll with fresh green tomato, jalapeño pepper, red onion, and chipotle aioli. The What's Shakin' Tuna Bacon Sandwich uses spring roll wrappers stuffed with kani and sushi rice to make "buns" for a sandwich of yellowfin tuna and applewood bacon.

Like the menu says: "Open your mind and your taste buds."

Vivo Italian Kitchen

What: Upscale Italian
Where: On the Plaza
Price Range: $$ - $$$
Hours: 4:00 p.m. to 11:00 p.m.; may open at noon for lunch during peak season.
Reservations: (407) 799-7440 or OpenTable.com

This sleek Italian bistro blends contemporary decor with the kind of Italian fare that avoids the usual red sauce clichés. The decor is in trendy blacks and whites with bold blond wood accents. Sinuous black metal tubes delineate round booths and a bar at the open kitchen in the rear lets you eavesdrop on the chefs as they make fresh pasta and fire up the entrees. Speaking of bars, Vivo has a very nice one, set apart from the dining area but still very much a part of the whole.

Among the appetizers ($4 to $13), the inexpensive *vasi*, mini mason jars filled with warm spreads and served with crisp slices of bread, are standouts,with the Tuscan bean and pesto combo especially winning. At the other end of the price spectrum, the spiedini, four rosemary accented grilled shrimp on a skewer is also a winner.

Pastas ($11 to $17) range from straightforward meatball and bolognese versions to a more exotic seafood mixture served over squid ink pasta. Most of the pastas are house made and it's always worth inquiring about the Pasta of the Day. Meat and poultry entrees ($14 to $33) are almost evenly divided between the moderately priced and the fairly expensive. At the lower end are chicken parmigiana, marsala, and picatta; at the upper end are a creamy risotto with short ribs and asparagus and a well-executed ribeye. Sides of veggies are on offer for $4.

At just $5, desserts are a bargain and the Nonna or Grandmother Cake, an orange-walnut cake with the chef's own sour cream gelato, is the go-to choice. The wine list ($32 to $99) is serviceable, although a wider selection of wines by the glass would be appreciated.

Bubba Gump Shrimp Co.

What: Seafood with a Southern flair
Where: At the entrance to CityWalk
Price Range: $$ - $$$
Hours: 11:00 a.m. to midnight
Reservations: None
Web: www.bubbagump.com

The infectious charm of the hit Tom Hanks film, *Forrest Gump,* suffuses the rambling, ramshackle bayou shrimp shack that greets you as you arrive at CityWalk. The wooden walls are covered with license plates, photographs from the film, little signs with pithy sayings, and flat-screen TVs that show the film over and over, without sound but with subtitles should you want to follow along. The place seems deceptively small from the outside, but it seats nearly 500 in a series of dining rooms and two bars. Cajun music and fifties rock plays constantly and everyone seems to be in a great mood.

The servers are every bit as peppy as the soundtrack, smothering you with attention and good cheer. A signaling system at each table uses license plates to flag down passing servers should you need anything and before your meal is through it may seem like everyone in the place has stopped by to see how you're doing or challenge you to a *Forrest Gump* trivia test.

Shrimp is the order of the day here. It's everywhere on the menu and the cooks obviously know their way around this tasty little crustacean. Everything sampled here is very good indeed, but if you need guidance, the menu helpfully calls out "Bubba's All Time Best" choices with a little Bubba

Gump shrimp logo. Appetizers ($5 to $16) feature breaded popcorn shrimp and the marginally more healthy Cajun shrimp, which is sauteed in butter and served with Gump's signature garlic bread for sopping up the sauce. Neither is too spicy. The Seafood Hush Pups also deserve special mention.

Salads and sandwiches ($10 to $15) include a Dixie Fishwich, a Shrimp Po Boy, and a BLT Shrimp Salad. The entrees ($16 to $28) showcase shrimp in a dazzling variety of guises, including fried, stuffed, sauced, and in a spicy New Orleans style preparation over rice. Separate lists feature "From The Grill;" "Forrest's Favorites," mostly non-shrimp dishes such as beer-battered fish and chips and fried chicken; and "Jenny's Catch," lighter entrees like Bourbon Street Mahi Mahi and chipotle-crusted tilapia. Desserts ($8 to $14) include an architecturally striking strawberry shortcake, Mama's Bread Pudding, and Key Lime Pie.

Bubba's offers a kids' menu ($6 with a $3 Build Your Own Sundae for dessert). There are also gluten-free choices.

There is, of course, a gift shop offering Gump T-shirts, souvenir glasses, and even the iconic "box of chocolates." But perhaps the best choice here is a container of Bubba Gump shrimp boil and the restaurant's own cookbook that will let you take the taste of Bubba Gump's home with you.

Fast Food at CityWalk

There are less elaborate, less costly dining choices in CityWalk for those looking for morning coffee, a quick bite, or a budget-saving alternative to a full-course, full-price blowout meal. There are also a few al fresco spots to grab a quick drink! This survey begins at the entrance to CityWalk, ascends Lombard Street, and proceeds down the Promenade

■ Starbucks

What:	Coffee, latte, and light snacks
Where:	As you enter CityWalk, just past Bubba Gump
Price Range:	$

Strategically located near the entrance to CityWalk to lure arriving guests, this is pretty much like every other Starbucks you've ever been in, except maybe larger — and with all the outdoor seating, larger still. If you like the jolt of Starbucks, note that this one opens at 7:00 a.m. and stays open late. There is free Wi-Fi (helpful if you're having trouble with Universal's occasionally balky Wi-Fi system). You can earn loyalty rewards here, but you can't redeem them. On the other hand, you can pay with a gift card.

■ Coldstone Creamery

What: Loaded ice cream
Where: Next to Starbucks
Price Range: $

Pick a flavor, pick a bunch of add-ins, and they'll smoosh it up while you watch, then put it in your choice of edible or non-edible container for easy on-the-go snacking

■ Red Oven Pizza Bakery

What: "Artisan" pizza
Where: Next to Coldstone Creamery
Price Range: $$

If you've been less than impressed with the pizza served in the parks, this casual eatery with open air seating will reassure you that decent pizza can be found at Universal. Pizzas must be ordered whole, no slices, but at just $12 to $14 per pie, enough for two people, who's complaining? Some of the more expensive choices are well worth sampling: pear and fig, prosciutto and arugula, and fennel sausage. Salads, too, if you must, plus beer and wine to wash it all down.

Make your selection and then walk to the cash register where, under the watchful gaze of King Umberto and Queen Margherita (she of the eponymous pizza) you place your order and pick up a numbered buzzer. Your order will then be delivered to your table in the shaded and air-cooled outdoor seating area. You can also order to go.

■ Cinnabon

What: Cinnamon buns
Where: Between the Cineplex and the Plaza
Price Range: $

Across the street from the Red Oven Pizza Bakery is this branch of the nationwide chain famous for its oversized, gooey, and delicious cinnamon buns at moderate prices. Seating is very limited inside and out. This place opens at 7:30 a.m. to snag the breakfast crowd; breakfast sandwiches are served until 11:00 a.m.

■ Menchie's Frozen Yogurt

What: Frozen yogurt
Where: On Lombard Street
Price Range: $

This chain has branches across the U.S. and around the world, so there's a good chance you know what to expect. For the uninitiated, they offer a bewildering array of flavors with an equally bewildering array of toppings. You put together your own and pay by weight (59 cents an ounce).

■ Bread Box

What:	Made to order sandwiches
Where:	Near the top of Lombard Street
Price Range:	$

The decor is bright and functional (check out that wall of colored lunch boxes). The sandwiches are made to order from fresh ingredients and served on very good bread. There are 14 choices, all priced at a budget-friendly $8. There are two salads and a few soups. Drinks include beer, wine, soft drinks, and a Nutella shake. The food here is excellent making Bread Box one of the best food values in CityWalk.

As at Red Oven, you place your order and it is delivered to your table. All seating is indoors and the porch swings at some tables are a nice touch even if they don't really swing.

■ Fusion Bistro Sushi & Sake Bar

What:	Walk-up Japanese food
Where:	Near the Cineplex upper exit and Bread Box
Price Range:	$ - $$

This small, sleek outlet outside the Cineplex's second-story exit, serves serviceable, if not exquisite, sushi rolls and nigiri. The stainless-steel bar isn't actually that inviting to sit at, but you can watch the chef inside through the window or on the closed-circuit TVs.

Appetizers ($3 to $8) include miso, edamame, and gyoza; rolls ($5 to $11) range from simple California to Dancing Eel. Bento boxes ($5 extra) include soup, salad, and an oddly addictive Mochi rice cake for dessert; they are a slightly better value than buying a la carte. Beverages include wine ($8), Japanese beer ($5 to $6), and hot or chilled sake ($5 to $9 per serving, $18 to $45 a bottle).

The sushi here is a cut above your local supermarket. For more refined versions of the genre you'll have to go to The Cowfish or schlep to the Orchid Court Lounge and Sushi Bar at Loews Royal Pacific (see *Chapter Five*).

■ Whopper Bar/ Panda Express/ Moe's Southwest Grill

What:	Walk-up indoor burgers, Chinese, and Mexican
Where:	Opposite Bread Box at the top of Lombard Street
Price Range:	$

Three familiar franchises fill this mall-style food court, strategically located near the upper exit of the Cineplex. Burger King's outlet is the first in a spin-off chain centered on their signature sandwich. For a little more than your local drive-thru ($9 with small drink and fries or onion rings) you can get a Whopper covered in gourmet toppings like guacamole, peppercorn bacon, and "angry onions." Panda Express serves passable stir-fry combo plates for $7 to $9, and Moe's tacos and burritos ($4 to $9) come with a free fresh salsa bar. A narrow balcony offers limited seating with a view of the plaza.

Tip: This is one of the only places on Universal property where you can comparison shop for soda — Panda's is the cheapest.

■ Fat Tuesday

What:	Walk-up daiquiri window
Where:	On the Promenade near the groove
Price Range:	$

Did you know that Louisiana allows drive-through alcohol sales? New Orleans staple Fat Tuesday has set up shop beside its hometown neighbor Pat O's to offer the next best thing: a stumble-through daiquiri bar. A chorus line of slushy machines spin merrily and dispense frozen concoctions ($7, or $10 to $15 in a 16- or 24-ounce souvenir cup with $6 or $9 refills) in flavors ranging from strawberry and mango to the aptly named "Cat 5 Hurricane" and "190 Octane." $1 Jello shots and "tooters" are available for those who really want to get their party on, along with beer and soda.

■ Hot Dog Hall of Fame

What:	Walk-up counter service
Where:	Across from the groove
Price Range:	$

Although touted by CityWalk as a major dining venue, this cheerful winner is, truth be told, just a hot dog stand, albeit one on steroids. The menu features dogs as served in New York, Boston, Chicago, L.A., and other places around the country. Natives of these locales can judge for themselves how successful the concept is, but there's no denying it's a lot of fun. The outdoor seating mimics ballpark seats and a giant screen broadcasts sporting events. Most dogs are $7 with a two-foot dog topping out at $15. There are six beers on tap ($6 to $7). The joint is open late, too, another plus.

■ Lone Palm Airport

What:	Walk-up bar with snacks
Where:	Opposite Margaritaville
Price Range:	$

Just outside Margaritaville stands a palapa-shaded bar that uses Jimmy Buffett's Hemisphere Dancer plane as the perfect backdrop. Makeshift tables are scattered about. It evokes the kind of beachside dives Jimmy sings about so eloquently. Sit at the bar and watch Buffett music videos while munching on snack food and sipping (what else?) margaritas.

■ Shoreline Patios

What:	Walk-up bars with snacks
Where:	Opposite Emeril's and Element
Price Range:	$

A trio of al fresco patios positioned along the waterside promenade offers an attractive eating option when the weather cooperates. Each provides casual cafe tables and benches to relax on as well as a bar serving coffee and pastries, cocktails, and/or appetizers. Take a breather here between adventures to admire the view across the canal. You can even catch a glimpse of the *Cinematic Spectacular*'s finale fireworks over Universal Studios Florida.

Tip: At the patio opposite Island Clothing, you can order from Red Oven Pizza Bakery and have it delivered.

■ ENTERTAINMENT ■
AT CITYWALK

There are two theatrical entertainment venues at CityWalk, both located conveniently on either side of Hard Rock Cafe. One hosts a resident attraction while the other welcomes touring artists.

Blue Man Group

> **What:** Avant garde theater performance
> **Where:** Across the waterway next to Hard Rock Cafe
> **Tickets:** Walk up prices (plus tax): Adults $70 to $105, kids $30 to $47, Sunday to Thursday; $80 to $115 and $35 to $52, Friday and Saturday; $10 less online.
> **Hours:** Varies widely. Call (888) 340-5476 or (407) 258-3626
> **Web:** www.blueman.com or www.universalorlando.com

Back in the early eighties, three "performance artists" created Blue Man Group in New York's seedy East Village. They were weird, hip, edgy, incomprehensible. They were the most avant of the avant garde. Today they are family entertainment. Such is cultural progress.

Now an international phenomenon, the Orlando edition of the troupe holds forth in an industrial-looking thousand-seat theater at the end of a long, winding pathway next to the Hard Rock Cafe. And just what awaits at the end of that path? Well, perhaps the greatest compliment that can be paid them is that it is pretty much indescribable. Three very bald, very blue, very silent guys in black pajamas (could they be space aliens?) appear on a stage that seems to be part of a strange factory and do a series of odd things, some of which take real skill, some of which are very funny, and some of which are just plain wacky. They are at once consummate masters of ceremony and befuddled innocents who seem constantly surprised by the presence of the audience.

Some of the best segments involve the trio's considerable skill as percussionists (a four-man, day-glo combo assists from overhead). And who could have guessed how much entertainment value there was in pouring colored liquids onto drum heads? There's plenty of audience interaction and the show wraps up with a psychedelic, booty-shaking finale that involves everyone and sends the crowd out in a festive mood.

Tip: Latecomers are subjected to very public humiliation. You have been warned.

So what's it all about? Some see a critique of our obsession with modern technology, others detect commentary on the pretensions of modern art. Perhaps the best advice is to check your brain at the door and let the fun of the evening take over. They do not recommend the show for children under three; that could be stretched to five or six.

It's unfair to compare this show to *La Nouba* over at Disney. *La Nouba* is a multi-million-dollar extravaganza. *Blue Man* is a three-man show that sticks close to its Off Broadway roots. It's an apples and oranges comparison.

Tip: The show lasts 1 hour and 45 minutes, there is no intermission, and beer vendors work the crowd beforehand.

The best seats in the house. All things being equal, the closer and more centrally located your seat, the better. The first four rows are designated as the "poncho zone" and cost $5 more than standard "Tier 1" seats. Those seated there are issued cheap plastic cover ups, just in case. But it's a far cry from a "splash zone" at SeaWorld and more marketing than anything else. Besides, the ponchos are a bit uncomfortable. Unless you're a die-hard fan, sitting a few rows farther back won't decrease your enjoyment one little bit. Zone 1, center is just about ideal. Zones 3 and 4 are on a steeper incline and offer good sight lines of the whole stage. "Tier 2" seats cost $10 less, but are in the extreme rear corners of the theater or have limited legroom.

Tickets can be ordered over the phone by calling (888) 340-5476 or (407) 258-3626 from 9:00 a.m. to 7:00 p.m. daily; you can also order online at the two websites above. Annual passholders and those holding park tickets for the day of performance get a $10 discount; Florida residents receive even more. Various special offers combining meals, park tickets, and hotel stays are offered from time to time. Check the web site.

The show schedule is somewhat erratic. Typically there are two shows a day at 6:00 p.m. and 9:00 p.m. But some days there is just one show at 8:00 p.m., or three shows at 3:00, 6:00, and 9:00 p.m. Some days there are none. Call or check the websites for show times during your visit.

For an extra $20 per person (more during busy times) you can get the VIP treatment, which includes access to the blacklit Bluephoria lounge above the entrance for 45 minutes before and after the show; a meet-and-greet with a Blue Man; a souvenir photo he will "sign" with his handprint; and two alcoholic (or non-alcoholic) beverages.

Hard Rock Live

What:	Rock performance space
Where:	Across the waterway next to Hard Rock Cafe
Tickets:	$15 and up, depending on the act
Hours:	Most shows start at 8:00 p.m.
Web:	www.hardrocklive.com

The Orlando Hard Rock Cafe may be the world's largest, but what really makes it special is its next door neighbor, Hard Rock Live, the chain's first live performance venue. It's a cutting-edge rock performance space packed with sound, light, and video technology, including two video walls flanking the stage. In its standard configuration the joint holds 1,800. If they pull out the seats and turn the first floor into a mosh pit they can pack in 2,500, which still makes it "intimate" by rock standards. At the other end of the spectrum, they can use flywalls and props to shrink the space to the size of an intimate club.

The large stage (60 feet wide and 40 feet deep) offers bands plenty of room in which to rock and the computerized lighting system, strobes, and fog machines create the kind of dazzling effects that rock fans used to have to roll up and bring with them. And the sound system could wake the Grateful Dead. In other words, the place totally rocks.

Given the limited capacity, it's unlikely that the real giants of rock will be able to play here (at least not too often), but Elton John has fluttered like a candle in the wind here and recent shows have featured current artists like The Killers, Matisyahu, and Dierks Bentley, alternating with classic acts like Weird Al Yankovic, Earth, Wind and Fire, Judas Priest, and Elvis — Costello, that is. Standups like Lisa Lampanelli, Howie Mandel, and Jim Gaffigan have appeared here, as have magicians Penn and Teller. "Classic Albums Live" features note by note recreations of famous albums by non-famous musicians.

If the music isn't blowing you away, you can repair to one of six bars and, depending on the show, concession stands offer noshes like hot dogs, wood-oven pizzas, or nachos prepared by the Hard Rock Cafe kitchen.

Ticket prices are moderate, with most acts checking in at between $25 and $50 with the occasional show rising to $150 or so. Every once in a while you can catch an evening of rocker wannabes for as little as $15. Tickets can be purchased at the box office, online at www.hardrocklive.com, or from Ticketmaster for a hefty additional fee. Balcony tables can only be purchased at the box office. Most shows begin at 8:00 p.m., with the box office opening at 10:00 a.m. Arrive early for your show, since the pre-entry security inspection can be slow. Information about upcoming events is available by calling (407) 351-5483 or online at the address above.

NIGHTCLUBS AT CITYWALK

As mentioned earlier, nightclubs at CityWalk are those entertainment venues that open only in the evening and serve either no food at all or a limited food menu. Fortunately, the food served in the clubs is very good indeed.

Note: All clubs have a **$7 cover charge** that clicks in at 9:00 p.m. See *The Price of Admission* and *What's The Best Price?* at the beginning of this chapter for advice on how to avoid or, at least, minimize these cover charges.

Red Coconut Club

What:	Hip, retro dance club
Where:	On the Promenade
Hours:	7:00 p.m. to 2:00 a.m. Monday to Saturday; 8:00 p.m. to 2:00 a.m. Sunday

It's the Rat Pack meets the Jetsons in this witty evocation of fifties-era Las Vegas-style futuristic chic. Step inside and it's as if you are entering the living room of Frank Sinatra's Palm Springs getaway. Continue on and you step onto the palm-fringed outdoor patio, where the swimming pool serves as the dance floor and many-pointed stars hover in the dark blue night sky above. But this isn't a nostalgia trip. The club has a hip, ironic edge that's very twenty-first century. The tone is captured perfectly by Paul Anka, in his best Sinatra mode, crooning "Smells Like Teen Spirit" just like Old Blue Eyes himself might have put it across at the Copacabana. If Kurt Cobain ever heard it, he'd kill himself all over again.

The club has a surprisingly large capacity, yet it manages to seem quite intimate. The upstairs balcony offers a great perspective on the dance floor and bandstand below. It is usually open only on weekends, but it is available for private rental throughout the week. There's music, too, of course, with a D.J. spinning nightly and a hip combo holding forth from a raised platform behind the patio bar on Fridays and Saturdays.

The band tailors its repertoire to suit the crowd, moving easily from laid-back sophistication to more upbeat and harder-edged selections. Late at night on weekends, the D.J. takes over again to keep the crowd rocking until closing.

Martinis and Cosmopolitans ($10 to $12) are the featured drinks here, but you can also get surreal specialty cocktails like a Moscow Mule (vodka, ginger beer, and lemon juice) or Man in the Moon (moonshine, bitters, and vermouth) for about $10 to $12. There's brief wine list, too, nearly all of it Californian. When it comes to champagne, the Club doesn't mess with success and offers a selection of French classics.

There is a brief and evolving menu of appetizer-sized nibbles ($8) including mini beef medallions, coconut shrimp, and jerk chicken flatbread. After 10:00 p.m., you can order pizza from Red Oven Pizza Bakery.

A happy hour (7:00 p.m. to 9:00 p.m. Monday to Saturday) offers discounts on select drinks. Thursday is "Ladies Night," with complimentary admission and drink specials for females.

What sets the Red Coconut apart from all other theme-park clubs is its bottle service. Order up a full bottle of premium liquor or champagne for your party ($100 to $450, 4 person minimum) and your table instantly becomes its own private club, complete with a red velvet rope limiting access to you and your guests. The bottle is delivered on a silver tray with your choice of two mixers. Pour it yourself or have your server do the honors. What a great way to impress your friends or business associates! And when you consider what it would cost to order drinks a la carte, it can be surprisingly cost-effective.

Bob Marley — A Tribute To Freedom

What:	Reggae club
Where:	On the Promenade
Hours:	4:00 p.m. to 2:00 a.m.; kitchen closes at 10:00 p.m.
	Sunday to Thursday, 11:00 p.m. Friday and Saturday
Reservations:	(407) 224-3663 or OpenTable.com
Web:	www.bobmarley.com

Reggae fans will appreciate this salute to Bob Marley, the Jamaican-born king of reggae, where the infectious backbeat of Marley's lilting music mingles with the spicy accents of island cooking. Created under the watchful eye of Marley's widow, Rita, who has contributed Marley memorabilia for the project, this venue is as much a celebration of Marley's vision of universal brotherhood as it is a restaurant or performance venue.

When Marley first hit the U.S. scene, he was regarded as something of a dope-smoking revolutionary barbarian. Like many black artists, he suffered the indignity of having his songs "covered" by white artists (like Barbra Streisand!). But music hath charms to soothe the conservative as well as the savage breast and Marley's infectiously charming music gradually became domesticated, despite his occasionally radical-sounding lyrics. Today, his lilting "One Heart" is the unofficial national anthem of Jamaica, made universally familiar through the magic of television commercials.

Marley was a member of the Rastafarians, a religious sect with roots in 1920s Harlem, that believes in the divinity of the late Emperor Haile Selassie and the coming of a new era in which the African diaspora will return in glory to the Ethiopian motherland. "Rastas" shun alcohol, adhere to a vegetarian diet, and smoke copious quantities of ganja, or marijuana, which is seen as a gift from God and something of a sacrament. The nightclub that bears his name violates all those principles; there's plenty of booze, meat on the menu, and no ganja.

One thing close to Marley's heart that does get full expression here is the theme of universal brotherhood. It is preached by the M.C. and practiced by the patrons, making Bob Marley's perhaps the most multicultural entertainment venue in Orlando, a place that turns up the volume and lives out the words of Marley's most famous song: "One love. One heart. Let's get together and feel all right."

The exterior is an exact replica of 56 Hope Road, Marley's Kingston, Jamaica home. Inside you will find two L-shaped levels, each with its own bar, opening onto a spacious palm-fringed courtyard with a gazebo-like bandstand in the corner. Because both levels are open to the courtyard, Marley's lacks central air-conditioning, but fans do a good job of keeping a breeze going.

The predominant color scheme is yellow, red, and green, the national colors of Ethiopia; the lion statues evoke Haile Selassie's title of Lion of Judah, a motif that is repeated in the mural on the bandstand. The walls are covered in Marley memorabilia and the sound system pumps out a steady stream of Marley hits.

The nighttime entertainment, which kicks off at about 9:00 p.m., typically consists of a house band of skilled reggae musicians performing a mix of Marley hits, other reggae classics, and the occasional pop standard adapted to the reggae beat. The music of the house bands is good, but not so good that it makes you forget how much better Bob Marley and the Wailers were. Still, their main job is to get people out onto the dance floor, and they accomplish that task easily. After a few drinks and once you are gyrating with the crowds, you'll find no reason to quibble.

The "Rastafarian Tings" ($4 to $6) are non-alcoholic. However, the "Island Favorites," "Frozen Tings," and "Extreme Measures" ($8 to $9), fueled with island rum and other potent potables, are designed to help get you past your inhibitions and onto the dance floor. Of course, Red Stripe, Jamaica's favorite beer, is also available.

The food is designed more as ballast for the drinks than anything else, but it is quite good and a nice introduction to Jamaican fare for the uninitiated. The portions are about appetizer size, so you could well sample several in the course of a long evening.

"Rita's Appetizers" ($6 to $15) include Stir It Up, a cheese fondue laced with Red Stripe and served with vegetables for dipping, and Jammin' Chips and Salsa. "Belly Full" entrees ($10 to $17) feature the "Catch a Fire" chicken sandwich, which is marinated in "jerk" seasoning (a sort of all-purpose Jamaican marinade), grilled, and served with a creamy cucumber dipping sauce. More adventurous eaters may want to try the oxtail stew or curry chicken. There are also both meat and vegetarian versions of Jamaican patties, filled flaky pastries. More substantial fish entrees ($14 to $18) include grilled mahi mahi and Rasta Mon's Fish Stew. Several dishes are served with yucca fries, which look deceptively like french fries but have a taste and texture all their own. Desserts ($6) are worth sampling, with the Is This Love mango cheesecake especially good. There's a kids' menu for $7.

A small shop counter in a downstairs corner hawks Marley T-shirts and polos as well as Marley CDs. This is probably as close as you'll get to finding the complete Marley discography in one place, a perfect chance to fill in the gaps in your collection. There is a small selection of books on reggae and Marley for those who would like to learn more.

Sundays are "Ladies' Night" with no cover and 2-for-1 specials until midnight for women.

Bob Marley's is a popular joint and on weekends can spawn long lines of people waiting for one of the 400 spaces inside to open up. Even early in the week, space can be hard to come by for those who don't arrive early. If you want to be in the thick of it, you'll definitely want to be downstairs. If you're not the dancing type, a row of stools along the railing of the upstairs balcony offers excellent sightlines to the stage. For a change of scenery, you can take your drink onto a second floor balcony that looks out over the Promenade.

Anyone looking for a fun evening of dancing and drinking and infectious music to go along with it will find little to complain about here. True Marley devotees will find everything they are looking for.

Everything but the ganja.

Pat O'Brien's

What: The original dueling pianos, plus New Orleans cuisine
Where: On the Promenade
Hours: 4:00 p.m. to 2:00 a.m.
Reservations: (407) 224-3663 or OpenTable.com
Web: www.patobriens.com

Step into Pat O'Brien's and you'll believe that you've been magically transported to the Big Easy. At least you will if you've ever visited the original Pat O'Brien's in New Orleans' French Quarter, because CityWalk's version is virtually a photographic reproduction. This was the first attempt to transplant the O'Brien's experience and word is that when O'Brien's owner visited CityWalk he marveled that Universal's design wizards had captured the place "right down to the cracks in the walls."

There are three main rooms at Pat O'Brien's. The Piano Bar houses the famed copper-clad twin baby grand pianos that are an O'Brien's trademark. This is strictly a bar, its brick walls and wooden beams hung with dozens of gaudy German beer steins that let you know this is a place for serious drinkers. Here a steady stream of superbly talented pianists keeps the ivories tickled almost constantly as patrons sing along, pound on the tables, and shout requests. In fact, Pat O'Brien's is credited with inventing the "dueling pianos" format that has been copied so often. The word seems to have gotten around that this is a great place to bring a bunch of old friends (or new acquaintances from the latest convention to blow through town) to drink and blow off some steam.

O'Brien's draws a somewhat older crowd than Marley's or Buffett's, especially when there are some big conventions in town. If you're old enough to remember when popular music meant songs with lyrics you could actually understand, you'll probably have a good time here, especially if you can carry a tune and aren't shy about singing along.

Across from the Piano Bar is a smaller version, called the Local's Bar, minus the pianos but with a jukebox and large-screen projection TV that always seems to be tuned to some sporting event. Out back is a delightful open-air patio dining area. Here, at night, the ambiance is highlighted by yet another O'Brien's trademark — flaming fountains. Upstairs is given over to private party rooms, which have exclusive access to the charming balcony overlooking the Promenade.

And speaking of drinks, Pat O'Brien's (for those who don't know) is the home of the Hurricane ($12), a lethal and lovely concoction of rum and lord knows what all else that has made the place famous worldwide. In fact, the original New Orleans location pulls in more money than any other bar its size in the world.

Pat O'Brien's hasn't skimped on the food side of the equation. Devotees of New Orleans' spicy Creole- and French-influenced cuisine won't be disappointed even though the presentation and service are decidedly casual. But the offhand style belies the sophistication of the cuisine. Prices are moderate, too, with nothing on the menu over $18 and many choices under $11.

The Jambalaya is a spicy medley of shrimp, chicken, andouille sausage, and rice flecked with vegetables. The blackened Louisiana redfish is a signature New Orleans dish and done well here. Perhaps best of all is the Cancun Shrimp appetizer, with its coconut-tinged frying batter and sweet, fresh fruit salsa. It's served over cole slaw and at $11 it's a real bargain. The Mardi Gras Gumbo appetizer comes in a small portion just right for the lighter appetite.

The Po' Boy sandwich is another Big Easy signature dish. It's a Creole take on the heroes and hoagies from up north. Pat O'Brien's version is a heaping portion of small shrimp served on an open-faced baguette with a rich Cajun mayonnaise on the side. Eating it as a sandwich is a bit of a challenge, but worth it as the bread, veggies, seafood, and rich Cajun sauce play off each other very nicely indeed. It's served with french fries dusted with paprika and ever so lightly spiced with cayenne before being fried to the perfect texture.

For dessert ($5 to $6) choose from the Strawberry Hurricane Cheesecake or Pat O's Bread Pudding, redolent of nutmeg and cinnamon and served with a whisky sauce that packs a 100-proof wallop. There is also a kids' menu, featuring simple meals for about $5 to $6.

Out front, facing the Promenade, you'll find a small gift shop offering Pat O'Brien's souvenir glassware and other gewgaws, as well as a window offering Hurricanes to go.

the groove

What:	High-tech, high-gloss disco
Where:	On the Promenade
Hours:	9:00 p.m. to 2:00 a.m.

the groove (the lower case is intentional) is CityWalk's dance club and it sets out to compete head to head with the legendary nightspots that have caught the public imagination in urban centers like New York, Chicago, and

Los Angeles. It is also the only venue (other than the Red Coconut Club) that does not come with a recognizable brand name. No Jimmy Buffetts or Bob Marleys to give this place instant name recognition. This joint stands or falls on its own merits.

It succeeds remarkably well by providing a place where a mostly young crowd (you must be at least 21 to enter) can come and boogie the night away in a cacophonous atmosphere that duplicates big city sophistication. The main difference is that here you will be let in even if you don't meet some snotty doorman's idea of what is currently cool and hip. Intimate it's not, with a maximum capacity of 1,277 on multiple levels, but with crowds comes excitement.

The design conceit is that you are in a century-old theater that is in various stages of renovation, but the dim lighting and pulsing light effects negate much of the intended effect. The various areas of the club provide ample space for those who want to thrash and writhe under pulsating lights to ear-splitting music while offering some refuge to those who just want to watch.

The main dance floor is dominated by a soaring wall of video monitors that operate separately and then coalesce to form a single image. Patterns of light swirl across the floor to disorienting effect. There is a small seldom-used stage for visiting groups. Most nights the nonstop sound assault is provided by a D.J., sometimes a name brand from out of town. The music is eclectic; set lists have transitioned from predominantly "progressive house" to a mix of current Top 40, EDM (electronic dance music), and Pop classics. On Fridays, DJ ET from local radio station 102 Jamz spins the latest urban dance beats. And there are go-go dancers flanking the stage on weekends.

Fortunately, there are some relatively quiet corners (50- to 80-seat bars actually) where you can get better acquainted with that special some-one you just met on the dance floor. These are the Red, Blue, and Green Rooms, respectively, and each is decorated differently. The Red and Green Rooms are dim and deliciously decadent but the Blue Room is lit with a ghastly pallor that will flatter only Goths and vampires and seems designed to convince you you've had too much to drink. When it all becomes too much, you can repair to a balcony over the Promenade and look down on the latecomers standing in line.

Rising Star

What: Karaoke club
Where: On the Promenade
Hours: 8:00 p.m. to 2:00 a.m.

Located in an octagonal building almost at the geographical center of CityWalk, Rising Star is your neighborhood karaoke bar given an extreme makeover. The canned "tiny orchestra" on a portable CD player is gone, replaced by a live band and backup singers with concert-quality lighting and sound systems. The only thing they can't upgrade are the vocal talents of the eager volunteers who line up for their shot at small-scale stardom.

The club's two-story design combines the intimate ambiance of a jazz club (its former incarnation) with the great sightlines of a conventional theater. A scattering of memorabilia from *Downbeat* magazine's Jazz Hall of Fame remains on the walls, with the rest covered by velvet curtains. The color scheme of soothing browns and rich reds, along with the plush banquettes, creates an aura of ultra-cool sophistication.

The format should be familiar: choose a song from their modest list of about 200 selections (classic rock standards and a smattering of Top 40), write it on a slip of paper, and wait your turn. You (and one friend) can join the band on stage, belting away with teleprompter assistance, while overhead video screens broadcast your performance to the back row. The musicians do a professional job of staying in time no matter how inebriated the intonations, though it's a wonder they don't go mad repeatedly playing "Baby Got Back," a perennial favorite. I wonder why.

The booze menu is fairly straightforward — beer ($6 to $7), wines by the glass ($6 to $8), and a variety of specialty shots and cocktails ($9 to $10). They don't serve their own food, but you can order pizza from Red Oven.

Rising Star opens at 8:00 p.m. and the band begins performing at 9:00. If you want to sing, get your request in early, as the club can fill up quickly, especially on weekends. On Sundays and Mondays the live band takes a break, so you will be singing to a much wider selection of prerecorded karaoke CDs.

SHOPPING IN
■ CITYWALK ■

The shopping here is fun without being overbearing, and the accent is on clothes of the casual variety and the accessories that go with them. Prices, on the whole, are surprisingly moderate. Oh sure, you can drop a bundle if you want, but there's plenty here to appeal to a wide range of budgets.

■ Need another souvenir?

As you've probably noticed by now, nearly every entertainment venue has its gift shop selling branded souvenirs. So it comes as a relief that the major retail spaces do not simply repeat the merchandise themes you found in the theme parks.

The one exception is the **Universal Studios Store** that, with its towering and colorful exterior signage, dominates the CityWalk Plaza. Here you will find a tasteful selection of touristy trinkets, with an accent on nicely designed (and, hence, moderately expensive) clothing. The merchandise mix changes frequently to take advantage of seasonal fads or the latest Universal film venture in need of targeted promotion. It's not as large as its sister store in Universal Studios Florida but if you are in desperate need of something to remind you of your visit to either of the theme parks, you should be able to find something suitable, including selected Wizarding World of Harry Potter merchandise.

P!Q (pronounced *pick*), a petite boutique sandwiched between Fresh Produce and the Island Clothing Store, offers knickknacks and novelties from French retailer Pylones, along with other manufacturers, that are "guaranteed to bring a smile to your face." They have a lot for kids, including some clever books. Think of it as a G-rated Spencer Gifts, minus the bachelor party gags.

For a souvenir that you'll never forget (without surgery) stop in for a tattoo at **Hart and Huntington** on Lombard Street. They also sell T-shirts and other gear of the sort that might freak your mom out.

■ Clothe thyself

Clothing, the kind that doesn't advertise anything, is offered at several locations here. Casual clothing with an emphasis on men's wear can be found at **Quiet Flight Surf Shop**. It is easy to spot on your right, near the Cineplex, as you enter CityWalk; the display window framed by the huge curling wave is the tip off. You can't actually buy a surfboard here, though there is a small selection of skateboards. Most of the space is devoted to casual clothing designed to make you look like a well-heeled surf bum. There are wildly colorful print shirts for men and equally colorful "baggies," the capacious swim trunks favored by surfers. Women get some attention with a selection of swimwear and casual poolside attire. Here you will also find the kind of accessories no well-dressed surfer should be without, from ultra-hip sunglasses to waterproof watches. They have a nice selection of "Croakies," colored bands that keep your glasses on while you ride those roller coasters in the parks.

Photo Op: Before you move on, check out that curling fiberglass breaker one more time. There's a riderless surfboard perfectly positioned in the curl. Step aboard for a nifty souvenir photo.

Continue through the store and it turns into the **Island Clothing Store**, with another entrance facing the waterway. This is a great place to pick up Tommy Bahamas and other high-end "tropical" shirts for men. Not only that, but these back-to-back shops make for a great air-conditioned shortcut when walking to or from the Universal Studios theme park.

Element, next to Island Clothing at the bottom of Lombard Street, is an offshoot of the professional skateboarding team of the same name. This shop sells customized skateboards, "Von Zipper" sunglasses, stylish sneakers, and any other apparel you need to accessorize your extreme sports lifestyle.

Fresh Produce, on the Plaza, features women's casual clothing in a limited palette of vibrant pastels as well as black and white. Many have a summery backyard feel. The designers, twin sisters from Colorado, describe their products as "make you feel good clothing." What will also make you feel good are the prices, which are surprisingly modest for the obvious stylishness of the clothes. Many ensembles can be put together for $100 or so.

For accessories to go with your new wardrobe, head to the **Fossil** shop, which carries a selection of handbags, belts, and other leather goods in a wide assortment of colors, along with men's and women's watches in their signature retro-styled tins. You'll also find a rack of sunglasses at prices that won't blind you.

CHAPTER FIVE:

THE LUXURY RESORTS

I n the hospitality industry, the word "resort" refers to a hotel that offers not just a high standard of luxury and extra amenities, but special recreational opportunities, either natural or man-made. Well, two world-class theme parks and a constantly evolving nighttime entertainment district surely qualify as a recreational opportunity.

So when the visionaries at Universal added Islands of Adventure and CityWalk to the original Universal Studios Florida they decided to go the extra mile and turn Universal Orlando into a true resort destination with distinctively themed luxury hotels surrounding the theme parks. To accomplish that they partnered with Loews Hotels to provide the hotel part of the equation. If you've never heard of Loews Hotels, you're forgiven. A smaller chain, Loews concentrates on operating a small portfolio of one-of-a-kind hotels of the four-diamond variety that seek to become the dominant hotels in their marketplace.

The Loews Portofino Bay Hotel, the Hard Rock Hotel (a separate brand managed here by Loews), and the Loews Royal Pacific Resort, described in this chapter, are "luxury" hotels that have been in operation now for over a decade. From now on, the hotels will be referred to by their shorter, "unofficial" names and nicknames.

Note: The three original luxury resort hotels have now been joined by a "moderate" resort, Cabana Bay Beach Resort, created by Universal and managed by Loews. Cabana Bay differs substantially from the luxury hotels and will be discussed in *Chapter Six*. A fifth hotel, Loews Sapphire Falls Resort has been announced for 2016 and will be touched on later in this chapter.

Honored Guests

Staying at one of the luxury resorts has some obvious advantages. For one thing, you will be staying almost literally at the gates to the theme parks. None of the these three hotels is more than a ten-minute complimentary boat ride from CityWalk, and all are within walking distance. For another, these are very nice hotels, far superior to the usual run of tourist hotels that ring Universal Orlando and continue down the tacky environs of International Drive. But there are other advantages; staying at one of the luxury resorts confers certain VIP privileges unavailable to the average run-of-the-mill tourist or even those staying at Universal's moderate resorts.

- *Early entry to the parks.* At press time, all on-site hotel guests get into Universal Studios Florida an hour before the general public, allowing them to explore the Diagon Alley attractions in relative privacy. The *Escape From Gringotts* ride currently doesn't offer Universal Express access (see below), but this privilege nearly makes up for it. At certain times, hotel guests may also be granted early access to Islands of Adventure. Whichever parks are involved, you'll be required to show a valid hotel key card at the gate to use this privilege.
- *Universal Express Unlimited Priority Access.* Perhaps the most talked-about perk of all is that guests at the three original luxury hotels get priority access at most of the rides and attractions in the theme parks. Cabana Bay is excluded and perks at Sapphire Falls have yet to be announced. Simply insert your room key in one of the computer kiosks in your hotel lobby and receive a Universal Express Unlimited card emblazoned with your photo. Show it in the parks to get immediate access to the Universal Express entrance to the ride. You can use this privilege as many times as you like. Of course, this may change in the future, so it's not guaranteed. Check with the concierge when you arrive.

  You must get a separate Express card for everyone in your party when you check in, since attendants are supposed to check the eligibility of everyone in the group. This perk is sometimes referred to as "Front-of-the-Line" or FOTL and some people think it means they are supposed to quite literally be the very first person in line. Not so. What it does mean is that your wait to ride will usually be cut to 15 minutes or less, although at extremely busy periods the wait can be somewhat longer.

It works just like the Unlimited Universal Express Pass system available to park visitors not staying in a luxury resort. (For more on Universal Express Plus, see *Chapter One: Planning Your Escape.*)

Certain rides, including *Escape From Gringotts, Forbidden Journey,* and *Pteranodon Flyers,* are excluded from the program. During very busy periods or at popular attractions, this perk may be restricted somewhat during part of the day, preventing you from riding the same ride many times in succession. However, enforcing such restrictions is left largely to the ride attendants, who may not always enforce it vigorously. Guests have reported that they experienced few if any restrictions, even when they were supposed to be in effect.

- *Priority seating.* This perk gets you the best seats for some shows and priority seating Sunday through Thursday nights at some restaurants in CityWalk and the theme parks. Check with the hotel concierge to see which shows and restaurants are offering this perk at the time of your visit.

- *Package delivery.* Any park visitor can get some shops to deliver their purchases to the front gate for later pick-up, but Universal hotel guests can have their purchases sent directly to their rooms, provided they are staying over till at least the next day. Packages are delivered the day after your purchase.

- *Charge privileges.* You can use your room key (which looks much like a credit card) to charge purchases in park shops and restaurants that accept credit cards. You pay just one bill when you check out.

- *Length-of-stay tickets.* Resort guests can purchase park passes valid for however long they are staying at the hotel. These tickets are usually booked as part of a package. They don't represent any great savings on park admission but they have the beneficial effect of giving you a better room rate. They can also come in handy if the length of your stay doesn't match one of the standard pass options. If you wish to purchase length-of-stay tickets once you have checked in, see the concierge.

- *Character Dining reservations.* Resort hotel restaurants play host to characters from the Universal stable of stars. Typically, these events happen a few times a week during the evening meal, and during breakfast at peak times. As a hotel guest, you will have priority when making reservations for these popular events. Check with the concierge for the nights and restaurants involved in the Character Dining experience during your stay.

Additional perks may be added. It's also possible that some may be changed or discontinued. So make sure to ask the concierge for the latest information when you check in. You are paying a premium to stay in such style so close to the parks, so you should take advantage of the privileges conferred by your status as an honored guest.

Perhaps the best perk is the excellent treatment you're sure to enjoy from Loews' famously guest-oriented staff. Whatever your need, you'll find the staff remarkably responsive to any requests.

Room Rates At A Glance

The hotels follow similar patterns when it comes to rooms and rates. Two hotels have "standard" rooms and larger, pricier "deluxe" rooms. In all hotels, the view from the room also affects the rate, with "pool" or "harbor" views costing more. All hotels in this chapter have a Club floor offering special amenities and perks for a price. Next come the suites. All hotels have "Kids' Suites," specially designed for families. For high rollers, there are larger, more elaborate suites with suitably larger, more elaborate price tags.

Hotel rates are notoriously volatile, rising and falling with the seasons, leisure travel patterns, and a variety of market conditions that are impossible to forecast. Since it's difficult to say exactly how much you will pay, the hope here is to provide some general guidelines about the "going rate" that will prove useful in considering your Universal Orlando Resort hotel choices. Then you can use the tips offered in *Getting A Good Deal* (below) to zero in on the best rate for the room you want.

The resort hotels recognize five distinct "seasons." The exact dates for each season change slightly from year to year depending on when certain holidays occur. Here, in ascending order of room cost, is a general overview of those seasons.

Value season. Roughly from early January to mid-February; from mid-August (when Florida kids head back to school) to early October; and from just after Thanksgiving to mid-December.

Regular season. From Spring Break (see below) to early June and from early October to just before Thanksgiving; and mid to late December.

Summer season. Early June to mid-August.

Peak season. The Presidents' Day period (mid-February to mid-March); Spring Break (late-March to mid-April); Memorial Day weekend;

and Thanksgiving weekend.

Holiday season. The two weeks around Easter and the Christmas/ New Year's holiday period, which typically begins a week before Christmas and ends a day or three after New Year's Day.

■ Standard Room Rates

The hotels play it close to the vest when it comes to room rates. Short of actually booking a room, it's hard to tell what a given room category will cost when. However, the following standard room rates, which are in effect during 2015, provide a basis for making some educated guesses. These are "starting from" prices, which means that the actual price quoted could be as much as $50 higher.

	Value	*Regular*	*Summer*	*Peak*	*Holiday*
Portofino Bay	$294+	$324+	$369+	$399+	$479+
Hard Rock	$269+	$304+	$369+	$389+	$464+
Royal Pacific	$234+	$269+	$304+	$319+	$404+

To these rates, add $30 per night for a room with a view, $60 to $100 for a "deluxe" room, and $125 to $160 for a club level room. The more expensive hotels add correspondingly more for each step up. Kids' Suites start at about $500 and go up to over $800; nonetheless, they sell out quickly. If you need to ask the price of the so-called "super luxury" suites, you probably . . . no, you *definitely* can't afford them.

Getting A Good Deal

While the resort hotels offer excellent value for the money, they are not precisely cheap. But the advantages of staying on site are so attractive that figuring out a way to make a stay at one of these great hotels fit into your budget will be worth the effort. Here, then, are a few suggestions on how to get the best possible deal on your resort hotel room rate.

Use a travel agent. A Universal specialist travel agent will know the best rates and the best dates to get them. And it won't cost you extra!

Book a package. Ask your travel agent about purchasing a package that includes an on-site hotel, theme park tickets, and perhaps airfare and car rental. You will probably wind up paying less than if you had booked all the elements separately.

AAA. Members receive a 20% discount.

Purchase an Annual Pass. Annual passholders to the theme parks receive a discount of about 30% off regular rates and are eligible for periodic special offers on a space available basis.

You First. Membership in Loews *You First*, the hotel chain's frequent lodger program, does not get you any discounts, but it qualifies you for some nice perks like free use of the fitness centers; food, spa, and golf credits; and room upgrades at check-in based on availability. You First is only valid at the Portofino and Royal Pacific; stays booked through third-party resellers are not eligible; and you'll need a couple of stays under your belt before getting the good stuff. You can enroll online at www.loewshotels.com or call (877) 563-9714 to have an application mailed to you. Hard Rock has its own, separate *All Access* club with similar perks, for a $25 membership fee. Visit hardrockcafe.com to join, or ask at check-in for a free membership. Be aware that you may not be able to combine these clubs with any additional discounts.

Go on the Internet. As a supplement to some or all of the above ploys, you should check out a Disney-oriented site called DISboards.com, which also has a discussion group devoted just to Universal Orlando. Scroll down on the home page until you see the link to "Universal Resorts & Hotels." This is where members post information on when they are going to the various resort hotels, the rate they got, and how they got it. It's a bit tricky to find the information you're looking for, but try searching the forum for "date rate."Another source of invaluable intelligence for the budget-conscious traveler is MouseSavers, which also covers cost-cutting for non-Disney parks. Visit www.mousesavers.com/universalorlando.html for details.

Go on the Internet, Part II. Once you have done your research, then you might want to try those hotel "discount" sites on the Internet. Among the more prominent are sidestep.com, hotels.com, and hotwire.com.

Making Reservations

If you are not using a travel agent to book a package vacation, you can do so yourself by calling (877) 801-9720. For the hearing impaired, there is a TDD line at (407) 224-4414. If you are calling from overseas or are already in Orlando, call (407) 363-8000 and ask to be transferred.

If you are interested in booking a room only, you can call Universal's central reservations number toll free at (888) 273-1311. Those calling from Orlando or overseas can dial (407) 503-1000 for Portofino Bay, (407) 503-

ROCK for the Hard Rock, and (407) 503-3000 for Royal Pacific Resort.

Good Things To Know About...

■ Access for Non-Guests

The resort hotels are tucked away in corners of Universal Orlando, carefully masked from the nearby streets, with grand entrance gates that have an air of exclusivity about them. That may be why many people mistakenly assume the resorts are closed to all but hotel guests. In fact, anyone can drop in for a visit and, if your vacation schedule affords the time, you should by all means come for a meal at one of the restaurants and a stroll through the very special grounds and public areas of the hotels. You can come by boat or on foot from the parks or you can drive in. If you drive, you can choose between valet and paid self parking. Non-guests must use the main entrances to the hotels since other entrances (like the pool areas) require a room key for access.

■ Business Centers

All resort hotels have a "business center" open Monday through Saturday for those who need to photocopy or fax something or use a computer. You can even find a notary should you need one. Most are conveniently located, although at the Royal Pacific Resort the business center is a good hike away in the adjoining conference facility. The fees charged won't surprise the average business traveler but might make others gasp.

■ Character Dining

All of the hotels offer "character dining" experiences at their main restaurants — Trattoria del Porto at Portofino, The Kitchen at Hard Rock, and Islands Dining Room at Royal Pacific. During these events, costumed characters such as Scooby Doo, Woody Woodpecker, Spider-Man, Shrek, and the Minions stroll the dining room, visiting with kids and posing for photos. Unlike character dining events at some theme park resorts, there is no separate charge for these events; if you are eating in the restaurant, you will be able to interact with the characters. Character dining takes place once or twice a week, typically between 6:30 p.m. and 9:30 p.m. If there is no character dining at your hotel during your stay, there most likely will be at another. You don't even need to be staying at any of the hotels to have dinner during these fun events. Since schedules and participating characters change from time to time, the best strategy is to call the hotel before your arrival and ask about the character dining schedule during your visit.

■ Concierge Service

The three luxury hotels offer concierge service. The concierge desk staff is extremely knowledgeable, not just about all things Universal, but about Orlando in general. They can offer tips on what else to see in the area, give you the latest weather report, where to shop, and where to find a baby sitter or get the perfect birthday cake for your kid. You can even stop by the concierge desk for information about and tickets to most local attractions. Although they stock plenty of brochures about Walt Disney World and can arrange transportation to get you there, Disney does not allow them to sell Disney tickets.

■ Checking In and Out

Standard check-in time at all hotels is 4:00 p.m.; if you arrive early, the front desk will happily give you your hotel keycard, which will let you create personalized Universal Express Unlimited passes (see above and *Chapter One*) for everyone in your party, and hold your baggage so you can go play in the parks. Check-out is at 11:00 a.m., and can be performed in person, "express," or via interactive television.

■ Did You Forget?

All hotels offer a service aimed at the forgetful among us, so if you forgot your toothbrush or razor you can call Star Service (see below) for a complimentary replacement.

■ Drugs

No, not that kind. We're talking medicine, the kind your doctor prescribes. The Loews resort hotels have partnered with a nearby pharmacy to provide 24-hour prescription service. For more information, call (407) 248-0437.

■ Game Rooms

All the hotels have small, unattended video arcades that seem to attract the under-15 crowd. Typically the games, none of them terribly elaborate, run on tokens with a token vending machine that accepts $1, $5, and $10 bills.

■ Golf

None of the resort hotels offers a golf course, but golfers needn't despair. The "Golf Universal Orlando" program has partnered with two nearby golf

Above: The funnies come to life. (Toon Lagoon)

Left: Bruce needs your help. (Marvel Super Hero Island)

Below left: Straight out of the movie. (Jurassic Park)

Below right: Like they say, you will get wet! (Toon Lagoon)

Above: What goes up...
(Marvel Super Hero Island)

Right: There are surprises
lurking in those bushes.
(Jurassic Park)

Below: Dudley Do-Right
and pals get their own Mt.
Rushmore. (Toon Lagoon)

Above: Hogwarts Castle throws open its door to Muggles.

Left: Are you in need of a wand?

Below: A typical Hogsmeade street scene, complete with butterbeer.

(All photos from The Village of Hogsmeade at The Wizarding World of Harry Potter)

Above: The Beauxbatons at the Triwizard Tournament.

Right: Go easy on the butterbeer!

Below left: Let's get Sirius.

Below right: Food fit for a wizard at the 3 Broomsticks.

(All photos from The Village of Hogsmeade at The Wizarding World of Harry Potter)

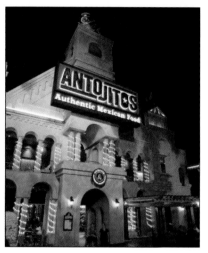

Above: Sushi with your burger?

Left: The tequila is muy autentico.

Below: Blue Man Group brings avant garde weirdness to Universal.

(All photos from CityWalk)

Hard Rock Hotel® at Universal Orlando.®

Top: Welcome to Portofino, Italy. (Portofino Bay Hotel)

Above: Live like a rock star. (Hard Rock Hotel)

Right: Relax in high style at the Villa Pool. (Portofino Bay Hotel)

Above: Elephants frolic in the lobby courtyard. (Royal Pacific Resort)

Left: Character dining. (Royal Pacific Resort)

Below: The Cabana Pool. [Cabana Bay Beach Resort]

Above: Cabana Bay Beach Resort has fifties flair.

Right: Homage to the vanished Tropicana Hotel.

Below: A family suite.

[All photos from Cabana Bay Beach Resort]

clubs — the Jack Nicklaus-designed Grand Cypress and Windermere Country Club, home to 63 holes between them — to make golfing easy for hotel guests. Perks include complimentary transportation and "special privileges." Rates and availability vary with the season. To make a reservation for a tee time, the best strategy is to call the golf concierge at your hotel prior to your arrival and let them do it. The numbers are (407) 503-1200 (PBH), (407) 503-2200 (HRH), and (407) 503-3200 (RPR). Or reserve online at www.universalorlando.com/golf.

■ Green Lodging

All hotels are "Green Lodging Certified," having passed eco-muster with the Florida Department of Environmental Protection inspectors. You'll find recycling bags in the rooms, and energy-saving compact fluorescent bulbs in the light sockets. Your bed will always have clean sheets upon check-in, but they'll only be changed every three days (unless you request otherwise). You can reuse towels by putting them back on the rack; only towels left on the floor are washed during your visit.

■ Hotel Hopping

Guests in the hotels are encouraged to visit the other on-site properties and take advantage of their restaurants, amenities, and special events like Dive-In Movies (see below). Your concierge will make dining reservations. Your hotel key will not work in the gated areas of other hotels, so show your key to an attendant, who will grant you access. You can, however, use your hotel key to charge purchases at any other hotel.

■ Internet Access

Loews offers two tiers of Internet service — "Premier" and "Premier Plus." The slower Premier is free, but if you want or need to take advantage of "media rich" sites (Netflix anyone?), you will have to shell out $14.95 a day to get something with a bit more bandwidth. Try the complimentary service first; I found it sufficed for most uses. If it's driving you nuts, ask for help in upgrading (they don't make it easy to find out how). No multi-day packages are offered.

■ Kids

Loews has a soft spot for kids. Kids under 18 stay free in a room with their parents and the hotels frequently run special promotions. Check when you make reservations to see if there are any special deals going on during your visit. When you check in, be sure to ask the desk clerk about Character Dining (described above) and Character Wake-Up Calls, tape-recorded telephone messages for your kids. All of the luxury hotels have special children's playrooms with supervised activities (see below) as well as special "Kids' Suites" designed to give families a little extra room.

■ Kids' Activities

The original three hotels all have special supervised activities programs for children aged 4 to 14. These center around large, colorful playrooms filled with fun things to do, from computer games, to arts and crafts, to movies shown on large screen TVs. The programs also take advantage of the hotel grounds for outdoor fun and games when appropriate.

These are typically evening programs, designed to let Mom and Dad go off to enjoy more adult nighttime entertainment knowing that their little darlings are being looked after and well entertained. So expect the programs to run from about 5:00 p.m. to 11:30 p.m., a little later on weekends. During busier periods and school holidays, hours can expand. Typically, only one kids' program is open, with the participating hotel rotating weekly and the other two programs closed, but since a guest at any hotel can use the program at any other hotel, this should not pose a problem.

Pricing varies from hotel to hotel and is subject to change without notice. $15 per hour per child and $15 for a meal is fairly common. If you think you might be interested in these programs, you will have to check with the hotel at check-in or shortly before arrival to ask about the current schedule and pricing arrangements. The concierge will be able to provide you with a flyer containing complete information on activities offered, hours, and pricing. The sections on the individual hotels provide information about locations and how to contact that hotel's kids' program. Private child care services provided by reputable outside agencies with licensed and bonded sitters can also be arranged. Ask your hotel concierge for assistance.

■ Mail

If you will need to receive mail or courier shipments while you are visiting the resort hotels, an increasingly likely scenario in our overworked world, have your mail sent to the address given below for each of the hotels. As long as your first and last name is on the letter or parcel, no special markings or additional notations are needed.

■ Microwave and Refrigerator

Microwaves and refrigerators are not included in standard rooms, but they may be rented for $16.88 (tax included) each per day by dialing Star Service.

■ Parking

Each resort hotel has its own parking lot. Self-parking is $20 per day for hotel guests, unless you take advantage of the valet parking service, in which case there is a $27 per day fee (plus tips, of course). If you fly into Orlando and plan to spend most of your time at the major attractions, you might want to consider foregoing a rental car during your stay and using shuttles and other options to get around Orlando. (See *Good Things To Know About...Transportation Elsewhere* below.)

For non-guests, there is a flat rate of $22 for self parking and $32 for valet service. If you come for a meal, ask to have your parking ticket validated at the restaurant and three hours of parking will be free.

■ Pets

Loews is a pet-friendly hotel chain and your furry friends are not only welcomed but pampered; they even get their own welcome gifts! If you'd like to bring a pet, be sure to let the hotel know when you make your reservation. A number of rooms in each hotel have been designated as pet rooms and a separate room service menu offers first-class pet dining for about $12.

You will be given a special sign to hang on your room latch to alert staff that a pet is in the room and you will have to make special arrangements with housekeeping since hotel policy is that no staff member will enter a room with a pet without the owner present. Up to date vaccination records are a must.

A $50 fee for "extra thorough cleaning" will be charged per night, up to $150 per stay. Maps provided by the hotels point out areas in which you can walk your pets. People with allergies should alert the hotel when making reservations to avoid being inadvertently placed in a pet room.

■ Room Service

There is 24-hour room service in the luxury hotels offering an abbreviated menu drawn from the main hotel restaurant. As you probably know, you pay a premium for room service, whether it is for a pet or a human. At the Universal resorts there is a $3 per order charge plus a 22% gratuity added to the bill.

■ Smoking

Loews hotels are smoke-free environments, except for designated outdoor areas. If you do light up in your room, you'll face a $200 cleaning fee.

■ Star Service

All the hotels offer "Star Service," a one-stop, one-phone-call solution for just about any need that might arise during your stay. It even has a special button on your in-room phone. The folks at Star Service seem to pride themselves on providing speedy answers to all your questions.

■ Transportation to the Parks

Once you arrive at the resort, it's possible to spend an entire vacation at Universal without riding any motorized vehicles (other than the ones inside the attractions), since all the hotels are at most a brisk 15-minute stroll from the action. All of the hotels are linked to the attractions and each other via attractively landscaped walking paths that allow pedestrians to avoid any vehicular traffic. The luxury hotels are also linked to CityWalk and the theme parks by complimentary water taxi. From the water taxi dock in CityWalk, it's a short walk to either park. If you want to go from hotel to hotel by boat, you will have to change boats at CityWalk.

All hotels, are served by shuttle buses that run about every half-hour from each hotel to a bus stop area near the entrance to Universal Studios Florida, but walking or taking the water taxi (where available) is a far quicker and more scenic way to get to the parks. If you prefer the bus, check with the concierge for details. Another option is the cadre of pedal-powered two-person rickshaws that ply the walkways. There is no set fee; the drivers work for tips. A few dollars per rider is customary.

■ Transportation Elsewhere

Complimentary bus shuttle service is also provided from all hotels to Wet 'n Wild and SeaWorld. Typically, there is one departure in the morning and, in the evening, one return from SeaWorld and one from Wet 'n Wild, although the schedule varies with park operating hours. Check with the concierge for more precise schedule information.

Mears Transportation operates on-demand shuttle services to and from Orlando Airport to the resort hotels, as well as scheduled shuttle service to and from each of the Universal Orlando Resort hotels and the Disney World parks. Limousine and town car services are also available. Check with the concierge for details.

If you prefer to do the driving yourself, all hotels have Hertz rental cars available. They can be reserved ahead but, if you decide you need a car at the last minute, chances are they will be able to accommodate you. Cars can be returned to the hotel or, for an additional fee, the Orlando Airport.

LOEWS PORTOFINO BAY HOTEL

5601 Universal Boulevard
Orlando, FL 32819
(407) 503-1000; fax: (407) 503-1010

A leisurely eight-minute cruise aboard a gracious nineteenth century motor launch takes you from CityWalk to one of the favorite getaways of Europe's fabled jet set — Portofino, Italy.

Well, okay, it's not really Portofino, Italy, but a near-photographic replica of the picturesque Ligurian fishing village that has long been a retreat for the rich and famous. And while you don't have to be famous to stay at this Portofino, it might help to be rich because the room rates place this property in the super-luxury range. If it's any consolation, staying at the Hotel Splendido (yes, that's its name) in the real Portofino will set you back $800 to $1,200 a night, while a room can be had at this Portofino Bay for $300 or so, at least at some times of the year.

If you're familiar with the real Portofino, you'll be amazed at how closely the architects and designers have come to re-creating the ambiance. If you're not, you might think the designers have cut corners by painting architectural details on the facades. Not so. This is exactly the way it's done in Portofino, Italy. It's called "trompe l'oeil," French for "trick the eye," and it's considered quite posh. The real trompe l'oeil accomplishment, however, is that what looks for all the world like a quaint fishing village made up of scores of separate homes, shops, courtyards, churches, palazzos, and alleyways is, in fact, a state-of-the-art luxury hotel whose 750 rooms have been artfully hidden behind those picturesque facades.

If you arrive by boat, you will walk from the dock to the large central piazza with all of Portofino arrayed before you. If you arrive by car, you will drive around the Bay to arrive at a portico entrance (dressed with vintage Fiats and Vespas for authentic flavor) where you can turn your vehicle over to a valet and step into a sumptuously appointed marble lobby. Either way, it's a spectacular introduction to a very special experience.

245

Orientation

Portofino Bay Hotel is located at the corner of Kirkman and Vineland Roads, but it turns its back to those streets and looks out on its own artificial harbor and across to Universal's Hard Rock Hotel and the theme parks beyond. The sole vehicular entrance is on Universal Boulevard near the Vineland Road entrance. You can also arrive by boat from CityWalk or walk onto the hotel property either from CityWalk and the Hard Rock Hotel or from Universal Boulevard.

The hotel wraps around "Portofino Bay," a small man-made harbor dotted with fishing boats and dinghies. A large open piazza faces the Bay and forms the focal point for the entire establishment. Most of the eateries and many of the shops face the piazza and the Bay.

The hotel's East Wing runs down one side of the Bay and the West Wing occupies the other, forming a rough "U." The section at the bottom of the "U" houses the hotel's main lobby area. Behind this, away from the Bay, are the extensive meeting rooms and banquet halls; they are located in such a way that vacationers and convention-goers need seldom cross paths or rub shoulders, except perhaps in the restaurants. Jutting out from the West Wing is the Villa Wing, offering larger rooms and easy access to the hotel's nicest pools and its spa facilities.

There is a downside to the layout, which is that your room can be quite a distance from the lobby and some of the hotel amenities.

Rooms and Suites

One nice thing about staying in a super-luxury hotel like Portofino Bay, which was refreshed inside and out with a fresh Mediterranean-inspired look in 2013, is that even the most modest room is going to be pretty special. And even the "average" guest is going to feel pampered by a level of service that the typical Orlando tourist never experiences.

All rooms have curvaceous headboards backing tall beds covered with Egyptian cotton linens and inviting plush comforters. All rooms include clock/radios with MP3 player connections and sleek 42-inch flat-screen televisions with HD channels. Especially convenient are terra cotta-colored marble his-and-hers dual bathroom sinks. Also common to all rooms are such thoughtful touches as lavishly stocked mini-bars, a coffee maker, plush bathrobes, an iron and ironing board, a hair dryer, and a safe. Every room benefits from keen attention to aesthetics, down to the coordinated colors of the carpet patterns and aqua-grey accent walls. About nine percent of the rooms have balconies; most of them are quite small but a few are large enough to allow al fresco dining.

Standard rooms are a comfortable 450 square feet, while deluxe rooms have 490 square feet of living space. Deluxe room bathrooms feature a separate shower stall, as well as the dual sinks, and have windows with louvered shutters over the tub that open onto the room. You may find the added perks well worth the added cost.

Beach Pool view rooms offer great views of the often dramatic Florida sunsets. Bay view rooms are ideal for those who want to feel as if they've been transported to the real Portofino. However, rooms in the Villa Wing that look out onto the Villa Pool offer a serenity that's hard to match.

Families with young children might want to consider one of the 18 recently reimagined Kids' Suites, which feature *Despicable Me*-inspired decor. All include a separate, Minion-filled kids' bedroom that is accessible only through the parents' room. Other multi-room options include a one-bedroom suite with parlor and a two-bedroom suite, ranging from 900 to 1,820 square feet. If you really want to treat yourself, consider the 2,725-square-foot Presidente Suite, with its spacious outdoor terrace.

See *Room Rates At A Glance*, above, to get an idea of the price range at Portofino Bay and how it compares to the other on-site hotels.

Amenities

The amenities here are as lavish in execution as the hotel itself and may encourage you to put off visiting the theme parks as you linger in the lap of luxury with a masseuse and a poolside waiter at your beck and call. The lobby alone, featuring comfortable armchairs and today's international newspapers on old-fashioned reading sticks, is an oasis of sophisticated repose.

■ Club Level

Ninety-seven rooms in the Villa Wing have been set aside to give select guests that extra level of service and exclusivity. It's essentially the same concept as that found on the "Concierge Level" at upscale business hotels. However, because the layout of the hotel makes it impossible to restrict access to the Club Level rooms and lounge area with elevators, the system here is slightly different.

The Club lounge is on the lobby level, near the Bar American, just past the hotel's ticket sales and auto rental counter. To gain admission, Club

Level guests must use their room keys. Once inside, they are treated to the largest Club lounge of all the resort hotels with free Internet access and a pool table along with more usual amenities like the *Wall Street Journal* and board games (to play there or take back to the room). There are also personal concierges on duty from 7:00 a.m. to 10:00 p.m.

There is a complimentary continental breakfast in the morning from 7:00 a.m., beverages and snacks throughout the day, light appetizers in the afternoon from noon to 3:00 p.m., free drinks from 5:00 p.m. to 7:00 p.m., and dessert at bedtime (8:00 p.m. to 9:30 p.m.).

■ Pools

There are three pools, ranging from the intimate to the lavish. The **Beach Pool** is the most extensive and the most fun. You'll find it nestled behind the West Wing. At one end it simulates a beach, with the ankle deep water surrounded by soft white sand; at the other end the pool is deeper, although never more than five feet. It surrounds a replica of the old lighthouse that stands along the Ligurian coast near Portofino. This crumbling ruin hides a short but speedy water slide that is a favorite with kids.

Nearby, against walls that mimic ancient aqueducts, are two small secluded spa pools with hot bubbling water and warm waterfalls that provide a very nice shoulder massage. Also close at hand is a large, separate children's play area, with a pirate ship to climb in and over and a wading pool that is constantly spritzed by a trio of fountains. Campo Portofino, the children's program (described below), is close by.

There are a few "cabanas," gaily striped canvas tents with overhead fans, electricity, flat-screen TVs, and small refrigerators. These can be rented for $100 per day (and up) and provide a modicum of privacy and a touch of class for your poolside lounging. All cabana rentals come with bottled water and include a small selection of soft drinks and fruit. Club Level guests sometimes receive a small discount. Make your reservations at the Beach Pool hut, call (407) 503-1200, dial 41745 from your room, or speak with the concierge.

The Beach Pool has its own poolside bar, Splendido's Pool Bar and Grill, so it's a great place to have a relaxed al fresco meal. Because of its popularity with kids, however, it can get noisy; so adults in search of peace and quiet might want to head elsewhere.

The **Villa Pool**, just a few steps from the Beach Pool and separated from it by a wing of the hotel, is much more elegant. The atmosphere is one of regal gentility. It's easy to imagine that you have your own palazzo or that you are a movie mogul cutting deals along the Italian Riviera. The layout of the pool is crisply formal with stately palm trees lining its borders and, at one end, an elaborate fountain backed by a raised balustrade.

There are more cabanas here; these start at $150 per day and come with the same amenities. Reserve them just as you would a Beach Pool cabana. There is a heated jacuzzi-like pool too, of course, and attendants are on hand to take food and drink orders at poolside. Just for fun, try out the immaculately groomed bocce ball courts; they make for a perfect no-cost date night. The official rules are posted nearby.

On peak-season Saturday nights there is a "Dive-In Movie" at the Beach Pool. A huge screen is set up at poolside so guests can watch while floating on rented rafts. The films are family fare of fairly recent vintage and never more racy than PG-13; the Harry Potter films are screened frequently.

A good place to go for some real privacy is the **Hillside Pool** tucked away at the end of the East Wing. Much smaller than the Beach Pool, it has the virtue of seclusion and quiet along with a view across the Bay.

Hours at the pools vary by season and occupancy. In summer, you will generally find the Beach Pool open 8:00 a.m. to 10:00 p.m. daily; the Villa Pool, 6:00 a.m. to 11:00 p.m.; and the Hillside Pool, 8:00 a.m. to 8:00 p.m.

■ Mandara Spa

Near the Beach Pool is a state-of-the-art spa. Never mind the serene but somewhat incoherent Malaysian theme: this is your perfect chance to feel like an Italian movie star. Mandara operates spas at luxury hotels from Vegas to Fiji and this one is among their finest. You can get the full treatment of massages, mud wraps, and facials, all with the latest "all-natural" and "therapeutic" ointments, oils, and unguents, of course. The heated massage tables are a particularly nice touch. Or you can simply have your hair and nails done in an elegant European salon setting. If you stroll in here and say, "Give me the works," be prepared to spend a bundle. The six-hour "Bliss for a Day" package, which includes lunch in addition to a dizzying regimen of facials, massages, makeup, manicure, pedicure, hair styling, and aromatherapy, costs $595. Less lavish packages of pampering start at $240 for "Men's Escape" or $340 for a "Sunrise Awakening"; a basic 50-minute massage starts at $130. Use of all spa and fitness center facilities is included with any service (see below).

■ Campo Portofino

Located near the Beach Pool, this indoor play area houses Portofino's children's activities program. For more information about the services offered here, see *Good Things To Know About...Kids' Activities* in the introductory section of this chapter. Make your reservations 24 hours in advance by calling 31200 on a hotel phone or (407) 503-1230 from outside.

■ Fitness Center

Adjacent to the Mandara Spa is a sleek health club (open 6:00 a.m. to 8:00 p.m. daily) offering the very latest in pec-pumping paraphernalia. Here you can exhaust yourself on treadmills, recumbent and standing bicycle machines, or stair climbers. For the die-hard traditionalist, there are also free weights. Access to the fitness center costs $10 per day ($25 for non-hotel guests), which entitles you to use all the facilities of the Spa, including showers, roman bath hot tubs, saunas, and steam rooms. You can also relax in the "quiet room" lounge, sipping herbal tea and snacking on dried fruit while you peruse periodicals in a comfy chair. If you are a customer of the Spa, staying on the Club level, a Premier Annual Passholder, or a member of You First, your access to the fitness center is free. Fitness-minded guests also use the paved walkway that surrounds the Bay or the path to Universal Studios Florida and back as a handy jogging trail.

Good Things To Know About...

■ Guest Laundry

Portofino Bay is apparently too posh for anything as down market as a coin laundry. You can either use the hotel's laundry service or carry your dirty duds to the Hard Rock Hotel and use the facilities there.

■ Meetings and Banquets

The hotel has over 42,000 square feet of meeting space, renovated in 2009, ranging from the magnificent 15,000-square-foot Tuscan Ballroom that can accommodate 1,280 for a sit-down dinner, to a sumptuous boardroom suite for 25. In addition to being beautifully appointed, with lavish hand-painted Italian murals, these facilities offer some of the most advanced telecommunications equipment available anywhere. That's made the Portofino Bay Hotel one of the most sought-after meeting venues in Orlando. If you'd like more information, simply call Conference Management at (407) 503-1130.

■ Musica della Notte

Every night at sunset, weather permitting of course, the piazza at Portofino comes alive with the "music of the night." Strolling musicians and classically trained singers appear on balconies and fill the night air with Italian favorites from opera, movies, and a cross-over style known as "popera" that blends classic opera and pop. There is no charge for this spectacle and guests from other hotels and even non-guests are welcome to take a motor launch over to Portofino Bay to enjoy the show.

■ Parking

The parking here is well-hidden and covered, making self-parking a more attractive option than at the other hotels, which have open lots.

■ Weddings

Looking for a very special place to tie the knot? Portofino Bay has quickly become a favorite spot for Orlando's discerning brides. There are two out-door gazebos that, when adorned with flowers, make lovely wedding cha-pels. One is above the Villa Pool in a palazzo-like setting; the other is in a courtyard near the main ballrooms and just steps away from a majestic curving staircase that was seemingly custom-designed for bridal portraits. And Universal Orlando, with its panoply of diversions, makes a terrific hon-eymoon destination. Call (407) 503-1120 for more information.

Dining at Loews Portofino Bay Hotel

Portofino Bay offers some superb gourmet dining, but reflecting the casual ambiance of its namesake, there are also casual, moderately priced eateries dotted around the property. Of course it's all Italian, in keeping with the hotel's theme. Unless you can be satisfied with a burger or a club sandwich, you'll have to travel to CityWalk or the parks for more varied fare.

Most of the hotel's eateries are positioned to take advantage of the pi-azza and the Bay. This survey begins on the western side of the Bay and heads around the piazza to the east, before describing two venues located elsewhere in the hotel. Guests who just can't drag themselves to one of these restaurants can take advantage of the hotel's 24-hour room service.

■ Bice

What:	Fine gourmet dining Northern Italian style
Where:	On the third level overlooking the Bay
Price Range:	$$$$+
Hours:	Daily, 5:30 p.m. to 10:00 p.m.
Reservations:	Recommended; (407) 503-1415 or OpenTable.com
Web:	orlando.bicegroup.com/

If the name Bice (pronounced BEE-chay) rings a bell, then there's a good chance you are an international jet setter with a generous expense account. The Portofino Bay Bice is yet another addition to a chain that spans the globe, with outposts in some 40 cities, most of them financial or mercantile capitals or resorts for the rich and famous. Bice was founded in Milan, Italy, in 1926 by Beatrice Ruggeri (Bice is an Italian diminutive for Beatrice). It was a family affair and still is, with the Ruggeri family still in control and still zealously maintaining its high standards. The atmosphere is one of hip, casual elegance. The main dining room is open and airy, with tall ceilings and large windows looking out onto the bay; black and white predominate, with elaborate flower arrangements adding a touch of color. Starched tablecloths on widely spaced tables add a certain formality to the trendy feel of the room, which can get extremely noisy when it's busy.

The best seats in the house. When the weather cooperates, the outdoor terrace's view of the harbor is marvelously romantic.

Each meal begins with bread accompanied by tasty tuna and sun-dried tomato spreads. The menu leans strongly to Northern Italian specialties. Antipasti and Insalate ($12 to $21) include Bice's signature tri-color salad with arugula, endive, and radicchio in a lemon dressing. Other starters include such standards as mozzarella with tomatoes and basil, prosciutto and melon, superbly sweet fried calamari, and tuna tartare. Primi Piatti (pastas and risottos) ($19 to $30) range from penne in a simple, but spicy, tomato sauce to fettuccine fra diavolo with shrimp. The Bice signature is Pappardelle al Telefono, broad pasta ribbons in a mozzarella and tomato cream sauce, a simple dish that is done to perfection.

Secondi Piatti ($28 to $46) include fish dishes such as swordfish, salmon and the like in simple sauces with vegetable accompaniments. Meat lovers will want to try the Ossobuco alla Milanese, another Bice specialty, a rich veal shank on a bed of saffron risotto. Other entrees include hearty steaks and chops and homey poultry dishes like grilled chicken breast. Side orders of vegetables ($9) are also available. Desserts ($10 to $13) cover the usual Italian bases with the Cioccolatissimo alla Bice the standout.

As you can see, the food here is not cheap, so you may want to take out a second mortgage if you plan on having wine with dinner. The extensive wine list ranges from $32 to $500. Expect to pay around $60 for a decent bottle. As you might expect, the list leans heavily to Italian wines, with a great selection of "Super Tuscan" wines listed from $40 to $450. Montalcinos start from $70 and the superior Brunello di Montalcino can be had for $75 to $190. Many wines can be ordered by the glass ($8 to $30).

At these prices, perfection seems a reasonable expectation. While we've had good experiences lately, past reports from other diners on food quality and service have been hit or miss. Instead of a full meal, try ordering appetizers at the bar. If you find yourself a fan, ask about their VIP club.

Tip: Bice will validate self-parking for non-hotel guests; valet parking will cost you $5, plus tax, with Bice validation.

■ The Thirsty Fish Bar

What:	Casual bar with snacks and cigars
Where:	Facing Portofino Bay, below Bice
Price Range:	$ - $$
Hours:	Opens nightly at 6:00 p.m., 5:00 p.m. on Saturday and Sunday
Reservations:	None

One of the few spots in the hotel that doesn't have an immediate echo in Italy, this casual bar is just a bit too tidy to be called funky. It caters to bayside strollers in need of liquid refreshment. This is primarily a drinking establishment. "Signature" cocktails ($13 to $14) include a Margarita Italiano and the Tuscan Limoni. You can also get a decent cigar.

Outdoor tables that spill into the piazza make The Thirsty Fish a great place to relax and survey the passing scene in the Italian fashion. On sultry summer nights (Thursday through Saturday) there may even be live music from 8:00 p.m. to 11:00 p.m.

■ Trattoria del Porto

What:	Casual dining
Where:	Facing the Harbor Piazza
Price Range:	$$ - $$$
Hours:	Breakfast daily 7:00 a.m. to 11:00 a.m.; dinner 5:30 p.m. to 10:30 p.m. Thursday through Monday
Reservations:	Not required but recommended during busier periods; (407) 503-3463 or OpenTable.com.

This spacious 300-seat restaurant serves first-rate, well executed American comfort cuisine at breakfast and dinner. Large windows look out onto the piazza, where there is plenty of al fresco seating. Should you care to eat outdoors, you'll be happily accommodated. The columns indoors are painted with fanciful scenes of commedia dell'arte figures cavorting under the sea with dolphins and seals. With its high ceilings, tile and mosaic accents in blue and gold, and polished wood trim, the Trattoria projects an air of laid-back elegance.

At breakfast, the Trattoria lays on a sumptuous buffet ($22 for adults, $12 for kids) that features made-to-order eggs and omelets. You can also order from a more traditional breakfast menu that features such favorites as Eggs Benedict and waffles adorned with fresh fruit.

At dinner, the restaurant's abbreviated menu shifts into "Tuscan Steak" mode, featuring filet mignon and hearty bone-in steaks ($32 to $34). Other entrees ($16 to $32) include slow-roasted chicken, mahi mahi, and pancetta-wrapped meatloaf. There is also a tapas-style "small plates" selection ($10 to $12) including charred calamari and chili-roasted shrimp. On Friday and Saturday (5:30 p.m. to 10:00 p.m.) Pasta Cucina, an all-you-can-eat, create-your-own-pasta-dish experience may be offered ($26 adults, $12 kids). A "foodies in training" kids' menu features simple dishes for $10. Desserts ($7) include a strawberry white chocolate cheesecake and a warm chocolate volcano cake.

The wine list is more than serviceable and includes a good selection of Italian wines. If the weather's fine, the tables in the large al fresco dining area on the piazza offer the best seats in the house.

Note: Kids are especially welcome. At the back of the restaurant there is a small dining area for little ones, featuring brightly colored toddler-sized tables, a large-screen TV showing appropriate kiddie fare, and big pillows for comfy after-meal sprawling. Some nights a magician will perform or a clown will drop by to create balloon animals. Other nights (typically Friday from 6:30 p.m. to 9:30 p.m.) there is Character Dining with various Universal stars; ask the concierge for the schedule.

■ Mama Della's Ristorante

What:	Home-style Italian dinners
Where:	Facing the Harbor Piazza, next to the Trattoria
Price Range:	$$$ - $$$$
Hours:	5:30 p.m. to 10:00 p.m.
Reservations:	Recommended; (407) 503-1432 or OpenTable.com

A lot of people will tell you this is their favorite Portofino Bay restaurant and it has attracted a dedicated local following. It isn't as fancy as Bice and the cuisine is more comforting than intriguing, but perhaps that is the attraction. Then, too, Mama Della's comes complete with Mama, a perfectly cast woman of a certain age who greets you warmly at the door and makes you feel as if you never left the Old Neighborhood even if you were never there to begin with.

The decor evokes a large and comfortable country home with its beamed ceilings and colorful wallpaper. Vintage family photographs and gaudy gold-framed floral paintings line the walls of the various rooms. Colorful pitchers, bowls, and other folk ceramics are displayed in niches. Adding to the casual air is an open galley kitchen in the back room where you can see chefs in baseball caps dishing up their homey specialties. And a festive note is contributed by a strolling singer offering popular Italian songs to an accordion accompaniment.

Among the appetizers ($9 to $17), you'll find the shrimp scampi, tender fried calamari, and mixed antipasto of cured meats, cheeses, and marinated vegetables especially noteworthy. A generous mixed salad for two costs $16, but the fresh bread and dipping oil are free.

The entrees ($23 to $39) can best be described as elevated Italian comfort food: chicken carbonara, fettuccine alfredo, lasagna, and the like. The veal dishes, prepared in various styles, are reliably spectacular and big enough for two to share; if the exquisite chop with mushroom sauce isn't listed, ask if the kitchen can improvise one. Many of the dishes here can be served "family style" on large platters for a group. Family style service typically means a modest discount off the individual price for each additional person.

Vegetable side dishes are not listed on the menu but can be ordered for about $7. Wine is served by the glass ($9 to $18) and bottle ($34 to $300+). Desserts ($6 to $9) range from simple sorbets and tiramisu to a fancy chocolate extravaganza.

■ Sal's Market Deli

What:	Casual sandwiches and pizza
Where:	Facing the Harbor Piazza
Hours:	Varies with the seasons and occupancy level, generally 6:00 a.m. to 11:00 p.m.
Price Range:	$$
Reservations:	None

Sal's offers a casual atmosphere patterned on the famed Peck emporium of Milan but reminiscent of New York's Little Italy, thanks to its marble-topped cafe tables and arched ceiling. It's a nice place to stop for a quick bite. Panini (grilled Italian sandwiches, $12) are served at the deli-like counter along with cold antipasto-style salads ($9 to $12).

At the back is a sort of pizza bar where you can order one of five styles of pizzas (small $13, large $15) and sit on a stool along a marble counter and watch it baking in the open-doored oven. A small pie can feed two people generously. This ain't Domino's, either. The pizza chefs here make their own dough, using a mixture of high-gluten flour for toughness and durum semolina for taste and a rich yellow color. (Special gluten-free pizzas are available on request.) The oven is a true pizza oven, with the base kept at a steady 600 degrees. The result is a crisper and firmer crust than you'll find over at the Trattoria or the Splendido Pizzeria. Sal's version of Pizza Salvatore, with a generous topping of mushrooms, sausage, and pepperoni, is especially good.

Tip: You can have your pizza made to go, a good thing to know if you are not staying in the hotel.

If you like wine with your pizza, you can get it by the glass for $5 to $7. Sal's is also a good place to grab a cup of coffee. Espresso and cappuccino are available, as is regular coffee. For a stronger cup ask for a Caffe Americano, a shot of espresso with steaming hot water added.

■ Gelateria Caffe Espresso

What:	Gelato
Where:	Facing the Piazza, past the Universal store
Hours:	Varies, generally 11:00 a.m. to 11:00 p.m.
Price Range:	$
Reservations:	None

After several years as an adjunct to Sal's, the Gelateria has moved to its own quarters. The Gelateria serves gelato, the creamy Italian ice cream, handmade daily on the premises. You can have it straight, in a sundae, or in a cream-topped milk shake. Sorbets and Italian ices are also served.

The move hadn't happened at press time, so details are sketchy. Back in the day, a small selection of cookies, muffins, pastries, and cakes was available here and, in the mornings, croissants, muffins, and fresh fruit were laid out, making this a good serve-yourself alternative to a room service breakfast. Presumably those functions will be left to Starbucks, next door.

■ Starbucks

What:	Coffee
Where:	Facing the Piazza, next to the Gelateria
Hours:	Daily, 6:00 a.m. to 8:00 p.m.
Price Range:	$
Reservations:	None

What can be said about Starbucks that hasn't been said before, often through gritted teeth?

■ Bar American

What:	Posh formal bar
Where:	Off the main lobby

Hours: Open selected nights 4:00 p.m. to 11:00 p.m.
Price Range: $$ - $$$
Reservations: None

There are vague echoes of Harry's Bar in Venice here, but Portofino's Bar American is very much its own room and in the fine tradition of up-scale hotel bars where patrons signal their status by swirling $200 snifters of fine brandy.

Luckily you can enjoy a drink and the refined atmosphere for less than that. Specialty cocktails are in the $15 to $16 range. There is a brief menu offering "Big Bytes" and "Nybbles" such as a 10-ounce Black Angus burger, chili roasted shrimp, and slow roasted tomatoes. Tiramisu and creme brulee ($7) are also served for dessert. Other specialties here include single malt Scotch ($12 to $35), and the aforementioned cognacs ($29 to $195).

■ Splendido's Pool Bar and Grill

What: Pizzeria
Where: At the Beach Pool
Hours: 11:00 a.m. to 5:00 p.m., but hours vary seasonally
Price Range: $$
Reservations: None

The name is a nod to the exclusive hotel in the real Portofino, but the atmosphere is far from deluxe. This laid back and ultra-casual poolside bar offers table service for about 50 people on a charming, shaded patio, while roving waiters serve loungers at both the Beach and Villa Pools.

Salads ($7 to $16) include Caesar, citrus arugula with locally caught fish, and a fruit plate. Sandwiches ($11 to $18) are served with salad, on-ion rings, or French fries and include a shrimp BLT, turkey wraps, folded quesadillas, and BBQ pulled pork. Appetizers ($7 to $13) feature root beer glazed baby back ribs and chicken satay with plum sauce. The pizza you get here ($12 to $14) is much the same as that served up in Sal's. But here you can eat it poolside, which, of course, makes it taste better. Italian ices and fruit smoothies round out the short menu. A kids' meal, including an entree, fries, and a beverage, is under $10.

The Splendido also serves up some fancy cocktails ($15 in a souvenir glass, $10 refills) designed to produce that perfect poolside buzz. The Riviera, to cite just one example, is a creative blend of Cruzan coconut rum, mango, and piña colada topped with a "strawberry lava flow."

As with all the poolside eateries at Universal Orlando, an 18% gratuity is automatically added to all bills.

Shopping at Loews Portofino Bay

Shopping is not the main focus at Portofino Bay Hotel. In fact, unlike many posh hotels around the world, this one has remarkably few shops. The ones it has can be roughly divided between the practical and the posh.

On the practical side is **Le Memorie di Portofino**, or Memories of Portofino, where you can pick up a variety of sundries and magazines along with pricey polo shirts bearing the hotel's handsome logo. If you don't like the paper dropped outside your door, you can come here for *The New York Times, Wall Street Journal,* and London's *Daily Mail.* Other reading matter includes glossy magazines and the latest thriller to take to the pool. There is also some posh Italian ceramic ware and resort wear emblazoned with the Portofino Bay logo.

Another place to stop into to pick up the necessities of resort life is **L'Ancora** (The Anchor) located near the boat dock. It thoughtfully purveys sunscreen and other items you might need as you head for the parks. This shop also stocks chips, nuts, and soft drinks to wash it all down with. In addition, about 50 percent of their business is in ultra-casual clothing.

As you might have guessed, there is an outpost of the **Universal Studios Store** in Portofino Bay. It stocks plenty of T-shirts and polo shirts, some of them quite nice. You'll also find a small selection of toys and plush dolls for the kids.

The remaining shops are for pampering yourself or that special someone. Once you've taken in the luxurious atmosphere of the hotel, you might want to rush to **Alta Moda** (High Fashion) for something you'll feel comfortable being seen in. They have thoughtfully provided the best in contemporary resort wear, with everything from Tommy Bahama clothes and fashion accessories, to swimwear, to lingerie, to evening wear for that special meal at Bice.

Another place to spend the money you didn't spend on a ticket to Italy is **Galleria Portofino**. It features the work of contemporary artists, alongside collectible prints of Dr. Seuss and comic characters and art inspired by Harry Potter, including prints by the artist who designed the book covers. In addition to paintings, there is some decorative statuary, colorful Britto housewares, and jewelry from a variety of artisans. If you'd rather take home artwork with your own face on it, **Family Art,** across the piazza, offers free photography sittings, and will print the results on anything from towels to tiles.

HARD ROCK HOTEL

5800 Universal Boulevard
Orlando, FL 32819
(407) 503-ROCK (7625); fax: (407) 503-ROLL (7655)

Imagine for a moment you are an aging rock star. Changing tastes and slumping record sales have reduced your income to pitiful new lows. Years of hard living and fiscal mismanagement have depleted your assets to the vanishing point. Your groupies have left you to your own devices in the palatial Beverly Hills mansion that you have filled with the memories and memorabilia of your high-flying years of hits and worldwide mega tours. Soon you will have to sell this last remnant of your once lavish lifestyle and move into a shabby condo. Then, inspiration strikes: you'll turn your mansion into a hotel! Paying guests will leap at the chance to experience, however vicariously, however briefly, what it must be like to live like a real live rock star.

That is the "backstory" of the Hard Rock Hotel. It's a story that will never be told in so many words to the guests who stay here, but it is the fanciful tale from which the architects and designers drew inspiration as they fashioned this flamboyant, flashy, and surprisingly elegant hostelry.

The 650-room Hard Rock Hotel draws on the architectural traditions of California's Spanish Mission style, with stucco arches and adobe-like touches, rising to seven stories at its highest point. With its gracious terraces and the towering palm trees that dot the 19 acres of manicured grounds, it looks more like the rambling mountaintop palaces of Hollywood's superstars than the well-appointed hotel it is.

Orientation

The Hard Rock Hotel is located on Universal Boulevard, just south of Vineland Road. Its huge front gates face toward the Portofino Bay Hotel, which lies, unseen, across the boulevard. For guests with hotel keys, there is also a side entrance near the dock where water taxis arrive from CityWalk.

The elegant main approach, an oval lawn flanked by stately palms, suggests pure luxury. The fountain out front, with its sculpture of spiraling guitars, adds a touch of whimsy. The pulsing rock music that subtly envelops guests as they walk over the marble-mosaic Hard Rock logo into the expansive lobby signals that a stay here is literally going to be an upbeat experience. The marble lobby gives way to a spacious sunken carpeted lounge overlooking the palm-dotted pool area out back.

The lobby lounge is decorated with clunky yet comfortable earth-toned furniture and some souvenirs that the unnamed rock star of the backstory has collected during his world tours, with coffee tables doubling as showcases for rare guitars once owned by rock masters.

The public areas of the lobby level are dominated by large-scale art paying homage to some of rock's greatest stars. A highlight is the massive blowup of the cover photo from the Stones' *Beggars' Banquet* album. This is a Hard Rock property, of course, so as you might expect, the ample collection of rock memorabilia spills out into the public areas and down the hallways. In fact, more than $1 million worth of rock memorabilia is scattered throughout the hotel, but judiciously so. Dial (407) 503-2233 and enter the code number on plaques next to display cases for related music trivia.

The lobby level, on the hotel's third floor, features the Palm Restaurant, the Velvet Bar, the Rock Shop, and the hotel's small meetings areas. Two floors below, at ground level, is The Kitchen, the hotel's main restaurant, and the extensive pool area. Also on this level are the fitness center and Camp L'il Rock for kids. A single bank of elevators gives access to all the hotel's floors.

The hotel wraps itself around the pool area out back, so the hallways of the upper floors, beautifully carpeted in blue and tan, curve gracefully. Where wings meet, the halls are punctuated by circular mini-lobbies with carpet medallions on the floor and rock memorabilia or rock portraits on the wall. The overall effect is quite classy; the rocker who owned this place obviously had exquisite taste — or hired a decorator who did.

For most people, the Hard Rock Hotel's best feature is likely to be its "ground-zero" location, next to Universal Studios Florida. As noted above, the actual front entrance to the hotel faces Universal Boulevard, looking across to the Portofino Bay Hotel, but the hotel grounds nestle up against the theme park. A side entrance on the ground level leads to a boat dock where you can pick up a motor launch for the short ride to CityWalk. If you prefer to walk, out back, past the pool, is a path that will take you directly to the front gates of Universal Studios Florida. You can leave the hotel on foot and, walking at a leisurely pace, be inside Universal Studios Florida in less than six minutes. It's the next best thing to actually staying inside the park.

Rooms and Suites

In general, the rooms are smaller than those at Portofino but just as nicely appointed. What you will find are beautifully designed and furnished rooms that would make the reputation of any big city "boutique" hotel. Most rooms, which avoid that boxy hotel room look with curved or angled walls, are "standard" rooms, 375 square feet, while the deluxe rooms are 400 square feet and feature a larger sitting area. Pool view rooms, especially those on floors five through seven, are highly recommended. You can reserve either a pool view or garden view room, but if you choose a deluxe room, the hotel will not be able to guarantee the view.

There is no rock memorabilia in the rooms, but the walls are decorated with black and white photos of rock history, in artful black frames with plenty of white matting. Each room has a different selection of photos from the hotel's collection. There are no labels, so your rock knowledge will be tested.

Every room boasts a 32-inch flat-screen television and a compact but powerful CD-radio player. All rooms also feature iHome clock/radios with built-in iPod docks. When you check in you will get a code allowing you to download three distinct iTunes playlists. Otherwise, you can tune the player to the local rock station, 101.1 FM, or 104.1 for classic rock on the weekends. Don't be surprised if you hear the dull throb of bass notes from other rooms lulling you to sleep and waking you up in the morning.

Rooms also boast soft bedding with huge bolsters and muted coverlets; only the stiff pillows leave something to be desired. Complimentary goodies include Keurig coffee and a copy of *Rolling Stone* magazine. And in what may be a subtle reference to a Beatles song, you'll even find a copy of Gideon's Bible. Gideon checked out and left it, no doubt, to help with some rocker's revival.

Hard Rock features a Club Level, with restricted access, on the seventh floor. For more on the Club Level, see *Amenities*, below. 800-square-foot Kids' Suites, similar to those offered at Portofino, are also available, as are 650-square-foot "King" Suites.

There is even a Graceland Suite, also named in honor of The King. But don't expect gaudy over the top furniture and pink Caddy fins on the bed. This is a beautifully appointed 2,375-square-foot suite of rooms with antiques, abstract paintings, and beautiful furnishings. The master bedroom features a flat-screen TV hanging on the wall and a glass-fronted fireplace that also opens onto a lavish shower area with a jacuzzi that can hold several people. (Groupies not included, presumably.)

Amenities

As a relatively small hotel on a smallish plot of land, the Hard Rock boasts fewer amenities than the nearby Portofino Bay, but what's here is choice.

■ The Pool

The Hard Rock's only pool, all 12,000 square feet of it, is like a jewel in a fine setting. The hotel itself almost completely encloses it. The open end looks out past a rocky hill topped by a 30-foot guitar and a forest of palm trees toward Universal Studios Florida. The far side of the pool is an extensive sandy beach, sporting a volleyball net, lounge chairs, and cabanas. The near side is dotted with more palm trees and still more lounge chairs. Two heated jacuzzi spas (one designated "adults only") offer soothing massages. As a screenwriter might put it in a pitch meeting, "It's Bel Air meets Palm Springs."

Like the Beach Pool at Portofino, the Hard Rock pool features a water slide, this one a bit longer (at 260 feet) and zippier. But the feature that will have everyone talking is the underwater sound system, which plays the same toe-tapping rock music you hear at poolside and throughout the hotel. It is possible to float lazily on your back, your ears below the water line, and groove to some of the greatest rock 'n roll ever recorded (though the sound is quite tinny). If you prefer, you can sit on underwater benches along the side where heated jets of water caress your back.

Near the pool is a concrete shuffleboard court that seems a bit incongruous. Yes, of course even rockers grow old, but it's still just a little difficult to picture Twisted Sister hanging out here.

A lot more "happening" is the beachclub bar (reviewed below). Attractive young servers roam the pool area taking orders for exotic drinks with names like Blue Suede Shoes and Hard Rockin' Lemonade.

Hollywood deal makers can spread out in one of the private tent-like cabanas that can be rented by the day. "Standard" cabanas range from $125 to $250 and "Beach Side" locations go for $150 to $290 depending on occupancy levels. Club Level guests get $40 off. There are no half-day rentals. All cabanas have a television, refrigerator, fresh water, fruit basket, towels, and a small selection of soft drinks. Call (407) 503-2236 to reserve one.

Most nights the pool hosts a "Dive-In Movie." A large screen is set up on the poolside beach so guests can watch while floating on rented rafts. The films include classic comedies and current blockbusters (think *Ghostbusters* and *Iron Man*) and are never racier than PG-13. On other nights there may be a "Dive-In Concert" or a D.J. may appear to keep the joint jumpin'.

If there's a downside to all this, it's probably that the pool is just too popular. So expect it to be crowded. The pool is open daily from 8:00 a.m. to 11:00 p.m. or midnight during warmer months. Access is through a gate that can be opened with your room key.

■ Club Level

The rooms and suites on the seventh floor have been set aside for those who insist on a little extra from their hotel stay. The concept is much like the Concierge Levels you may have encountered at those high-priced hotels that cater to business travelers, except this one has the hip, rock star name "Club 7."

For starters, access to the seventh floor is strictly limited. Just to make sure you are not bothered by the riff-raff, you have to insert your room key into a slot in the elevator before it will take you to seven. Once there, you can step into a spacious lounge staffed with friendly hosts and hostesses, who serve as your personal concierges from 7:30 a.m. to 10:00 p.m. This is where you come in the morning for a complimentary continental breakfast and to glance through the tony out-of-town papers high rollers insist upon. The lounge serves refreshments throughout the day; hors d'oeuvres, beer and wine in the evening; and cookies and milk before bedtime.

Club Level guests can borrow from a collection of 500 rock CDs for private listening in their rooms. If they're feeling more sociable, the Club lounge offers two large screen TVs with DVD players in an area with very comfy seating. Club level guests also receive free access to the hotel's fitness center and a discount on those pricey poolside cabanas (see above).

■ Camp L'il Rock

Hard Rock's kiddie club is located on the ground floor not far from the pool. For more information about the services offered here, see *Good Things To Know About...Kids' Activities* in the introductory section of this chapter. Make your reservations 24 hours in advance by calling 32230 on a hotel phone or (407) 503-2230 from outside.

■ Workout Room

The "Body Rock" compact fitness center on the ground floor has a small selection of treadmills, weight machines, and free weights. After your workout, you can relax in a steam room or sauna and then change in the locker room. There is a $10 per day fee; multi-day passes are available. Club Level guests and All Access members get in free. Hours are 6:00 a.m. to 10:00 p.m. Kids 13 through 17 are allowed, but only if they have adult supervision.

Joggers can take off for a loop around either the Bay at Portofino Bay in one direction or CityWalk in the other.

Good Things To Know About...

■ Guest Laundry

The Hard Rock Hotel has small guest laundry rooms on the second and fourth floors near the elevators, each with two washers and two dryers. The cost is $3 to wash, $3 to dry.

■ "Picks" Guitar Loans and "MIX" D.J. Lessons

If the hotel's theme puts you in a musical mood, Hard Rock will give you one of 20 awesome Fender axes to annoy your suitemates with. The guitar is free for your stay, but you must provide a refundable $1,000 credit card deposit. If spinning is more your speed, daily D.J. lessons in the lobby during peak seasons will teach you to "MIX like a Pro."

■ Meetings, Weddings, and Banquets

There is very little meeting space at the Hard Rock. The largest space is the Avalon Ballroom, 3,000 square feet divisible into three separate sections, with a total capacity of 300 people. Two smaller rooms, the Apollo Boardroom and the Fillmore Meeting Room, are suitable for receptions or small meetings. For more information, call (407) 503-2100.

■ Parking

Parking is outdoors in two lots that flank the impressive main entrance. Finding a good spot (or any spot!) can sometimes be a challenge. Valet parking is another option; the Palm will validate for all diners.

■ Velvet Sessions

On the last Thursday of most months, the Velvet Bar (see below) spills out into the lobby for Velvet Sessions, "a rock and roll cocktail party," and a guest rock band pumps up the volume from 6:30 p.m. to 9:00 p.m. or later. Past acts have included Modern English, Bret Michaels, Cheap Trick, Joan Jett, Eddie Money, and Gin Blossoms. Various liquor companies use the events to tout new brands and concoctions, and presumably a good time is had by all. Tickets are $29 online, $35 at the door, $75 for VIP, but can go higher for big names. Visit www.velvetsessions.com to find out the latest.

Dining at the Hard Rock Hotel

There are two full-service restaurants at Hard Rock, one offering gut- and wallet-busting steaks for the expense account crowd in the evenings, the other serving up moderately priced casual fare all day long. An ice cream parlor doubles as a casual, take-out breakfast spot in the morning. Guests who are too pooped to pop or too old to stroll can call on the hotel's 24-hour room service.

■ Palm Restaurant

What:	Steak house
Where:	On the lobby level, near Velvet, with outside entrance
Price Range:	$$$$+
Hours:	Monday to Thursday 5:00 p.m. to 10:00 p.m.; Friday and Saturday 5:00 p.m. to 11:00 p.m.; Sunday 5:00 p.m. to 9:30 p.m.
Reservations:	Not required but highly recommended, especially on weekends; (407) 503-7256 or OpenTable.com

The original Palm opened in New York in 1926 and over the years developed a reputation as a place where movers and shakers gathered to devour mammoth steaks and cut big deals. In the intervening years, the Palm has branched out to many other cities and has now established itself in Orlando. Those who know the original will find the Hard Rock incarnation familiar, if larger.

Like the other branches, the walls of this one are filled with colorful caricatures of regular patrons and local celebrities from the business world and the media. The dark wooden wainscoting and room dividers evoke an earlier, male-dominated era when the steak house was something of a boy's club. The waiters in long white meat cutters' aprons complete the vintage picture.

The Palm fits the spirit of Hard Rock and is equally popular with tourists and high-rolling locals. It's a great place to come in a celebratory mood with a bunch of friends who don't mind shouting to make themselves heard as they tuck into huge slabs of prime aged meat or crack open a five-pound lobster, all washed down with some pricey wines. Figure a bare minimum of $75 per person for the standard Palm blowout meal, much more with cocktails and wine. Those looking for a quiet table in the corner or a moderately priced meal should look elsewhere.

Steaks are the center of attention here and they are quite good. They range in price from $46 to $60, with a mammoth 32-ounce double steak for two going for $100. Three-pound lobsters start at $75; at times you can get a four-pounder for two with salads and sides for $99. If you don't know exactly what you want, rely on the server's recommendation. Steak and lobsters at the Palm are traditionally accompanied by a number of side dishes served for one ($8) or "family style for two or more" ($12). The creamed spinach is justly famous and the brussels sprouts are addictive.

For those not into thick slabs of steak or gargantuan crustaceans, the Palm offers a selection of fairly standard Italian veal dishes ($25 to $34). For lighter appetites, two of the Palm's signature salads are worth recommending. The Gigi ($16) is a blend of tomatoes, bacon, onions, chopped shrimp, and green beans in a light vinaigrette and the Monday Night Salad ($13) is mixed greens, pimentos, onions, tomatoes, anchovies, and radishes.

Desserts ($10) are fairly pedestrian versions of old standbys and strike some as a tad overpriced. They include New York cheesecake, carrot cake, key lime pie, and creme bruleé.

From 5:00 p.m. to 7:00 p.m. Sunday through Friday, the bar takes half off of "Prime Bites" (including steakburgers, crab cakes, and lobster sliders), beer, wine, and premium cocktails, a fantastic value. Repeat diners should ask their server about the 837 Club; you can earn points toward a free lobster for your birthday.

The Palm has two entrances. One leads from the hotel lobby down a stately corridor lined with psychedelic day-glo posters from the heyday of San Francisco acid rock; the other offers access from the hotel's front drive for those arriving by car.

■ Velvet Bar

What:	Trendy watering hole
Where:	Off the main lobby lounge
Price Range:	$ - $$
Hours:	5:00 p.m. to 2:00 a.m. daily (1:00 a.m. kitchen closes, 1:30 a.m. last call)
Reservations:	None

Flat-screen TV screens on the wall provide a never-ending flow of music videos for the crowds that gather in this intimate, postmodern lounge. It has quickly proved to be the place for groups of friends to meet before an evening at the hotel or CityWalk.

The decor continues the same "rock star rummage sale" motif that fills the lobby. To this are added some wonderfully tacky faux zebra chairs, abstract art, and portraits of rock stars in a mish-mash that makes you feel like you've had a bit too much to drink before you take your first sip. A well-placed divider splits the room into a bar area and a more secluded lounge area, and servers prowl the bar and the adjacent lobby lounge taking orders.

If you like your libations on the elaborate side, a selection of colorfully named "heavy metal" cocktails ($11 to $14) like Bri's Bongwater and Mexican Bishop should satisfy your craving. For serious drinkers there is cognac ($14 to $263) and single malt Scotch ($14 to $47). There is a brief menu of "nibbles" ($11 to $18) including shrimp cocktail, fried gator tail, and salads, along with more substantial "big bites" plates ($13 to $34) of BLT and NY strip. Hookah water pipes ($25) and cigars ($6 to $19) are also available.

A daily happy hour runs from 5:00 p.m. to 7:00 p.m., with discounts on select mixed drinks and draft beers. Trivia and video games are played on occasion, and live music is offered every Friday with no cover charge.

■ The Kitchen

What:	Casual all-day dining
Where:	On the ground floor with an entrance facing the pool
Price Range:	$$ - $$$
Hours:	7:00 a.m. to 11:00 p.m. daily
Reservations:	Not required but accepted at (407) 503-DINE (3463) or OpenTable.com

This artfully casual eatery features "New American" cuisine in a glamorous open setting that seems to run the length of the hotel. The long main dining area features an open kitchen and a brick pizza oven. There is a separate, more intimate dining room at the far end for private parties, a small bar area, and a "Kids' Crib," a separate area where kids can dine apart from their hectoring parents. In keeping with the kitchen theme, many dishes are served in what appear to be cooking utensils like colanders and frying pans. The entire restaurant looks out through generous glass walls to the pool area and there is an outdoor seating area where the tables are shaded by snazzy square canvas umbrellas.

Breakfast is the most traditional meal, as the counters by the open kitchen are transformed into a sumptuous buffet. You can choose the full Breakfast Buffet ($19.50, $31.50 with unlimited mimosas and Bloody Marys, $10 for kids), or you can order a la carte from a menu of standards ($12 to $18), from bacon and eggs to waffles with fruit, all of them well executed.

Lunch and dinner share most of the same menu items. Flatbreads are $14 to $15, with toppings like smoked chicken, ricotta, mozzarella, and garlic. Main dishes ($15 to $37) range from a simple Mac and Cheese to Seared Ahi Tuna and filet mignon, and include straightforward interpretations of corvina, chicken pot pie, and rotisserie chicken. Otherwise, there are salads and sandwiches ($7 to $18). From 3:00 p.m. to 5:00 p.m., a smaller subset of "light fare" from the lunch menu is served.

The food is good without making an attempt to be exceptional. In the center of the restaurant is a "chef's table" where you can sit at a curving counter and watch a sous chef prepare the evening's specials. A tilted overhead mirror gives you a good view of the techniques being employed. On rare occasions, visiting rock stars like Dee Snyder and Vince Neil have done cooking demos here and "Kids Can Cook, Too" is a regular event.

Universal cartoon characters make the rounds here from 6:00 p.m. to 9:00 p.m. on Wednesday and Saturday. Tuesday and Thursday from 5:00 p.m. to 7:00 p.m. is "Kids Can Cook, Too" night, with supervised activities for little chefs. For the adults, there are wine specials on Monday and Wednesday, discount martinis on Tuesday and Thursday, and cheap Bloody Marys all Sunday. On Fridays, strolling magicians prestidigitate tableside for your pleasure.

■ Emack & Bolio's

What:	Ice cream parlor and grab & go market
Where:	On the ground floor on the way to the pool
Price Range:	$ - $$
Hours:	6:30 a.m. to 11:00 p.m. daily
Reservations:	None

In the morning, Emack & Bolio's serves up quick, easy-to-carry breakfast items like yogurt, fruit cups, Starbucks coffee, and pastries. There are also take-to-your-room snacks and drinks. Its main line of business, however, is upscale, high-fat, premium ice cream and fruit smoothies that have made it one of the hotel's most popular "dining" spots.

The ice cream flavors have cutesy Ben & Jerry's-style names, often with a rock and roll twist. A single scoop costs $3.75 and a pint goes for $7.50. Sundaes start at $5.50, but why not round up seven friends and splurge on a $24 Emack Attack?

■ beachclub

What:	Bar and snacks al fresco
Where:	By the pool
Price Range:	$ - $$
Hours:	11:00 a.m. to 10:00 p.m., later when it's busy
Reservations:	None

The pool enjoys its own casual bar serving light fare, with optional poolside service. The circular bar is open to the pool and raffishly decorated with rusted metal sculptures of musicians. Tables spill out from under the conical roof, but roaming servers will take your order and fetch your food and drink anywhere in the pool area. You can order up a daiquiri, margarita, or other fancy drink ($9 to $12) or opt for a non-alcoholic smoothie ($6).

The abbreviated menu ranges from the sort of salty snacks that will encourage you to order another beer, to salads and sandwiches, to simple desserts. The sandwiches ($10 to $16) range from wraps and burgers (including veggie burgers) to more refined fare. Or you can build your own pizza ($10 and up). Salads ($10 to $16) range from a simple dish of mixed greens to Caesar salad with shrimp. The desserts ($4 to $6) include ice cream treats from Emack & Bolio's. As with all the poolside eateries at Universal Orlando, an 18% gratuity is automatically added to all bills.

Shopping at Hard Rock Hotel

"Love all. Serve all. Sell all a tchotchke." That's not really the Hard Rock motto, of course, but it's hard to escape noticing that the Hard Rock empire must make as much money selling branded clothing, souvenirs, and memorabilia as it does selling burgers, shakes, and booze. So it's fitting that the only shop is the coyly named **Rock Shop** just off the main lobby.

Most of the room in this spacious emporium is given over to souvenir clothing, from T-shirts to snazzy leather jackets with equally snazzy price tags. If you have arrived only to discover that your wardrobe isn't what it should be, you can remedy that here. There are some sexy bikinis for women, but precious little for the guys. A small section is devoted to the latest in earbuds and earphones.

You'll find some nice things for kids here, too, including black leather jackets. Almost as an afterthought, a corner of the shop is given over to a small selection of the sort of sundries you usually find in a hotel gift shop. You will have to head to Le Memorie di Portofino shop in Portofino Bay's lobby for a larger selection.

Tip: Inside the shop is a interactive display screen that provides information on the memorabilia inside the hotel as well as at Hard Rocks around the world.

LOEWS ROYAL PACIFIC RESORT

6300 Hollywood Way

Orlando, FL 32819

(407) 503-3000; fax: (407) 503-3010

Like the Hard Rock, the Royal Pacific Resort has a "backstory" that subtly informed the design of the hotel and the themes of its restaurants. This one involves the Royal Pacific family of companies, a made-up travel and transportation conglomerate that flourished in the 1930s, the "Golden Age of Travel." Its holdings included Royal Pacific Airways, a fleet of dashing sea planes that linked the sprawling island chains of the South Pacific, and Royal Pacific Steamship Lines, a fleet of luxury ocean liners that plied the tropical seas. The Royal Pacific Resort, it would seem, is the latest jewel in the Royal Pacific crown, a luxury getaway located somewhere in Bali. Of course, none of this is terribly overt. It's a muted story, told with subtlety — a welcome message in the in-room hotel directory, the retro art on the travel posters in your room, and the occasional display case of memorabilia dotted around the property, not to mention the Royal Pacific Airways Grumman Albatross sea plane floating near the water taxi dock. Everything here has been inspired by, rather than copied from, Indonesia and Fiji, so the hotel reminds you of the South Seas while remaining very much its own place.

If the fictional Royal Pacific was a company of the thirties, the present seven-story hotel is very much of the twenty-first century. Its public spaces are open, airy, and luxurious, tastefully decorated with genuine Indonesian woodcarvings and other art works. Its lobby is gorgeous, the most exotic of the three resort hotels. Its amenities are state of the art and the dining venues, including a snazzy restaurant by Emeril Lagasse, are a cut or three above standard hotel fare.

The hotel's facade, which reflects its Balinese inspiration, is a rather featureless mustard-colored slab, but the lush greenery growing along it provides visual flair and grows lusher every year. The exterior looks even better at night, when artfully placed spotlights and the shadows cast by palm trees add texture and depth to the building's flat surfaces.

While the other hotels have meeting space — Hard Rock a little, Portofino Bay somewhat more — the Royal Pacific was designed as a full-fledged convention hotel. The attached convention center is vast. In fact, all of Portofino Bay's meeting space could fit into Royal Pacific's Grand Ballroom with enough space left over to swing quite a few cats. Of course, with its fabulous and fun pool and its proximity to two great theme parks, the Royal Pacific has drawn a large leisure and family business as well.

Orientation

Your Royal Pacific Resort experience begins when you cross a broad, thatched-roofed, bamboo-accented bridge over an artificial river. Step into the massive rectangular lobby and you enter a Balinese demi-paradise. Pause to admire the intricately carved Indonesian wood panels hanging on the walls on either side of the entrance. The lobby completely surrounds a glassed-in, orchid-accented courtyard pool. Statuary elephants cavort in its shallow depths while fountains in the form of Southeast Asian temple statuary constantly replenish its waters. At night, with a crescent moon high overhead, this courtyard is ravishingly romantic.

To the left of the courtyard pool is the reception area, to the right an elegant staircase that descends two stories to the hotel's main restaurant and the swimming pool area. Also to the right, just around the corner and past the staircase, is a spacious seating area complete with expansive views and the elegant Orchid Court Lounge bar with an adjoining sushi bar. The floor to ceiling windows overlooking the pool area evoke the open-air pavilion architecture that represents the finest in Balinese living.

The hotel's 1,000 rooms are arrayed off the lobby in three Y-shaped, seven-story wings, called Towers. Tower 1, The Windward, is to your right as you enter, Tower 2, The Leeward, is to your left, and Tower 3, The Royal, which houses the hotel's Club Level rooms on its seventh floor, is directly opposite the main entrance. (In your four-digit room number, the first digit indicates which tower you're in and the second digit denotes the floor.)

The swimming pool is located between the Windward and Royal Towers, and beyond the pool the rides and attractions of Islands of Adventure form an antic skyline. The space between the Leeward and Royal Towers, in contrast, is given over to a quiet croquet lawn and open spaces, such as the Wantilan Pavilion, designed for outdoor events. The Leeward and Windward Towers frame the main entrance.

The lobby is on the third level. Most of the dining and other amenities will be found two floors below. From the Islands Dining Room, the hotel's main restaurant, a covered walkway hugs the building as it makes its way past the pool to Tchoup Chop, another creation of Emeril Lagasse, and the vast convention center beyond that is attached to the hotel.

The water taxi dock is near Tchoup Chop, most convenient to rooms in the Royal Tower and a longish walk past the pool from the lobby area. From the water taxi stop, the "Garden Walkway" runs along the shore of the Bali Sea, past the pool and on to CityWalk. It takes less than ten minutes to stroll there at a leisurely pace. The main entrance can be reached by foot from the Garden Walkway, but is most conveniently reached by car.

Rooms and Suites

Compared to the wide-open public spaces, the rooms seem small. They are decorated in pale pastels like lime and mango, with sisal-style carpeting and rattan touches in the furniture evoking the tropics and making the space seem airier. Flat-screen TVs add a sleek modern touch, while the bamboo patterned screens and vintage posters from Bali remind us that we are a world away. A number of other small touches in the rooms echo the hotel's backstory and are fun to look for.

Since the Royal Pacific was designed as a convention hotel, there is one distinct difference from the other hotels: all rooms are standard rooms. There are no slightly larger rooms designated as "deluxe rooms" as there are at Portofino and the Hard Rock. Most rooms have a compact vanity area with a sink just outside the bathroom (which has no sink), while others have full bathrooms. All rooms have 32-inch (or larger) flat-screen televisions, Keurig coffee makers for that morning jolt of java, iHome clock/radios with iPod docks, as well as the usual blow dryer for damp hair and an iron and ironing board. A mini bar is also provided.

The next step up from a 335-square-foot standard room is a suite. Like the standard rooms, the 28 "king suites" were designed with the convention trade in mind. Starting at 670 square feet, they are the nicely appointed two-room suites you would expect in any business hotel; aside from the extra space, they feature the same amenities as in the standard rooms. The Royal Pacific has eight Jurassic Park-themed "Kids' Suites," complete with dinosaur murals and raptor-cage headboards, as well as a Club Level with restricted access in the Royal Tower. For more on the Club Level, see *Amenities*, below.

For high rollers, the best option is The Captain's Suite, located on the seventh floor Club Level of the Royal Tower. It is exquisitely decorated with Indonesian art and fabrics and features a full kitchen and a guest bathroom off the entry foyer. All the super luxury suites at the luxury hotels are grand and splashy, but this one is the most quietly elegant, the kind of place you could imagine yourself having as a permanent residence. It also has the best view in the hotel, a sweeping vista of the pool area and Islands of Adventure. Compared to the rates for other luxury suites at Universal, The Captain's Suite here is a positive bargain.

Pool view rooms are obviously much sought after. Unfortunately, the hotel has just 173 such rooms, so your odds of getting one are approximately one in six. The hotel will try to honor requests for a specific view but they cannot guarantee them.

See *Room Rates at a Glance,* at the beginning of this chapter, to get an idea of the price range at Royal Pacific and how it compares to the other on-site hotels.

Note: The Royal Pacific is rumored to undergo a complete refurbishment starting in early 2015 so the rooms may look quite a bit different when you visit.

Amenities

One thing you might expect of a hotel with "resort" in its name is a spa, but Royal Pacific lacks this amenity, directing its guests to the Mandara Spa at the Portofino Bay Hotel. For the rest, the choices are limited but well executed.

■ Club Level

The rooms and suites on the seventh floor of the Royal Tower have been set aside for those who enjoy that extra little bit of pampering. The concept is much like that used at the Hard Rock, and if you've enjoyed Club Level service there, you'll no doubt want to see how the Royal Pacific compares.

As at the Hard Rock, access is strictly limited; a slot in the elevator reads your room key before it will take you to seven. At the end of the corridor, you will find a spacious V-shaped lounge. Picture windows looking out across Interstate 4 to the International Drive area give this room an edge over similar rooms at the other hotels. It is staffed with friendly hosts and hostesses, who serve as your personal concierges from 7:00 a.m. to 9:30 p.m. Head here in the morning for a complimentary continental breakfast (7:30 a.m. to 10:00 a.m.) and to glance through the tony out-of-town newspapers so important to the elite. The lounge serves refreshments throughout the day; hors d'oeuvres, beer, and wine in the evening; and "Sweets Hour" before bedtime.

Club Level guests can use the Internet-enabled computer and printer in the lounge. They also receive free access to the hotel's fitness center and discounts on poolside cabanas.

■ Lagoon Pool

The Royal Pacific may have only one pool, but it's the largest in the city of Orlando (although not, it should be noted, in the greater Orlando area). It sprawls languorously between the Windward and Royal Towers beside the Bali Sea end of the winding waterway that links all the resort hotels with CityWalk. The heated pool is like a small tropical sea itself, with an irregular, sinuous shape and even a tiny palm-dotted island. It's shallow, too, designed more for playing than serious swimming, with no spot deeper than about four feet, seven inches.

One side is dominated by the superstructure of the Royal Bali Sea, a ship of the Royal Pacific line that seems to have run aground and buried itself in the sand. Actually it's an elaborate water play area (think *Curious George* over at Universal Studios) that gushes cold, bracing water from every conceivable orifice, while kids man a battery of water cannons, never seeming to tire of squirting each other and unsuspecting swimmers who venture too close to shore. This is Royal Pacific's answer to the water slides at the other resorts and kids love it.

On this side, the pool bottom slopes gently up to water's edge, affording little ones easy entry. Nearby is a white sandy beach area and a fenced children's play area complete with wading pool and sandbox (pails included). Close by is an ice cream parlor. It's just a walk-up kiosk, but it dispenses a surprising variety of fast-melting treats.

Near the middle, the pool narrows to accommodate a volleyball net strung from shore to shore and an impromptu game between former strangers always seems to be in progress. The opposite side is more adult-oriented. Here you will find the **Bula Bar and Grille** (reviewed below), three cabanas, a red-topped pool table, and two hot tubs, one somewhat larger than the other. Between the pool and the hotel is a concrete shuffleboard court; you will often see a ping-pong table in this area when the weather cooperates.

Cabanas are small canvas-sided shelters with a TV, ceiling fan, and a small, modestly stocked fridge. Full-day rentals (9:00 a.m. to pool closing) are $200; Club Level guests get full day rentals starting at just $75. Rentals are handled by the staff at The Gymnasium (see below) and cabanas can be reserved by calling (407) 503-3235.

On Friday and Saturday nights at sunset (plus Tuesdays during the summer), near the Bula Bar end of the pool, the wail of conch shells and the sonorous singing of a Samoan chieftain signal the start of a brief "torch lighting ceremony." A trio performs ten minutes of drumming, hula dancing, and fire juggling, concluding with a hula contest for the kids. Many people drift over to watch from the shallow water.

There is a constant schedule of games, activities, and enticements around the pool throughout the day, from **free** smoothies and chilled cucumber slices to cannonball competitions. On select nights, a screen is set up poolside for a family-friendly Dive-In Movie, usually featuring a tie-in to the parks; animated films like the *Shrek* series are popular.

Just outside the fenced-in pool area is the "Garden Walkway" that takes you to CityWalk. The gates are usually open during the day, but after 9:00 p.m. you will need your room key to gain entry.

■ Volleyball Court

Also just outside the pool, on the very edge of the Bali Sea, is a splendidly inviting white sand regulation volleyball court. It's first come, first served and **free**. Grab a ball at the pool towel hut.

■ The Mariners' Club

Just past the Game Room is Royal Pacific's children's playroom. For more information about the services offered here, see *Good Things To Know About... Kids' Activities* in the introductory section of this chapter. Make your reservations 24 hours in advance by calling 33230 on a hotel phone or (407) 503-3230 from outside.

■ The Gymnasium

This sleek, modern, but rather spartan fitness room is close by the Lagoon Pool, just past the Treasures of Bali shop as you head to the convention center. The equipment is state-of-the-art but free weights are also available for the old-fashioned pumping iron crowd. The fee is $10 per day; it includes use of the sauna, steam bath, and a unisex whirlpool room, which is a particularly lovely place to hang out and relax. Club Level guests and You First members (Blue level or higher) receive complimentary use of the fitness facilities. Kids 14 through 17 are allowed, but only if they have adult supervision. The Gymnasium is open daily from 6:00 a.m. to 8:00 or 9:00 p.m.

■ Croquet Lawn

Far from the frenzied activity of the pool area, on the other side of the Royal Tower wing, is a meticulously groomed croquet lawn, where the harried executive can come to unwind and practice those tricky cannon shots. You can pick up **free** mallets and balls at The Gymnasium.

Good Things To Know About...

■ Guest Laundry

Each Tower has a guest laundry room. In the Royal Tower, it is on the second level. In the other two towers, it is on the bottom floor with an outside entrance. There are three washers and three dryers in each room. The cost is $3 per load to wash and the same to dry. Soap costs $1, and the machines accept both quarters and credit cards; buying soap requires cash.

■ Meetings and Banquets

Loews Royal Pacific was designed as a convention hotel, with some 75,000 square feet of meeting space. The Grand Ballroom alone is 41,500 square feet. The convention area, which is adjacent to but quite separate from the hotel itself, is spacious and airy and decorated with a South Seas nostalgia theme. The walls are dotted with fanciful 1930s-style travel posters and memorabilia. For more information, call (407) 503-3100.

■ Parking

There is less guest parking available at the Royal Pacific than at the other resort hotels, which means that if you are self-parking, finding an empty space can sometimes be a challenge. One choice is to park at the rear of the hotel in the convention center parking area. Or you might want to consider paying the extra money for valet parking to avoid the hassle. Diners at Tchoup Chop can get their valet parking validated; use the convention entrance.

Dining at Loews Royal Pacific Resort

The food at Royal Pacific is entirely of the sit-down, table service variety, except for the morning selection at the Orchid Court Lounge, which has a grab-and-go informality. Prices ranging from moderate to expensive at the sit-down venues. The good news is that the food served here is worth the premium prices charged. Those looking for a quick bite or more moderately priced fare will have to travel to CityWalk.

■ Orchid Court Lounge and Sushi Bar

What:	Lounge bar with sushi at night
Where:	In the main lobby
Price Range:	$ - $$$
Hours:	6:00 a.m. to midnight; sushi 5:00 p.m. to 11:00 p.m.
Reservations:	None

This elegant lobby bar and lounge area is awash in the gorgeous orchids from which it takes its name. It serves up exotic drinks ($12 to $15) ranging from martinis to elaborate "South Seas" concoctions like ginger juleps and lemongrass mojitos. They arrive garnished with colorful little umbrellas or enormous tropical palm leaves. Wine is available by the glass.

In the morning, from 6:00 a.m. to 11:00 a.m., the bar at the Orchid Court turns into a cafeteria line serving an a la carte continental breakfast featuring cereal, fruit, and a variety of breakfast sandwiches, breads, and pastries. It has proven to be a popular option and the lines are frequently quite long. Careful! If you have a hearty appetite the cost can quickly approach that of the buffet breakfast downstairs at the Islands Dining Room. One saving grace is that coffee refills are free and unlimited until 11:00 a.m.

From 5:00 p.m. to 11:00 p.m., the **Orchid Court Sushi Bar** operates at the opposite end of the lobby from the bar. Here you can get your favorite maki or sashimi specialties prepared to order by a team of experienced sushi chefs. This section of the lobby has been partitioned off, creating a de facto restaurant, which makes the sushi bar a perfectly good choice for dinner if you're in the mood for sushi.

Prices are moderate ($4 to $10 per pair of nigiri, $6 to $16 for rolls) although some of the sushi and sashimi platters can be quite pricey ($32 to $110). Some of the rolls are quite creative, like the Tropical (salmon and tuna with mango and kiwi) and Pacific (four fishes with cucumber wrapping and ponzu sauce).

For non-sushi fans, there's "The Other Menu," featuring Big Plates ($13 to $18) like a burger, a chopped Asian salad, and the Orange Ginger Chicken from Islands Dining Room, and Little Plates ($8 to $15) like vegetable spring rolls, calamari, and tuna tartare.

Happy hour runs from 5:00 p.m. to 7:00 p.m. and 9:00 p.m. to 11:00 p.m. offering $4 drafts, $6 wine, and $5 well drinks.

■ Islands Dining Room

What:	Full-service dining
Where:	Directly below the lobby overlooking the pool
Price Range:	$$$ - $$$$+

Hours:	Breakfast 7:00 a.m. to 11:00 a.m. Monday to Friday, 7:00 a.m. to 12:00 p.m. Saturday and Sunday; dinner 5:00 p.m. to 10:00 p.m. daily.
Reservations:	Not required but highly recommended Call (407) 503-3463 or OpenTable.com

The hotel's large main dining room (the restaurant seats 380) is styled in the Indonesian fashion with louvered walls and ceiling fans hand-fashioned from silken hand fans. Indonesian carved wooden panels divide the room into separate seating areas. Floor to ceiling windows seem to bring the pool area indoors and huge carved frogs from Indonesia stand sentinel-like, adding a whimsical touch. Alcoves along one side of the room serve as added dining space, or buffet lines, one of them set aside for the special evening kids' buffet ($14), complete with kiddie-sized tables and chairs, a great way to give the grown-ups a mealtime break.

Most breakfast tastes can be accommodated — there are Hawaiian pancakes and Tahitian french toast — with the typical a la carte breakfast running just under $20. Unless, of course, you order one of the fancier Eggs Benedict offerings, in which case your bill could easily approach $22, the price of the sumptuous, all-you-can-eat breakfast buffet that includes made-to-order eggs and omelettes. The kids' version of the breakfast buffet is $12.

For dinner, Islands Dining Room offers a pan-Asian, but quite Americanized, menu. Don't expect authenticity. The flavors are muted so as not to offend sensitive palates, but the ingredients are impeccably fresh, making veggie-rich dishes a good choice.

The starters ($8 to $10) feature spring rolls, Sui Mai dumplings, and crab rangoon served in bamboo baskets. Salads ($10 to $16) include a wonderfully simple "Seven Leaf" with a choice of dressing, and an Asian chopped salad. Entrees ($17 to $30) feature some hearty American meat dishes like pork chop and a ribeye steak, along with a goodly selection of Chinese inspired dishes. A popular choice is the Family Dining option ($38 for two), which lets you pick two Chinese entrees, served with a vegetable stir fry and your choice of rice or noodles.

The Islands Dining Room features Character Dining (Scooby-Doo and Gru are common sightings) on various evenings from 6:45 p.m. to 9:15 p.m.; check with the concierge for the schedule during your visit. You may also occasionally see a hula dancer moving from table to table or hear strolling Pacific islands musicians. On Fridays and Saturdays (5:00 p.m. to 9:00 p.m.) you can enjoy the Wok Experience, a select-your-own stir-fry station ($24 adults, $14 kids 3 to 9). A Polynesian buffet is offered very occasionally for the same price.

■ Jake's American Bar

What:	Bar and light meals
Where:	Downstairs, near Islands Dining Room
Price Range:	$$ - $$$
Hours:	11:00 a.m. to 1:30 a.m.; limited "late nite" menu from 11:00 p.m.
Reservations:	Not required but available at OpenTable.com

Jake McNally was quite a guy, a sea plane pilot for Royal Pacific Airways who won the "World Series of sea plane racing" in 1927. Jake's exploits in love were as dismal as his airborne feats were glorious. Dumped by the love of his life, Jake disappeared and is rumored to be flying from one backwater dive to another trying to forget. This bar is a tribute to his memory by his friends, who have donated memorabilia to help decorate the joint. It's all made up, of course, but this fanciful story forms the basis for one of the most successful themed restaurants in all of Universal Orlando Resort.

The decor is colonial men's club and casual, echoing the open architecture of the South Seas, where any breeze is welcome. In fact, it's worth peeking into Jake's just to marvel at the ceiling fans. Also a great deal of fun is the Jake McNally memorabilia and the framed love letters that grace the walls.

The food is as jaunty as the decor with the accent on casual bar fare that won't overly tax the wallet, another reason Jake's has become so popular with guests. The "Pre-Flight" section of the menu ($7 to $16) consists of appetizer-like nibbles such as tender calamari, hot wings, and pretzel rods, but the $16 charcuterie board is hefty and shareable. For veggie lovers there are Caesar and garden salads, with the mixed greens a light-bite winner, especially with the ginger soy dressing. Slightly more substantial are the "Final Approach" sandwiches and burgers ($12 to $17) and "En Route" flatbreads and pizzas ($13 to $15). The most expensive items on the "Cruising Altitude" menu (available after 5:00 p.m.) is the 10-ounce Ribeye Steak ($30), the same one served in Islands Dining Room.

Of course, Jake's is a bar and dining is not mandatory. Jake's would make an excellent choice for drinks before (or after) dining at Islands. Happy hour is 3:00 p.m. to 5:00 p.m. daily. Along with the usual, the bartenders here whip up a variety of lethal "South Seas" concoctions with don't-tell-me-I-didn't-warn-you names like Tsunami. Setting new heights for exotic concoctions is the flaming Mt. Kumuneyewanadrinkya, a 32-ounce behemoth with at least eight ounces of rum and other booze lurking in its depths.

If you stop by for a nightcap, you should check out the small outside seating area under the bridge where you can enjoy the lingering warmth of a summer night with a waterfall providing a romantic soundtrack. A limited "late nite" menu ($10 to $18) will take care of those midnight munchies.

Happy hour runs from 1:00 p.m. to 5:00 p.m. offering $4 drafts, $6 wine, and $5 well drinks.

■ Bula Bar and Grille

What:	Casual poolside dining
Where:	By the pool, near the Royal Tower
Price Range:	$ - $$
Hours:	11:00 a.m. to 10:00 p.m., kitchen closes at 8:00 p.m. (varies seasonally)
Reservations:	None

An inviting palapa-like bar beckons thirsty swimmers with exotic drink concoctions ($15, with souvenir cup) ranging from Mai Tais to potions with names like "Witch Doctor," whose lengthy list of ingredients might give even the heartiest boozer pause. Other drinks are available as well, of course, with beers going for $6 to $7. Non-alcoholic Tropical Smoothies (about $6) in strawberry, mango, and passion fruit flavors are also on tap for those who want to get into the South Seas swing of things and still walk.

Snacks and light meals are available from the Grille part of the establishment, cooked up in a small kitchen a few paces away. They range in price from $8 to $15 and include "loaded" nachos with a cheddar cheese sauce, fish tacos, Korean barbequed steak wrap, and (at about $14) the Kona Half Pound Burger. The food here is surprisingly substantial and quite good, making the Bula Bar an option for your main meal of the day. Many people seem to agree since there is now seating available for well over 100.

Happy hour runs from 11:00 a.m. to 1:00 p.m. and 7:00 p.m. to 9:00 p.m. offering $4 drafts, $6 wine, and $5 well drinks. As with all poolside eateries at Universal Orlando, an 18% gratuity is automatically added to all bills.

On the other side of the pool, **Bula Ice Cream** is a walk-up window serving everything from simple cones ($4 to $5) to the 15-scoop Captain Jake's Buried Treasure ($40).

■ Tchoup Chop

What:	Another Emeril's extravaganza
Where:	Near the convention center
Price Range:	$$$ - $$$$+
Hours:	Lunch 11:30 a.m. to 2:30 p.m. daily; dinner 5:30 p.m. to 10:00 p.m. daily
Reservations:	Highly recommended; (407) 503-2467 or OpenTable.com

Located at the point where the Royal Pacific Resort meets the massive convention center attached to the hotel, Tchoup Chop (pronounced "chop chop") is to Royal Pacific what Bice is to Portofino Bay, the signature restaurant for the hotel and a destination in its own right. And being an Emeril Lagasse restaurant, the cooking is as bold as the decor.

Guests arriving by boat from CityWalk pass through a carved wooden moon gate and cross an open patio to reach the restaurant. The dining area, carefully designed according to feng shui principles, is a riot of blue tile, orange glass chandeliers, pale beige bamboo and rattan and dark teak furniture. A long, narrow pool bedecked with lily pads runs down the middle with a chic and well-stocked bar at one end. The overall effect is at once vibrant and soothing. Unfortunately, the design has been spoiled somewhat by an ungainly curtain that's been installed as a partition for private parties.

Facing the entrance is an open kitchen and food bar that allows "interactive" experiences between chefs and diners. Tchoup Chop was destined to become instantly popular and the Lagasse touch has kept the place humming well after the initial curiosity was satisfied. So if you plan to dine here, be on the safe side and book your dining reservation when you book your hotel room.

Fortunately, the food lives up to the hype and Chef de Cuisine Ryan Vargas has revamped the menu. The cuisine is inspired both by the Polynesian islands of the South Pacific and Asian cooking techniques, with the fresh seafood of the Gulf of Mexico and the nearby Atlantic playing a strong supporting role. But don't expect a re-run of Trader Vic's, which is the stereotype of a Polynesian restaurant, or even Emeril's over at CityWalk for that matter. Here the emphasis is on relatively straightforward preparation of superb ingredients. Get a burger for your kid and it will be made from the finest beef. The menu changes with admirable regularity as the chefs take advantage of the seasonal availability of fish and produce, so it's difficult to predict what will be available when you visit. However, a survey of past dishes will give you some idea and help whet your appetite. Rest assured that everything sampled here has ranged from excellent to life-altering.

Your meal begins with complimentary prawn chips with a tangy peanut dipping sauce. Appetizers ($6 to $14) might include Emeril's take on steamed pork and vegetable dumplings, crunchy shrimp with chili sauce, and Kiawe smoked baby back ribs, all very good. Dinner soups and salads ($7 to $10) range from simple miso soups to an elaborate salad with bacon and a soft fried egg. A limited menu of sushi rolls ($8 to $9) is offered.

Entrees ($19 to $39) include innovative takes on filet mignon, short ribs, and salmon, which might be crusted with macadamia nuts and served with coconut purple sticky rice. The roasted duck breast with gingered pear chutney is notable, as is the five-spice braised lamb shank. Meats are often served over mashed potatoes laced with roasted garlic or wasabi paste. Desserts ($5 to $10) also change too often to keep up with. Suffice it to say, they're all terrific. Be sure to ask about the evening's specials, as they are almost always exquisite. If the options are overwhelming, a four-course Chef's Tasting Menu ($60; wine pairing $35 extra) will simplify your choices.

Sake ($12 to $100 per cold bottle; $9 for a 10-ounce hot carafe) features in the culinary concept here, much as wine would in a fine French restaurant, with a small but choice selection of premium brands available. A more traditional wine list is also available ($10 to $15 per glass, $40 to $220 bottles).

At lunch, Tchoup Chop serves an abbreviated menu, with an emphasis on sandwiches ($10 to $14), rice and noodle bowls ($10 to $14), and bento boxes ($15).

Tip: Tchoup Chop owns a small outdoor "tiki bar" that serves all the elaborate cocktails ($13 to $14) served inside. What is less well known is that you can order anything else on the menu here to be served outside. It makes for a fun blending of the elegant and the casual. The daily happy hour (5:00 p.m. to 8:00 p.m.) features full-sized appetizers, including ribs and egg rolls, for just $5, plus drinks as low as $4.50. It may be the best bargain in all Orlando.

■ Wantilan Luau

What:	Hawaiian-themed dinner show
Where:	On the Wantilan Terrace
Price Range:	Adults, $63 (plus tax); children age 3-9, $40
Hours:	Saturday nights year round, Tuesday nights seasonally; registration at 5:00 p.m., 6:00 p.m. seating
Reservations:	Required; (407) 503-3463 or see the concierge

Wantilan is Indonesian for "gathering place," and at the outdoor Wantilan Terrace, on Saturday nights, the hotel gathers its guests together with that tried-and-true staple of warm weather tourism, a Hawaiian luau complete with roast suckling pig on your plate and Hawaiian hams on stage, but thankfully no poi.

The generous buffet meal starts with fruits and salads, continues with Lomi Lomi Chicken and Ahi Poke salads, the "Catch of the Day," Teriyaki Chicken, fire-grilled beef, and the aforementioned Pit-Roasted Suckling Pig, before wrapping up with a dessert station with goodies like White Chocolate Macadamia Nut Pie and Chocolate Banana Cake. Macadamia-crusted goat cheese with kim chee is served for the non-carnivores. Wine, beer, Mai Tais, and soft drinks are included in the price and a cash bar is available. The entertainment is as rich and filling as the meal, featuring a medley of Polynesian song stylings and hula dancing.

Check-in begins at 5:00 p.m., and seating starts at 6:00 p.m. Be prepared for a slow and somewhat disorganized process. For an extra $7 per person ($5 for kids) you can secure "Priority Seating" with a guaranteed table near the stage. There is a cancellation fee of $20 per person unless you cancel prior to noon on the day of the performance.

Shopping at Loews Royal Pacific Resort

Shopping here is muted and low key, which after the mercantile madness of the theme parks is a refreshing change of pace. Off the lobby, you will find **Toko Gifts**, a small shop that at first glance seems entirely devoted to casual clothing and souvenirs, all with Royal Pacific and Universal logos. Peek around the corner at the back and you will find magazines, sundries, and snacks of the sort you'd expect at any hotel lobby store. Right next door, **Mas** stocks a lovely selection of exotic handcrafts and distinctive decorative items, perfect for a last-minute gift.

More elaborate is **Treasures of Bali**, located near the pool on the way to the convention wing. This is the place to come if you forgot to pack your swim gear. Swimsuits for men and women are stocked here, along with a variety of balls and toys suitable for pool play. You will find some very nice resort wear for after-pool occasions, much of it with a South Seas flavor. A small selection of Indonesian crafts can be found here and, if you poke around in the back of the shop, you'll discover some magazines and popular novels for poolside reading.

■ SAPPHIRE FALLS ■ RESORT

Adventure Way

Orlando, FL 32819

Opening in the summer of 2016, Loews Sapphire Falls Resort is a 1,000-room, Caribbean-themed hotel catering to the meeting and convention trade. While the hotel will have plenty of meeting space of its own, an air-conditioned walkway will connect the new resort to both the existing convention center and the Royal Pacific Resort. Indeed, the new hotel is sometimes referred to as an "extension" or "expansion" of the Royal Pacific.

Located at the intersection of Hollywood Way and Adventure Way, with its main entrance on Adventure Way, just across from Cabana Bay Beach Resort, this will be the fifth on-site hotel. It is described as a tropical paradise featuring elaborate waterfalls, inspired by the rivers and waterfalls of the Caribbean islands.

The existing system of waterways will be extended from Royal Pacific to allow water taxi service to whisk Sapphire Falls guests to CityWalk and beyond. There will also be shuttle bus service to the parks in addition to walking paths.

While Universal has announced that guests here will enjoy early park entry, no mention was made of Express Access to rides and attractions. It seems likely that room rates will be similar to or slightly lower than those at Royal Pacific, but higher than at Cabana Bay. In fact, there is speculation that after its refurbishment, Royal Pacific will raise its rates, so that Sapphire Falls will become the least expensive of the luxury hotels, which might serve to justify the lack of Express Access. Of course, all this is speculation, subject to change.

Note: There has been some scuttlebutt that Sapphire Falls will be a "value" resort on the model of Cabana Bay (see *Chapter Six)*, but considering that it will be a Loews hotel, will cater to the convention and meeting trade, and be connected to CityWalk by water taxi, it's reasonable to expect that its amenities will be more in line with the other hotels discussed in this chapter. Only the apparent lack of front-of-the-line access for guest suggests otherwise.

Orientation

The concept art shows a water taxi arriving at a dock with a cascading waterfall, somewhat reminiscent of Jamaica's Dunn's River. The renderings also depict what seems to be a covered walkway that crosses the waterfall to reach a wing of guest rooms. Past that walkway, presumably, lies the resort's pool "complete with waterfalls, a white sand beach, a water slide, a children's play area, and cabana rentals." The pool will also reportedly feature a fire pit, the latest instant cliche in hotel amenities.

Other amenities that have been announced include valet parking, full concierge service, a fitness center, a business center, and a pet-friendly policy. There will also be 131,000 square feet of meeting space — that's in addition to Royal Pacific's 141,000 square feet!

It appears that, like Royal Pacific Resort, six- or seven-story wings will radiate out from a central lobby, wrapping around the pool, the waterway to CityWalk, and other areas. Sapphire Falls' 1,000 new rooms will include 77 suites, bringing the total number of on-site hotel rooms to 5,200, perhaps another reason that Express Access will not be an amenity here.

Little is known of the dining options at the new hotel, but it has been announced that it will have at least one sit-down dining venue with splendid water views. Also promised are a poolside bar and grill, a grab-and-go Caribbean marketplace, and a "themed" lobby bar.

Universal Orlando

CHAPTER SIX:

CABANA BAY BEACH RESORT

After a burst of activity that saw a lone theme park, Universal Studios Florida, expand into Universal Orlando Resort with the addition of Islands of Adventure, CityWalk, and three luxury resort hotels, Universal took a breather. A long breather. But there was still a lot of land left over on Universal property crying out for development. What next, a lot of us wondered? And wondered. And wondered.

I suspect it was the enormous success of Harry Potter's arrival that re-ignited Universal's creativity and opened its wallets. Still, expansion presented challenges. Yes, there was demand for more on-site hotel rooms, but what about the cherished perks of the luxury resorts — front-of-the-line privileges prominent among them? Adding more tourists with FOTL access might create "Express" lines just as long as the regular lines and dilute the value of a very special resort amenity.

While I obviously wasn't privy to the planning discussions, I think Universal made the very wise decision to create a second category of on-site hotel, one that appeals to families on a budget. The Cabana Bay Beach Resort fills that role quite nicely, offering proximity to the parks to a demographic that had been priced out of the luxury resorts. The trade-off is that, in exchange for lower room rates, those staying in this new "value" resort would have to forego some of the perks available to those at the luxury resorts. The end result is that Universal captures a wide swath of lodging customers who might otherwise have stayed elsewhere while preserving the very special perks that justify the higher rates at the luxury properties. It's a classic example of win/win.

Not The One Percent

While not precisely second-class citizens, guests at Cabana Bay can expect a very different experience from that enjoyed by guests at the luxury resorts. If you have stayed at one of the luxury resorts and expect Cabana Bay to be just the same, you will be disappointed. If you are new to Universal's on-site hotels and believe Cabana Bay will have all the wonderful perks you've heard about, you will also be bummed out. In fact, lack of knowledge about what this new hotel does and does not provide has been the source of a great many guest complaints. My goal in this chapter is to make your decision to stay at Cabana Bay an informed one.

With that in mind, here's a brief overview of the perks you will **not** receive as a Cabana Bay Beach Resort guest. Other points worth noting will be covered in *Good Things To Know . . .* below.

- *No Universal Express Access.* Guests at Cabana Bay are not entitled to the front-of-the-line privileges that are the most cherished perk of those staying at the luxury resorts, although at press time they are accorded early admission to Diagon Alley at Universal Studios Florida.
- *No water taxis.* The waterway system that serves the luxury hotels does not extend to Cabana Bay, so there are no water taxis to take you to CityWalk. Instead, the hotel provides an efficient bus service to CityWalk (see below).
- *A lower level of service.* The service you receive at Cabana Bay Beach Resort will be just as gracious and friendly as at the luxury resorts. There will just be less of it. At Cabana Bay, **none** of the following is offered:
    Bellman service
    Valet parking
    Concierge services
    Business center
    Fine dining in the hotel
    Room service (other than pizza delivery)
    Club level floor
    Super luxury suites
    Spa (although there is a complimentary fitness center)
    Special kids' program
    Priority seating at CityWalk restaurants
    Meeting space
    Loews YouFirst credit for your stay

Cabana Bay Beach Resort Overview

6550 Adventure Way

Orlando, FL 32819

(407) 503-4000; fax: (407) 503-1010

Wow! This may be one of the snazziest budget hotels in Orlando. It certainly compares favorably to Disney's "value" resorts down the Interstate, as many people who have stayed at both will attest. If you cast a jaundiced eye on the place and examine the decor closely, you'll be able to tell that the architects and interior designers were working on a very strict budget, which only makes what they have accomplished all the more impressive. To start with, the place is huge — 1,800 rooms accommodating a reported 9,000 guests (although I, for one, wouldn't much like to be packed in five to a room!). It stretches a full third of a mile from one end to the other.

The word "retro" is used far too often these days, but it is absolutely appropriate when discussing the design of Cabana Bay. The architects have drawn on two primary inspirations: the fabled (and now vanished) Americana Hotel of Bal Harbour, Florida, which opened in 1956, and the exuberant, futuristic stylings of fifties seaside motels (sometimes referred to as Raygun Gothic), which reflected the optimism of a prosperous nation on the brink of the space age. What the designers lacked in budget they made up for in space; the public areas are vast, which adds a sense of grandeur but can make them look a little bare in places.

The furnishings, too, reflect a 1950s notion of what was hip and of the moment. Sinuous curves on the banquettes, self-consciously "modern" designs for chairs, coffee tables, and the like do a wonderful job of evoking the era. But nothing says late-fiftiess like the color palette used in the public spaces and rooms — orange and blue predominate, with bright pastel accents.

For a value-priced hotel, the entrance is rather grand, a horseshoe shaped driveway, accented with vintage cars. The soaring lobby is almost a carbon copy of the Americana, right down to the soaring palm trees in the center, and the lobby bar conjures up a *Mad Men* age when every evening started with a cocktail or three.

Whereas Portofino Bay and Royal Pacific are Loews brands and Hard Rock is its own brand managed by Loews, Cabana Bay is a Universal property. Loews merely manages it.

Orientation

Cabana Bay Beach Resort is located at the corner of Turkey Lake Road and Hollywood Way, with the sole entrance on Adventure Way. The orientation is north-south with the entrance facing east. Like Caesar's Gaul, the resort is divided into three parts.

The central, two-story lobby building wraps around an impressive horseshoe-shaped driveway accented with vintage cars from the 1950s. (The selection changes regularly, so check back during your visit.) This building houses most of the dining and entertainment venues for the hotel.

To the north are three separate four-story buildings called Starlight, Thunderbird, and Castaway, all popular names for fifties motels. Their names are announced in bright, flowing neon script at the roofline, so it's impossible to get lost. They surround the so called Cabana Courtyard, whose amenities are described later. All of the rooms in this section are "family suites" and are accessed via exterior walkways.

To the south of the lobby building two long, seven-story wings, named Americana and Continental after two now-vanished hotels of the era, define the Lazy River Courtyard. Most of the rooms in this section are standard rooms, although a portion of the Continental wing is devoted to family suites. Rooms here are accessed by an interior corridor and most rooms have floor to ceiling windows, although a few have large round windows.

Rooms and Suites

Universal gets high marks for creating rooms that allow them to keep the rates low while looking pretty darn good. Naturally, there are some trade-offs. For starters, the rooms are small; even the family suites are smaller than the rooms in many Quality Inns you may have stayed in. On the plus side, however, they look terrific. Using a mid-twentieth-century palette of orange and blue with accents in red, green, and bright pastels, the interior decor evokes the 1950s, but with some decidedly twenty-first century touches.

Rooms come in two flavors: 300-square-foot "standard" rooms and 430-square-foot "family suites" The standard rooms feature two queen-size beds a small table, a mini-fridge, and a flat-screen TV. The family suites have the same two beds, with a sofa bed in the compact "living room," and an additional flat-screen TV in the "bedroom."A sliding panel provides some privacy to those sleeping while an ingenious three-part bathroom arrangement — bath/shower with sink, vanity area with sink, and a tiny commode room — allow several family members to get ready for the parks at the same time. Suites also have a "kitchenette," which may not match your definition of the term. There is a mini fridge, a small microwave, a sink, and a fair amount of shelf space above.

Guests staying in any of the Cabana Courtyard family suites must brave the elements to reach the lobby building, while those staying in the less expensive standard rooms of the Lazy River Courtyard can enter the lobby building directly, an important consideration during Orlando's increasingly frequent afternoon monsoons.

Cabana Bay distinguishes between "regular" rooms and suites and so-called "poolside" rooms and suites. This simply means that the room faces one of the courtyards. In the Cabana Courtyard, because of the exterior walkways and palm trees, not every room offers a view of the pool. Thanks to their floor to ceiling windows, poolside rooms facing the Lazy River Courtyard offer a much better view, especially from the higher floors.

With the family crowd in mind, fully half of the rooms and suites connect to the room next door, allowing large families to stay together and smaller families to spread out a bit.

Room Rates At A Glance

As mentioned in *Chapter Five*, the resort hotels recognize five distinct "seasons," which are reflected in room pricing. I refer you to that chapter for a refresher course in how those seasons are defined.

Since Cabana Bay is a new property, predicting room rates is difficult. Here is a best guess as to the "starting from" rates for a standard room by season.

	Value	Regular	Summer	Peak	Holiday
Cabana Bay	$119+	$139+	$154+	$179+	$199+

To these rates, add $30 per night for a "poolside" room and $50 or more for a family suite.

Getting A Good Deal

Much of what was said under this same heading in *Chapter Five* applies to Cabana Bay. However, there are some intriguing facts that set Cabana

Bay apart that have some people debating whether staying here is a good deal with the same intensity that Walowitz and Koothrappali might invest in deciding which superpower was the coolest. Here are the most frequently cited variables: Cabana Bay does not offer FOTL privileges; it charges for parking and high-speed Internet, and is the farthest hotel from the parks; also the fact that FOTL access can be purchased in the parks, the fact that (for now at least) neither of the blockbuster Harry Potter attractions honors FOTL, the rise and fall of rates with the seasons, privileges granted by various annual pass options, the size of your party, and others I'm sure I'm overlooking.

The calculation can be torturous when you take into account the givens (room rates and the cost of Express passes), the variables (season, number of people in your party, rates at Royal Pacific), the conundrums (can you get along without FOTL in the off season?), and the imponderables (the value you personally put on convenience and specific amenities).

Depending on the season and the size of your party, the raw price difference between staying at Royal Pacific and Cabana Bay might be less than what you'd spend on Unlimited Universal Express Passes. Then again, there are indications that after its planned 2015 refurbishment, Royal Pacific may no longer be the bargain it seems today. On the other hand, there will be times when a small party staying in a standard room during the off-season (when crowds are less of an issue), or a family of six (too large for standard rooms at the other hotels) in a family suite, can save a bundle at Cabana Bay.

Finally, it must be said that some budget-minded people will look at the cost of a Cabana Bay stay, weigh it against the inconveniences (small rooms and suites, the difficulty of self catering, the distances from the parks, no breakfast included, and so forth) and decide that staying off-site is the better option for them.

Amenities

Cabana Bay Beach Resort isn't as luxurious as its cousins, so you won't find a club level concierge here. But you will find plenty of family-friendly fun.

■ Pools

Cabana Bay features two elaborate swimming areas, one for each courtyard. The **Cabana Courtyard pool** is a 10,000-square-foot behemoth with a narrow "zero entry" point at one end. The pool never gets deeper than three feet, nine inches. It is dominated by a cantilevered tower with four circular platforms jutting out from it. Those on the cutting edge of the Baby Boom will recognize it as the kind of diving platform that graced many public pools in the days before lawyers decided no one should have any fun. Here it serves as theming for a short but zippy 100-foot water slide.

There is a spacious kiddie water play area near the dive tower and, on the opposite side of the pool, a sandy area with beach buckets and shovels, two ping pong tables with balls provided, and several other kids' games.

There are 17 cabanas that offer a modicum of privacy. They have two lounge chairs, a small table with chairs, a fridge, a safe, and a flat-screen TV; just four bottles of water are provided gratis. Rental is $50 a day on weekdays, $100 on weekends. They offer all-day rentals only and there are no discounts available. Rentals are handled by the Atomic Tonic bar (see below). Near Atomic Tonic is a single eight-person hot tub. It is frequently packed in the evenings.

The pool is pretty deserted during the day when most guests are at the parks. You may want to take a day off from the thrill rides, rent a cabana, stock its fridge with cold beer and snacks, and just chill out.

Outside the pool area, in the northwest corner of the courtyard, you will find six shaded concrete **picnic tables**, with an inlaid checkerboard, and an electrical outlet close at hand.

The **Lazy River Courtyard pool** is a sinuous 8,000-square-foot affair with a zero-entry point at the north end. This one reaches a depth of five feet in the middle. There is also a 6,000-square-foot sandy beach, crammed with lounge chairs for sunbathers. But the big draw here is Universal's first **Lazy River**, whose 700 feet flow a little more rapidly than the name would suggest. To fully enjoy it, you will have to buy a tube from the Tube Shack; there are no rentals. Tubes range from $3 for tyke-sized models to $16 for more elaborate versions with a mesh bottom. The most popular seems to be the $8 plain-vanilla adult tube. You can save a bit of money by buying a tube at a nearby Walgreen's or Target.

Like the Cabana Courtyard pool, this one is also deserted during the day but there are no cabanas here. Both pools are heated during cooler weather.

■ Kids' Club

There is no on-site childcare offered at Cabana Bay, but guests are welcome to take advantage of the clubs located at the three luxury hotels ($15 per child, per hour).

■ Jack LaLanne Physical Fitness Studio

If you've done Beach Body or PX90 you owe a debt of gratitude to Jack

LaLanne, the guy who at age 54 beat a 21-year-old Arnold Schwarzenegger in an informal bodybuilding contest. LaLanne was the first fitness guru of the television age and he remains a legend. While Schwarzenegger still holds forth in *Terminator 3-D* over at IOA, the memory of LaLanne (who died in 2011 at 96) is honored in Cabana Bay's fitness center, located on the second floor of the lobby building.

LaLanne's Studio is notable for a number of things — its sheer size, which dwarfs most hotel fitness centers, the number of exercise machines, and the LaLanne memorabilia, provided by his widow. Most impressive, however, is the fact that the facility is **free** to guests. In addition to the treadmills and such, there are dumbbells and locker rooms.

■ Galaxy Bowl

A few steps away from the Physical Fitness Studio is a spiffy 10-lane bowling alley that evokes the days of yore when bowling alleys took the trouble to look nice. It also bears more than a passing resemblance to the lanes in *The Big Lebowski*. No sightings of The Dude so far, however.

The Dude would probably quail at the prices, too — $11 per game (kids $5) and $4 for shoe rental. On the plus side, beer is cheap by resort hotel standards, just $8 for 24 ounces. You can bowl for a third to half the price at Kings Bowl Orlando, which has a similar retro look and is just a short drive away on International Drive. The number is (407) 363-0200. But I suspect that bowling is not the first thing on the minds of most Cabana Bay guests.

■ Game-O-Rama Arcade

The hotel brochure claims there are "retro" touches in this noisy arcade, which got me hoping for some vintage pinball machines from before everything went electronic. But other than Skee-Ball there's nothing particularly retro about it. Too bad. On the other hand, those vintage machines are probably too valuable to expose to the depredations of twenty-first century tourists. If you must, this place is next door to Galaxy Bowl.

Good Things To Know About...

■ Access for Non-Guests

Non-guests are every bit as welcome here as they are at the other resort hotels. Feel free to take the shuttle from CityWalk for a visit. If you want to drive, check the section on parking, below.

■ Character Dining

While Universal characters occasionally make appearances in the public areas, typically on weekends, there is no character dining here, so take advantage of the opportunities offered at the other resorts or, better yet, in the parks where you will get to interact with more characters.

■ Charge Privileges

You can use your room key (which looks much like a credit card) to charge purchases in park shops and restaurants that accept credit cards. You pay just one bill when you check out.

■ Early Entry To The Parks

At press time, Cabana Bay guests were being admitted to Universal Studios Florida an hour before the general public, allowing them to explore Diagon Alley in relative privacy. From time to time, guests may be granted early access to Islands of Adventure as well. Whichever park is involved, not all attractions will be available at that early hour. You will be required to show a valid hotel key card and personal identification at the park gate to use this privilege; this is why every member of your party will be issued a separate room key with their name on it at check in.

■ Guest Laundry

There are laundry facilities on the ground floor of each building in the Cabana Courtyard and two in each of the Lazy River Courtyard wings (on the third and sixth floors). There are four washers and four dryers in each room. The cost is $3 to wash and the same to dry. The machines accept quarters only. Soap is $1. Change machines are located in each laundry room. Note that these high efficiency washers use a special low sudsing variety of detergent, so if you are bringing your own, plan accordingly.

■ Golf

Cabana Bay offers the same access to nearby golf course enjoyed by guests at the luxury resorts. See *Chapter Five* for more information.

■ Hotel Hopping

You are more than welcome to visit the other on-site properties, although you will have to make your own dining reservations. Your hotel key will not work in the gated areas of other hotels, so show your key to an attendant, who will grant you access. You can, however, use your hotel key to charge meals and other purchases at any other Universal hotel.

■ Internet Access

Cabana Bay offers two tiers of Internet service — "Premier" and "Premier Plus." The slower Premier is free, but if you want or need to take advantage of "media rich" sites (Netflix anyone?), you will have to shell out $14.95 a day to get something with a bit more bandwidth. Try the complimentary service first; I found it sufficed for most uses. If it's driving you nuts, ask for help in upgrading (they don't make it easy to find out how). No multi-day packages are offered.

■ Kids

There are no organized children's activities at Cabana Bay, but guests can take advantage of the programs at the other resorts. The Universal Tickets desk in the lobby can help you make arrangements. The **Fun in the Sun Rec Center** next to Game-O-Rama on the second floor of Cabana Bay's lobby building is put into use during inclement weather. Films are shown, board games are deployed, and kids can also take advantage of four Xbox consoles.

■ Length-of-Stay Tickets

Resort guests can purchase park passes valid for however long they are staying at the hotel. These tickets are usually booked as part of a package. They don't represent any great savings on park admission but they have the beneficial effect of giving you a better room rate. They can also come in handy if the length of your stay doesn't match one of the standard pass options. If you wish to purchase length-of-stay tickets once you have checked in, stop by the Universal Tickets desk in the lobby near the entrance.

■ Luggage Service

While there is no doorman and no bellmen, a small crew of friendly guys at the lobby entrance will help you stow your luggage if you arrive early in the day and restow it when you check out so you can enjoy the parks on your last day. They will also summon a taxi from the nearby stand.

■ Package Delivery

Cabana Bay guests can have their purchases sent to the hotel front desk, provided they are staying over till at least the next day. Packages are delivered the day after your purchase.

■ Parking

All parking is self service, outdoors, and costs an additional $10 a day. You must swipe your key card to enter and exit the parking areas. If you'd like to stop by just to check the hotel out, look for Check-In Parking near the entrance; you should be able to leave you car there for an hour or so without paying. Otherwise, you will pay the full $10 daily rate even if you stay just a few hours; instead of using a key, you must press a button at the parking gate to get a ticket.

■ Pets

Loews brands itself as a pet-friendly chain, but this is a Universal property managed by Loews and Universal says no pets allowed.

■ Self Catering

The theme harkens back to family vacations at the beach, and the price points will probably appeal to families traveling on a budget, and the term "Family Suites" and "kitchenette" will probably convince some that it will be possible to eat at least some meals in the room. Well, maybe.

The kitchenettes are extremely basic, with a mini fridge, a small, low-power microwave, a small sink, and a two-cups-at-a-time coffee maker with a limited supply of coffee provided. While there is shelf space, there are just a few plastic plates and utensils. Thus, doing anything other than making sandwiches or reheating leftovers brought home from CityWalk will be a challenge. And the standard rooms provide only a mini fridge. So if you are thinking of self catering, plan and pack carefully.

■ Smoking

Cabana Bay is strictly non-smoking in all rooms and public areas. Smoking areas are in each Courtyard and at the four corners of the resort.

■ Star Service

All the hotels offer "Star Service," a one-stop, one-phone-call solution for just about any need that might arise during your stay. It even has a special button on your in-room phone. The folks at Star Service seem to pride themselves on providing speedy answers to all your questions.

■ Transportation To The Parks

As noted earlier, there is no water taxi service to CityWalk. In its place, Cabana Bay has a very efficient shuttle bus service that departs from the semicircular driveway of the lobby building. Buses, which are highly reminiscent of Disney's Magical Express, depart every seven or eight minutes and take four minutes to arrive at a drop-off point near the escalators to the Hub. From there, you walk through CityWalk to the parks.

■ Transportation Elsewhere

Complimentary bus shuttle service is provided to Wet 'n Wild and Sea-World. The schedule varies with park operating hours and time of year, but typically there are a few departures from CityWalk (*not* from the hotel!) in the morning with return service scheduled for late afternoon. Check with the Universal Tickets counter in the lobby for more precise schedule information and to make reservations.

Mears Transportation operates on-demand shuttle services to and from Orlando Airport to the resort hotels, as well as scheduled shuttle service to and from each of the Universal Orlando Resort hotels and the Disney World parks. Limousine and town car services are also available. Check with the concierge for details. If you'd rather drive yourself, there is a Hertz rental counter in the lobby near the check-in counter. Cars can be returned to the hotel or, for an additional fee, Orlando International Airport. The number is (407) 503-3156.

■ Walking To The Parks

It is possible to walk to the parks. A gate at the northwest corner of the property leads to the intersection of Hollywood Way and Turkey Lake Road; cross Hollywood Way, turn right and walk down the north side of the street. In about 15 minutes you'll arrive in CityWalk near Jimmy Buffett's. It's about as far as walking from Portofino Bay. Depending on where your room is located and how many people are waiting for the bus, this option might get you to the parks more quickly.

At press time a pedestrian bridge was under construction at the northeast corner of the resort property. It will take you over Adventure Way to a winding path on the south side of Hollywood Way to Royal Pacific Resort, where the path spirals down to the waterway path leading from RPR to Jimmy Buffett's. Opinion is divided on whether this route will take less time.

Eating at Cabana Bay Beach Resort

The food at Cabana Bay is almost entirely of the fast food variety, most of it served cafeteria style. The good news is much of it is quite tasty. Only the modest Galaxy Bowl Restaurant offers table service. Reservations? Ha! More varied fare is available at CityWalk and the parks, but that's a schlep.

Most of the hotel's eateries are located in the lobby building, although the Hideaway Bar in the South Courtyard offers some simple food choices. There is room service of a sort; from noon to midnight, you can have pizza delivered to your room. And many folks get their orders at the Bayliner Diner (see below) to go.

Tip: Those who are always ready to sample a new cocktail will be pleased to know that every bar at Cabana Bay has its own selection of specialty concoctions.

■ Bayliner Diner

What:	Food court
Where:	In the lobby building on the ground floor
Price Range:	$ - $$
Hours:	Daily, 7:00 a.m. to 11:00 p.m.

Rather than a retro diner, as the name might suggest, Bayliner is a very contemporary food court much like the ones you find in every mall in America. The subtle difference is that here the various stands are unbranded and distinguished by their specialties. For the most part, their name says it all.

Step up to the Deli Station, the Burger Station, the self-serve Salad Station, or the Dessert Station and you'll know what you're getting before you read the menu. Only the International Station, which is a personal favorite, is a little difficult to decipher. It serves dishes from around the world like Brazilian Churrasco, ginger-soy glazed salmon, and Swedish meatballs, all of which are very good.

The prices are surprisingly modest; the Brazilian Churrasco is the most expensive item here at $12.50. Most items are in the $9 to $10 range. There is also a "Grab and Go" station offering pre-wrapped sandwiches and the like to take to your room or to poolside.

You can visit several stations to construct your meal before heading to the check out counter. If you've picked up a beer, you may be "carded," even if you're a grizzled old coot. It's a bizarre bit of legal overkill that puts you to the inconvenience of always having to carry ID, even when you're coming from the pool. Thankfully, this policy is rarely enforced.

Once you've paid, you step into what may be the largest food court seating area you've ever seen. It's a huge two-story space with hundreds of seats and a smaller number of booths. Both ends are dominated by two enormous screens that show a never ending montage of TV clips and ads from the fifties and sixties. I may be wrong here, but I think the latest clip is the one showing the Beatles' 1964 arrival on our shores.

Depending on your family's habits, you might save money with a **Sonic Fill**, an ingenious cup with a chip that can be activated to provide unlimited beverages (coffee, tea, or soft drinks) for one, two, or three days ($9, $12, and $15) or for the length of your stay ($18).

Breakfast is served until 11:00 a.m. and once again the stations specialize. One whips up omelets to order, another does pancakes, a third does waffles, and so forth. The bacon, egg, and cheese croissant offered at the Deli counter is especially good. You can get a very nice breakfast here for around $10.

■ Galaxy Bowl Restaurant

What:	Casual, table service dining
Where:	In the bowling alley
Price Range:	$ - $$
Hours:	Daily, 11:00 a.m. to 10:00 p.m.

Although it is modest, this 32-seat eatery that overlooks the Galaxy Bowl lanes is the only place at Cabana Bay that offers table service. The food is of the fast food variety, but quite good of its kind. The bacon cheeseburger with "signature sauce" (a mayo blend) is sturdy and the fries are intriguingly spiced (or substitute a very tasty cole slaw). If the menu looks familiar, you've probably seen most of the choices at Bayliner Diner. Sandwiches and burgers are $8 to $10, salads are $4 to $10 (Caesar salad with shrimp). There's pizza, too (about $10).

There is a small bar area nearby, separated from the dining area by the shoe rental kiosk.

■ Atomic Tonic

What:	Poolside bar with snacks
Where:	Cabana Courtyard pool area
Price Range:	$
Hours:	Daily, 10:00 a.m. to 10:00 p.m.

This modest walk-up bar is semi-shaded but otherwise open to the elements. It serves its own selection of specialty drinks ($9 and up) as well as beer and soft drinks. Food choices are quite limited, a few bags of chips and a limited selection from the "Grab and Go" station at Bayliner Diner. There is no waiter service.

■ Hideaway Bar & Grille

What:	Poolside bar with light meals
Where:	Lazy River Courtyard pool area
Price Range:	$ - $$
Hours:	Daily, 10:00 a.m. to 10:00 p.m.

This is the nicer of the two poolside bars. It is tucked away under a low overhang giving it a cozy, cave-like atmosphere, but if you like you can take your drinks upstairs where a spacious patio with a fire pit overlooks the pool. While the bar whips up specialty drinks ($9 and up), a nearby walk-up window offers many of the food items you enjoyed at the Bayliner Diner's Burger Station. There is also an excellent selection of beer on draft. Canned beers include some interesting craft brews. There is no waiter service.

■ Delizioso Pizza

What:	Pizza delivery service
Where:	As close as your room phone
Price Range:	$ - $$
Hours:	Daily, noon to midnight

Forget Dominos and don't expect flyers to be slipped under your door. Cabana Bay offers its own version of this Orlando tourist dining staple. There's even a tiny pizza slice icon on a button on your in-room phone. The pizzas come from the Pizza Station at Bayliner Diner, so if you liked the pizza there and are willing to pay a bit more ($12 to $16), why not?

■ Swizzle Lounge

What:	Lobby bar
Where:	Off the hotel lobby
Price Range:	$ - $$
Hours:	Daily, 5:00 p.m. to 11:00 p.m.

Return with us now to those thrilling days of yesteryear when real men started drinking early and pretty much never stopped. The location in Cabana Bay's spacious lobby will let you conjure up visions of Don Draper heading south to Bal Harbour to sign up the next big account. The cocktails here ($9) tend to the traditional — Manhattans, Side Cars, White Russians, and the like.

■ Starbucks

What:	Coffee and snacks
Where:	Off the hotel lobby
Hours:	Daily 6:00 a.m. to 10:00 p.m.
Price Range:	$

This may be the prettiest Starbucks I've ever seen. It's long, narrow, and curved, with an artful room divider of coffee cups strung on wire. Murals on the wall depict vintage photos of the mermaids at one of Florida's oldest tourist attractions, Weeki Watchee Springs, an apparent reference to the mermaid in the Starbucks logo. As for the rest, if you've ever been to a Starbucks you know it all.

Shopping at Cabana Bay Beach Resort

Shopping is virtually non-existent here compared to the other hotels, but you will find a **Universal Gift Shop** selling a limited selection of souvenirs from the parks, including a few wands from The Wizarding World of Harry Potter. You can also pick up T-shirts, bathing suits, sun screen, and other sundries. Newspapers, too.

CHAPTER SEVEN:

STAYING NEAR THE PARKS

If you aren't staying at one of Universal Orlando's on-property hotels, you may want to consider staying close by. The following hotels are located along Major Boulevard (Orlando 32819), just opposite the Kirkman Road entrance to the Universal Orlando property. They are listed in order of their distance to CityWalk, with the nearest listed first. Major Boulevard is also served by the Super Star Shuttle (see *Chapter One*) and some properties offer shuttles to Disney (fees may apply). The price range refers to the cost of a standard double room, from low season to high, as follows:

$	Under $100
$$	$100 - $150
$$$	$150 - $200
$$$$	Over $200

Be aware that at particularly busy times the cost of a room can soar to astronomical levels, regardless of what it says here.

■ DoubleTree Hotel

5780 Major Boulevard
(800) 222-8733; (407) 351-1000; fax (407) 363-0106
www.doubletreeorlando.com
A sleek corporate-style hotel (there's a convention center attached) that is a favorite with upscale overseas visitors.
Price Range: $$ - $$$$

303

Amenities: Large pool, five restaurants, playground, exercise room, business center, shops, wireless Internet (free basic with fee to upgrade to high-speed), $12 per day self-parking, $20 valet

■ Holiday Inn

5905 South Kirkman Road
(800) 465-4329; (407) 351-3333; fax (407) 351-6404
www.hihuniversal.com

Standard mid-range hotel with ten-story all-suite tower.
Price Range: $$ - $$$$
Amenities: Pool, volleyball, self-service laundry, fitness center, business center, free wireless Internet, free self-parking, restaurant next door

■ Hyatt Place

5895 Caravan Court
(800) 233-1234; (407) 351-0627; fax (407) 351-3317
www.orlandouniversal.place.hyatt.com

Upscale hotel chain.
Price Range: $$ - $$$
Amenities: Outdoor heated pool, fitness center, 42-inch flat-screen TVs, free hot breakfast, Starbucks 24-hour coffee bar, free wireless Internet, free self-parking

■ Days Inn

5827 Caravan Court
(800) 327-2111; (407) 351-3800; fax (407) 363-2793
www.daysinn.com

Typical budget-class motel.
Price Range: $ - $$
Amenities: At press time, amenities were being refurbished and upgraded; call for details

■ Baymont Inns and Suites

5652 Major Boulevard
(877) 229-6668; fax (407) 354-3299
www.baymontinns.com

Spartan budget motel.
Price Range: $ - $$

Amenities: Pool, free continental breakfast, free parking, free wireless Internet

■ Comfort Suites

5617 Major Boulevard
(800) 424-6423; (407) 363-1967; fax (407) 363-6873
www.choicehotels.com
All-suite hotel.
Price Range: $$ - $$$
Amenities: Pool, free hot breakfast, shuttle to Universal, free parking, free wireless Internet

■ La Quinta Inn

5621 Major Boulevard
(800) 531-5900; (407) 313-3100; fax (407) 313-3131
www.lq.com
Standard budget motel.
Price Range: $$ - $$$
Amenities: Pool, free hot breakfast, all rooms with refrigerator/microwave, business center, free wireless Internet, shuttle to Universal, free parking

■ InTown Suites

5615 Major Boulevard
(800) 553-9338; (407) 370-3734; fax (407) 363-4650
www.intownsuites.com
Budget all-suite property with kitchenettes; weekly rentals only, limited office hours, and no Sunday check-ins.
Price Range: $$ - $$$
Amenities: Pool, 42-inch flat-screen TVs, HBO, free wireless Internet, free parking

■ Extended Stay America

5620 Major Boulevard
(800) 398-7829; (407) 351-1788; fax (407) 351-7899
www.extendedstayamerica.com
Budget-priced all-suite property with well-equipped kitchenettes, including pots, pans, dishes, a microwave, and a coffee maker.
Price Range: $ - $$
Amenities: Laundry room, free wireless Internet, free parking

■ Extended Stay America

5610 Vineland Road
(800) 398-7829; (407) 370-4428; fax (407) 370-9456
www.extendedstayamerica.com
 Mid-range all-suite property, a more upscale variant of the Extended Stay America formula.
 Price Range: $ - $$
 Amenities: Laundry room, pool, free grab-and-go breakfast, free wireless Internet, free parking

■ Holiday Inn Express

5605 Major Boulevard
(877) 863-4780; (407) 363-1333; fax (407) 363-4510
www.hiexpress.com
 Eleven-story hotel with both standard rooms and suites.
 Price Range: $$ - $$$
 Amenities: Outdoor pool, exercise room, free hot breakfast, free shuttle to Universal, Wendy's next door, free parking, free wireless Internet

■ Fairfield Inn & Suites

5614 Vineland Road
(800) 936-9417; (407) 581-5600; fax (407) 581-5601
www.marriott.com
 Standard budget hotel with some suites.
 Price Range: $$ - $$$
 Amenities: Outdoor whirlpool, exercise room, free hot breakfast, free parking, free wireless Internet, refrigerators and microwaves in suites

■ Best Western Plus Universal Inn

5618 Vineland Road
(800) 780-7234; (407) 226-9119; fax (407) 370-2448
www.bestwestern.com
 Renovated and upgraded mid-range motel chain.
 Price Range: $$ - $$$
 Amenities: Pool, business center, refrigerator/microwave, free parking, free hot breakfast, free wireless Internet

CHAPTER EIGHT:

DINING AT A GLANCE

As Napoleon once said, "A family visiting a theme park travels on its stomach." With that in mind, here is a quick look at Universal Orlando's many dining options — all 105 of them! The table that follows, lists the restaurant name, its location, its type, the cuisine featured, and the estimated price range. Locations are abbreviated as follows:

Universal Studios Florida (USF): Front Lot (FL); Hollywood (Hwd); KidZone (KZ); World Expo (WE); Harry Potter: Diagon Alley (HP); San Francisco (SF); New York (NY); Production Central (PC).

Islands of Adventure (IOA): Port of Entry (PoE); Seuss Landing (SL); Lost Continent (LC); Harry Potter: Hosgsmeade (HP); Jurassic Park (JP); Toon Lagoon (TL) Marvel Super Hero Island (MS).

Resort Hotels: Portofino Bay (PBH), Hard Rock (HRH), Royal Pacific Resort (RPR), and Cabana Bay (CB).

Price is based on the cost of an "average" meal at each restaurantbased on its type (entree, non-alcoholic beverage, and appetizer or dessert at full-service restaurants). Prices are as follows:

$	Under $15
$$	$15 - $25
$$$	$25 - $40
$$$$	Over $40

Restaurant	Location	Type	Cuisine	Price
Antojitos	CityWalk	Full-service	Mexican	$$ - $$$
Atomic Tonic	CB	Poolside bar	Snacks	$
Backwater Bar	IOA/PoE	Bar	n/a	$
Bayliner Diner	CB	Cafeteria	American	$ - $$
Bar American	PBH	Bar	Italian	$$ - $$$$
beachclub	HRH	Poolside	American	$ - $$
Ben & Jerry's	USF/NY	Walk-up	Ice cream	$
Bev Hills Boulangerie	USF/Hwd	Cafeteria	American	$
Bice	PBH	Full-service	Italian	$$$$+
Blondie's	IOA/TL	Cafeteria	American	$
Bob Marley	CityWalk	Full-serve, club	Caribbean	$ - $$$
Bone Chillin' Bev.	USF/PC	Bar	n/a	$
Bread Box	CityWalk	Cafeteria	Sandwiches	$
Bubba Gump	CityWalk	Full-serve, Bar	Seafood	$$ - $$$
Bula Bar and Grille	RPR	Full-serve, Bar	American	$ - $$
Bumblebee Man's	USF/WE	Walk-up	Tacos	$
Burger Digs	IOA/JP	Cafeteria	Burgers	$
Cafe 4	IOA/MS	Cafeteria	Italian	$
Cafe La Bamba	USF/Hwd	Cafeteria	Latin	$ - $$
Capt America Diner	IOA/MS	Cafeteria	Burgers	$
Cathy's Ice Cream	IOA/TL	Walk-up	Ice cream	$
Chez Alcatraz	USF/SF	Bar, Walk-up	Snacks	$
Cinnabon	CityWalk	Walk-up	American	$
Cinnabon	IOA/PoE	Walk-up	American	$
Circus McGurkus	IOA/SL	Cafeteria	American	$
Classic Monsters Cafe	USF/PC	Cafeteria	American	$
Cletus' Chicken	USF/WE	Walk-up	Fried chicken	$
Coldstone Creamery	CityWalk	Walk-up	Ice cream	$
Comic Strip Cafe	IOA/TL	Cafeteria	Various	$
Cotton Candy	IOA/MS	Walk-up	Snacks	$
Cowfish	CityWalk	Full-service	Sushi/Burgers	$$ - $$$
Confisco Grille	IOA/PoE	Full-service	Eclectic	$$ - $$$
Croissant Moon	IOA/PoE	Cafeteria	American	$
Delizioso Pizza	CB	Pizza delivery	Italian	$ - $$
Doc Sugrue's Kebabs	IOA/LC	Walk-up	Mid Eastern	$
Duff Gardens	USF/WE	Outdoor bar	Snacks	$
Emack & Bolio's	HRH	Walk-up	Ice cream	$
Emeril's	CityWalk	Full-serve, Bar	Eclectic	$$$ - $$$$
Eternelle's Elixir	USF/HP	Walk-up	Water	$
Fat Tuesday	CityWalk	Walk-up bar	n/a	$

Restaurant	Location	Type	Cuisine	Price
Finnegan's	USF/NY	Full-serv, Bar	Irish/British	$$
Fire Eaters Grill	IOA/LC	Walk-up	Mid. Eastern	$
Florian Fortescue's	USF/HP	Walk-up	Ice cream	$
Fount. Fair Fortune	USF/HP	Bar	Butterbeer	$
Frozen Ice	IOA/MS	Walk-up	Snacks	$
Frying Dutchman	USF/WE	Walk-up	Fried fish	$
Fruit	IOA/MS	Walk-up	Fruit, snacks	$
Fusion Sushi	CityWalk	Walk-up	Japanese	$$
Galaxy Bowl	CB	Full-service	American	$ - $$
Gelateria Caffe Esp.	PBH	Cafeteria	Italian	$
Green Eggs and Ham	IOA/SL	Walk-up	Fast food	$
Hard Rock Cafe	CityWalk	Full-serv, Bar	American	$$ - $$$
Hideaway Bar	CB	Poolside	American	$ - $$
Hog's Head Pub	IOA/HP	Bar	n/a	$
Hop on Pop	IOA/SL	Walk-up	Ice cream	$
Hopping Pot	USF/HP	Walk-up bar	British	$
Hot Dog Hall of Fame	CityWalk	Walk-up	Hot dogs	$ - $$
Ice Cream	IOA/MS	Walk-up	Ice cream	$
Islands Dining Rm	RPR	Full-service	Asian	$$$- $$$$
Jake's American Bar	RPR	Full-serv, Bar	American	$$ - $$$
Jimmy Buffett's Margaritaville	CityWalk	Full-serv, Bar Nightclub	Caribbean	$$ - $$$
KidZone Pizza	USF/KZ	Walk-up	Fast food	$
Krusty Burger	USF/WE	Walk-up	Burgers	$
Lard Lad	USF/WE	Walk-up	Donuts	$
Leaky Cauldron	USF/HP	Cafeteria	British	$$
Lisa's Teahouse	USF/WE	Walk-up	Healthy	$
Lombard's Seafood	USF/SF	Full-service	American	$$ - $$$
Lone Palm Airport	CityWalk	Walk up, Bar	Snacks	$
Louie's Italian Rest.	USF/NY	Cafeteria	Italian	$
Luigi's	USF/WE	Walk-up	Pizza	$
Mama Della's Ristorante	PBH	Full-service	Italian	$$$- $$$$
Mel's Drive-In	USF/Hwd	Cafeteria	Burgers	$
Menchie's	CityWalk	Walk-up	Frozen yogurt	$
Moe's SW Grill	CityWalk	Walk-up	S'western	$
Moe's Tavern	USF/WE	Bar	n/a	$
Moose Juice...	IOA/SL	Walk-up	Soft drinks	$
Mythos	IOA/LC	Full-service	Eclectic	$$ - $$$
NBA City	CityWalk	Full-serve, Bar	American	$$ - $$$

Restaurant	Location	Type	Cuisine	Price
Orchid Court	RPR	Bar	n/a	$ - $$
Orchid Court Sushi	RPR	Full-service	Japanese	$ - $$$
Palm Restaurant	HRH	Full-service	Steaks, seafd	$$$$+
Panda Express	CityWalk	Walk-up	Chinese	$
Pat O'Brien's	CityWalk	Full-serv, Bar Nightclub	New Orleans	$$ - $$$
Pizza Predattoria	IOA/JP	Walk-up	Pizza	$
Red Coconut Club	CityWalk	Nightclub	Eclectic	$ - $$
Red Oven Pizza	CityWalk	Cafeteria	Pizza	$$
Richter's Burger Co.	USF/SF	Cafeteria	Burgers	$
Sal's Market Deli	PBH	Cafeteria	Italian	$$
SF Pastry Company	USF/SF	Cafeteria	American	$
Schwab's Pharmacy	USF/Hwd	Cafeteria	Ice cream	$
Shoreline Patios	CityWalk	Walk-up	Snacks, Drinks	$
Splendido's Pool Bar	PBH	Poolside	Italian	$$
Starbucks	CityWalk	Coffee house	Coffee	$
Starbucks	CB	Coffee house	Coffee	$
Starbucks	IOA/PoE	Coffee house	Coffee	$
Starbucks	PBH	Coffee house	Coffee	$
Starbucks	USF/NY	Coffee house	Coffee	$
Swizzle Lounge	CB	Bar	n/a	$
Tchoup Chop	RPR	Full-service	Asian fusion	$$$-$$$$
the groove	CW	Nightclub	Drinks	$ - $$
The Kitchen	HRH	Full-service	American	$$ - $$$
Thirsty Fish Bar	PBH	Bar	Italian	$
Three Broomsticks	IOA/HP	Cafeteria	British	$$
Thunder Falls Terrace	IOA/JP	Cafeteria	Barbecue	$$
Trattoria del Porto	PBH	Full-service	Italian	$$ - $$$
Universal Cineplex Concessions	CityWalk	Walk-up	Snacks	$
Velvet	HRH	Bar	American	$ - $$
Vivo Italian Kitchen	CityWalk	Full-serv, Bar	Italian	$$ - $$$
Wantilan Luau	RPR	Dinner show	Polynesian	$$$$
Watering Hole	IOA/JP	Bar	n/a	$
Whopper Bar	CityWalk	Walk-up	Burgers	$
Wimpy's	IOA/TL	Walk-up	Burgers	$

Note: The replacement for NASCAR Sports Grille is not included here.

Index

This Index lists rides, attractions, and restaurants mentioned in the text, along with other topics of interest. Where appropriate, the location of each entry is indicated by the following abbreviations: (CB) - Cabana Bay Beach Resort; (CW) - CityWalk; (HR) - Hard Rock Hotel; (IOA) - Islands of Adventure; (PB) - Portofino Bay Hotel; (RP) - Royal Pacific Resort; (USF) - Universal Studios Florida; (WDW) - Walt Disney World Resort.

Come Back Next Year!